The Birds of Panama

A FIELD GUIDE

GEORGE R. ANGEHR

ROBERT DEAN

A Zona Tropical Publication

FROM

COMSTOCK PUBLISHING ASSOCIATES

a division of

Cornell University Press

Ithaca and London

First published 2010

Cornell ISBN: 978-0-8014-7674-7 (pbk.: alk. paper)

Zona Tropical ISBN: 978-0-9798804-5-2

Printed in China
10 9 8 7 6 5 4 3 2 1

Zona Tropical Editor in Chief: John K. McCuen
Book design: Zona Creativa S.A.
Designer: Gabriela Wattson

I dedicate this book to my mother, Rose, for all her support through the years.

George R. Angehr

This is for the cadre of largely unsung conservationists working to protect birdlife throughout the neotropics.

Robert Dean

Contents

Introduction

Panama holds an extraordinary diversity of birds for a country its size. As of 2010, a total of 978 species had been recorded, more than in the United States and Canada, and all in an area about the size of the state of South Carolina. This diversity owes much to Panama's location at the intersection of the two American continents and two oceans. Many birds typical of North America reach their southern limits here, while many basically South American species extend no farther north. Millions of migrants, using the country as a bridge between the continents, pass through en route between breeding areas in the north and wintering sites in the south. In addition, marine species of both the Atlantic and the Pacific reach Panama's coasts. With its complex geological history and rugged and diverse topography, Panama also has a host of national and regional endemics: 107 of the species recorded are found only in Panama or are shared with just a few other countries, mainly Costa Rica and Colombia.

A major advantage for birders is that much of this wealth of birdlife is easily accessible. There are excellent birding areas within a few minutes of downtown Panamá City. An excellent road system provides access to many other sites, and there are a growing number of comfortable hotels and other tourism facilities in prime birding areas. Panama's small size means that most parts of the country can be reached within an hour's flight of Panamá City. All this makes it possible to see a large number of species in a short amount of time.

Despite all its advantages, Panama is still relatively little known as a birding destination. We hope that this guide will contribute to increased awareness of just how much Panama has to offer.

ABOUT THIS BOOK

The objective of this book is to provide a compact guide that is easy to use in the field and that provides the key information needed to identify all species likely to be encountered in Panama. Brief species accounts highlight the most significant field marks or behaviors that distinguish each species from those most similar to it. A condensed summary of information on habitat, range, and vocalizations is also included. A range map allows quick evaluation of where the species is most likely to be encountered. Most important, the guide features an illustration of each species on the page facing its text account, so the user does not have to flip back and forth between the description and the illustration.

All species known or thought to breed in Panama are illustrated, as are all regularly occurring migrants, with the exception of a few that are almost identical to other species. A few rare migrants or vagrants are described in text accounts in the main body of the book without an accompanying illustration. However, some of the rarest vagrants (two records or fewer), as well as species believed to have reached Panama with human assistance, are included only in the list of additional species on page 393, and a complete list of all species recorded in Panama begins on page 405. The most significant variations due to sex, age, or breeding condition are illustrated, as are most subspecies that can be identified in the field.

For those who wish more information on the natural history of Panama's birds, we highly recommend *A Guide to the Birds of Panama* by Robert S. Ridgely and John A. Gwynne (Princeton, second edition, 1989). One of the first modern field guides to any area in the tropics, this book contains a wealth of additional information on plumages, habitat, ecology, behavior, range, breeding, migratory movements, and vocalizations. Those who seek detailed information about where to see birds in Panama, should consult my *A Bird-finding Guide to Panama* (Cornell University Press, 2008), co-authored with Dodge and Lorna Engleman.

TAXONOMIC ISSUES

The species-level classification of birds, as with other organisms, often varies between scientific authorities. The most prevalent modern classification standard is the Biological Species Concept, which regards species as consisting of interbreeding groups of organisms that do not regularly interbreed with other such groups where they come into contact. Unfortunately, this concept cannot be applied directly when the ranges of two groups do not meet. In such cases classification necessarily becomes somewhat subjective; isolated groups are generally considered to belong to separate species when they differ as much or more than two related species of the same group that do occur together.

Many of Panama's birds vary geographically, and often isolated populations (such as those on different mountain ranges or on offshore islands) can be quite distinctive. Whether to call such isolated populations subspecies of a single species or regard them as distinct species can be difficult to judge. In the nineteenth century, many of these forms were classified as separate species. From the 1930s to the 1960s, a period of taxonomic "lumping" took place, and forms that had been considered separate species were combined as subspecies within a single species, often on the basis of little or no actual data. In recent decades, there has been a trend, in large part based on information from molecular genetics, of re-splitting these lumped species back into their original components, as well as making additional splits.

For this book, we used the checklist of the American Ornithologists' Union (AOU) as our basic authority for species limits, scientific and English names, and the sequence of families and species. (In a number of cases, we have not strictly followed the AOU sequence for family and species due to design issues or in order to place similar-looking species on the same page so they can be compared directly.) In some instances, however, we chose to recognize species the AOU has not yet accepted, based on published references. We expect that the AOU will eventually recognize a majority of them.

The following is a list of the species included in this book that the AOU does not presently recognize. In the species accounts, we note the difference in treatment.

Galapagos Shearwater (*Puffinus subalaris*). We follow Austin et al. (2004) in recognizing this species as distinct from Audubon's Shearwater *P. lherminieri*. This species occurs off Panama's Pacific coast, while Audubon's is found on the Caribbean coast.

Brown-backed Dove (*Leptotila battyi*). We follow Wetmore (1968), Ridgely and Gwynne (1989), Monroe and Sibley (1993), Baptista et al. (1997), and Gibbs et al. (2001) in recognizing Brown-backed Dove *L. battyi* as distinct from Gray-headed Dove *L. plumbeiceps*. The species is a Panama national endemic, found only on Coiba and Cébaco islands and in the Azuero Peninsula.

Azuero Parakeet (*Pyrrhura eisenmanni*). Originally described as a subspecies of Painted Parakeet *Pyrrhura picta* (Delgado 1985), this isolated form was recommended for full species status by Joseph (2000); genetic work by Ribas et al. (2006) also suggested a change in status. It is a Panama endemic, restricted to southwestern Azuero Peninsula.

Escudo Hummingbird (*Amazilia handleyi*). Originally described as a full species by Wetmore (1968), most references have included it as a subspecies of Rufous-tailed Hummingbird *A. tzacatl* without explicit justification. Given its much larger size and substantial ecological differences (it occurs in all habitats on Escudo de Veraguas Island, including forest, whereas Rufous-tailed, on the mainland, is mainly restricted to open areas), in the absence of published data supporting a merger we prefer to continue to recognize it as a separate species. A Panama national endemic, the species is restricted to the 400-hectare Escudo de Veraguas Island off Bocas del Toro.

Blue-throated Toucanet (*Aulacorhynchus caeruleogularis*). We follow Navarro et al. (2001) and Puebla-Olivares et al. (2008) in recognizing Panamanian and Costa Rican populations as a species distinct from Emerald Toucanet *A. prasinus* and other extralimital forms, but include the subspecies of eastern Darién (*A. cognatus*), which Navarro and Puebla-Olivares and their colleagues proposed as a separate species, as part of *A. caeruleogularis*. The morphological character they propose as separating the two taxa, a red spot at the base of the culmen in *A. caeruleogularis*, is mostly limited to westernmost Chiriquí, and birds from Ngöbe-Buglé eastward resemble *A. cognatus* in lacking it (Angehr, unpublished data). More genetic data will be needed to determine the precise relationship between these two taxa.

Coiba Spinetail (*Crainioleuca dissita*). We follow Ridgely and Gwynne (1989) and Monroe and Sibley (1993) in recognizing this species as distinct from the South American Rusty-backed Spinetail *C. vulpina*, with which it was considered conspecific by Wetmore (1972). The species is a Panama national endemic, restricted to Coiba Island.

Canebrake Wren (*Thryothorus zeledoni*). We follow Kroodsma and Brewer (2005) in recognizing Canebrake Wren as distinct from Plain Wren *T. modestus*. In Panama, Canebrake Wren is restricted to western Bocas del Toro, while Plain Wren occurs on the Pacific slope from western Chiriquí to eastern Panamá Province, and on the Caribbean slope from northern Coclé to eastern Colón Province.

In four cases we use English names that differ from those employed by the AOU. For two of those, we opt for names used by Ridgely and Gwynne (1989) that are more descriptive and appropriate for the species in question: Speckled Antshrike instead of Spiny-faced Antshrike (*Xenornis setifrons*), and Southern Nightingale-Wren instead of Scaly-breasted Wren (*Microcerculus marginatus*). To avoid confusion with the manakins of the Family Pipridae, we refer to Nutmeg Mannikin (*Lonchura punctulata*) and Tricolored Mannikin (*Lonchura malacca*) as Nutmeg Munia and Tricolored Munia, respectively.

PLAN OF THE BOOK

Family Accounts. For each family of birds, we provide a brief introduction that describes its global distribution, feeding habits, and sometimes other aspects of its ecology. We also discuss behavior, habitat preferences, and other information that applies to all or most members of the family in Panama and that may aid in recognition. In this section we also mention the major identification problems within the family and the features to observe in order to distinguish similar species.

Species Accounts. A text account is provided for each species included in the guide, giving the basic information needed for identification. This includes the following:

> **Range Maps.** Most text accounts are accompanied by a range map (the only exceptions being Great Frigatebird, which has only been recorded far offshore, and White-faced Whistling-Duck and Sedge Wren, which have

probably been extirpated from Panama). The maps are color coded to indicate the species's status in the mapped area. It should be emphasized that bird distribution in many parts of Panama is very imperfectly known, particularly on the Caribbean slope, much of which is difficult to access, and in Darién. The mapped ranges in many cases represent a "best guess" at the actual distribution. It is quite likely that additional work will produce many extensions in range compared to what is shown by the present maps.

Purple = breeding resident. Note that the species may not necessarily breed throughout the entire mapped area. This color is used to indicated the entire range of a given species in the country, except in cases where areas occupied by breeding populations are distinct from those in which nonbreeding migrants occur. Isolated records, away from the main known range of the species, are shown as dots. Dots are also used for records of rare species whose range is poorly known.

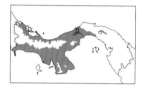

Solid blue = nonbreeding resident. A species that does not breed in Panama, but in which individuals remain resident in the country for a significant part of the year (typically the northern winter, but sometimes other periods). This is also used for those nonbreeding species with no clear seasonal pattern of occurrence. Areas where species occurs both as a transient and a nonbreeding resident are shown as solid blue. Isolated records are shown as dots.

Hatched blue = transient. A species that does not breed in Panama, but in which individuals are present in the country for relatively brief periods of time in transit to other areas. Isolated records of transients are shown as solid blue dots.

Red = breeding migrant. A species that breeds in Panama, but migrates out of the country during the nonbreeding season.

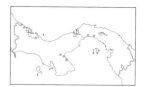

Green = vagrant. A species that has been recorded in Panama only a very few times. Green is also used to indicate records of breeding or migrant species outside their typical range that are probably wandering individuals.

Species Name. Both the English common name and the scientific name are given. As described in the previous section, names conform to the American Ornithologists' Union, except as noted.

Measurements. Total body length is given in inches (rounded to the nearest half-inch) and centimeters (rounded to the nearest centimeter). Body length is the measurement from the tip of the bill to the tip of the tail; for some species with extremely long tail feathers this measurement is given separately. For species in which males and females differ substantially in size, separate measurements are given for each, indicated by "M" and "F," respectively. Wingspans, abbreviated "WS," are given for larger species that are commonly seen in flight, including raptors and seabirds. Most body-length measurements are based on those provided in Wetmore's *Birds of the Republic of Panama*, supplemented by information in other references as necessary.

While measurements provide a general idea of a bird's size, they should be used with care when making field identifications. Obviously a bird's proportions must be taken into account—a long-billed, long-tailed hermit hummingbird is much smaller in actual body size than a short-billed, short-tailed flycatcher, which has the same total length. Posture, distance, lighting, and many other factors can also influence perception of a bird's size. However, when two species of similar proportions are compared side-by-side under the same conditions, relative length can provide valuable information for identification.

Field Marks. The first few sentences of the text account describe the features that distinguish the species from similar ones. The most significant field marks to be looked for are highlighted in bold. Exceptions include a species that is essentially unmistakable, or conversely when it is so similar to another species that a number of subtle characteristics need to be taken into account. We have used nontechnical terms in describing field marks as much as possible, but for the sake of brevity technical terms are used where appropriate. Descriptions of these technical terms can be found in the Anatomical Features section starting on p. xxiv.

In species in which plumage varies due to age and sex, generally adult male plumage is described first, then adult female, then immature plumage. (In species in which immature plumage differs between the sexes, generally the immature male plumage is discussed after that of the adult male, and immature female after that of the adult female.) In some species the first plumage after hatching, held for a short period of time, differs from later immature plumages; this is identified as "young immature."

Most resident breeding species in Panama show little if any difference between breeding and nonbreeding plumages. (An exception is the male

Red-legged Honeycreeper.) Some species, however, develop brighter colors in their bare parts or long plumes during the breeding season. In contrast, many migratory species, especially shorebirds and warblers, have highly distinctive breeding plumages but molt into drabber colors during the nonbreeding season. They are much more likely to be seen in the latter condition in Panama, but may appear in breeding plumage for short periods when they first arrive in the fall or before departure in the spring. In the text accounts, these differing plumages are referred to as "breeding" and "nonbreeding."

In some species, especially raptors, nightjars, owls, and some seabirds, distinct color forms are found within the same population. We refer to these variant forms as "morphs"; some other references, such as Ridgely and Gwynne's guide, call them "phases." For brevity, we refer to subspecies as "races"; when several subspecies as a group share similar characters, we refer to them jointly as a "form."

Relative Abundance. This term is related to the probability of encountering the species on a given day in the field. (This includes recording it by call; many species are heard far more often than they are seen.) Bear in mind that it applies only for the appropriate habitat, time of day, and season for each species. Also note that these are relative terms, and apply only when comparing similar types of birds. Large birds such as hawks are often more detectable at a distance than smaller birds such as flycatchers; in absolute terms, a "common" hawk is much less numerous than a "common" flycatcher. The term is also only an approximation across the range of the species in Panama, since species frequently vary in abundance in different parts of the country. Where there are substantial differences in commonness in different parts of Panama or at different elevations, this is mentioned, but in a book of this kind it is impossible to discuss such variation in great detail. The following terms are used to describe relative abundance:

- Abundant: Recorded every day in the field, often in large numbers.
- Very common: Recorded almost every day, but usually not in such large numbers as the previous category.
- Common: Recorded on substantially more than half of all days in the field.
- Fairly common: Recorded on about half of all days in the field.
- Uncommon: Recorded on substantially fewer than half of all days in the field, but more common than the following category.
- Rare: Recorded on fewer than 10% of all days in the field.
- Very rare: Few records in Panama; experienced observers may not encounter the species in years of field work. The species, however, is believed to breed in the country, or to occur regularly as a migrant.

- Vagrant: A nonbreeding species that has been recorded only a very few times in Panama, and that is not expected to occur with any regularity.
- Local: A species that appears to be absent from much of its potential range, not being found in areas which otherwise seem suitable for it in terms of habitat. This term may be used in conjunction with the other abundance categories: for example, "locally common."

Migratory Status. A large majority of Panama's birds are breeding residents— that is, they occur in Panama year-round. However, a significant number reach Panama only as long-distance migrants—they are present in Panama only during their nonbreeding season. By far the largest number of these breed in the United States, Canada, and in some cases Mexico and northern Central America. Because of this, we describe the occurrence of these species in Panama relative to the northern seasons. (In Panama itself, there is little seasonal change in temperature. Instead, seasons are determined by changes in rainfall. Locally, the sunny dry season, which occurs in most of the country from mid-December to mid-April, is called the *verano* ["summer"]. The rainy season, from mid-April to mid-December, is called the *invierno* ["winter"].)

"Winter residents" are migrants that remain in Panama throughout the northern winter (and usually during parts of fall and spring). "Transients" are migrants that pass through Panama in spring and fall en route to wintering grounds in South America. Many species occur both as transients and as winter residents; these are generally much more common during the migratory period in spring and fall than they are during winter months. In some species (particularly shorebirds), a few individuals, usually immatures, may linger in Panama throughout the northern summer. Populations of some breeding residents are augmented during the northern winter by the arrival of migrants that bred farther north. For a few rare migrants, whose records are too few to characterize the period of occurrence, the term "migrant" is used without the characterization as either transients or winter residents. Note that migrants may turn up in almost any habitat in addition to their typical one, and even appear in unusual locations such as offshore islands during the migratory period. During the period of winter residence they are more apt to be found in the habitats characteristic of their species.

A small number of species arrive in Panama as migrants from South America, or from elsewhere in the tropics. Only one species of land bird that breeds in South America, Brown-chested Martin, regularly migrates to Panama; however, a few other species may occur rarely, such as Chapman's Swift, Southern Martin, or the southern race of Blue-and-white Swallow. Some marine species breed in the Galápagos or other island groups in the tropics, or else in the South Temperate Zone or the Antarctic. To avoid confusion, the seasonal occurrence of these species is described individually, without reference to the northern seasons.

Only five species breed in Panama but migrate out of the country entirely during their nonbreeding season: Plumbeous Kite, Swallow-tailed Kite, Common Nighthawk, Piratic Flycatcher, and Yellow-green Vireo. These cases are described individually in the species texts, without reference to northern seasons. Besides these, all the species not described in the texts as winter residents, transients, migrants, or vagrants can be assumed to be breeding residents, present in Panama year-round.

Panama Range. A brief description of range is given in the text; consult the small range map accompanying the account for details. The map of Panama on the inside front cover will also help interpret the range description. Species's ranges on Panama's Pacific and Caribbean slopes are usually given separately. These two slopes are separated by the Continental Divide, which in most of Panama runs along the crest of the higher mountain ranges, usually closer to the Caribbean than to the Pacific, except in northern Coclé, the Canal Area, and Panamá Province. Range is generally described from west to east; for example, "on Pacific slope eastward to southern Coclé" means the species occurs from the Costa Rican border in Chiriquí as far as southern Coclé; "on Caribbean slope from western Colón Province eastward" means it occurs from western Colón Province to the Colombian border in Kuna Yala. Note that some species whose range is mostly on one slope may barely reach the other slope in a few areas, especially in foothills where there are low passes through the mountains. Two areas where this regularly occurs are Fortuna in central Chiriquí and Santa Fe in Veraguas. "Western Panama" means Panama west of the Canal Area, and "eastern Panama" means Panama east of the Canal Area.

Panama traditionally has included nine provinces: Bocas del Toro, Chiriquí, Veraguas, Los Santos, Herrera, Coclé, Panamá, Colón, and Darién. (We distinguish the provinces of Panamá and Colón from the cities of the same name by adding the word "Province" afterward.) In addition there is the Comarca de Kuna Yala (previously called San Blas), a provincial-level semi-autonomous homeland of the Kuna indigenous group. Recently, additional provincial-level comarcas have been created for other indigenous groups. The Ngöbe-Buglé comarca includes parts of what were formerly central and eastern Bocas del Toro, northeastern Chiriquí, and western Veraguas. The Emberá-Wounaan comarca, which consists of two sections, includes parts of what were formerly Darién province. These changes should be kept in mind when consulting older references such as Ridgley and Gwynne.

In addition to these official divisions, we also refer to the Canal Area. This informal designation indicates the area formerly included in the U.S.-administered Canal Zone, which reverted to Panamanian control at the end of 1999, plus the adjacent cities of Panamá and Colón. (The northern part of the former Canal Zone is now part of Colón Province, and the southern part belongs to Panamá Province.) Because the Canal Area is an area of overlap between the avifaunas of western and eastern Panama, and because it preserves substantially more forest than the lowlands immediately to the east and west of it, it is convenient to refer to it by a single term.

It is worth commenting on some of the more typical distributional patterns found in Panama's birds. In lowland birds, two broad groups can be distinguished: species that prefer wetter, more humid conditions, and those that prefer drier habitats, whether dry forest, woodland, or grassland. The first group tends to have ranges that include the entire Caribbean slope but that extend to the Pacific slope mainly in eastern Panama, including Panamá Province and Darién. The second type usually has ranges confined mainly to the Pacific slope, extending eastward to eastern Panamá Province or sometimes western Darién. Birds typical of foothills and highlands sometimes have ranges extending throughout all of Panama's mountains but often are confined to either the mountains of western Panama or those of eastern Panama, not both; the dividing line is usually the Canal Area, the lowest point between the mountain chains.

It should be remembered that species will be found within the mapped range only where appropriate habitat occurs. In particular, since much of Panama's western Pacific slope has been deforested, birds restricted to forest are found only very locally, where sufficiently large patches remain to provide adequate habitat.

Altitudinal Range. Many birds are restricted to a specific altitudinal range, some being typical of lowlands, while others favor foothills and highlands. In the text, we give the known altitudinal range in feet (usually rounded to the nearest 100) and meters (rounded to the nearest 50). These limits should be regarded as approximate. For species for which specific elevational limits are not well known, this range is expressed in more general terms. "Lowlands" are areas from sea level to 2,000 ft (600 m); "foothills" from 2,000 to 4,000 ft (600 to 1,200 m), and "highlands" are areas above 4,000 ft (1,200 m). Bear in mind that birds are often less common near the upper or lower limits of their altitudinal ranges. Some species also engage in seasonal altitudinal migration and may be less common at some altitudes at certain times of year. On occasion, highland or foothill birds may turn up in the lowlands (this is particularly likely on the wetter Caribbean slope), or vice versa.

Foraging Height. Many birds typically forage in a particular zone above the ground where they are most likely to be encountered. Knowing this zone may help in locating them, and is sometimes also an important clue for identification. For birds found in forest, forest edge, or woodland, we indicate the zone above the ground where the species spends most of its time. The categories used include "on ground," "lower levels" (from ground level to about 10 feet above the ground), "middle levels" (from about 10 to 30 feet above the ground), and "upper levels" (everything above 30 feet including the canopy); the word "canopy" used alone indicates the very top layer of the forest, within about 10 feet of the upper level of leaves. Keep in mind, however, that these zones are rather flexible, and that birds typically found in upper levels may descend lower at the edge of clearings or to feed in fruiting shrubs, and birds that usually forage low may range higher to feed on fruit or flowers above their normal zone. Some species such as doves and others that are usually near the ground may call from high perches during the breeding season.

Habitat. Most birds have particular habitats where they are typically found, although many occur across a range of habitats. A few of the habitat terms used in this guide require some explanation. "Forest" indicates a wooded area with a closed canopy—that is, the crowns of trees are close enough to virtually touch. In most lowland forests in Panama, the canopy is at least 30 feet above the ground, and usually much higher. In general, this category does not distinguish between primary forest or mature secondary forest, since most forest birds occur in both. In some cases, we indicate that a species has a preference for wetter or drier forest. "Woodland" means a wooded area in which the trees are spaced so widely that their canopies do not touch; usually it is shorter than forest and results from a disturbance of closed canopy forest. The space between trees is often filled with dense shrubs or saplings. "Gallery forests" are those found along water courses in otherwise mostly treeless terrain; they are common especially on the western Pacific slope. "Mangroves" are a special forest type found between the low- and high-tide lines in coastal areas; the trees that grow in them have special adaptations that permit them to grow in salt water. Mangrove forests are usually of only moderate height, but they can be very tall in estuaries on the Pacific coast. "Forest edge" and "woodland edge" indicate the border between forest or woodland and more open areas, and include the edges of clearings, roads, and other spaces within forest or woodland. Such edges are often characterized by dense vegetation, including thickets and tangles of vines and lianas. "Second growth" as used here refers only to young second growth, usually less than five years old and 10 feet high. Such regenerating vegetation is common in areas where forest has been cut down for timber or where fields have been allowed to regrow; it usually consists of a dense tangle of saplings, shrubs, and large herbs, sometimes including rank grasses. Allowed to continue to regenerate, such areas will revert to woodland in a fairly short period of time. "Shrubby areas" are those consisting mainly of shrubs with few or no trees. "Scrub" is a vegetation type found mainly on the Pacific coast, often in drier or coastal areas, which includes woody vegetation that is maintained at a short height due to continual disturbance such as burning, poor soil, or other factors. "Grasslands" are areas in which grasses are the dominant vegetation and that mostly lack woody vegetation; this term includes pastures as well as natural grassy areas. "Open areas" is a general term for areas without extensive woody vegetation (but which may include scattered trees), including grasslands, agricultural fields, golf courses, airstrips, parks, and gardens. "Swamps" are wooded areas with standing water covering the soil for most of the year; "marshes" are areas with standing water most of the year that lack trees but instead are dominated by grasses, large herbs, and other nonwoody vegetation.

Vocalizations. The sounds produced by birds are often a key clue for identification. This is especially true in the tropics, where so many species are secretive and frequent dense vegetation. For reclusive, nocturnal, or canopy species, calls may be the most common way that a bird is detected. In a few cases, certain species are so similar in other characteristics that differences in voice are the only reliable way to distinguish them. For the groups of birds in which sound is often important for identification, the species account includes transcriptions of vocalizations, examples of the most common calls and songs that each species produces. (Some groups of birds, such as most seabirds, herons, swifts, and swallows, do not commonly produce distinctive sounds.) Bear in mind that most species have a variety of vocalizations used in different circumstances, and due to space limitations it is impossible to include all of them. You may well hear a species give calls that differ from the ones described here.

Behavior. Where appropriate, we include characteristic behaviors that may be useful for identification. We also indicate whether the species is likely to be found in groups, either of its own species or with mixed flocks of other species. In tropical forests, many species forage together, most likely as a defense against predators by ensuring that many pairs of eyes are alert for danger. Mixed flocks in the lower levels and middle levels of the forest are often composed of small insectivorous species such as antbirds, flycatchers, warblers, and others, while flocks in the upper levels and canopy typically include frugivorous species such as tanagers and honeycreepers. In open grassy areas flocks of small granivorous birds like seedeaters and grassquits are often found. Another type of association unique to the tropics is the group of species that habitually follow army-ant swarms. Army ants are nomadic, and large swarms scour the leaf litter on the forest floor in search of insects and other small arthropods. Many birds follow these swarms, feeding on insects frightened into flight by the ants rather than the ants themselves. These include species of typical antbirds, antthrushes, antpittas, woodcreepers, cuckoos, and tanagers. Some species join in opportunistically, but others are obligate ant-followers, rarely being found away from a swarm.

Regional and National Endemics. Panama has a large number of regional and national endemics that may be of particular interest to the visiting birder. In this book, we categorize as "regional endemics" those species that qualify as "restricted-range species" according to the definition of BirdLife International, that is, those with a total world range of less than 19,300 sq mi (50,000 km²), approximately the size of Costa Rica. Panama has a total of 107 such regional endemics. Of these, 11 are national endemics, species that have so far been found only within Panama's borders. (Some of these probably also occur in Colombia but have not yet been recorded there due to the remoteness of the areas in which they are likely to be found.)

BirdLife International has identified more than 200 "Endemic Bird Areas" (EBAs) throughout the world, in which two or more restricted-range species occur together. Panama includes parts of five such EBAs. Species accounts of regional endemics in Panama include a two-letter code indicating in which EBAs they are found. These codes and the corresponding EBAs are as follows:

CL (Caribbean Lowlands) = Central American Caribbean Slope EBA (includes Caribbean slope lowlands from Honduras to Panama).
WH (Western Highlands) = Costa Rica and Panama Highlands EBA (includes highlands of Costa Rica and of western Panama).
PL (Pacific Lowlands) = South Central American Pacific Slope EBA (includes Pacific slope lowlands of Costa Rica and Panama).
EL (Eastern Lowlands) = Darién Lowlands EBA (includes lowlands of eastern Panama and western Colombia).
EH (Eastern Highlands) = Darién Highlands EBA (includes highlands of eastern Panama and extreme western Colombia).

In addition, Escudo de Veraguas Island (**EV**) has a single endemic species, Escudo Hummingbird. Regional endemics that are also Panama national endemics are indicated with an asterisk (*). These are as follows:

Brown-backed Dove
Azuero Parakeet
Escudo Hummingbird
Glow-throated Hummingbird
Stripe-cheeked Woodpecker
Coiba Spinetail
Beautiful Treerunner
Yellow-green Tyrannulet
Pirre Bush-Tanager
Green-naped Tanager
Yellow-green Finch

Illustrations. Most species are illustrated on the page facing the text account. For a few species, a text account is provided without a corresponding illustration; these include very rare species, and some that are virtually identical to an illustrated species. To the extent that space has permitted, the illustrations include as many of the major plumage variations found in a species as possible, including male, female, immature, breeding and nonbreeding, color morphs, and distinctive subspecies. Slight differences, such as that between adult and duller immature plumage, or minor color variations between subspecies, usually are not shown. When a single illustration is provided for a species, and its plumage type is unlabeled, it can be presumed to depict an adult; in such cases there are only minor differences between the sexes and between adults and immatures. When there are significant plumage differences within a species, these are mentioned in the text, and the illustrations are labeled to indicate the plumage that is depicted.

All birds on the same page are generally illustrated to the same scale. Birds in flight are shown at a smaller scale than perched birds on the same page; however, they are at the same scale as other birds in flight on that page. (The only exception is hummingbirds, in which perched birds and flying birds are shown at the same scale.) If there is a change in scale within a page, this is indicated by a horizontal line spanning the page. Bear in mind that scale may change from page to page due to design considerations; this is true even within the same family.

For More Information on Panama's Birds

Our knowledge of Panama's birds is constantly growing, in large part due to observations made by birders, both residents in the country and those who are just visiting. You can contribute to our understanding of Panama's birds by sending reports of rare species, or observations of birds outside of their typical range or seasonal occurrence, to the author at angehrg@si.org. The best source for up-to-date information on birds in the country is the Panama Audubon Society, the leading organization promoting the appreciation and conservation of Panama's birds (http://www.panamaaudubon.org; e-mail: info@panamaaudubon.com). Birders can share their own observations, and also see records submitted by others, by visiting eBird Panama (http://ebird.org/content/panama), maintained by the Panama Audubon Society in collaboration with the National Audubon Society and the Cornell Laboratory of Ornithology. In addition, Xenornis (http://www.xenornis.com; e-mail: xenornis@hotmail.com), a website hosted by Darién Montañez, provides information on recent observations of rare or unusual birds in Panama.

Panama's amazing wealth of birdlife is not yet as well known to birders as it deserves. We hope that this book will serve you well in getting to know and enjoy the birds of Panama.

REFERENCES

Angehr, G.R., D. Engleman, and L. Engleman. 2008. *A Bird-Finding Guide to Panama*. Cornell University Press, Ithaca, New York. [Panama edition published by the Panama Audubon Society in 2006 as *Where to Find Birds in Panama: A Site Guide for Birders*]

Austin, J. J., V. Bretagnolle, and E. Pasquet. 2004. A global molecular phylogeny of the small *Puffinus* shearwaters and implications for systematics of the Little-Audubon's Shearwater complex. *Auk* 121: 847–864.

Baptista, L. F., P. W. Trail, and H. M. Horblit. 1997. Family Columbidae (Pigeons and Doves). In J. del Hoyo, A. Elliot, and J. Sargatal (eds.), *Handbook of the Birds of the World*. Vol. 4. *Sandgrouse to Cuckoos*, pp. 60–245. Lynx Edicions, Barcelona.

Delgado, F. 1985. A new subspecies of the Painted Parakeet (*Pyrrhura picta*) from Panama. In P. A. Buckley, M. S. Foster, E. S. Morton, R. S. Ridgely, and F. G. Buckley (eds.), *Neotropical Ornithology*, pp. 17–20. American Ornithologists' Union, Washington, D.C.

Gibbs, D., E. Barnes, and J. Cox. 2001. *Pigeons and Doves: A Guide to the Pigeons and Doves of the World*. Yale University Press, New Haven, Conn.

Joseph, L. 2000. Beginning an end to 63 years of uncertainty: The Neotropical parakeets known as *Pyrrhura picta* and *P. leucotis* comprise more than two species. *Proceedings of the Academy of Natural Sciences of Philadelphia* 150: 279–292.

Kroodsma, D. E., and D. Brewer. 2005. Family Troglodytidae (Wrens). In J. del Hoyo, A. Elliot, and D. A. Christie (eds.), *Handbook of the Birds of the World*. Vol. 10. *Cuckooshrikes to Thrushes*, pp. 356–448. Lynx Edicions, Barcelona.

Monroe, B. L., Jr., and C. G. Sibley. 1993. *A World Checklist of Birds*. Yale University Press, New Haven, Conn.

Navarro, A. G., A. T. Peterson, E. López-Medrano, and H. Benítez-Díaz. 2001. Species limits in Mesoamerican *Aulacorhynchus* Toucanets. *Wilson Bulletin* 114: 363–372.

Puebla-Olivares, F., E. Bonaccorso, A. E. de los Monteros, K. E. Omland, J. E. Llorente-Bousquets, A. T. Peterson, and A. G. Navarro-Siguenza. 2008. Speciation in the Emerald Toucanet (*Aulacorhynchus prasinus*) complex. *Auk* 125: 39–50.

Ribas, C. C., L. Joseph, and C. R. Miyaki. 2006. Molecular systematics and patterns of diversification in *Pyrrhura* (Psittacidae) with special reference to the *picta-leucotis* complex. *Auk* 123: 660–680.

Ridgely, R. S., and J. A. Gwynne. 1989. *A Guide to the Birds of Panama: With Costa Rica, Nicaragua, and Honduras*. 2nd ed. Princeton University Press, Princeton, N.J.

Wetmore, A. 1968. *The Birds of the Republic of Panama. Part 2. Columbidae (Pigeons) to Picidae (Woodpeckers)*. Smithsonian Institution, Washington, D.C.

Wetmore, Alexander. 1972. *The Birds of the Republic of Panama. Part 3. Passeriformes: Dendrocolaptidae (Woodcreepers) to Oxyruncidae (Sharpbill)*. Smithsonian Institution, Washington, D.C.

Anatomical Features

See Glossary, page 397, for definitions of other terms.

THE BILL

culmen The top edge of the upper mandible in profile is called the *culmen*.

upper mandible

lower mandible

The bill (or beak) comprises the upper and lower mandibles. The term ***decurved*** describes a bill that has a downward curve.

cere Birds' nostrils are located on top of the base of the upper mandible. In some families (e.g., hawks, falcons, owls, and parrots), the nostrils open through a fleshy covering called a *cere*.

Note: The unfeathered parts of a bird (i.e., beak, cere, orbital area, legs, and feet) are referred to as the ***bare parts***.

THE EYE AREA

supraloral The area above the lore.

lore The area between the base of the bill and the eye.

superciliary The line of feathers extending from the base of the bill to above and behind the eye (thus including the supraloral feathers) is known as the *superciliary*.

eye-line (or eye-stripe) When the lore and the postocular stripe are of the same color and set off from the surrounding feathers, they form an eye-line.

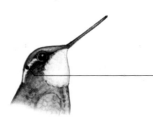

postocular stripe When a differently colored line of feathers extends behind the eye, it is referred to as a *postocular stripe*. Note that some birds show only a postocular spot.

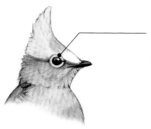

eye-ring Most species of birds have a narrow ring of very short feathers around the eye. When these feathers are of a different color than the surrounding ones, they form an eye-ring.

orbital skin In some species, the area around the eye (and sometimes beyond) is featherless. This bare area is referred to as *orbital skin*, or, when it forms a circle, as an *orbital ring*.

spectacles

Sometimes an eye-ring is the same color as the lore; the resulting pattern is called *spectacles*.

mask

A mask is an area of darker color (usually black or blackish) around the eye, often extending to the area around the base of the bill and/or the ear coverts.

CROWN, FORECROWN, AND NAPE

nape

crown

The entire top of the head is called the *crown*. The anterior portion of the crown is called the *forecrown* or *forehead*, especially if distinctly colored. The back of the neck is known as the *nape*.

forecrown

crown patch Some species, including many of the tyrant flycatchers, have a colorful crown patch of erectile feathers that is generally kept concealed beneath the crown feathers.

crest When most or all of the crown feathers are capable of being raised, they are termed a *crest*.

hood The term *hood* has variable usage, though it generally indicates that the crown and nape (and often also the cheeks and lower throat) are of a single color (with the forehead, eye area, and chin of a differing color).

cheek, ear patch The **ear coverts**, or cheek, are a distinct group of short feathers that cover the ear opening, which is located just below and behind the eye. When the feathers of the ear coverts, or sometimes just those along their outer border, are of a different color and contrast with the feathers surrounding them, the result is an ear patch.

moustachial stripe A line of differently colored feathers just below the ear coverts and above the malar.

chin
lateral throat stripe, submalar stripe
throat
malar stripe

The area extending down from the base of the lower mandible between the cheek and throat is known as the *malar*, and when it is distinctly colored, it is called a *malar stripe*. A line between the malar and the throat is referred to as a *lateral throat stripe* or *submalar stripe*. The throat extends on the underside of the head from the base of the lower mandible to the upper breast. The part of the throat directly below the lower mandible is called the *chin*.

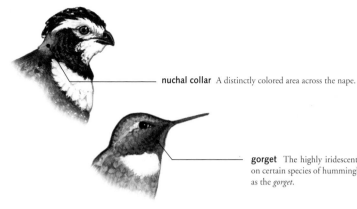

nuchal collar A distinctly colored area across the nape.

gorget The highly iridescent throat feathers on certain species of hummingbirds are known as the *gorget*.

Tᴀɪʟ ꜰᴇᴀᴛᴜʀᴇꜱ

subterminal band A distinctly colored band above the tail tip is called a *subterminal band*.

tail corners The tips of the outer tail feathers are referred to as the *tail corners*.

central tail feathers The innermost two feathers are referred to as the *central tail feathers*.

graduated tail A tail in which the feathers become gradually shorter from the center to the sides.

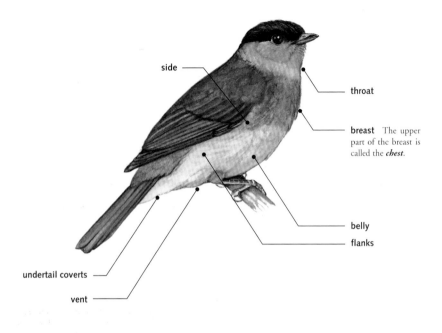

side

throat

breast The upper part of the breast is called the *chest*.

belly

flanks

undertail coverts

vent

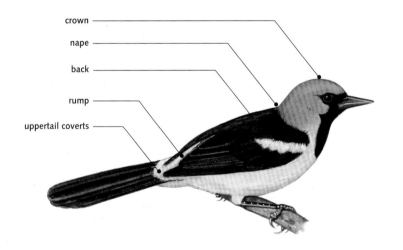

crown

nape

back

rump

uppertail coverts

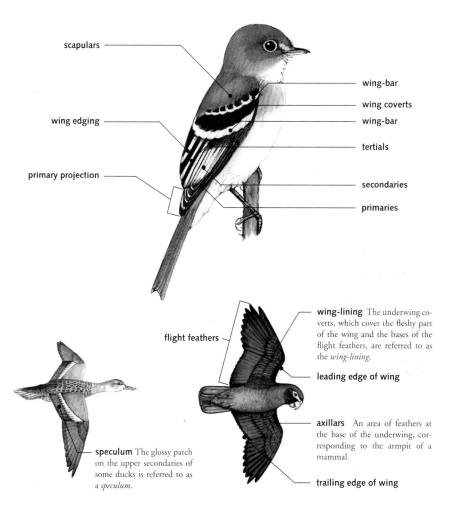

scapulars

wing edging

primary projection

wing-bar
wing coverts
wing-bar
tertials
secondaries
primaries

flight feathers

wing-lining The underwing co-verts, which cover the fleshy part of the wing and the bases of the flight feathers, are referred to as the *wing-lining*.

leading edge of wing

axillars An area of feathers at the base of the underwing, cor-responding to the armpit of a mammal.

trailing edge of wing

speculum The glossy patch on the upper secondaries of some ducks is referred to as a *speculum*.

Features on the wings often help in identification. The feathers covering the juncture of the wing and body, corresponding to the shoulder, are known as the *scapulars*. The several rows of feathers that cover the base of the flight feathers are the wing coverts. When the tips of these feathers are distinctly colored, they form wing-bars.

The flight feathers are composed of three contiguous sets of feathers, which, from the inner to the outer portion of the extended wing, are known as *tertials* (three innermost feathers), *secondaries*, and *primaries*. When the wing is folded, these feathers stack up with the innermost of the three tertials on top and the outermost of the nine or ten primaries on the bottom.

A feature that is sometimes useful in identification is the distance that the tip of the outermost folded primary extends beyond the longest secondaries and tertials; this is known as the *primary projection*.

The term *wing edging* is used to describe a lighter color on the edge of each flight feather (and often wing covert as well); this lighter color imparts a striped look to the wing.

Adult Vultures and Raptors in Flight

Turkey Vulture, p. 36
WS 67 in (171 cm)

Black Vulture, p. 36
WS 58 in (146 cm)

King Vulture, p. 36
WS 73 in (185 cm)

Zone-tailed Hawk, p. 48
WS 51 in (128 cm)

Common Black-Hawk, p. 48
Caribbean race
WS 44 in (112 cm)

White Hawk, p. 46
WS 42 in (108 cm)

Short-tailed Hawk, p. 50
dark morph
WS 36.5 in (93 cm)

Great Black-Hawk, p. 48
western race
WS 49 in (124 cm)

Barred Hawk, p. 46
WS 46 in (118 cm)

Crane Hawk, p. 44
western race
WS 37 in (94 cm)

Solitary Eagle, p. 48
WS 66 in (168 cm)

Crested Caracara, p. 58
WS 47 in (120 cm)

Gray-headed Kite, p. 38
WS 39 in (100 cm)

Black Hawk-Eagle, p. 54
WS 52 in (131 cm)

Ornate Hawk-Eagle, p. 54
WS 46 in (117 cm)

Plumbeous Kite, p. 40
WS 31 in (78 cm)

Mississippi Kite, p. 40
WS 31 in (79 cm)

Osprey, p. 38
WS 59 in (150 cm)

Illustrations are not to uniform scale.

Cooper's Hawk, p. 44
WS 30 in (76 cm)

Sharp-shinned Hawk, p. 44
WS 21.5 in (55 cm)

female

Hook-billed Kite, p. 38
WS 35 in (88 cm)

Double-toothed Kite, p. 40
WS 26 in (66 cm)

Broad-winged Hawk, p. 50
pale morph
WS 33.5 in (85 cm)

Gray Hawk, p. 50
WS 33 in (84 cm)

White-tailed Hawk, p. 52
pale morph
WS 51 in (130 cm)

Short-tailed Hawk, p. 50
pale morph
WS 36.5 in (93 cm)

Black-and-white Hawk-Eagle, p. 54
WS 48 in (122 cm)

Swainson's Hawk, p. 52
pale morph
WS 50 in (127 cm)

Swainson's Hawk, p. 52
dark morph
WS 50 in (127 cm)

Harris's Hawk, p. 52
WS 42 in (106 cm)

Red-tailed Hawk, p. 52
resident race
WS 49 in (124 cm)

Red-tailed Hawk, p. 52
pale morph migrant race
WS 49 in (124 cm)

Savanna Hawk, p. 46
WS 51 in (130 cm)

Black-collared Hawk, p. 42
WS 51 in (129 cm)

Peregrine Falcon, p. 60
WS 38 in (96 cm)

Swallow-tailed Kite, p. 40
WS 50 in (128 cm)

Species Accounts and Illustrations

Color Code for Maps

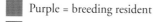 Purple = breeding resident

Solid blue = nonbreeding resident

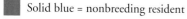 Hatched blue = transient

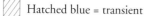 Red = breeding migrant

Green = vagrant

See page xiii for a more detailed explanation of color codes.

Abbreviations

M = male
F = female
WS = wingspan

Endemic Bird Areas within Panama:
CL = Caribbean lowlands
WH = western highlands
PL = Pacific lowlands
EL = eastern lowlands
EH = eastern highlands
EV = Escudo de Veraguas Island

Regional endemics that are also Panama national endemics are indicated with an asterisk (*).

TINAMIDAE. These partridge-like ground birds, found only in the neotropics, are actually more closely related to ostriches, rheas, and other large flightless birds. Their small heads, plump bodies, and very short tails give them a distinctive appearance. Panama's species are extremely secretive and far more often heard than seen. On occasion one may be spotted walking quietly along a trail, or flushed into explosive flight from the forest floor. The porcelain-like eggs (beautifully colored blue, green, or purplish) are incubated exclusively by the male.

Highland Tinamou
Nothocercus bonapartei

15 in (38 cm). Slightly smaller than Great Tinamou (little elevational overlap). Distinguished by mostly **rufous underparts** (especially so on throat) and **small buff spots on wings and back**. In area of overlap (western Pacific slope), Great has chestnut (not grayish) crown. Rare. Occurs in forest, in western highlands eastward to Fortuna area in central Chiriquí; above 4,600 ft (1,400 m). Call a resonant *kuh-ow*, repeated at approximately 1-second intervals in a long monotonous series.

Great Tinamou
Tinamus major

17 in (43 cm). Largest tinamou. Mostly **olive-brown**, with **blackish markings on back, wings, and flanks**. Race on western Caribbean slope has dusky crown; races on western Pacific slope have chestnut crown; race in eastern Panama (both slopes) has chestnut crown and slight crest. Distinctly larger than Little and Choco Tinamous; distinguished from Highland Tinamou by brown (not rufous) underparts, lack of buffy spots on back, and (in area of overlap) chestnut crown. Inhabits forest. Common on entire Caribbean slope; common on Pacific from western Panamá Province eastward (local on western Pacific slope, mostly in foothills); to 5,000 ft (1,500 m). Call a series of quavering whistles, deeper and more resonant than that of Little Tinamou; most often heard at dawn and dusk.

Little Tinamou
Crypturellus soui

8.5 in (22 cm). **Smallest** tinamou. **Yellowish legs** and **lack of any barring or spotting** distinguish it from other tinamous. Varies from rusty brown to grayish depending on race and sex (females of some races are more rufous than males). Common on both slopes to 5,000 ft (1,500 m); occurs in second growth, woodland, scrub, and forest edge. Call a series of high quavering whistles, similar to that of Great Tinamou but thinner and higher pitched.

Choco Tinamou
Crypturellus kerriae

10 in (26 cm). Only tinamou with **red legs**. Mostly dark reddish brown, with grayish head (blackish on crown); obscure blackish barring on wings, tail, and thighs; and small pale spots on wings. Rare. Occurs in forest in eastern Darién, to at least 2,500 ft (750 m). Call a mournful, three-noted *hooo-hooo-ah*, repeated at long intervals. **EL**

Highland Tinamou

eastern Panama

western Caribbean slope

Great Tinamou

rusty brown race

Little Tinamou

grayish race

Choco Tinamou

ANATIDAE. Ducks, found worldwide, are familiar to everyone. Panama species can be distinguished from other aquatic birds such as grebes, sungrebes, coots, and gallinules by their broad flattened bills. Ducks occur in Panama mainly in freshwater habitats, although some species may also be found in mangroves and estuaries. Only two species are both common and widespread: the resident Black-bellied Whistling-Duck and the migrant Blue-winged Teal. Panama's resident species nest mostly in tree holes, except for the Masked Duck, which nests on the ground near water. In species in which male and female plumages differ, males may molt (from late summer to autumn) into eclipse plumage, a drab plumage like that of females. Identification of females and males in eclipse often depends on details of size, shape, and plumage. In flight, wing pattern can be an important distinguishing feature.

Black-bellied Whistling-Duck   *Dendrocygna autumnalis*

17.5 in (44 cm). Adult's **bright pink bill and legs** are diagnostic; color pattern also distinctive. Immature similar but much duller; bill and legs gray. In flight, all plumages show **broad white wing stripe**. Formerly uncommon, now common and apparently spreading in lowlands on much of the Pacific slope; uncommon and local on Caribbean slope. Found on lakes, ponds, and rice fields, and also in mangroves and estuaries. Call (from which the local name *güichichi* is derived) is a series of shrill somewhat harsh whistles, *whit-WHEE-chi-chi-chi* (variable in stress and number of syllables), given mainly in flight.

Fulvous Whistling-Duck   *Dendrocygna bicolor*

18.5 in (47 cm). Mainly **pale cinnamon-brown** (darker on back), with **white stripes along flanks**. Immature similar to adult but slightly duller; distinguished from immature Black-bellied Whistling-Duck by cinnamon (not gray) head. In flight, all plumages show **all-dark wings** and a **white U-shaped rump band**. Formerly known only as a vagrant, but has recently colonized Panama, and a small breeding population is now established at Las Macanas Marsh, Coclé. Call a thin whistle *WHEER-chi-chi-chi,* harsher and often with fewer syllables than that of Black-bellied Whistling-Duck.

White-faced Whistling-Duck   *Dendrocygna viduata*

15.5 in (40 cm). **Front half of head white**; bill dark. Otherwise mainly brown, with black neck and belly and chestnut chest. Immature duller; front half of head grayish buff. In flight, **wings and rump are entirely dark**. Formerly bred very locally in eastern Panamá Province, but extirpated by hunting in 1940s; last record of vagrants 1976. **Not illustrated. No map.**

Muscovy Duck   *Cairina moschata*

M 31.5 in (80 cm); F 23.5 in (60 cm). Very large. **Mostly black** with greenish gloss. Males, much larger than females, have reddish warts on face and base of bill and a prominent crest. In flight, from both above and below, adults show a **large white wing patch** (very small or absent in immature). Domesticated Muscovies, often kept in rural areas, are best told from wild birds by tameness and habitat and, frequently, by white patches on head or body in addition to those on wing. Rare; found in lowlands in both freshwater wetlands (mostly in wooded areas) and in mangroves. On Pacific slope occurs mainly in eastern Panamá Province and Darién (local elsewhere); on Caribbean, found in Bocas del Toro and Canal Area. Mostly silent; male hisses, female gives a weak quack.

adult

immature

adult

Black-bellied Whistling-Duck

adult

adult

Fulvous Whistling-Duck

male

male

Muscovy Duck

American Wigeon
Anas americana

19.5 in (50 cm). Male's **white crown** distinctive; on female, combination of **grayish head** and contrasting **cinnamon sides and flanks** is distinctive. Both sexes have **short bluish bill**. In flight, male shows **large white wing patch**; female shows white line on wing coverts; white wing markings absent in immature. Rare and irregular winter resident (Oct to April) in freshwater habitats in lowlands eastward to eastern Panamá Province.

Mallard
Anas platyrhynchos

24 in (61 cm). Male (not illustrated) has **bright green head**, narrow white collar, **chestnut chest**, and **bright yellow bill**. Male Northern Shoveler is smaller, with longer bill, white chest, and chestnut flanks. Female distinguished from similar species by larger size and **orange bill with dark spot on upper mandible**. Vagrant, with most recent record from Pacific side of Canal Area (1992). Found in freshwater habitats; mallards seen in Panama are most likely escaped domestic stock.

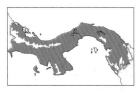

Blue-winged Teal
Anas discors

14 in (36 cm). Small. Male's **white crescent on front of head** is distinctive. Female distinguished from similar female Northern Shoveler by much shorter bill; from female Northern Pintail by shorter neck and tail; very similar to female Cinnamon Teal (p. 8) but has slightly shorter bill. In flight, both sexes show prominent blue wing patches (shared by Northern Shoveler and Cinnamon Teal). By far the most common migrant duck (transient and winter resident, from Sept to April; rare in summer), occurs in freshwater habitats throughout the country, to 4,600 ft (1,400 m).

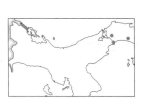

Northern Shoveler
Anas clypeata

19 in (48 cm). Strikingly **long spatulate bill** is longer than head. Male's bold pattern distinctive. Female resembles female Blue-winged and Cinnamon Teals (p. 8); distinguished by much longer bill and larger size. In flight, both sexes (like both teals) show prominent bluish wing patches (grayer in female). A rare migrant to freshwater habitats in lowlands, eastward to eastern Panamá Province.

Northern Pintail
Anas acuta

25 in (64 cm). **Long-necked and slender** compared to other migrant ducks, with **long pointed tail** (much longer in male). Male has brown head with **white stripe extending up side of neck**. In flight, both sexes show white stripe on rear edge of speculum (green in male, bronzy in female). Rare winter resident (Oct to March) in freshwater habitats in lowlands of western Panama, mainly in Bocas del Toro but with a few records eastward to eastern Panamá Province.

Green-winged Teal
Anas crecca

14 in (35 cm). On male, **green and chestnut head** is diagnostic. Female has a smaller, thinner bill than other female teals and female Northern Shoveler. In flight, shows green speculum with buffy bar above it. Vagrant, with one record from Pacific side of Canal Area (1996). Found in freshwater habitats.

7

American Wigeon

Mallard

Blue-winged Teal

Northern Shoveler

Northern Pintail

Green-winged Teal

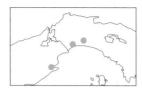

Cinnamon Teal
Anas cyanoptera

14 in (36 cm). **Rich chestnut** male nearly unmistakable; distinguished from male Masked Duck by dark bill and absence of black on face. Female almost identical to female Blue-winged Teal (p. 6) but has somewhat longer bill. Vagrant in freshwater habitats in lowlands.

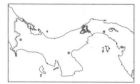

Masked Duck
Nomonyx dominicus

13.5 in (34 cm). Small and compact. Breeding male distinctive; mostly **rich chestnut** with **black face**, black spots on back, and **blue bill**. Female has strongly **striped, black and buff face** and barred back; immature and eclipse male are similar to female. In flight, both sexes have prominent **white patch on secondaries.** Shy and retiring, often remaining hidden in aquatic vegetation; dives and also submerges slowly, like a grebe. Rare and local in freshwater habitats with thick vegetation, including shallow ponds, marshes, and the edges of lakes and sluggish rivers, to 4,600 ft (1,400 m). Mostly silent; males give a long *kuri-kuroo,* often repeated; females give a short hiss.

Ring-necked Duck
Aythya collaris

17.5 in (44 cm). **Bluish gray bill with white band and black tip** is diagnostic. Male similar to male Lesser Scaup but has **black back, gray flanks**, and a prominent vertical white mark just behind black chest; female distinguished from female Lesser Scaup by **white eye-ring** and faint vertical white mark on side of chest. In flight, both sexes distinguished from Lesser Scaup by **gray** (not white) **secondaries**. Like scaup, feeds by diving. Very rare winter resident (Dec to Feb) in freshwater habitats, with scattered records from Chiriquí, Herrera, the Canal Area, and eastern Panamá Province; to 4,600 ft (1,400 m).

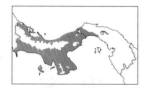

Lesser Scaup
Aythya affinis

15.5 in (40 cm). Male's **black head** (glossed purple), **neck, and chest** distinguish it from all except male Ring-necked Duck, from which it differs by **unmarked bluish bill, gray back**, and **whitish flanks**. Female mostly dark brown with **distinct white patch on face at base of bill**; further distinguished from female Ring-necked Duck in **lacking eye-ring**. In flight, both sexes show **white stripe across secondaries**. Like Ring-necked and Masked Ducks, dives to feed (unlike all other Panama ducks). Rare winter resident (Nov to March) in freshwater habitats eastward to eastern Panamá Province; to 4,600 ft (1,400 m).

Comb Duck
Sarkidiornis melanotos

M 24 in (61 cm); F 20.5 in (52 cm). Large. **Mainly white**, with small black dots on head and neck and **blackish back, sides, flanks, and wings**. Male has large rounded comb on base of bill (absent in female). Status uncertain; probably vagrant but possibly a very rare breeder; recorded in eastern Panamá Province (1949) and Darién (1959).

White-cheeked Pintail
Anas bahamensis

18 in (46 cm). Resembles Northern Pintail (p. 6), including **pointed tail**, but both sexes are mostly brown, with black spotting on underparts. **White cheeks and throat** are diagnostic; also note gray bill with **pink spot on base**. Inhabits mangroves, estuaries, and other coastal wetlands; sometimes found on freshwater ponds. Vagrant; one record from Costa del Este in eastern Panamá City (1996). **Not illustrated**.

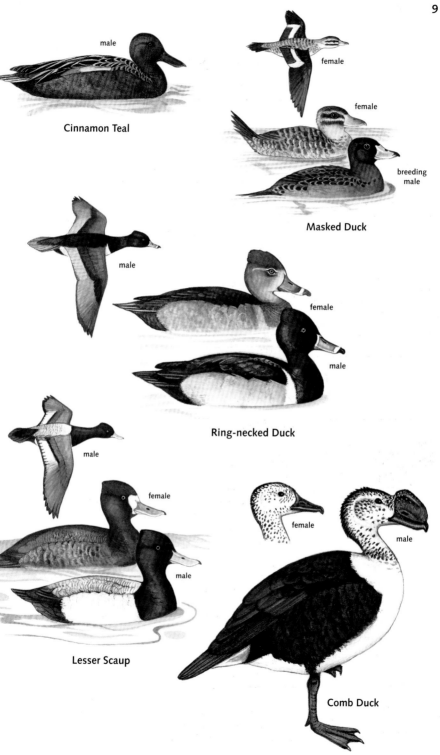

male

Cinnamon Teal

female

female

breeding male

Masked Duck

male

female

male

Ring-necked Duck

male

female

male

Lesser Scaup

female

male

Comb Duck

CRACIDAE. These mainly neotropical birds resemble pheasants and turkeys but are only distantly related to them. Though largely arboreal, curassows spend much of their time on the ground, and fly strongly (if only for short distances). They feed mostly on vegetable matter, especially fruit. Curassows and guans are primarily forest birds, while chachalacas favor second growth and scrub. The larger species are favorite game for hunters, and have become scarce near populated areas.

Gray-headed Chachalaca   *Ortalis cinereiceps*
21 in (53 cm). Pheasant size. Mainly **grayish brown** (head and neck gray, with small bare red patch on throat); **tail tipped buff.** In flight shows prominent **chestnut primaries.** Occurs in lowlands throughout the country, in flocks of up to about a dozen. Common in middle and upper levels of woodland, second growth, and shrubby areas. Primary call is a high-pitched *wheek!* repeated frequently, especially when alarmed.

Crested Guan   *Penelope purpurascens*
32 in (81 cm). Nearly as long as Great Curassow but much more slender. Mainly **dark olive-brown**, with **whitish streaking on neck and breast** and prominent **bare red throat.** Rare near populated areas, but can be fairly common in protected areas and in remote regions; to 7,000 ft (2,100 m). Found in middle and upper levels of forest, usually in pairs or small groups. Gives loud honking calls, especially when disturbed; in display, makes a whirring sound with wings.

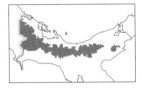

Black Guan   *Chamaepetes unicolor*
26 in (66 cm). Smaller than Crested Guan; distinguished by **all-black plumage** and **bare blue facial skin.** Fairly common where protected. Occurs in western foothills and highlands eastward to Coclé; mainly between 3,000 and 8,200 ft (900 and 2,500 m), but down to 1,500 ft (450 m) on Caribbean slope. Found in middle and upper levels of forest (occasionally on ground). Usually in pairs, sometimes in small groups. Main call similar to that of Crested Guan but lower and softer; in display, makes a loud rattling sound with wings. **WH**

Great Curassow   *Crax rubra*
M 35.5 in (90 cm); F 32 in (81 cm). **Very large** with **prominent crest.** Male **black with white vent and undertail coverts**; yellow knob on base of bill (absent in immature). On female, crest is barred with white; color varies from rufous brown (with tail strongly barred with buff) to blackish (with unbarred tail); lacks yellow knob on bill. Rare to uncommon; very local in forests in protected areas and remote regions, to 5,700 ft (1,900 m). Usually in pairs, occasionally in small groups; mostly on ground, taking refuge in trees when flushed. Males produce an extremely low-pitched booming call during the breeding season; when alarmed, both sexes give a high-pitched *wheep.*

Gray-headed
Chachalaca

Crested Guan

Black Guan

female
rufous morph

male

Great Curassow

ODONTOPHORIDAE. New World quails, while very similar in appearance to the quails and pheasants of the Old World (family Phasianidae), are not closely related to them. They feed mostly on seeds, fruit, and other vegetable matter but supplement this with insects and other small animals. Generally they are found in small groups (called coveys), running swiftly on the ground and only flying when startled or closely pursued. The Crested Bobwhite occurs in open country, while the other species live in forest. Wood-quails have crests that are not very apparent except when raised in excitement. All species are shy and secretive, their presence revealed mainly by musical calls. These vocalizations are actually duets, the male performing one part and the female the other.

Marbled Wood-Quail
Odontophorus gujanensis

10 in (26 cm). **Red orbital skin** is diagnostic. Less distinctively patterned than other Panama quails. Fairly common in forest on Caribbean slope, from northern Coclé eastward, and on Pacific from eastern Panamá Province eastward; rare and local in westernmost Chiriquí; to 5,000 ft (1,500 m). Call a rollicking *koo-ku-wha-koo* repeated many times, often for several minutes.

Black-eared Wood-Quail
Odontophorus melanotis

9.5 in (24 cm). Male's **blackish throat**—in combination with unmarked **chestnut breast and belly**—is diagnostic. Female has less black on throat (sometimes lacking) and blackish orbital skin. Only other quail with rufous crest is Spotted Wood-Quail, which occurs mostly at higher elevations. Rare in forest on Caribbean slope; local on Pacific in Veraguas, Panamá Province, and Darién; mainly in foothills, from 1,500 to 3,500 ft (450 to 1,050 m), but sometimes to sea level or above 5,000 ft (1,500 m). Call a repeated *KLA-coo* or *coo-KLAK*.

Tacarcuna Wood-Quail
Odontophorus dialeucos

9.5 in (24 cm). Combination of **white face** and **white chest separated by blackish band** is diagnostic. Poorly known; reported to be common in forest in its very limited known range, on Cerro Tacarcuna in Darién; 4,000 to 4,800 ft (1,200 to 1,450 m). Call undescribed. **EH**

Black-breasted Wood-Quail
Odontophorus leucolaemus

9 in (23 cm). Only quail with **black breast**. Variable; in some individuals white throat is reduced or absent, or underparts are mostly brown. Uncommon; occurs in forest of western Panama eastward to Coclé, in foothills and highlands, from 3,300 to 5,300 ft (1,000 to 1,600 m). Call a repeated, fast, high-pitched *WI-chi-chi WU-chi*. **WH**

Spotted Wood-Quail
Odontophorus guttatus

10 in (25 cm). Combination of **white spots on breast** and **blackish throat streaked with white** is distinctive. Some individuals are brighter rufous. Black-breasted Wood-Quail, which overlaps in range and habitat, lacks rufous on head and usually has white throat. Fairly common in forest of western Chiriquí, in highlands, from 3,600 to 8,000 ft (1,100 to 2,400 m). Call a repeated *KEE-a-whit ah KOO-whit* (slower in tempo than that of Black-breasted Wood-Quail).

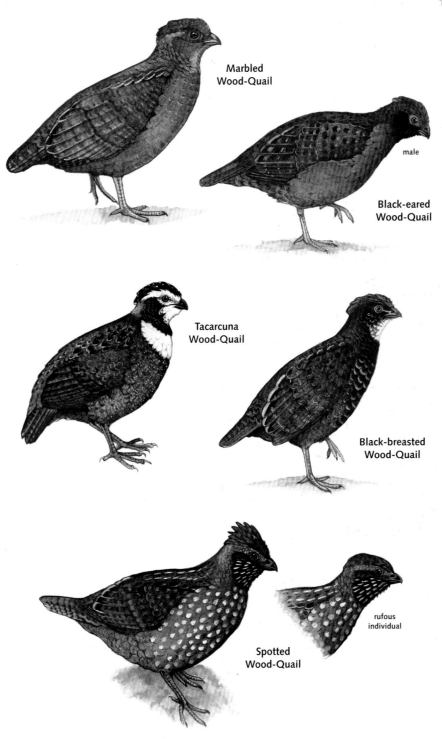

Marbled
Wood-Quail

Black-eared
Wood-Quail

male

Tacarcuna
Wood-Quail

Black-breasted
Wood-Quail

Spotted
Wood-Quail

rufous
individual

Tawny-faced Quail
Rhynchortyx cinctus

7 in (18 cm). Smaller than other forest quails. On male, **tawny face** and **gray chest** are both distinctive; on female, **whitish superciliary** and **black-and-white barred lower breast and belly** are unique. Rare and local in forest from western Colón Province eastward, to 4,800 ft (1,450 m). Usually in pairs, less often in small coveys. Call, reminiscent of that of Great Tinamou (p. 2), is a hesitant, mournful series of five to eight notes (sometimes more) changing in pitch and spacing, usually with the last two or three more closely spaced than the rest.

Crested Bobwhite
Colinus cristatus

8 in (20 cm). **Heavily white-spotted underparts** distinguish it from all other Panama quails except the Spotted Wood-Quail (p. 12), which occurs in different habitat and has a mostly blackish throat. Throat of male varies from rufous to buffy or white. Female similar to male, but with shorter, darker crest and black streaking on throat. Fairly common in areas with tall grass and scrub; occurs on Pacific slope eastward to western Panamá Province, to 4,600 ft (1,400 m). Call a distinctive whistled *bob, bob-white.*

Grebes

PODICIPEDIDAE. These aquatic birds are highly specialized for diving. They superficially resemble ducks but have lobed toes instead of completely webbed feet and are virtually tailless. When swimming, grebes sometimes slowly submerge their bodies, leaving only the head and neck above water. Panama's two species inhabit quiet freshwater habitats with standing or floating vegetation, including marshes, ponds, lakes, and sluggish rivers. They make floating nests of aquatic vegetation.

Least Grebe
Tachybaptus dominicus

8.5 in (22 cm). Distinguished from Pied-billed Grebe by smaller size, **slender pointed black bill**, prominent **yellow eye**, and generally darker coloration. In breeding birds throat is black; in nonbreeders it is whitish. Immature has striped head. In flight, shows **white patch on flight feathers**. Fairly common, to 4,600 ft (1,400 m). Call a nasal *ahnk*; also gives a prolonged *churrrr* like that of White-throated Crake (p. 62).

Pied-billed Grebe
Podilymbus podiceps

12.5 in (32 cm). Larger than Least Grebe and further distinguished by **short broad whitish bill** (with black band in breeding season), **dark eye**, paler coloration, and, in flight, lack of white wing patch. Throat black in breeding plumage, whitish in nonbreeding. Immature has striped or mottled head. Common in western and central Panama, becoming rare east of eastern Panamá Province; to 4,600 ft (1,400 m). Resident breeding population is augmented by northern migrants in winter. Call is a loud *kuk-kuk-kuk-kuk, kuh-cow, cow-cow-cow,* presented in a varying series; also a rapid *kikikikikikiki.*

female

male

Tawny-faced Quail

female

male

Crested Bobwhite

breeding adult

nonbreeding adult

Least Grebe

breeding adult

nonbreeding adult

Pied-billed Grebe

PROCELLARIIDAE. The members of this cosmopolitan family are highly pelagic, spending their lives at sea except when breeding. Many species are very similar, and identification often requires the recognition of subtle differences of pattern and flight style. Fortunately, the only three species known to occur regularly in Panama— Sooty, Audubon's, and Galapagos Shearwaters—are easily distinguished by size, pattern, and range.

Sooty Shearwater   *Puffinus griseus*

17.5 in (44 cm); WS 40 in (102 cm). Combination of all-dark body and long slender pointed wings showing **silvery whitish** (rarely gray) **wing-linings** is distinctive. Glides low over water on stiff wings; rarely flaps. Fairly common transient (mainly June to Sept, peaking in Aug) off Pacific coast, usually well offshore. Breeds in Southern Hemisphere.

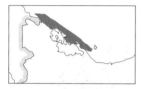

Audubon's Shearwater   *Puffinus lherminieri*

12 in (30 cm); WS 28 in (71 cm). Much smaller than Sooty Shearwater, with **white underparts** and relatively shorter and more rounded wings. Fluttery flight distinctive, with a series of shallow flaps interspersed with short glides. No range overlap with very similar Galapagos Shearwater. Breeds on small islets off coast of Valiente Peninsula in Ngöbe-Buglé; could occur elsewhere in Caribbean.

Galapagos Shearwater   *Puffinus subalaris*

12 in (30 cm); 25 in (63 cm). Similar to Audubon's Shearwater but no range overlap; in comparison with Sooty Shearwater note Galapagos's **white underparts**. Somewhat variable; some individuals have an underwing pattern much like Audubon's, while others have dark smudgy markings on the white areas. Fairly common transient from April to Aug and Oct to Dec (most common in April and from Oct to Nov). Occurs on Pacific in Gulf of Panama (south of Pearl Islands) and off Darién. Breeds in Galápagos. Considered a subspecies of Audubon's Shearwater by AOU. **Not illustrated**.

Wedge-tailed Shearwater   *Puffinus pacificus*

18 in (46 cm); WS 40 in (100 cm). Legs flesh-colored. Occurs in two color morphs. Dark morph, entirely dark brown, is distinguished from most Sooty Shearwaters by **dark wing-linings**. Pale morph, brown above and white below, is much larger than similar Galapagos Shearwater. Vagrant in Gulf of Panama and off coast of Darién. Breeds on islands in Pacific and Indian Oceans. **Not illustrated**.

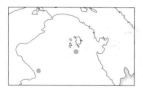

Galapagos Petrel   *Pterodroma phaeopygia*

16.5 in (42 cm); WS 36 in (91 cm). Blackish above; white below (**white extends onto forehead**, giving a distinctive capped appearance). Vagrant in Gulf of Panama. Breeds in Galápagos. **Not illustrated**.

Parkinson's Petrel   *Procellaria parkinsoni*

18 in (46 cm); WS 45 in (115 cm). All dark; **heavy bill is whitish with black tip**. More heavily built than Sooty Shearwater and lacks Sooty's slender dark bill and its (usually) silvery whitish wing-linings. Vagrant off Pacific coast. Breeds in New Zealand. **Not illustrated**.

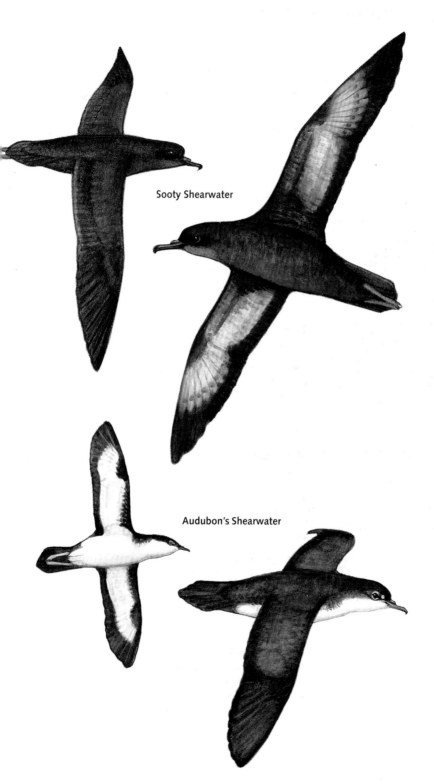

Sooty Shearwater

Audubon's Shearwater

HYDROBATIDAE. These small pelagic seabirds are found worldwide. Most have a distinctive fluttering flight, sometimes "dancing" on the surface of the sea with their feet touching the waves. Identification is often difficult; the three species that occur regularly in Panama can be distinguished by color pattern, size, and tail shape.

Wedge-rumped Storm-Petrel   *Oceanodroma tethys*
7.5 in (19 cm); WS 14.5 in (37 cm). Very large **triangular white rump patch** is diagnostic. At times a fairly common migrant off Pacific coast, especially from June to Aug (recorded Feb to Nov). Breeds in Galápagos and off coast of South America.

Black Storm-Petrel   *Oceanodroma melania*
9 in (23 cm); WS 17 in (43 cm). Distinguished from Least Storm-Petrel by much larger size and **deeply forked tail**. Uncommon migrant off Pacific coast; recorded nearly all year, but most numerous in June and Nov. Breeds off Baja California.

Least Storm-Petrel   *Oceanodroma microsoma*
5.5 in (14 cm); WS 13.5 in (34 cm). Distinguished from Black Storm-Petrel by much smaller size and **wedge-shaped tail** (shape can be hard to see at sea). Sometimes common as a migrant off Pacific coast, with peaks of abundance from Feb to April and in Aug (recorded nearly all year). Breeds off Baja California.

Tropicbirds

PHAETHONTIDAE. This family of just three species occurs in tropical waters throughout the world. Adults are characterized by extremely long central tail feathers. Tropicbirds fly gracefully and catch fish by plunge-diving.

Red-billed Tropicbird   *Phaethon aethereus*
20 in (51 cm), not including very long central tail feathers; WS 44 in (112 cm). Adults distinguished from all other mainly white seabirds by **very long white tail feathers** and **red bill**. Immature lacks long tail feathers and has yellow bill; black eye-stripe extends around back of head. Breeds on Swan Cay off Colón Island in Bocas del Toro; not recorded elsewhere on Caribbean coast but likely occurs there. Very rare off Pacific coast.

White-tailed Tropicbird   *Phaethon lepturus*
15 in (39 cm), not including very long central tail feathers; WS 36 in (93 cm). **White, unbarred back** and bold black line along shoulders distinguish adult from all plumages of Red-billed Tropicbird; also note that adult White-tailed has yellow bill. Immature similar to immature Red-billed, but black eye-stripe does not extend around back of head; also has less black barring on back. Vagrant off western Caribbean coast. **Not illustrated**.

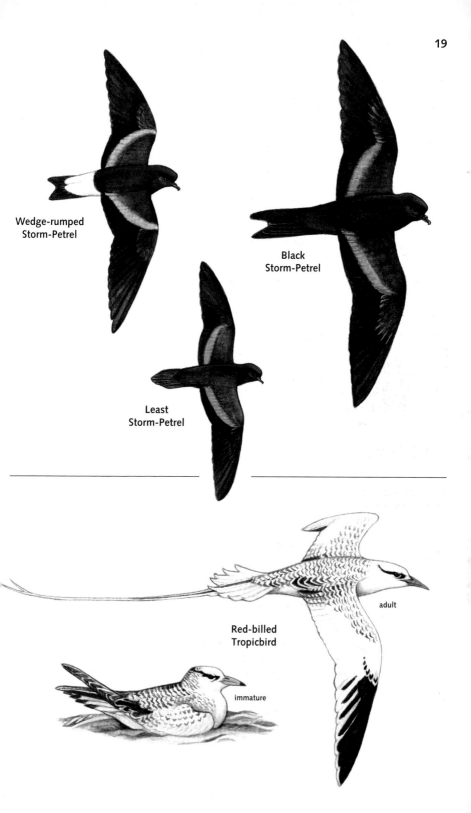

Wedge-rumped
Storm-Petrel

Black
Storm-Petrel

Least
Storm-Petrel

Red-billed
Tropicbird

adult

immature

SULIDAE. These large seabirds are found throughout the world. Boobies occur in tropical waters, gannets in temperate regions. They plunge-dive to feed, often from considerable heights. In flight, pointed wings and long pointed tails are distinctive. Also note pointed conical bills. In Panama, the Brown Booby is the sole species commonly seen from shore; this and Blue-footed Booby are the only species that breed in the country.

Masked Booby
Sula dactylatra

34 in (86 cm); WS 60 in (152 cm). Adult mainly **white with black flight feathers and tail**; legs grayish to yellowish. Distinguished from very similar Nazca Booby by **yellow** (not orange) **bill**. Compare also with white morph of Red-footed Booby (p. 22). Immature, mainly brownish above with grayish bill, is distinguished from Brown Booby (p. 22) by broad white collar across hindneck. Vagrant off Caribbean coast; possible on Pacific but no definite records.

Nazca Booby
Sula granti

34 in (86 cm); WS 60 in (152 cm). Mainly **white with black flight feathers and tail**, this species is very similar to the Masked Booby, but adult has **orange to orange-pink bill**. Unlike immature Masked Booby, most immature Nazcas lack white collar on hindneck (a few have narrow or incomplete collar). Immatures that lack collar are similar to Brown Booby (p. 22); distinguished from adult Brown by white underparts extending higher up chest, more extensive white on underwing, and yellow eyes; from immature Brown by clean white underparts; distinguished from immature Blue-footed Booby by white underparts extending higher up chest. Uncommon transient (Sept to Nov and April to June) on Pacific, south of Pearl Islands and off Darién; one record of an immature from Caribbean coast near Colón.

Blue-footed Booby
Sula nebouxii

32 in (81 cm); WS 62 in (157 cm). Breeding adults have **bright blue feet** (duller blue-gray in nonbreeders and immatures). **White patches on upper back and rump** of adult are distinctive. Immature differs from adult Brown Booby (p. 22) by grayish bill and lack of clean-cut division between dark breast and white lower underparts; from immature Brown by whiter belly. On Pacific only; common around nesting islands in Bay of Panama and near Pearl Islands, but rarely seen from shore.

Peruvian Booby
Sula variegata

29 in (74 cm); WS not recorded. Very similar to Blue-footed Booby but adult has **pure white head**; legs blue-gray (never bright blue). On immature, uniform brown streaking on head, neck, and underparts distinguish it from immature Blue-footed. Thousands invaded Gulf of Panama from normal South American range during strong El Niño event of 1983. None seen since but likely to occur again if such conditions repeat.

Masked Booby

adult

immature

Nazca Booby

adult

immature

Blue-footed Booby

immature

breeding adult

breeding adult

Peruvian Booby

immature

adult

Brown Booby
Sula leucogaster

28 in (71 cm); WS 57 in (145 cm). **Yellow bill, yellowish feet**, and clean-cut division between dark upperparts and white underparts distinguish adults from similar immatures of other boobies. Immature is darker below than other immature boobies. Male of Pacific race has pale head. By far the most common Panama booby; breeds on islands off both Pacific and Caribbean coasts.

Red-footed Booby
Sula sula

27 in (68 cm); WS 60 in (152 cm). Adult's **red legs** diagnostic in all plumages; white tail (present in some morphs) is also diagnostic. Several color morphs occur. White morph smaller than Masked Booby (p. 20) and further distinguished by white (not black) tertials and black patch on underside of wing near wrist. White-tailed brown morph is mostly brown, but rear of body and tail are white. Brown morph is entirely dark brown; it is more uniformly colored than immature Brown Booby (as are immatures of all morphs). Vagrant off Caribbean coast; one record from Pacific.

Pelicans

PELECANIDAE. This small family is found throughout the tropics and in some temperate regions. Pelicans are large birds distinguished by long bills with capacious throat pouches that are used to catch fish. Most species are found in freshwater habitats, but Panama's only regularly occurring species, the Brown Pelican, is mainly coastal.

Brown Pelican
Pelecanus occidentalis

51 in (130 cm); WS 79 in (200 cm). Enormous size and very large bill make this species essentially unmistakable. In breeding adults back of neck is brown, front is white; in nonbreeders neck is entirely white; in immatures it is completely brown. Brown Pelicans often glide low over the water or soar higher in lines or V-formations; they fish by plunge-diving. Very common on both coasts, breeding on islands off Pacific. Sometimes seen soaring far inland, evidently crossing between coasts.

American White Pelican
Pelecanus erythrorhynchos

65 in (165 cm); WS 108 in (274 cm). Mostly **white** (primaries and outer secondaries black), with **orange bill and legs**. Note that from a distance the Brown Pelican can look whitish when in strong sunlight. Vagrant, with a few records from Herrera and eastern Panamá Province. **Not illustrated**.

Albatrosses

DIOMEDEIDAE. Highly adapted for soaring, albatrosses have extremely long narrow wings and spend most of their lives far at sea (except when nesting on remote islands). They pluck squid and other marine life from the water's surface without alighting.

Waved Albatross
Phoebastria irrorata

35 in (89 cm); WS 92 in (250 cm). Much larger than any shearwater or petrel. Distinguished from all other albatrosses by combination of large, heavy **all-yellow bill, completely white head** (tinged yellow on crown and nape in adult), and **slaty lower breast and belly** marked with very narrow white barring. Back and rump slaty with fine white barring, more extensive on rump. Vagrant at sea off Darién and south of Pearl Islands. Breeds in Galápagos. **Not illustrated**.

adult

immature

adult

male Pacific race

Brown Booby

adult white morph

adult brown morph

adult brown morph

Red-footed Booby

nonbreeding adult

immature

breeding adult

Brown Pelican

PHALACROCORACIDAE. These long-necked, long-tailed aquatic birds are found worldwide in both freshwater and marine environments. They catch fish underwater by diving from the surface. Cormorants often swim low in the water, sometimes with just the head and neck exposed. Only the Neotropic Cormorant regularly occurs in Panama.

Neotropic Cormorant　　　　*Phalacrocorax brasilianus*
27 in (68 cm); WS 40 in (101 cm). Distinguished from the Anhinga by **shorter neck and tail, shorter bill (with hook at tip)**, and lack of white on wings. Adult **mostly black**; immature brownish, paler below. Common on both coasts and on larger lakes and rivers; occasionally on smaller streams; to 4,600 ft (1,400 m). Breeds in colonies on offshore islands, in mangroves, and on Lake Bayano.

Guanay Cormorant　　　　*Phalacrocorax bougainvillii*
28.5 in (73 cm); WS not recorded. Distinguished from Neotropic Cormorant by **white breast and belly** (with brown cast in immature); adults also have white chin. Breeding adults have blue-black upperparts; in nonbreeding adults and immatures these are brownish. Immature shows contrast between dark neck and pale breast and belly, unlike immature Neotropic Cormorant. Irregular visitor to southern Darién and Gulf of Panama, mainly in El Niño years; most recent records in 1983.

Darters

ANHINGIDAE. These cormorant-like birds are found in freshwater habitats in tropical and subtropical regions throughout the world. Darters hunt fish by swimming underwater and spearing prey with their long pointed bills. Like cormorants, they often swim with only the head and long slender neck exposed.

Anhinga　　　　*Anhinga anhinga*
32.5 in (83 cm); WS 45 in (114 cm). Distinguished from Neotropic Cormorant by relatively **longer neck, longer fan-shaped tail, longer pointed bill**, and **white wing coverts**. Male mainly black; female has buffy head and neck. Sometimes soars, its long pointed wings and long neck and tail giving it a distinctive cross-shaped silhouette. Uncommon on lakes, ponds, and rivers in lowlands throughout the country.

Frigatebirds

FREGATIDAE. This small group of graceful seabirds occurs in tropical oceans worldwide. Frigatebirds are highly adapted for soaring, and in fact they never alight on the water's surface as their plumage is not waterproof. They are well known for their habit of pursuing and harassing other seabirds (boobies, gulls, and others) until they drop their food, which the frigatebirds then steal and eat. They also pluck food from the surface of the sea with their long, slightly hooked bills.

Magnificent Frigatebird　　　　*Fregata magnificens*
40 in (102 cm); WS 91 in (230 cm). Extremely long pointed wings and **deeply forked tail** distinguish this species from all but vagrant Great Frigatebird (p. 26). Male mostly black; female has white breast; immature has white head and breast. Immatures undergo a complex series of changes over several years as they gradually acquire adult plumage. Males inflate their red throat pouches to enormous size in breeding display. Very common along coasts, especially on Pacific, where it breeds on offshore islands. Occasionally seen soaring far inland.

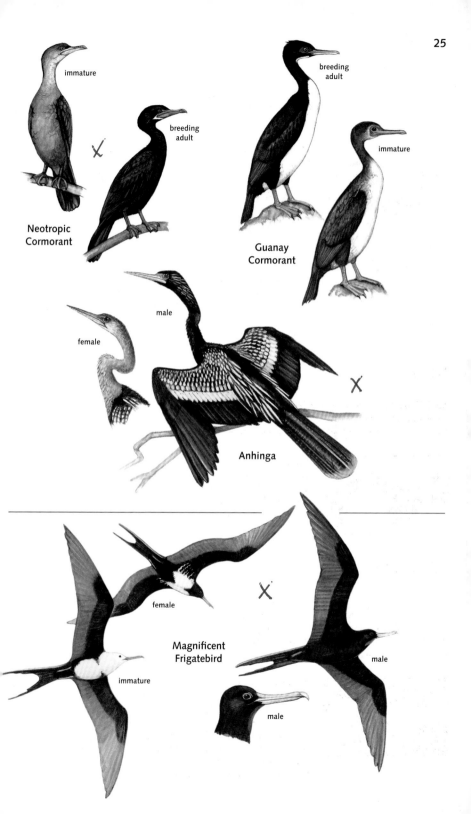

Neotropic Cormorant

immature

breeding adult

Guanay Cormorant

breeding adult

immature

Anhinga

female

male

Magnificent Frigatebird

female

immature

male

male

Great Frigatebird *Fregata minor*
37 in (93 cm); WS 86 in (218 cm). All plumages distinguished from those of very similar Magnificent Frigatebird (p. 24) by prominent pale bar across wing (above secondaries). Female and older immature Magnificents also show narrow white barring on axillars; this is always lacking in Great. Female has pale grayish or brownish throat contrasting with black head and white breast; immature usually has tawny head. Vagrant far offshore of western Pacific coast; one record (2003). **Not illustrated. No map**.

Herons & Egrets

ARDEIDAE. These long-necked, long-legged wading birds occur throughout the world. Most have long straight bills that they use to catch fish, small vertebrates, and insects. Panama species, which vary greatly in size, occur mainly in freshwater and coastal habitats, with the exception of the Cattle Egret, which frequents pastures and other grassy areas. All-white species may be distinguished by combination of size, bill color, and leg color. Herons fly with neck folded, while storks, ibises, and spoonbills fly with neck extended. In the species accounts, "heron" is used as a generic term for all members of the family, including bitterns and egrets.

Rufescent Tiger-Heron *Tigrisoma lineatum*
27 in (68 cm). On adult, rich **rufous head and neck** distinguish it from other tiger-herons. Immature, heavily barred with black and buff (especially on wings), lacks yellow throat of immature Bare-throated Tiger-Heron. Immature Fasciated is nearly identical but is smaller and has shorter bill; probably best distinguished by habitat. Uncommon. Occurs on entire Caribbean slope; on Pacific slope, from eastern Panamá Province eastward; to 1,800 ft (550 m). Found in forested streams, lake edges, and swamps.

Fasciated Tiger-Heron *Tigrisoma fasciatum*
24 in (61 cm). Adult is the darkest tiger-heron. Distinguished from Bare-throated Tiger-Heron by **darker sides of head and neck** and **white** (not bare yellow) **feathered throat**. Immature nearly identical to immature Rufescent, but is smaller with shorter bill. Fasciated is typically found in different habitat than Rufescent. Rare. Occurs on entire Caribbean slope and on Pacific slope from eastern Panamá Province eastward; mainly in foothills, to at least 4,300 ft (1,300 m), but occasionally in lowlands. Found along forested streams (usually rapidly flowing ones).

Bare-throated Tiger-Heron *Tigrisoma mexicanum*
30 in (76 cm). **Bare yellow throat** diagnostic in all plumages. Common on Pacific offshore islands, including Coiba and Pearl Islands; rare along mainland Pacific coast, including adjacent mangroves and freshwater marshes, and on large freshwater lakes; one record from easternmost Caribbean coast.

Agami Heron *Agamia agami*
28 in (71 cm). In all plumages, exceptionally **long thin bill** and **long neck** are distinctive; on adult, combination of **green back** and rich **chestnut neck and underparts** is also distinctive. Immature dark brown above, with blackish crown, white throat, and underparts streaked with black and buff. Rare. Occurs in lowlands on entire Caribbean slope, and on Pacific slope from Canal Area eastward. Found along forested streams and in marshes.

Rufescent
Tiger-Heron

Fasciated
Tiger-Heron

Bare-throated
Tiger-Heron

Agami Heron

adult

immature

adult

immature

adult

immature

adult

Great Blue Heron
Ardea herodias

40 in (102 cm). This and Cocoi are largest herons. In any plumage, distinguished from Cocoi by **rufous thighs**. Adult also differs from adult Cocoi in **central white crown stripe** (lacking in immature) and **grayish neck**. Common winter resident (mostly Sept to April), a few present in summer; on larger rivers and lakes, in marshes, and along coasts; to 5,300 ft (1,600 m).

Cocoi Heron
Ardea cocoi

40 in (101 cm). Distinguished in any plumage from Great Blue Heron by mostly **white thighs**; on adult, note **white neck** (not grayish) and all-black crown. Immature, with grayish neck, is similar to immature Great Blue (both have all-black crown), but the latter has rufous thighs, and its neck is not pure gray, instead showing a brownish cast. Uncommon on Pacific slope, from eastern Panamá Province eastward; vagrants occur as far west as Herrera; found on larger rivers and lakes and in marshes.

Great Egret
Ardea alba

35.5 in (90 cm). Largest white heron. Combination of **yellow bill** and **black legs** distinguishes it from much smaller Snowy Egret, white-morph Reddish Egret, and immature Little Blue Heron; much larger with longer neck than Cattle Egret (p. 30). Common in all freshwater habitats and on both coasts, to 4,600 ft (1,400 m). Breeds along Pacific coast in colonies in wetlands and on offshore islands; local population supplemented by migrants in winter.

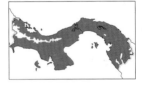

Snowy Egret
Egretta thula

22 in (56 cm). **Thin black bill** and (on adult) **black legs** with **bright yellow feet** distinguish it from other white herons. On immature, backs of legs are greenish yellow; distinguished from immature Little Blue Heron by lack of dusky tips on primaries (often hard to see). Common along both coasts; uncommon inland, in freshwater habitats; to 4,600 ft (1,400 m). Breeds along Pacific coast in colonies in wetlands and on offshore islands; local population supplemented by migrants in winter.

Little Blue Heron
Egretta caerulea

22.5 in (57 cm). In all plumages, distinguished from other herons (except very rare Reddish Egret) by **two-tone bill**, which is usually grayish near base and black at tip (in immatures, sometimes pinkish, greenish, or yellowish near base). Adult slaty gray with reddish cast on head and neck. Immature all white with dull green legs and inconspicuous dusky tips to primaries; when molting into adult plumage, immature is white with irregular splotches of dark gray. Common migrant (some present all year). Found inland, in freshwater habitats, and on both coasts, to 4,600 ft (1,400 m). Very rare breeder in Panama.

Reddish Egret
Egretta rufescens

30 in (76 cm). Has both dark and white morphs. In both morphs: on adult, **two-tone, pink and black bill** and **shaggy neck** are distinctive; immature has all-dark bill and dark gray legs, distinguishing it from smaller Little Blue Heron in any plumage. Very rare migrant, with scattered records from Veraguas, Herrera, Coclé, Panamá, and Colón Provinces. Feeds in shallow water, where it displays distinctive, very active foraging behavior, dashing about and often spreading wings.

adult

Great Blue
Heron

immature

adult

Cocoi
Heron

immature

adult

Great Egret

Snowy Egret

adult
dark morph

immature
dark morph

adult

molting
immature

Reddish
Egret

Little Blue
Heron

adult
white morph

Tricolored Heron
Egretta tricolor

24 in (61 cm). Combination of **dark upperparts** and **white belly** is diagnostic in all plumages; has proportionally longer neck and longer bill than Little Blue Heron (p. 28). Immature has bright rufous head, hindneck, and wing coverts. Common inland, in freshwater habitats, and on both coasts, to 4,600 ft (1,400 m). Breeds in colonies along Pacific coast (in wetlands near coast) and on offshore islands; local population supplemented by migrants in winter.

Cattle Egret
Bubulcus ibis

20 in (51 cm). Chunkier than other white herons. Nonbreeding adult distinguished from other white herons (except much larger Great Egret, p. 28) by **yellow bill**. Breeding adults have buffy patches on head, breast, and back and **red bill and legs**. Immatures have black bill and legs. Very common; occurs throughout the country to 4,600 ft (1,400 m), in grassy locations, especially near cattle or in wetter areas. Follows livestock or farm equipment to feed on the small animals they stir up.

Capped Heron
Pilherodius pileatus

22.5 in (55 cm). **Blue bill and facial skin** (brighter when breeding) are diagnostic; of the white herons, Capped is the only species with black crown. Breeding adults have notably buffy tinge below; on immature, crown streaked with gray. Uncommon on Pacific slope, from Canal Area eastward; rare on Caribbean slope in Canal Area; on rivers and in marshes.

Green Heron
Butorides virescens

18 in (47 cm). Small and stocky. Distinguished from similar Striated Heron by **dark chestnut sides of head and neck**, and from smaller Least Bittern by darker coloration and lack of buffy wing patch. A dark morph with a chocolate brown neck occurs in Bocas del Toro. Immature is duller and not distinguishable from immature Striated Heron. Common in western Panama as far east as Canal Area, uncommon in eastern Panama; to 4,600 ft (1,400 m). Found in freshwater habitats and along both coasts. Local population supplemented by migrants in winter.

Striated Heron
Butorides striata

18 in (47 cm). **Gray (or buff) sides of head and neck** distinguish Striated from very similar Green Heron; immatures not distinguishable. Common in eastern Panama, from Canal Area eastward; less common westward, to eastern side of Azuero Peninsula. Found in freshwater habitats and along coasts.

Least Bittern
Ixobrychus exilis

11.5 in (29 cm). Smallest heron. Prominent **buffy wing patch** (especially visible in flight) distinguishes it from the larger Green and Striated Herons and all rails. Resident race has rufous neck and sides of head; in migrants, neck and sides of head are cinnamon. Secretive and difficult to see, usually keeping to dense vegetation. Uncommon and local. Found in lowlands, in freshwater marshes; probably widespread but known with certainty from only a few localities, due to reclusive habits.

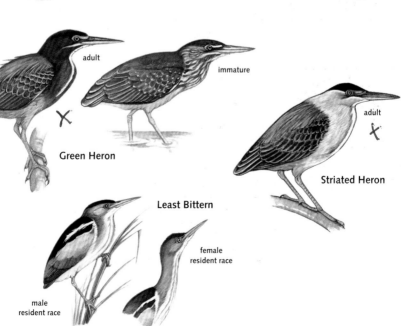

immature

adult

Tricolored Heron

breeding adult

nonbreeding adult

Cattle Egret

breeding adult

Capped Heron

adult

immature

Green Heron

adult

Striated Heron

Least Bittern

male resident race

female resident race

Black-crowned Night-Heron
Nycticorax nycticorax

24 in (61 cm). On adult, **black crown and back** in combination with **whitish underparts** (pale gray on neck) are distinctive. Immature very similar to immature Yellow-crowned Night-Heron but has yellow lower mandible and larger white spots on wing coverts. Fairly common in freshwater marshes and swamps in lowlands and along coast; more common on Pacific slope than on Caribbean. Mainly nocturnal, roosting by day in vegetation near water. Breeds in colonies along Pacific coast, in wetlands near the coast and on offshore islands; local population supplemented by migrants in winter.

Yellow-crowned Night-Heron
Nyctanassa violacea

22 in (56 cm). On adult, **striped head** and uniformly **gray underparts** are distinctive. Immature very similar to immature Black-crowned Night-Heron but has stouter, all-dark bill and smaller white spots on wing coverts. Common on Pacific coast; uncommon on Caribbean coast, and inland on rivers and marshes in lowlands; rare in highlands; to 4,600 ft (1,400 m). Mainly nocturnal, but along coasts often seen by day. Breeds in colonies along Pacific coast, in wetlands near the coast and on offshore islands; local population supplemented by migrants in winter.

Boat-billed Heron
Cochlearius cochlearius

19.5 in (50 cm). Extremely **broad flat bill** is diagnostic. Somewhat similar in plumage to Black-crowned Night-Heron, but adult has black sides and flanks, rusty belly, and (in most of Panama) buffy neck; immature has brown back and wings lacking any spotting. Birds from southeastern Darién have paler gray backs and white necks. Uncommon on Caribbean slope, local on Pacific slope; in lowlands. Found in mangroves and along rivers and marshes. Mainly nocturnal, roosting by day in dense vegetation over water.

Storks

CICONIIDAE. These large, long-legged waders resemble herons, but, unlike them, they fly with their necks extended and often soar. Storks use their large bills to feed on fish, frogs, rodents, and other small animals in shallow water or wet grassy areas.

Jabiru
Jabiru mycteria

52 in (131 cm). **Enormous size, huge slightly upturned bill,** and **red at base of neck** should preclude confusion. In flight, **wings** (including flight feathers) are **entirely white.** Immature has brownish gray cast. Vagrant, with scattered records from Bocas del Toro eastward to eastern Panamá Province. Found in freshwater marshes and rice fields.

Wood Stork
Mycteria americana

36.5 in (93 cm). Distinguished from other white wading birds by **heavy, slightly decurved bill** and (in flight) by **black flight feathers** extending length of wing. (White Ibis, p. 34, has black only on tips of wings.) Adult has bare blackish neck (mostly feathered in immature). Uncommon on Pacific slope; rare on Caribbean slope, in Bocas del Toro and Canal Area. Occurs in lowlands, in marshes and swamps.

adult

immature

Black-crowned
Night-Heron

adult

Yellow-crowned
Night-Heron

adult
buff-necked
race

immature
buff-necked
race

immature

Boat-billed
Heron

adult

adult

Jabiru

adult

immature

Wood Stork

THRESKIORNITHIDAE. Members of this family occur worldwide but are most common in the tropics. These heron-like waders have distinctive bills—decurved in the case of ibises and flat and widened at the tip in spoonbills. Ibises probe mud to obtain food, while spoonbills use sweeping movements of the bill to sift food from shallow water. Unlike herons, ibises and spoonbills fly with their necks outstretched.

White Ibis   *Eudocimus albus*

23 in (58 cm). **Decurved red bill** and **red legs** distinguish adult from white herons, as do **black wing tips** in flight. Immature is mostly brown; told apart from other dark ibises and Whimbrel (p. 76) by its white rump, breast, and belly (contrasting with rest of body) and its pinkish bill. Fairly common along Pacific coast, on mudflats, in mangroves, and in adjacent wetlands; very rare on Caribbean coast in Bocas del Toro and Canal Area. Breeds in colonies around Gulf of Panama and on offshore islands.

Scarlet Ibis   *Eudocimus ruber*

23 in (58 cm). Identical in shape to White Ibis, but adult is entirely **bright red** (except for black wing tips). Immature often indistinguishable from immature White, but sometimes shows pink on rump. Found in mangroves, mudflats, and other coastal wetlands; also in freshwater marshes. Vagrant, one record, near Pacific entrance of Panama Canal (1967). **Not illustrated**.

Glossy Ibis   *Plegadis falcinellus*

20 in (51 cm). Glossy is slimmer than Green Ibis and has thinner neck and much longer legs; usual habitat also differs, as it tends to forage more in the open. In good light, breeding adult's head and neck appear bronzy chestnut; nonbreeding adult and immature are duller and have small white speckles on head and neck. Very local, but regularly occurs in Herrera and eastern Panamá Province, in freshwater marshes and rice fields; a few records from Caribbean side of Canal Area. Recently confirmed breeding in Panama, and apparently spreading.

Green Ibis   *Mesembrinibis cayennensis*

19.5 in (50 cm). Stocky, with thicker neck and shorter legs than Glossy Ibis. In good light, it appears mainly **bronzy green** (brightest on neck and chest). Rare and local on Caribbean slope and, on Pacific, from eastern Panamá Province eastward. Found in lowlands, along forested rivers and in swampy forest (sometimes at edge of more open marshes).

Buff-necked Ibis   *Theristicus caudatus*

29 in (74 cm). Larger than other ibises. **Buffy lower head and neck** are diagnostic; also note chestnut crown and black facial skin. Back is gray; wings are blackish with a **large white patch on wing coverts**; lower underparts are black. Legs are red. Found in wet grasslands and open areas with ponds and marshes. Vagrant; two records from eastern Panamá Province (1950, 1958). **Not illustrated**.

Roseate Spoonbill   *Platalea ajaja*

30 in (76 cm). In all plumages, **spoon-shaped bill** is diagnostic; on adults, note distinctive **pink plumage** (immature much paler). Uncommon on Pacific coast; a few records from Caribbean coast in Bocas del Toro and Canal Area. Found on mudflats, in mangroves, and in adjacent wetlands.

adult

White Ibis

immature

breeding
adult

Glossy Ibis

Green Ibis

breeding
adult

immature

Roseate Spoonbill

CATHARTIDAE. Found only in the Americas, these large soaring birds resemble the vultures of the Old World but are not closely related. They feed mainly on carrion that is located by sight as the birds soar (Turkey Vultures also have an acute sense of smell that enables them to detect food concealed below the forest canopy). New World vultures have hooked bills for tearing flesh from carcasses but lack the talons and grasping feet of other birds of prey. Panama species can often be set apart by shape and style of flight, even at great distances.

Black Vulture
Coragyps atratus

25.5 in (65 cm); WS 58 in (146 cm). Entirely black except for prominent **white patch at base of primaries** (visible in flight). **Black head** distinguishes it from adults of other species. Immature Turkey Vulture is more slender; immature King Vulture is much larger and usually has some white below. In flight has relatively shorter, broader wings and tail than Turkey and Lesser Yellow-headed Vultures; soars on flat wings, interspersing bursts of flapping with short glides. Abundant around cities and towns and in coastal areas; common in other open areas throughout the country; rare in extensively forested habitats; to at least 4,600 ft (1,400 m).

Turkey Vulture
Cathartes aura

27 in (69 cm); WS 67 in (171 cm). **Red head** distinguishes adult from other vultures. In flight, **underwings are two-toned**, with silvery gray flight feathers that contrast with dark wing-linings. Immature has dark head; distinguished from Black Vulture by more slender build; from immature King Vulture by smaller size and lack of white in plumage. Resident race has whitish band across back of neck (also often a whitish crown); migrants have whitish crescent below eye. Much smaller Zone-tailed Hawk (p. 48) resembles Turkey Vulture in flight, in both appearance and flight style. Soars with wings held above horizontal in a shallow V, teetering from side to side; rarely flaps. Very common nearly throughout the country, including in cities, towns, and open areas, and over forest; to at least 4,600 ft (1,400 m). During migration (Oct to Nov and late Feb to early April) enormous flocks composed of tens of thousands of birds pass through, mainly on the Caribbean slope in western Panama, and on the Pacific slope from Panamá City eastward.

Lesser Yellow-headed Vulture
Cathartes burrovianus

23 in (59 cm); WS 62 in (158 cm). Very similar to Turkey Vulture but smaller; at close range, distinguished by mostly **yellow or yellow-orange head** (dark in immature). Like Turkey Vulture, in flight shows **two-toned underwings** and flies with wings in shallow V; however, tends to fly lower than that species, often skimming only a few yards above the ground (sometimes flies higher). From above, has **indistinct whitish patch at base of primaries** produced by pale feather shafts (much less prominent than wing patch of Black Vulture). Fairly common on Pacific slope, from Chiriquí to eastern Panamá Province, over pastures and marshes in lowlands; rare in immediate area of Panamá City and in Darién.

King Vulture
Sarcoramphus papa

30 in (76 cm); WS 73 in (185 cm). Very large. Adult easily identified by mostly **white plumage with black flight feathers and tail** and, at close range, by **multicolored head**. Immature mainly blackish brown (including head), gradually becoming whiter below with age; distinguished from other vultures by large size and, at close range, pale eye. In flight, King Vulture shows broader wings and a shorter tail than other vultures; soars on flat wings, often very high; on immature, **wings are uniformly colored from below**. Uncommon on both slopes, to 5,000 ft (1,500 m), usually over forested areas, occasionally over grassland or pasture.

adult

adult

immature

Turkey Vulture

adult
resident race

Black Vulture

adult

adult

adult

immature

adult

King Vulture

adult

adult

Lesser Yellow-headed
Vulture

adult

ACCIPITRIDAE. Found worldwide, these diurnal birds of prey have hooked beaks and powerful, grasping feet for catching, killing, and dismembering prey. Panama's species vary greatly in size, ranging from the tiny Pearl Kite to the enormous Harpy Eagle, the heaviest bird of prey in the world. Their habits are also diverse; some species, for example, hunt in flight, while others catch prey by pouncing from exposed perches or by ambushing from hidden places in dense foliage. Identification is often a challenge, as many species occur in several color morphs, and immature birds often go through a complex series of plumages before reaching adulthood. Shape, habitat, and behavior can provide important clues.

Osprey
Pandion haliaetus

23 in (58 cm); WS 59 in (150 cm). Brown above, white below; **white crown** is separated from underparts by **broad dark stripe through eye**. Immature similar but marked with paler streaks above and buffier streaks below. In flight, underwings mostly whitish, with dark patch at wrist; flies with **wings crooked at wrist**. Common transient and winter resident (Oct to April); a few birds (mainly immatures) present in summer. Found along coasts and, inland, on larger bodies of water, to at least 4,600 ft (1,400 m). Feeds mainly on fish, which it catches by plunging feet first into the water. Call a high yelping *heeaaa!*; also a series of short high whistles.

Gray-headed Kite
Leptodon cayanensis

19 in (48 cm); WS 39 in (100 cm). **Head appears small** for body. On adult, **gray head** contrasts with **blackish back** and white underparts. Immatures occur in two color morphs, with some intermediates, but all have yellow to yellow-orange bare parts. Pale immature resembles Black-and-white Hawk-Eagle (p. 54), but the latter has black lores, orange cere, and feathered legs. Dark morph immature more heavily streaked on chest than intermediate morph immature; both resemble streaked immatures of several other species; best distinguished by shape. In flight, broad rounded wings and long tail recall hawk-eagles, but contrasting **black wing-linings** and **white body** are diagnostic. Often soars. Uncommon on both slopes, to 6,600 ft (2,000 m). Found in upper levels of forest. Call a rapidly repeated *kek-kek-kek-kek-kek*; also a distinctive catlike *eee-oww!*

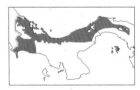

Hook-billed Kite
Chondrohierax uncinatus

18 in (45 cm); WS 35 in (88 cm). Extremely variable, but, in all plumages, **large hooked bill, pale eye with orange spot in front**, and **greenish lores** are distinctive. Adult male slaty gray above, usually barred gray and white below; adult female dark brown or gray above with rufous collar on hindneck, barred brown and white below; immature dark brown above with narrow whitish collar on hindneck, whitish below. Dark morph almost entirely blackish except for single white tail band. Soars occasionally; in flight has **broad paddle-shaped wings**, indented near body. Uncommon and local in lowlands on both slopes (rare at higher elevations); not recorded from Darién or from western Pacific slope (except in Chiriquí); to 4,600 ft (1,400 m). Occurs in upper levels of forest; favors swampy areas. Feeds on tree snails. Call a whinnying *whi-hi-hi-hi-hi-hii-uh*.

Pearl Kite
Gampsonyx swainsonii

8.5 in (22 cm); WS 19.5 in (50 cm). **Very small**. Combination of **buffy forehead and cheeks**, white underparts, and **rufous sides, flanks, and thighs** is diagnostic. Occurs in open areas in lowlands. Uncommon on entire Pacific slope; very rare on Caribbean slope, in Bocas del Toro and Canal Area; to 2,000 ft (600 m). Often seen perched on wires along roadsides. Call a high-pitched whistling *ki-ki-ki-ki-ki-ki-ki*.

adult

adult

Osprey

X

adult

Gray-headed Kite

adult

intermediate immature

pale morph immature

adult female

Hook-billed Kite

Pearl Kite

adult dark morph

adult female

adult male

immature

Swallow-tailed Kite

Elanoides forficatus

22.5 in (57 cm); WS 50 in (128 cm). **Long forked tail** makes this species unmistakable. Exceptionally graceful in flight. Often soars in small groups of up to 20. Occurs on both slopes but more common on Caribbean slope. Uncommon in lowlands, common in foothills and highlands; to 6,000 ft (1,800 m). Found in canopy and in flight above forest. Breeds in Panama, migrating to South America in nonbreeding season (absent Oct to early Jan); flocks of migrants from farther north pass through from late July to early Sept and return early Jan through March. Call a series of high twittering whistles, usually given in flight.

White-tailed Kite

Elanus leucurus

15.5 in (39 cm); WS 37.5 in (95 cm). Combination of **black shoulders (brownish in immature)** and **white tail** is diagnostic. Common on Pacific slope; more local on Caribbean slope; to 4,600 ft (1,400 m). Found in open areas, where it perches conspicuously on wires or tall trees. When hunting, often hovers. Call a whistling *kee-oo*.

Double-toothed Kite

Harpagus bidentatus

12.5 in (32 cm); WS 26 in (66 cm). In all plumages, **dark central stripe on white throat** is diagnostic. In flight, resembles *Accipiter* species (p. 44), but **fluffy white undertail coverts** are often conspicuous, projecting on either side of rump. Fairly common on both slopes, to 4,600 ft (1,400 m); in middle and upper levels of forest. Often soars; frequently follows troops of white-faced monkeys (sometimes other monkeys) to catch the insects and other small animals that their foraging stirs up. Call a high thin *wheet!* or *whit-whee-up!*

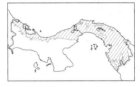

Mississippi Kite

Ictinia mississippiensis

13.5 in (34 cm); WS 31 in (79 cm). Similar to the more common Plumbeous Kite, but when perched, wings on Mississippi extend only slightly past end of tail; adult further distinguished by paler head that contrasts with back, **all-dark tail**, absence of rufous in wings, and **whitish patch on secondaries** (visible from above, both when perched and in flight). Immatures of both species have tail bands, but they are fainter in Mississippi; immature Mississippi is browner above, has rufous (not blackish) streaks below, and lacks rufous in wing. Uncommon transient, in Oct and from mid-March to late April; in western Panama, mostly on Caribbean slope; in eastern Panama, on both slopes. Often in flocks of several hundred, soaring over almost any habitat.

Plumbeous Kite

Ictinia plumbea

13.5 in (34 cm); WS 31 in (78 cm). **Long wings, extending well past end of tail**, distinguish Plumbeous from other mostly gray raptors, including very similar Mississippi Kite. Adults are further distinguished from that species by a darker head (no contrast with back), **two narrow white bands on underside of tail**, **rufous in wing**, and lack of whitish patch on secondaries. Immature Plumbeous has more distinct tail bands than immature Mississippi, is blacker above, has blackish (not rufous) streaks below, and shows some rufous on the primaries. Uncommon on both slopes, to at least 4,600 ft (1,400 m). Breeds in Panama, migrating to South America in nonbreeding season (absent mid-Oct to mid-Jan); flocks of migrants from farther north pass through from early Aug to early Oct and return early Feb to mid-March. Frequently soars, catching insects in flight; often perches in tops of tall trees. Calls include high-pitched whistles and twitters.

Swallow-tailed
Kite

adult

adult

White-tailed
Kite

immature

adult

Double-toothed
Kite

adult

immature

adult

Mississippi
Kite

adult

adult

immature

adult

immature

Plumbeous
Kite

Snail Kite
Rostrhamus sociabilis

17.5 in (44 cm); WS 42 in (107 cm). In all plumages, extremely **slender, hooked bill** distinguishes it from all species except probably vagrant Slender-billed Kite; note also red to orange-yellow cere and legs. **White basal half of tail** is shared only by Great Black Hawk (eastern race, p. 48), which is larger and has a different shape. Adult female resembles immature but is blacker above and has heavier dark streaking below and red-orange cere and legs. Flies slowly and buoyantly over marshes and lakes with floating vegetation, searching for apple snails (whose flesh it extracts from the shell with its specialized bill). Following introduction of apple snails, has recently become common in the Canal Area (on and near Lake Gatún) and in southern Coclé (around Las Macanas Marsh); rare and erratic elsewhere. Call a harsh creaky *ka-ka-ka-ka-ka*.

Slender-billed Kite
Helicolestes hamatus

15 in (38 cm); WS 33.5 in (85 cm). In all plumages, resembles male Snail Kite, but **tail is shorter and lacks white at base** (immature has two or three thin whitish tail bars); **eyes of adults whitish** (dark in Snail Kite). Status uncertain; probably vagrant but possibly a very rare resident. Two records from eastern Darién (1958, 1959). Inhabits wooded swamps. **Not illustrated**.

Black-collared Hawk
Busarellus nigricollis

21 in (52 cm); WS 51 in (129 cm). Adult's **bright cinnamon-rufous body, whitish head**, and **black chest patch** make it unmistakable. Immature duller, but black chest patch still obvious. Very rare on eastern Pacific slope in lowlands; a few old records from elsewhere. Found on rivers and lakes and in marshes. Feeds on fish that it catches from water surface. Call a hoarse whistled *wheeerah*.

Northern Harrier
Circus cyaneus

18 in (46 cm); WS 43 in (110 cm). In all plumages, combination of **white rump** and **long, banded tail** distinguishes it from other raptors (except vagrant Long-winged Harrier). Swainson's Hawk and immature White-tailed Hawk (p. 52) show a pale U on uppertail coverts but are larger and bulkier and have a different shape. Rare transient and winter resident, mostly on Pacific slope; occurs in lowlands, in grassy areas and marshes. Flight style distinctive: quarters back and forth low over open areas, with long wings held slightly above horizontal in a shallow V (note that Swainson's may soar with wings in this posture).

Long-winged Harrier
Circus buffoni

21 in (53 cm); WS 54 in (137 cm). Similar in shape and behavior to Northern Harrier, but, from above, all morphs show **distinct gray areas in flight feathers**. Pale-morph male mostly black above with **white rump**; chest black, rest of underparts whitish; tail barred gray and black. Pale-morph female similar to male but brownish above, chest and underparts streaked brown. Dark morph (both sexes) mostly black, rump barred white, tail barred gray and black. Immature similar to pale-morph female. Vagrant, with records from Tocumen Marsh in eastern Panamá Province and El Real in Darién.

Snail Kite

adult male

Black-collared Hawk

adult

adult male

immature

adult

immature

Northern Harrier

adult female

immature

adult male

Long-winged Harrier

adult male pale morph

adult female pale morph

immature

Sharp-shinned Hawk
Accipiter striatus

11.5 in (29 cm); WS 21.5 in (55 cm). Slender with short rounded wings and a long tail (like other *Accipiter* species). Combination of **slate-gray back** and **rufous barring on breast** distinguishes it from Tiny Hawk. Lacks dark central stripe on throat that characterizes Double-toothed Kite (p. 40). Immature similar to Merlin (p. 58), but has **yellow eyes** and wings that do not extend past base of tail. See also nearly identical (but vagrant) Cooper's Hawk. Uncommon winter resident (late Oct to late March) in western foothills and highlands; very rare elsewhere; to at least 8,200 ft (2,500 m). Found in middle and upper levels of woodland and forest edge. Hunts from cover and so usually unobtrusive; occasionally soars. Call a high staccato *kew-kew-kew-kew-kew*.

Cooper's Hawk
Accipiter cooperii

17 in (42 cm); WS 30 in (76 cm). Almost identical to Sharp-shinned Hawk, but larger, with heavier build and proportionately larger head, **darker crown** (contrasting with nape), and **rounded tail tip** (square on Sharp-shinned). Vagrant, with two records from Chiriquí.

Bicolored Hawk
Accipiter bicolor

16 in (40 cm); WS 28 in (70 cm). On adult, combination of mostly light gray underparts, dark gray upperparts, and **contrasting blackish crown** is distinctive; **rufous thighs** diagnostic but often concealed in belly feathers. Immatures are variable; brownish above, usually showing **pale collar on hindneck**; may be whitish, cream, buffy, or rufous below. Immature resembles some forest-falcons (p. 56) but lacks prominent yellow orbital ring of Barred and Slaty-backed (Slaty-backed lacks collar on hindneck) and prominent dark crescent on cheek of Collared (and also has shorter tail). Rare on both slopes, somewhat more numerous in western Panama; to at least 5,000 ft (1,500 m). Found at all levels of forest. Call a sharp *keh-keh-keh-keh-keh-keh-keh*.

Tiny Hawk
Accipiter superciliosus

9 in (23 cm); WS 17 in (43 cm). **Very small**. Adult distinguished from Sharp-shinned Hawk and Double-toothed Kite (p. 40) by **blackish** (not rufous), **very fine barring on breast**; from Barred Forest-Falcon (p. 56) by **distinct dark cap** and absence of yellow orbital skin. Immatures occur in brown and rufous morphs; similar species with barring below differ in having gray backs. Rare on entire Caribbean slope; rare on Pacific slope from eastern Panamá Province eastward; to 4,000 ft (1,200 m). Found in upper levels of forest. Call a shrill *kree-ree-ree-ree*.

Crane Hawk
Geranospiza caerulescens

18 in (46 cm); WS 37 in (94 cm). Slender, with a small head. Birds in western Panama are blackish, in eastern Panama more grayish. Exceptionally **long orange-red legs** distinguish it from other mostly dark raptors; distinguished from Plumbeous Hawk (p. 46) and male Snail Kite (p. 42) by **gray** (not red) **cere**. Immature browner than adult, with whitish wash on face and more distinct whitish barring below. In flight, all plumages show **white crescent across base of primaries**. Uncommon in lowlands from Canal Area eastward (both slopes); rare and local in lowlands on western Pacific slope; unrecorded on western Caribbean but probably occurs there. Found at all levels in swampy forest and marshes. Uses long legs, which it can bend backward as well as forward, to probe bromeliads and tree holes for small animals. Occasionally soars. Call a thin whistling *wheeer*.

adult

adult

immature

adult

Sharp-shinned Hawk

adult

adult

Cooper's Hawk

immature

Bicolored Hawk

whitish immature

adult

buffy immature

adult western race

adult western race

immature

adult male

immature rufous morph

Tiny Hawk

Crane Hawk

Barred Hawk   *Leucopternis princeps*

21 in (54 cm); WS 46 in (118 cm). Combination of **blackish chest** with **finely barred lower breast and belly** is diagnostic. In flight, has notably broad wings and short tail; frequently soars. Uncommon in foothills and highlands; mostly above 1,500 ft (450 m); a few records from lowlands. Found at middle and upper levels of forest. Call, often given in flight, a loud whistled *keEEE-ur*, slurred upward at the end and sometimes followed by a long series of *weep* notes.

Plumbeous Hawk   *Leucopternis plumbeus*

14 in (35 cm); WS 30 in (75 cm). Combination of **orange cere and legs** and **single white tail band** distinguishes it from other dark raptors. In flight (from below), **wings mostly white with dark tips**. Immature similar, but has whitish barring on thighs, whitish flecks on belly, some dark barring on underwings, and may have a second tail band. Rare on Caribbean slope, from Veraguas eastward, and on Pacific slope from western Panamá Province eastward; to about 3,300 ft (1,000 m). Found in upper, middle, and (sometimes) lower levels of forest. Call a high thin *wheeeee-urr*.

Semiplumbeous Hawk   *Leucopternis semiplumbeus*

13.5 in (34 cm); WS 23 in (58 cm). **Orange (or orange-red) cere, base of bill, and legs** distinguish it from other raptors that are **dark above** and **white below** (for example, pale-morph Short-tailed Hawk, p. 50, and Slaty-backed Forest-Falcon, p. 56). Immature has white streaking on head and back and black streaking on chest. In flight, wings are **mostly white below**. Uncommon on entire Caribbean slope; uncommon on Pacific slope from Canal Area eastward. Found in upper, middle, and (sometimes) lower levels of forest in lowlands. Call a long whistled *wheee-EEP!*

White Hawk   *Leucopternis albicollis*

20.5 in (52 cm); WS 42 in (108 cm). **Mostly white plumage (including back)** makes this species essentially unmistakable. Fairly common on both slopes, to 4,000 ft (1,200 m), rarely higher. Occurs in upper, middle, and (sometimes) lower levels of forest. Frequently soars. Call a harsh, high-pitched *hee-EE-ah*, often given in flight.

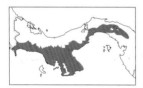

Savanna Hawk   *Buteogallus meridionalis*

21.5 in (55 cm); WS 51 in (130 cm). Coloration, mostly **dull cinnamon-rufous**, is unique; very rare Black-collared Hawk (p. 42) is brighter rufous, has white head, black chest patch, and lacks white in tail. In flight, **wings are mostly rufous above and below**. Immature blackish brown above; long legs, creamy face, and rufous barring on secondaries and thighs are distinctive. Fairly common on most of Pacific slope (uncommon to rare in western Chiriquí and Darién); rare on Caribbean slope; found in lowlands. Favors open grassy areas. Perches on low branches or fences; often stands or walks on ground; soars frequently. Call a plaintive *WHEeer*, loud at first and then fading off.

Barred Hawk

Plumbeous
Hawk

adult

adult

Semiplumbeous
Hawk

adult

White Hawk

Savanna Hawk

adult

adult

Common Black-Hawk
Buteogallus anthracinus

19.5 in (50 cm); WS 44 in (112 cm). Adult's **yellow lores** distinguish it from all other black raptors except for eastern Panama race of Great Black-Hawk (see description). In flight, note **very broad wings** and **short tail**. Race on Pacific coast, formerly considered a separate species (Mangrove Black-Hawk), often shows rufous wash on secondaries. Also compare with Zone-tailed Hawk, dark-morph Short-tailed Hawk (p. 50), Crane Hawk (p. 44), and Solitary Eagle. Immature very similar to immature Great Black-Hawk, but has **dark facial streaking and malar stripe**, and fewer, slightly wider tail bars; also resembles immature Gray Hawk (p. 50) but has barred undertail coverts. Common on both coasts, sometimes occurring inland along larger rivers and lakes. Usually found near water, perching on trees or other vegetation; frequently soars. Call a series of loud high whistles, first rising in volume and then trailing off: *whee-whee-whee-whee-WHEE-WHEE-WHEE-weh-weh*.

Great Black-Hawk
Buteogallus urubitinga

24 in (61 cm); WS 49 in (124 cm). Larger than Common Black-Hawk but otherwise very similar. Both species have **very broad wings** and a **short tail**. Western Panama race distinguished from Common by **slaty** (not yellow) **lores**, white on uppertail coverts, and **two** (not one) **white tail bands**. Eastern Panama race shares yellow lores of Common but **entire base of tail is white**; also usually shows **white barring on thighs**, white flecks on underwing coverts, and less (or no) white at base of primaries. Immature is similar to immature Common but has more (and narrower) tail bands and lacks dark malar stripe. Compare also with Solitary Eagle. Uncommon on both slopes, to 6,000 ft (1,800 m). Found in upper levels of forest; usually near water, but less so than Common. Soars frequently. Call, often given in flight, is a high, prolonged whistling scream—very different from call of Common.

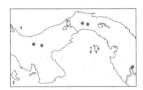

Solitary Eagle
Harpyhaliaetus solitarius

27.5 in (70 cm); WS 66 in (168 cm). Very similar to Great Black-Hawk but larger and **slaty gray** instead of blackish. (Beware, however, of color variation due to lighting: black-hawks can look grayer in strong light, and this species may appear darker when backlit.) Great Black-Hawk usually has white barring on thighs; in western Panama has slaty (not yellow) lores; in eastern Panama entire base of tail is white. Immature also similar to immature black-hawks, but has **heavy streaks on chest** (almost forming a band) and **dark thighs**. In flight, has **exceptionally broad wings**, widest near body; **very short, squared-off tail**; and **legs that reach almost to tail tip** (legs of black-hawks reach only to tail band). Very rare, with scattered records from Veraguas eastward to near Colombian border. Mainly in forest. Favors steep foothills, mostly from 1,600 to 5,000 ft (500 to 1,500 m). Frequently soars. Call, often given in flight, is a shrill prolonged series of whistles: *wheet-wheet-wheet-wheet-wheet* (similar to call of Black Hawk-Eagle, p. 54).

Zone-tailed Hawk
Buteo albonotatus

20 in (51 cm); WS 51 in (128 cm). Has a more **slender body and longer tail** than other dark raptors. Dark-morph Short-tailed Hawk (p. 50) lacks obvious tail bands; black-hawks are larger and have longer legs. In flight, very similar to Turkey Vulture (p. 36), soaring with **two-tone wings** held above horizontal in shallow V and teetering from side to side, but note feathered black head, yellow bill and legs, and (in adult) **white tail bands**. Uncommon on Pacific slope; on Caribbean slope recorded from Canal Area and eastern Kuna Yala; occurs mainly in lowlands and foothills. Found in open areas. Call a high thin scream *keeYEEEEER*.

adult
Caribbean
race

adult
western
race

**Common
Black-Hawk**

adult
Caribbean
race

immature

**Great
Black-Hawk**

adult
western
race

immature

adult
eastern
race

adult

**Solitary
Eagle**

adult

immature

adult

**Zone-tailed
Hawk**

adult

immature

Roadside Hawk
Buteo magnirostris

14 in (36 cm); WS 31 in (78 cm). On adult, combination of **gray head and chest** and **rufous barring on breast** distinguishes it from other similar raptors. In flight, **rufous patch in primaries** is diagnostic. In most of Panama, tail is banded with rufous (appearing mostly reddish at a distance) but in Bocas del Toro, Kuna Yala, and eastern Darién, tail is banded with gray. Immature distinguished from other streaked raptors by rufous-barred thighs. Common on Pacific slope, uncommon on Caribbean slope; to 5,000 ft (1,500 m). Occurs in open and scrubby areas, and in lower and middle levels of woodland. Soars infrequently. Call a nasal, sharp *kee-YOOuuu.*

Broad-winged Hawk
Buteo platypterus

14.5 in (37 cm); WS 33.5 in (85 cm). Adult, barred with rufous below, somewhat resembles Double-toothed Kite (p. 40) and Roadside Hawk, but head is brown (not gray); note **dusky malar stripe**. In flight, **undersides of wings are mostly white with dark border**, and **tail is prominently banded black-and-white**. Rare dark morph has dark brown body and wing-linings but still has whitish (with dark border) flight feathers and banded tail. Immature distinguished from most other streaked raptors of similar size by **dusky malar stripe**, except for immature Gray Hawk, which has whitish (not dark) cheeks and usually a whitish band across uppertail coverts. Abundant transient, in flocks of up to tens of thousands (late Sept to early Nov and March to early April), often in company of Turkey Vultures (p. 36) and Swainson's Hawks (p. 52). In western Panama, passage is mainly on Caribbean slope; from the Canal Area east, passage is mainly on Pacific slope. Soars frequently (migrating birds in particular rarely use flapping flight). Very common winter resident throughout the country, to 6,500 ft (2,000 m). Found at low and middle levels of forest and woodland. Call a high whistle on one pitch, with a short note at the beginning: *titeeeeee.*

Gray Hawk
Buteo nitidus

16 in (41 cm); WS 33 in (84 cm). **Pearly gray** adult is distinctive; distinguished from Roadside Hawk by **dark** (not rufous) **barring** that is finer and extends higher on chest, and by lack of rufous in primaries; most populations of Roadside also differ in having a rufous-barred tail. Immature set apart from other streaked immatures by **whitish cheek separated from whitish superciliary by dark eye-line**; note also bold teardrop-shaped spotting on breast. In flight (from below), underwings are pale; from above, shows U-shaped whitish band at base of tail. Uncommon in most of country (not recorded from western Caribbean slope); to 4,000 ft (1,200 m). Found in open and scrubby areas, relatively open woodland, and at forest edge. Soars fairly often. Call a shrill descending whistle *KEEEeeer.*

Short-tailed Hawk
Buteo brachyurus

15.5 in (40 cm); WS 36.5 in (93 cm). Pale morph best recognized by **dark cheeks giving hooded appearance, white forehead, and lack of prominent tail-banding**. White-tailed Hawk (p. 52) also appears hooded, but sides of head are lighter gray and tail is mainly white. Less common dark morph is most similar to Zone-tailed Hawk (p. 48), but stockier, with shorter wings and tail; adult Zone-tailed has prominent tail-banding. In flight, both morphs show **whitish patch in primaries** and **dark gray secondaries**; all flight feathers have dark tips. Immature similar to respective adult morph, but pale morph has whitish streaks on head and dark morph has whitish spotting below. Uncommon on both slopes, to about 4,600 ft (1,400 m). Usually found in open areas (occasionally over forest). Often seen soaring. Call a high thin *keeeaa.*

adult gray-tailed race

Roadside Hawk

adult pale morph

Broad-winged Hawk

immature

adult gray-tailed race

rufous-tailed race

adult pale morph

immature pale morph

adult dark morph

adult pale morph

adult

Gray Hawk

Short-tailed Hawk

adult

immature

adult pale morph

immature pale morph

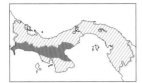

Swainson's Hawk
Buteo swainsoni

19.5 in (49 cm); WS 50 in (127 cm). Combination of **dark chest** and **contrasting white throat and white lower breast and belly** distinguishes pale-morph adult from similar species. Dark morph is similar to immature White-tailed Hawk, but that species usually has white patch on breast. In flight, has **long pointed wings**, often held above horizontal in shallow V-shape, and **long tail**; both morphs have dark flight feathers and pale undertail coverts. Abundant transient (from mid-Oct to mid-Nov and March to early April), soaring in flocks of up to tens of thousands, often with Turkey Vultures (p. 36) and Broad-winged Hawks (p. 50). In western Panama, migrates mainly on Caribbean slope and in highlands; in eastern Panama, migrates on Pacific slope and in highlands. Rare winter resident on western Pacific slope, in open areas in lowlands. Call a thin scream: *wheeeeeah.*

White-tailed Hawk
Buteo albicaudatus

20 in (52 cm); WS 51 in (130 cm). Resembles pale-morph Short-tailed Hawk (p. 50) in pattern (particularly hooded appearance) but is **grayer** (not so blackish) **above** and has **rufous patch on shoulders**. In flight, **white tail with single black subterminal band** is diagnostic. Rare dark morph is almost entirely slaty gray, including on shoulders, but shares white tail. Immature is dark brownish above and below but usually has **whitish patch on breast** and white streaking on belly; tail is pale grayish, without subterminal black band. Rare on Pacific slope, eastward to eastern Panamá Province; a few records from western Caribbean slope; to 6,000 ft (1,800 m). Occurs in open grassy areas. Often soars. Call a high harsh *ke-yeeer keHAK keHAK keHAK.*

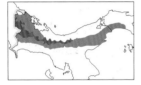

Red-tailed Hawk
Buteo jamaicensis

20.5 in (52 cm); WS 49 in (124 cm). On adult, **bright rufous tail** is distinctive. Roadside Hawk (p. 50) has dull reddish tail in most of Panama but is smaller and has rufous in wings. Resident race has **rufous belly and thighs**; a few individuals are more extensively rufous below than shown. Migrants highly variable; pale morph migrants often have **dark streaks forming a band across belly**; other migrant morphs may be heavily streaked below, mostly rufous, or mostly blackish. Immature of resident race has cinnamon tail with narrow dark bands; migrant immature usually has grayish tail with faint bands. In flight, pale-morph migrant adult and immature show **dark leading edge to forewing**. Resident race uncommon; occurs in western highlands, mainly above 5,000 ft (1,500 m), in upper levels of forest and in adjacent cleared areas. Migrants rare; recorded as far east as eastern Panamá Province (including in lowlands). Often soars. Call a hoarse rasping scream, falling in pitch and trailing off: *kree-ar-r-r-r-r .*

Harris's Hawk
Parabuteo unicinctus

20.5 in (52 cm); WS 42 in (106 cm). **Rufous shoulders and thighs** are diagnostic in all plumages. Immature streaked below. In flight, **basal half of tail is white**. Vagrant in open areas; recorded in Bocas del Toro, Veraguas, and eastern Panamá Province.

adult pale morph

adult dark morph

Swainson's Hawk

adult pale morph

adult pale morph

immature pale morph

White-tailed Hawk

adult pale morph

adult pale morph

adult resident race

adult pale morph migrant race

Red-tailed Hawk

adult resident race

immature resident race

adult

adult

immature

Harris's Hawk

Crested Eagle
Morphnus guianensis

33 in (84 cm); WS 57 in (146 cm). Closely resembles Harpy Eagle (particularly immature of that species) but distinguished in all plumages by **single-pointed crest** and longer, less massive legs. Pale-morph adult lacks Harpy's black chest band; dark morph is heavily barred or (rarely) entirely dark below. Hawk-eagles have completely feathered legs. In flight, pale morph shows **white wing-linings**; on dark morph wing-linings are barred but less heavily so than on Harpy. Very rare on Caribbean slope; also very rare on Pacific slope, in the southwestern Azuero Peninsula and from eastern Panamá Province eastward. Inhabits lowlands and foothills, in upper levels of forest. Occasionally soars. Call is a sharp *wheet!* (sometimes doubled).

Harpy Eagle
Harpia harpyja

38 in (96 cm); WS 74 in (188 cm). One of the largest and most powerful birds of prey in the world. The Harpy Eagle (especially in immature plumage) is similar to Crested Eagle but has heavier build; distinguished in all plumages by **double-pointed crest** and shorter, **extremely thick legs** (2 in [5 cm] in diameter). Adult has **black chest band**. In flight, **wing-linings are barred (or spotted) with black**. Rare on Caribbean slope and on Pacific slope from eastern Panamá Province eastward; in lowlands and lower foothills. Found in upper levels of forest. Despite its size, rather difficult to observe as it does not soar and spends much of its time in the forest canopy hunting monkeys, sloths, and other large prey. Call a high-pitched whistle: *FEEEEooooo.*

Black Hawk-Eagle
Spizaetus tyrannus

25 in (64 cm); WS 52 in (131 cm). Adult distinguished from other dark raptors by **completely feathered legs with white barring**. On immatures, combination of **streaked underparts** and **barred feathered legs** is distinctive. In flight, no other dark raptor has such **prominent black-and-white banding on flight feathers**. Common on both slopes to over 5,500 ft (1,650 m). Found in middle and upper levels of forest and woodland. During middle of day, often soars high and calls frequently, giving a loud whistled *whut-whut-whut-WHEEER!*

Ornate Hawk-Eagle
Spizaetus ornatus

23.5 in (60 cm); WS 46 in (117 cm). Adult, with **tawny sides of head and neck** and **boldly barred underparts,** is virtually unmistakable. Immature distinguished from Black-and-white Hawk-Eagle, immature pale-morph Gray-headed Kite (p. 38), and immature Crested Eagle by **barred flanks and thighs**; from latter two, further distinguished by **completely feathered legs**. Rare in lowlands; uncommon in foothills and highlands, to over 5,100 ft (1,500 m). Found in middle and upper levels of forest. Soars occasionally, usually fairly low over forest. Call a loud whistled *wheer-whe-whe-whe-whe-we-up.*

Black-and-white Hawk-Eagle
Spizaetus melanoleucus

22 in (56 cm); WS 48 in (122 cm). Similar to immature Ornate Hawk-Eagle and immature pale-morph Gray-headed Kite (p. 38), but has **black lores** and **orange cere**; further distinguished from Ornate by **unbarred flanks and thighs** and from Gray-headed Kite by **completely feathered legs**. In flight (from below), wings are mostly white; from above or head-on, shows distinctive **white leading edge on forewing**. Very rare and local; recorded on the Caribbean slope, in Bocas del Toro and the Canal Area, and on Pacific slope, in the Chiriquí highlands and from eastern Panamá Province eastward; one record from Veraguas (specific location not cited); to 5,500 ft (1,650 m). Found in forest canopy. Soars frequently. Call a series of whistles: *klee-klee-klee.*

adult pale morph

adult pale morph

adult pale morph

adult

adult

adult dark morph

immature

Crested Eagle

Harpy Eagle

immature

adult

Black Hawk-Eagle

adult

adult

immature

immature

Ornate Hawk-Eagle

adult

Black-and-white Hawk-Eagle

FALCONIDAE. Members of this cosmopolitan family resemble raptors of the family Accipitridae, differing only in minor anatomical features. Panama's species are diverse in form and habits. The true falcons (genus *Falco*) have pointed wings and are swift fliers that pursue birds and other prey in flight. Forest-falcons (genus *Micrastur*) are *Accipiter*-like ambush-hunters; secretive and inconspicuous, they are far more often heard than seen. The caracaras feed on carrion or the larvae of social insects, while the Laughing Falcon is a snake specialist.

Barred Forest-Falcon
Micrastur ruficollis

13.5 in (34 cm); WS 21 in (53 cm). **Fine dark barring below** (including vent) distinguishes adult from all except Tiny Hawk (p. 44); differs from that species by **yellow orbital skin**, absence of dark cap, and narrower, more widely spaced white tail bands. Immature variable; may have whitish to buff underparts, with a varying degree of dark barring; usually has **pale collar on hindneck**; distinguished from immature Collared Forest-Falcon by lack of dark crescent on cheek; individuals with unbarred underparts distinguished from immature Bicolored Hawk (p. 44) by yellow orbital skin and narrow tail bars. Uncommon on both slopes; relatively more common in foothills, to 5,400 ft (1,600 m). Found in lower levels of forest. Sometimes follows army-ant swarms to prey on the insects they flush—or on other birds attracted to the swarm. Call, often given at dawn or dusk, is a sharp barking *ehnk!*, sometimes repeated in series: *ehnk-EHNK-ehnk-enkh-enkh.*

Slaty-backed Forest-Falcon
Micrastur mirandollei

16.5 in (42 cm); WS 27 in (68 cm). Adult distinguished from those immature Barred Forest-Falcons that lack barring on underparts by **slate-gray** (rather than brownish) **upperparts**, and from immature Bicolored Hawk (p. 44) by narrower tail bands and **yellow orbital skin**. Immatures of both Barred Forest-Falcon and Bicolored Hawk usually have pale collar on hindneck. Semiplumbeous Hawk (p. 46) is stockier, with a single broad white tail band. Immature browner above, whitish below; in place of barring, either scalloped, streaked, or mottled with a dusky tone. Rare on Caribbean slope, from northern Coclé eastward (may occur on western Caribbean slope); also rare on Pacific slope, from eastern Panamá Province eastward; to 4,600 ft (1,400 m). Inhabits lower levels of forest. Call a series of nasal *annh* notes, rising slightly in pitch and accelerating.

Collared Forest-Falcon
Micrastur semitorquatus

20.5 in (52 cm); WS 31 in (79 cm). Pale-morph adult (underparts can be either white or buff) has **light collar on hindneck**; distinguished from immature Bicolored Hawk (p. 44) and immature Barred Forest-Falcon by **dark crescent on cheek**. Pale-morph immature may lack collar and have a less distinct cheek pattern; these less distinctive individuals, along with rare dark-morph adult and immature, can be identified by **bare greenish facial skin**, lanky shape, and **long legs and tail**. Uncommon on both slopes, to 6,500 ft (1,950 m). Found in lower levels of forest. Call a mournful, slowly repeated *aoww . . . aoww . . . aoww . . . aoww* (often given at dawn and dusk).

Red-throated Caracara
Ibycter americanus

19.5 in (50 cm); WS 44 in (110 cm). Very distinctive—almost suggesting a guan or curassow—but note **bare red facial skin** and **red legs**. Common locally, from eastern Panamá Province eastward, to 5,000 ft (1,500 m). Formerly occurred in western Panama, but now mostly gone except in Bocas del Toro. Found in middle and upper levels of forest. Travels in noisy flocks, raiding wasp and bee nests for their larvae. Gives very loud, ringing calls reminiscent of a macaw: *KOW! KOW! KOW! ca-KOW! ca-ca-KOW!*

adult

immature

**Barred
Forest-Falcon**

adult
dark morph

**Collared
Forest-Falcon**

immature
pale morph

adult

**Slaty-backed
Forest-Falcon**

adult
pale morph

**Red-throated
Caracara**

Crested Caracara
Caracara cheriway

23 in (58 cm); WS 47 in (120 cm). **Bare red facial skin** and **white neck** distinctive. In flight shows prominent **white patches in primaries**, white rump, and mostly white tail with dusky barring. Immature similar, but has paler facial skin; overall browner, with white areas replaced by buff. Yellow-headed Caracara also has pale patch in primaries but is much smaller and lacks dark cap and belly. Very common on Pacific slope, eastward to eastern Panamá Province; rare on Caribbean slope in Canal Area and Bocas del Toro. Found in open areas in lowlands. Feeds on carrion and sometimes on small live animals; often seen on ground, especially near highways, where it forages for roadkill. Call a harsh cackling.

Yellow-headed Caracara
Milvago chimachima

17 in (43 cm); WS 34.5 in (88 cm). On adult, **buffy head, neck, and underparts** are distinctive. Laughing Falcon has broad black mask and differs in shape and habits. In flight, both adult and streaked immature show **prominent buffy patch in primaries**; much larger Crested Caracara has white wing patches and a dark cap and belly. Very common on Pacific slope, eastward to eastern Panamá Province; less common (but increasing) on Caribbean slope, from northern Coclé to eastern Colón Province; common in urban areas; to 4,600 ft (1,400 m). Occurs in open areas. Feeds on carrion; often seen along roadsides where it feeds on roadkill. Call a grating, whistling screech *khyeeeeer!*

Laughing Falcon
Herpetotheres cachinnans

19 in (48 cm); WS 32.5 in (83 cm). **Broad black mask** is diagnostic; larger and stockier than Yellow-headed Caracara. In flight shows **buffy patch in primaries**. Rare on both slopes, to 4,300 ft (1,300 m). Found in canopy of forest and in woodland and open areas with scattered trees; often perches conspicuously on exposed branches. Loud resonant call (*gwa-co!*) repeated for several minutes (often starts out with a single *guah* note that suggests call of Collared Forest-Falcon, p. 56); also produces a cackling laugh: *heh heh heh heh heh.*

American Kestrel
Falco sparverius

9.5 in (24 cm); WS 22 in (56 cm). Both sexes are distinguished from other raptors by **distinctive facial pattern** and mostly **rufous back and tail**. Immature male has white breast with dark streaking. Merlin is similar in size but has only faint facial pattern and has gray or brown back and tail. Migrants are more heavily spotted (above and below) than form that breeds locally, which has recently colonized Panama from Colombia. Uncommon transient and winter resident (early Oct to early April), on the Pacific slope eastward to eastern Panamá Province; rarer on the Caribbean slope; to at least 5,300 ft (1,600 m). Rare as a resident breeder, from western Panamá Province eastward. Found in open areas; frequently seen on wires or other exposed perches. Often hovers when hunting (mainly for insects). Call a high squeaky *ki-ki-ki-ki-ki.*

Merlin
Falco columbarius

11 in (28 cm); WS 25 in (63 cm). Distinguished from other falcons by **lack of distinctive head pattern**; further distinguished from American Kestrel by gray or brown (not rufous) back and **lack of rufous in tail**. Immature similar to adult female. Set apart from immature Sharp-shinned Hawk (p. 44) by dark eyes and narrower, pale tail bands. Rare transient and winter resident (late Sept to mid-April) mainly along coasts; also inland in open areas (up into highlands). Mainly silent in Panama; call similar to that of American Kestrel.

adult

adult

Yellow-headed
Caracara

adult

immature

Crested
Caracara

immature

adult

adult male
migrant race

adult female
migrant race

Laughing
Falcon

American
Kestrel

adult
male

Merlin

adult
female

Aplomado Falcon   *Falco femoralis*

15.5 in (40 cm); WS 35 in (89 cm). Prominent **pale superciliary** (extending back to encircle crown) is diagnostic; note also **blackish band across lower breast** and **rufous-tawny underparts**. Immature has more extensive black streaking on white breast and is buffier below. In flight, **pale trailing edge on inner flight feathers** distinguishes it from other falcons. Uncommon in Herrera, Los Santos, southern Coclé, and western Panamá Province; in open areas in lowlands. Vagrant elsewhere. Call a high *ee-ee-ee*.

Bat Falcon   *Falco rufigularis*

10 in (26 cm); WS 23 in (59 cm). **Dark head** (except throat) **without moustachial mark** distinguishes it from other *Falco* falcons, except very rare Orange-breasted. Throat and upper breast vary from white to buff, sometimes grading into cinnamon or orange-rufous just above breast band and on sides of neck; birds with cinnamon or orange-rufous very similar to Orange-breasted (see description). Uncommon on both slopes, to at least 4,000 ft (1,200 m). Found in upper levels of forest and in adjacent clearings with tall trees; often seen on high exposed perches. Most active at dawn and dusk. Call, a high shrill *kee-kee-kee-kee-kee*, is similar to that of other falcons.

Orange-breasted Falcon   *Falco deiroleucus*

14 in (36 cm); WS 30.5 in (77 cm). Very similar to much more common Bat Falcon. Orange-breasted is slightly larger, with **proportionately larger head, bill, and feet**; has **wider, less even, white scalloping on black breast band; upper breast and sides of neck are always orange-rufous**, contrasting strongly with **pure white** (never buff) **throat**. Bat falcons with extensive orange on upper breast tend to have buff throats. Immature has dark barring on thighs and belly (absent on immature Bat Falcon). Very rare from Coclé eastward, with old records from Chiriquí. Occurs in upper levels of forest in highlands. Nests on cliffs, and most likely seen in their vicinity.

Peregrine Falcon   *Falco peregrinus*

17 in (43 cm); WS 38 in (96 cm). In all plumages, distinguished from other falcons by **broad moustachial mark**. Uncommon transient and winter resident (Oct to early May), mainly along coasts and around larger bodies of water; may occur elsewhere. Often found near concentrations of shorebirds and other aquatic birds; sudden flight of flocks is frequently a sign that a Peregrine is patrolling the area. Usually silent in Panama; call a harsh *kek-kek-kek*.

Sunbittern

EURYPYGIDAE. The single member of this neotropical family resembles a heron although it is more closely related to rails. The Sunbittern forages for small aquatic animals by walking slowly along forested streams. Its bulky nest, made of mud and vegetable matter, is placed on a tree branch, often over water. A concealed eye-spot pattern (chestnut, buff, and black) on the wings can be flashed to startle predators; this pattern is also prominent in flight.

Sunbittern   *Eurypyga helias*

18.5 in (47 cm). **White stripes on black head** distinguish it from all herons; also differs in shape and proportions from the tiger-herons and Agami Heron (p. 26), which occur in the same habitat. Uncommon; mainly on Caribbean slope and in Darién; local on Pacific slope. Occurs in lowlands and lower foothills, to 3,000 ft (900 m). Found along smaller streams in forest. Call a haunting, high-pitched, rising whistle.

adult

Aplomado
Falcon

Bat Falcon

adult

Orange-breasted
Falcon

adult

adult

Peregrine
Falcon

immature

Sunbittern

RALLIDAE. Most members of this nearly worldwide family live in wetlands, though a few species favor other habitats. They generally feed on both plant and animal matter. The majority of rails and crakes (referred to jointly as rails in the accounts that follow) are highly secretive, and are thus far more often heard than seen. Individuals may call within a few feet of an observer yet remain entirely hidden within thick vegetation. They are more likely to be seen near dawn and dusk, when they sometimes forage in more open areas. Gallinules, moorhens, and coots are easier to observe, as they often swim in open water or feed at the water's edge.

Ruddy Crake   *Laterallus ruber*
6 in (15 cm). Combination of **unbarred rufous underparts** and mostly **gray head** is distinctive; note also dark bill and greenish legs. White-throated Crake has barred flanks; Uniform Crake (p. 64) is larger, with yellowish bill and red legs. One record, in a marsh near Changuinola, Bocas del Toro (2006); probably a vagrant, but perhaps just overlooked due to inconspicuous habits.

White-throated Crake   *Laterallus albigularis*
5.5 in (14 cm). Combination of **bright rufous breast** and **barred flanks** is diagnostic. Bocas del Toro race has grayish crown and sides of head. Immature has grayish breast; distinguished from Gray-breasted Crake by lack of rufous on nape. Common on entire Caribbean slope; also common on Pacific slope, both in Chiriquí and from western Panamá Province eastward; to 4,600 ft (1,400 m). Found in wet grassy areas, including damp meadows and roadside ditches. Very hard to see; presence revealed mostly by its call, an abrupt descending *chuuuuurrrrrr*, given at frequent intervals.

Gray-breasted Crake   *Laterallus exilis*
5.5 in (14 cm). Combination of **gray head and neck** and **bright rufous nape** is diagnostic. Immature duller and lacks chestnut nape. Distribution poorly known due to secretive habits; apparently rare, with scattered records from both slopes, to 4,600 ft (1,400 m). Found in wet grassy areas and at edge of marshes. Call a high-pitched *teet-tee-tee-tee-tee-tee*, with first note higher and longer than notes that follow; also gives a descending *chuurrr* (like that of White-throated Crake but not as loud or harsh).

Black Rail   *Laterallus jamaicensis*
6 in (15 cm). **Darker** than any other rail, especially on head and breast. **White speckling on back and rump** is diagnostic; also note black bill. One record of a pair that was apparently breeding in a wet grassland in eastern Panamá Province (1963). Call a sharp rapid *ki-ki-doo!*

Gray-necked Wood-Rail   *Aramides cajanea*
13.5 in (34 cm). **Largest rail. Black rump, tail, and underparts** distinguish it from all except probably vagrant Rufous-necked Wood-Rail, from which it differs by **gray head and neck**. Fairly common throughout the country to 4,600 ft (1,400 cm). Occurs near streams and in swamps and mangroves. Call a loud ringing series of clucks and hoots: *kuk kuk, kuk-WHOOT kuk-WHOOT kuk-WHOOT kuk-WHOOT kuk-whoot-whoot whoot-whoot.*

Rufous-necked Wood-Rail   *Aramides axillaris*
10 in (26 cm). Distinguished from larger Gray-necked Wood-Rail by **rufous head and neck**; distinguished from smaller Uniform Crake (p. 64) by **gray patch on back** and black on rump, tail, and underparts. Status uncertain, with scattered records from both coasts; probably vagrant but possibly a very rare resident. Found in mangroves. Call a loud *pik-pik-pik.*

Ruddy Crake

White-throated Crake

adult

adult
Bocas del Toro
race

Gray-breasted Crake

adult

Black Rail

Gray-necked
Wood-Rail

Rufous-necked
Wood-Rail

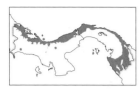

Uniform Crake
Amaurolimnas concolor

8 in (20 cm). More **uniformly colored** than other rails; smaller and has shorter bill than wood-rails (p. 62). Note also **yellow bill** and **red legs**. Very rare, with scattered records from both slopes. Occurs in dense vegetation in wet areas; sometimes also found in areas near water, in either forest or second growth. Call a series of whistles slurring upward: *tuwheet tuwheet tuwheet tuwheet tuwheet tuwheet.*

Sora
Porzana carolina

8 in (20 cm). In all plumages, combination of **yellow bill** and **barring extending to sides** (not just on flanks) is diagnostic. Adult has **black facial mask** and gray breast. Immature has smaller mask and buffier breast; distinguished from much smaller Yellow-breasted Crake by lack of distinct white superciliary. Fairly common winter resident (late Sept to early April), mostly in lowlands but sometimes higher; to 4,600 ft (1,400 m). Found in freshwater marshes and in wet grassy areas. Makes a variety of calls, including a high-pitched, descending whinny (*ko-WHEee-e-e-e*) that slows at the end; a whistled *kerWHEE*; and a high-pitched *kek*.

Yellow-breasted Crake
Porzana flaviventer

4.5 in (12 cm). **Smallest rail**, and only species with **distinct whitish superciliary** and **black eye-line**. Very local; known mainly from middle Chagres Valley, but scattered records elsewhere; in lowlands. Found in dense vegetation in freshwater marshes and around lakes and large rivers. Call a high-pitched *kreeer.*

Colombian Crake
Neocrex colombiana

8 in (20 cm). **Red legs** and **yellow-green bill with red base** distinguish it from all but Paint-billed Crake. It differs from that species in having **buffy** (not barred) **lower underparts** and a gray (not brown) crown. Very rare (most recent record 1984); recorded in Tocumen Marsh (eastern Panamá Province) and near Caribbean coast in Canal Area. Occurs in freshwater marshes. Call a slow series of whistled notes: *tuee tuee tuee tuee.*

Paint-billed Crake
Neocrex erythrops

8 in (20 cm). **Red legs** and **yellow-green bill with red base** are shared only with Colombian Crake, from which it is distinguished by **barred lower underparts** and brown (not gray) crown. Very rare; recorded in Tocumen Marsh (eastern Panamá Province) and in western Bocas del Toro. Found in freshwater marshes. Call a chirping *kukKUKtuKUK.*

Spotted Rail
Pardirallus maculatus

10 in (25 cm). **Bold black-and-white spotting and barring** make this species unmistakable. Immature is browner with reduced spotting and barring. Very rare. Recorded mainly from Tocumen Marsh in eastern Panamá Province; other records from Canal Area (near Caribbean coast) and from western Kuna Yala. Found in freshwater marshes and mangroves. Call a repeated rasping, groaning screech.

Uniform Crake

Sora

immature

adult

Yellow-breasted Crake

Colombian
Crake

Paint-billed Crake

Spotted
Rail

adult

Clapper Rail

Rallus longirostris

14 in (36 cm). **Larger** and has **longer bill** than other rails; distinguished from wood-rails (p. 62) by prominent **black-and-white barring on flanks and belly**. Only one record, from Bocas del Toro, where it may be a rare resident in coastal wetlands. Call a series of dry clicks that accelerate and then slow.

Purple Gallinule

Porphyrio martinica

11 in (28 cm). Brilliant **deep blue and bright green** adult is unmistakable. Immature is distinguished from immature Common Moorhen and American Coot by **brownish** (not gray) **head and neck**. Immature jacanas (p. 72) have different shape and distinct white superciliary and black line behind eye. Common in freshwater marshes and around the edges of lakes, ponds, and larger rivers; to 4,600 ft (1,400 m). Walks on floating plants and climbs about in thick vegetation at water's edge; swims only occasionally. Call a sharp *kik!*

Common Moorhen

Gallinula chloropus

12 in (30 cm). **Red bill and frontal shield** and **white line on flanks** distinguish adult from American Coot. Immature distinguished from immature American Coot by darker bill, from immature Purple Gallinule by gray (not brown) head and neck, and from both by **white line on flanks**. Common in freshwater marshes and on larger lakes and ponds; to 4,600 ft (1,400 m). Often swims in open water. Has various clucking calls.

American Coot

Fulica americana

14 in (36 cm). **Stout white bill** (whitish gray in immature), **white frontal shield**, and lack of white line on flanks distinguish it from all plumages of Common Moorhen. Immature Purple Gallinule has darker bill and brown (not gray) head and neck. Uncommon winter resident (Oct to late April) in western Panama; becomes rarer eastward, extending as far as eastern Panamá Province; to 4,600 ft (1,400 m). Found on lakes and ponds, usually seen swimming; feeds by diving. Calls include a variety of cackling notes.

Finfoots

HELIORNITHIDAE. This family of aquatic birds contains just three species, one each in the tropics of Africa, Asia, and the Americas. Their toes are lobed (as in the true grebes) rather than fully webbed (as in ducks). Diet consists of small aquatic animals, often taken from the surface of the water or from adjacent vegetation.

Sungrebe

Heliornis fulica

11.5 in (29 cm). **Black-and-white striped head and neck** distinguish it from all ducks and grebes. Nonbreeding female resembles male. Immature grebes and some plumages of Masked Duck (p. 8) have stripes on head, but these are less distinct and do not extend to neck. Uncommon in western Bocas del Toro and in Canal Area; uncommon and local in eastern Panamá Province and in Darién; found in lowlands. Occurs on quiet bodies of fresh water bordered with dense vegetation, including ponds, lakes, and slow-moving rivers and streams. Very secretive and wary, often diving suddenly at first hint of disturbance. Sometimes swims with just head and neck exposed. Gives a hollow-sounding yelping call: *gwoop-woop-woop-woop*.

Clapper
Rail

adult

Purple
Gallinule

immature

adult

Common
Moorhen

immature

American
Coot

adult

immature

Sungrebe

male

breeding
female

ARAMIDAE. The Limpkin, sole member of its family, is related to cranes and rails. Found in freshwater habitats, from Florida to northern Argentina, it feeds mainly on apple snails.

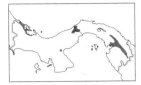

Limpkin
Aramus guarauna

24 in (60 cm). **White streaking on head and neck** distinguishes it from most herons and ibises; on race found on western Caribbean slope, streaking extends to back and wings. Both immature and nonbreeding adult Glossy Ibis (p. 34) show small white speckles on head and neck but have bills that are more decurved and bare facial skin. Immature night-herons (p. 32) have much shorter bill and legs. Uncommon in Bocas del Toro, northern Ngöbe-Buglé, southern Herrera (Las Macanas Marsh), Canal Area, and Darién. Found in marshes and swamps and borders of larger lakes and rivers. Call a loud wailing *caRAUuuu!*

Plovers & Lapwings

CHARADRIIDAE. Members of this family occur throughout much of the world. These shorebirds resemble sandpipers (pp. 74-85) but are generally stockier and have shorter, thicker bills and larger eyes. Some species occur mainly in coastal habitats, while others prefer grasslands. Plovers and lapwings feed on crustaceans, insects, and other small animals. Many species are highly migratory, though a few species breed locally in Panama.

Southern Lapwing
Vanellus chilensis

12 in (31 cm). Its **crested head (mostly gray)** and **black breast** make this species unmistakable. In flight, shows conspicuous white line across wing coverts and a white rump. Formerly uncommon; now common on Pacific slope from Coclé eastward; uncommon and local elsewhere on Pacific and on Caribbean (in Canal Area); to 4,300 ft (1,300 m). Found in areas with short grass, usually near water. Often in pairs and small groups; frequently gives loud raucous alarm calls when disturbed: *KEER KEER KEER KEER.*

Black-bellied Plover
Pluvialis squatarola

11 in (28 cm). In nonbreeding plumage, combination of **overall gray plumage** and **short, thick black bill** distinguishes it from all other shorebirds except the much rarer American Golden-Plover (see for distinctions). In flight, **black axillars** diagnostic; also note **white rump and base of tail** and **distinct white wing stripe**. Distinctive breeding plumage seen occasionally in April and May and in Aug (compare American Golden-Plover). Common transient and winter resident (mostly Sept to April); a few present in summer; occurs along the coast, mostly on mudflats but sometimes on beaches and grassy areas. Call a plaintive whistle: *ker-wheee-ur.*

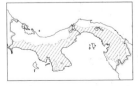

American Golden-Plover
Pluvialis dominica

10 in (25 cm). Very similar to much more common Black-bellied Plover but smaller and has thinner bill. In nonbreeding plumage, **whitish superciliary is more distinct** than on Black-bellied; in breeding plumage, has all-black underparts (no white on belly) and upperparts flecked golden yellow (not gray). In flight, shows **gray axillars, dark tail**, and only a faint wing stripe. Rare transient (recorded mainly late Aug to early Nov and in March and April); a few present in winter and summer. Mostly on or near coasts (primarily Pacific), usually in areas with short grass but sometimes on mudflats. Call a high *kur-ur-wheet!* (sharper in tone than call of Black-bellied Plover).

Limpkin

eastern
race

Southern
Lapwing

nonbreeding
adult

nonbreeding
adult

Black-bellied
Plover

breeding
adult

nonbreeding
adult

nonbreeding
adult

American
Golden-Plover

breeding
adult

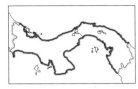

Collared Plover   *Charadrius collaris*

5.5 in (14 cm). Distinguished from all plumages of Semipalmated and Snowy Plovers by **lack of collar across hindneck** (note also that Semipalmated has orange base to bill rather than all-dark bill). Distinguished from larger Wilson's Plover by **shorter, more slender bill**. During nonbreeding season (July to April), fairly common in central Panama (both coasts), on beaches and at edge of mudflats. During breeding season, evidently disperses inland to nest on gravel banks of streams and rivers. Call a sharp *whit!*

Wilson's Plover   *Charadrius wilsonia*

6.5 in (17 cm). In any plumage, its **exceptionally thick bill** distinguishes Wilson's from other small plovers. Breeding female has brown breast band, sometimes with a rufous tinge. Note also pinkish legs; Semipalmated Plover has yellowish or orange legs. Breeds in Panama, with numbers augmented by migrants in winter. Fairly common on Pacific coast, uncommon on Caribbean; found on beaches and mudflats. Call a whistled *wheet!*

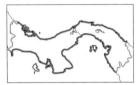

Semipalmated Plover   *Charadrius semipalmatus*

6 in (15 cm). Distinguished from other small plovers by **yellowish to orange** (not pinkish or gray) **legs**. On breeding adults, base of bill is orange or yellow; in nonbreeding plumage, bill mostly black; immature has all-black bill. Very common transient (arrivals begin in early July; largest flocks occur Sept to Nov and late March through April); common winter resident; fairly common in summer. Occurs on both coasts, on beaches and mudflats. Call a whistled *kur-WHEE.*

Killdeer   *Charadrius vociferus*

9.5 in (24 cm). **Double breast band** is diagnostic. In flight, shows **orange rump and base of tail**. Uncommon transient and winter resident (late Oct through March, occasionally to mid-April); very rare breeder near Las Macanas Marsh (Herrera). Found in areas with short grass, not necessarily near water. Call a loud *kill-dee!* or *kill-dee-dee!*

Snowy Plover   *Charadrius alexandrinus*

6 in (15 cm). Upperparts are much **paler gray** than in other small plovers, and Snowy has only **incomplete breast band**; differs also in having **gray** (not pinkish or yellowish) **legs**. Vagrant, with records from Bocas del Toro and western Panamá Province; inhabits sandy beaches. Call a trilling *pur-wheet!*

Oystercatchers

HAEMATOPODIDAE. Members of this small distinctive family are found almost throughout the world, mostly along coasts but sometimes inland. The long, laterally compressed bill is used to pry open shellfish.

American Oystercatcher   *Haematopus palliatus*

17 in (43 cm). **Long red bill** and **all-black head** are diagnostic. Locally common on Pacific coast; two records from Caribbean; on beaches and rocky shores. Call a loud whistled *wheeep!*

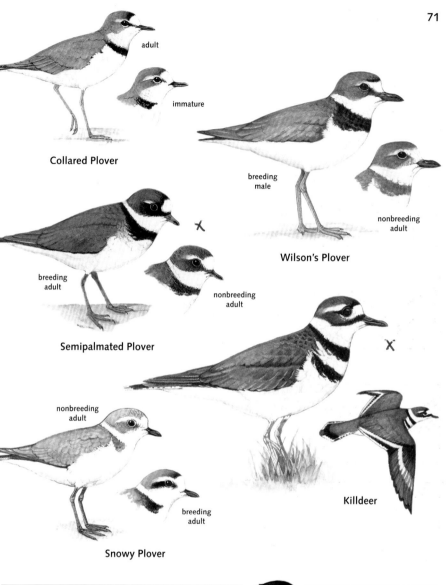

adult

immature

Collared Plover

breeding
male

nonbreeding
adult

Wilson's Plover

breeding
adult

nonbreeding
adult

Semipalmated Plover

nonbreeding
adult

breeding
adult

Snowy Plover

Killdeer

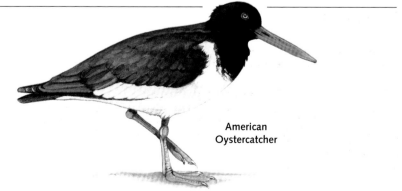

**American
Oystercatcher**

RECURVIROSTRIDAE. This small family of long-legged shorebirds is found throughout much of the world. Stilts have long straight bills, while avocets have bills that curve upward. Stilts feed mainly on insects, and avocets on crustaceans, but both also take other kinds of aquatic invertebrates.

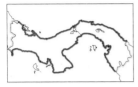

Black-necked Stilt
Himantopus mexicanus

14 in (36 cm). **Exceptionally long red (or pinkish) legs** are diagnostic; also note **pied plumage** and **thin, straight black bill**. Fairly common along both coasts; relatively more common on Pacific. Found on coastal mudflats and in shallow brackish and freshwater habitats (such as marshes and salt ponds) near coast. Occurs all year, but more numerous Sept to March, probably due to presence of migrants. Breeds locally around Gulf of Parita and perhaps elsewhere. Call, often given in alarm, is a long series of sharp *kek* notes.

American Avocet
Recurvirostra americana

18 in (46 cm). **Slender black upturned bill** is diagnostic; also note **black-and-white pattern**. Vagrant; so far only recorded on salt ponds at Aguadulce (Herrera), and in western Panamá Province. Call a piping *wheet!*

Jacanas

JACANIDAE. Members of this small family occur in freshwater environments throughout the tropics and in some parts of the subtropics. Jacanas have extraordinarily long toes that allow them to walk on floating vegetation, where they feed on a variety of aquatic plants and animals and build their nests. In most species, females are polyandrous, guarding male harems, in which each male incubates one of the female's egg clutches. In all plumages, both Panama species are distinguished from any other waterbird by their very long toes and, in flight, greenish yellow flight feathers.

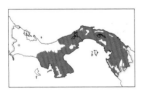

Wattled Jacana
Jacana jacana

8.5 in (22 cm). Combination of **red, two-lobed frontal shield** and **red wattles on sides of bill** is diagnostic. Adult usually all black; a few individuals have some chestnut on wings, back, or rump (adult Northern Jacana has all-chestnut body). Immature very similar to immature Northern, but rudimentary frontal shield and wattles are pinkish and crown is paler. Common on Caribbean slope, from northern Coclé eastward; and on Pacific slope, from western Veraguas eastward. Occurs in lowlands, on ponds and slow-moving streams with abundant floating vegetation. Calls similar to those of Northern Jacana.

Northern Jacana
Jacana spinosa

8.5 in (22 cm). **Yellow, three-lobed frontal shield** is diagnostic. Adult distinguished from Wattled Jacana by **chestnut body** (note that a few Wattled Jacanas have some chestnut on wings, back, or rump); immature very similar to immature Wattled, but rudimentary frontal shield is yellowish and crown is darker. Common on Caribbean slope in Bocas del Toro, and on Pacific slope, eastward to western Veraguas; to 4,600 ft (1,400 m). Found on ponds and slow-moving streams that have abundant floating vegetation. Noisy; calls include a harsh *scraa* (often given in flight).

Black-necked
Stilt

breeding
adult

nonbreeding
adult

American
Avocet

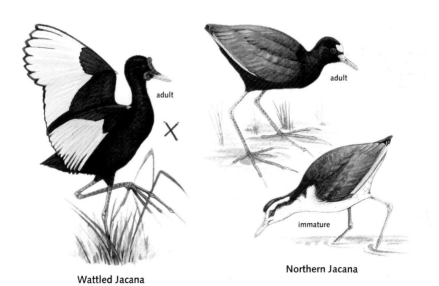

adult

adult

immature

Wattled Jacana

Northern Jacana

SCOLOPACIDAE. Most members of this cosmopolitan family occur along coasts or in other aquatic environments, although a few favor drier habitats such as grasslands. All species found in Panama are migrants that breed farther north, mostly in the northern United States and in Canada. Some individuals, especially immatures, may remain in Panama throughout the northern summer. Many species are quite similar to one another, especially in the drab nonbreeding plumages in which they usually occur in Panama (although breeding dress may be seen just after arrival or before departure); immature plumages can also present identification problems. The small sandpipers of the genus *Calidris* (Semipalmated, Western, Least, White-rumped, and Baird's, pp. 78-83), collectively known as "peeps," are especially difficult to distinguish. Length and shape of bill, length and color of legs, behavior, and habitat can be important keys to identification.

Greater Yellowlegs
Tringa melanoleuca

13 in (33 cm). In all plumages, **long bright yellow legs** distinguish it from all but very similar Lesser Yellowlegs. Differs from that species by proportionately **longer bill (distinctly longer than head) that is paler at base** and usually appears slightly upturned. In breeding plumage, darker and more speckled; breeding Lesser is not as dark, has less speckling above, and has less extensive barring on flanks. In flight, combination of plain wings, white rump, and mostly white tail distinguishes it from all sandpipers but Lesser Yellowlegs and Stilt Sandpiper (p. 82). Common transient and winter resident (mostly Aug to April); rare in summer. Occurs throughout the country to 4,600 ft (1,400 m). Found mainly on coastal mudflats; also in and near shallow freshwater habitats and in wet grassy areas. Call, a loud sharp whistle, usually consists of three or four notes: *tew-tew-tew* (Lesser Yellowlegs has one- or two-note call).

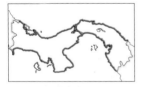

Lesser Yellowlegs
Tringa flavipes

9.5 in (24 cm). Very similar to Greater Yellowlegs (including flight pattern); distinguished by a **thinner and proportionately shorter bill (about same length as head)** that is straight (not upturned) and **all dark**. In breeding plumage, somewhat darker and more speckled above; breeding Greater is even darker and more speckled, and has more extensive barring on flanks. Common fall transient (late Aug through Nov); uncommon winter resident; uncommon spring transient (up to April); rare in summer. Found in lowlands throughout the country, mostly in shallow freshwater habitats and wet grassy areas; less common on coast. Call is a sharp whistle of one or two notes: *tiw-tiw* (that of Greater usually has three or four notes).

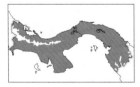

Solitary Sandpiper
Tringa solitaria

8.5 in (21 cm). **Olive green legs** and prominent **white eye-ring** distinguish it from Greater and Lesser Yellowlegs (which are similar in shape). In flight, shows plain wings and dark center of tail and rump; from below, underwings are entirely dark. In breeding plumage, darker and more spotted. Bobs head and teeters tail when nervous, but not as constantly as Spotted Sandpiper (p. 76). Common transient and winter resident, mostly from late Aug to early April; also, rarely, in late July and in late April. Occurs throughout the country to 4,600 ft (1,400 m), in shallow, mainly freshwater habitats. Call a sharp high-pitched *peek-peek* or *pik*.

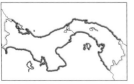

Willet
Tringa semipalmata

14 in (35 cm). In nonbreeding plumage, distinguished by **moderately long grayish legs** and relatively **stout straight bill**; more uniformly colored than similar species. In flight, **bold black-and-white wing pattern** is diagnostic. Very common transient and winter resident (mostly Aug to April); common in summer. Found on both coasts. Calls include a loud grating *kreee-up* and a high-pitched *kee-dit!*

Greater
Yellowlegs

nonbreeding
adult

Lesser
Yellowlegs

nonbreeding
adult

nonbreeding
adult

Solitary
Sandpiper

nonbreeding
adult

nonbreeding
adult

nonbreeding
adult

breeding
adult

Willet

Wandering Tattler

Tringa incana

11 in (28 cm). In nonbreeding plumage, distinguished by combination of **yellow legs, moderately long dark bill**, and **uniformly grayish plumage** (including flanks). Teeters and bobs when foraging, like much more common Spotted Sandpiper. Very rare transient; most records from March to April, with one record in Sept and one in late Feb; possible winter resident. Found on rocky shores, mostly on Pacific coast.

Spotted Sandpiper
Actitis macularius

6.5 in (17 cm). In nonbreeding plumage, note **distinct brown smudge on sides of breast** and **white mark extending up side** (in front of wing). In breeding plumage, prominent rounded spots on breast are distinctive. When foraging on ground, recognized by its almost **constant teetering**; flies with short bursts of rapid wing beats interspersed with glides. Very common transient and winter resident, mostly from early Aug (rarely late July) to mid-May (rarely late May); to at least 4,600 ft (1,400 m). Found almost anywhere near water, from coastal areas to small mountain streams.

Whimbrel

Numenius phaeopus

17 in (43 cm). **Long decurved bill** distinguishes it from all other shorebirds except for the Long-billed Curlew, which is much rarer and lacks **pale median crown stripe**. Immature White Ibis (p. 34) has white breast and belly and pink bill. Very common winter resident (mostly early Sept to April); rare in summer. Occurs on both coasts, though more common on Pacific. Found mostly on beaches and mudflats; sometimes also in nearby wet grassy areas. In flight, gives a high-pitched *ki-ki-ki-ki-ki-ki*, with all notes on the same pitch.

Long-billed Curlew
Numenius americanus

24 in (61 cm). **Lack of median crown stripe** distinguishes it from Whimbrel, as does its **much larger** size and **buffier** coloration. Adult has much longer bill than Whimbrel, but some immatures have bills similar in length. In flight, note **cinnamon wing-linings**, shared only with Marbled Godwit. Very rare fall transient and possible winter resident; recorded mid-Aug to Dec, in and near Canal Area, and in southern Coclé. Found on mudflats, salt ponds, and in nearby grassy areas.

Marbled Godwit
Limosa fedoa

17 in (43 cm). Combination of **long, slightly upturned bill** and **mostly buffy plumage** is diagnostic. In breeding plumage, has fine barring on underparts. Uncommon transient and winter resident (Aug to May); rare in summer. Recorded mostly from upper Bay of Panama (mainly east of Panamá City), with a few records elsewhere. Found on coastal mudflats and nearby wet grassy areas.

Hudsonian Godwit
Limosa haemastica

15 in (38 cm). Note **long, slightly upturned bill**, similar to that of Marbled Godwit. In nonbreeding plumage, distinguished from that species by **uniformly gray** coloration; in breeding plumage, dark rufous breast is distinctive. In flight, note **black wing-linings, black tail with white band across base and rump**, and **white wing stripe**. Vagrant, with just two records: one near Colón City (Oct) and one in eastern Panamá Province (late Sept). Found on coastal mudflats and in grassy areas. **Not illustrated.**

nonbreeding
adult

breeding
adult

**Wandering
Tattler**

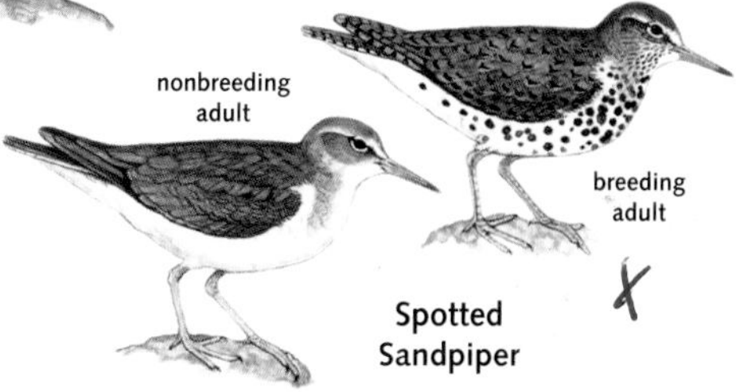

nonbreeding
adult

breeding
adult

**Spotted
Sandpiper**

Whimbrel

**Long-billed
Curlew**

nonbreeding
adult

**Marbled
Godwit**

Ruddy Turnstone
Arenaria interpres

9 in (23 cm). In all plumages, note **distinctive pattern on head and breast** and **orange legs**. In flight, shows striking pattern of **white stripes on back, white wing stripe**, and **black tail with white base**. Common transient and winter resident (Aug to April); uncommon in summer. Occurs along coast; favors rocky or gravelly areas but also found on mudflats or grassy areas near shore. Flight call is a squeaky rattle.

Surfbird
Aphriza virgata

9.5 in (24 cm). Best distinguished from all similar species by **short stout bill with orangish or yellowish base**; also note **yellowish legs**. In breeding plumage, prominent black spotting below and rufous scapulars are distinctive. In flight, shows striking pattern of **white wing stripe** and **white tail with black tip**. Fairly common (but local) transient and winter resident (recorded Aug to Feb, but probably occurs later); one summer record, in June. Occurs on rocky shores on Pacific (most records from near Panamá City).

Red Knot
Calidris canutus

9 in (23 cm). Most similar to the two dowitchers (p. 82), but distinguished by much **shorter bill** and **chunkier shape**. Larger than other *Calidris* sandpipers. In flight, note **pale gray rump and tail**. Rare transient (from Sept to Oct and from March to April); a few birds present in winter and summer. Found on coastal mudflats and beaches, and occasionally in nearby wet grassy areas.

Sanderling
Calidris alba

7 in (18 cm). In nonbreeding plumage, **paler** than other sandpipers; also note **black shoulders**. In breeding plumage, rufous head and neck are distinctive. Immature has black speckling on back. In flight, shows more **prominent white wing stripe** than other *Calidris* species. Fairly common transient and winter resident (early Aug to late May); very rare in summer. Occurs mostly on Pacific coast, on sandy and pebbly beaches. Typically seen in small flocks, running rapidly back and forth at the very edge of the waves.

Dunlin
Calidris alpina

8.5 in (21 cm). In nonbreeding plumage, which is very drab brownish gray, note relatively **long bill that droops slightly at tip**. In breeding plumage, black belly patch is diagnostic; in immature, belly is speckled with black. Nonbreeding Red Knot is larger and has straight bill. Western Sandpiper (p. 80) also has drooping bill but is much smaller. See also White-rumped (p. 80) and Stilt Sandpipers (p. 82). Vagrant; recorded Sept to March. Occurs on mudflats along both coasts. Call a distinctive prolonged buzzy trill.

Curlew Sandpiper
Calidris ferruginea

8.5 in (21 cm). In nonbreeding plumage, very similar to Dunlin, but is paler gray above, has bill that curves more evenly along its length (rather than just near tip), longer legs, and pale superciliary that is more distinct. In flight, note **white rump** (Dunlin has dark rump). In nonbreeding plumage, distinguished from nonbreeding Stilt Sandpiper (p. 82) by shorter, blackish legs. In breeding plumage, head and breast are entirely dark rufous; breeding Red Knot is chunkier and has shorter bill and dull olive legs. Vagrant; one record on mudflats in Panamá City (2008). **Not illustrated.**

breeding
adult

Surfbird

breeding
adult

Ruddy Turnstone

nonbreeding
adult

nonbreeding
adult

breeding
adult

Red Knot

breeding
adult

Sanderling

nonbreeding
adult

nonbreeding
adult

breeding
adult

Dunlin

nonbreeding
adult

Least Sandpiper
Calidris minutilla

5.5 in (14 cm). Distinguished from Semipalmated and Western Sandpipers by **yellowish legs**, but note that in poor light, or when stained with mud, legs can appear dark. Least is also browner overall, and breast is darker, with more distinct margin between it and white belly; bill is shorter and thinner. Common transient, mostly Sept to Oct (but some may arrive in late July) and from March to April; fairly common winter resident. Most often found around freshwater lakes and ponds and in wet grassy areas but also forages on higher parts of mudflats. Call a high thin rising *wheeedup!*

White-rumped Sandpiper
Calidris fuscicollis

6.5 in (17 cm). **Wing tips extend beyond end of tail**; has longer wings than all other *Calidris* species except for Baird's Sandpiper. At close range, **reddish base of lower mandible** is diagnostic. Has heavier build and, in nonbreeding plumage, is grayer than Baird's. In flight, **narrow white rump band** distinguishes it from other small sandpipers, except the Stilt Sandpiper (p. 82), which is otherwise quite different. Rare transient, mostly Sept to Oct and April to May; a few records from summer. Found on mudflats and in wet grassy areas. Call a distinctive high mouselike squeak: *tseet-tseet.*

Baird's Sandpiper
Calidris bairdii

7 in (18 cm). **Wing tips extend beyond end of tail**; has longer wings than all other *Calidris* species except for White-rumped Sandpiper. Distinguished from White-rumped by more slender body, **all-black bill**, and, in flight, rump with dark center. In nonbreeding plumage, browner than other *Calidris* except for Least, which has yellowish (not black) legs; also note **buffy breast with fine streaks**. Rare fall transient, Sept to Oct; very rare in spring. Found in wet fields with short grass. Call a low rough *kreeep!*

Semipalmated Sandpiper
Calidris pusilla

6 in (15 cm). Very similar to Western Sandpiper, especially in nonbreeding plumage. Bill is straight and on average shorter than in Western (but lengths overlap). In breeding and immature plumages, lacks rufous on scapulars seen in Western. Differs from Least Sandpiper by its black legs. Very common transient and winter resident, from Aug to April; uncommon in summer. Occurs on coastal mudflats, especially those on Pacific coast; sometimes on shores of freshwater lakes and ponds; less numerous than Western. Call a rough *chert*, slightly lower and harsher than that of Western.

Western Sandpiper
Calidris mauri

6 in (15 cm). Very similar to Semipalmated Sandpiper, especially in nonbreeding plumage. Bill often droops slightly at tip and on average is longer than in Semipalmated (but lengths overlap). In breeding and immature plumages, distinguished by rufous on scapulars. Differs from Least Sandpiper by its black legs. Abundant transient and winter resident, from Aug to April; fairly common in summer. Occurs on coastal mudflats, especially those on Pacific; sometimes on shores of freshwater lakes and ponds. Call a thin *cheep*, somewhat higher than that of Semipalmated.

breeding adult

nonbreeding adult

Least Sandpiper

note narrow white rump band

White-rumped Sandpiper

nonbreeding adult

Baird's Sandpiper

nonbreeding adult

breeding adult

Semipalmated Sandpiper

nonbreeding adult

breeding adult

Western Sandpiper

nonbreeding adult

Pectoral Sandpiper
Calidris melanotos

9 in (23 cm). **Sharp demarcation between finely streaked breast and white underparts** is distinctive; also note **yellow legs** and **pale base of bill**. Least Sandpiper (p. 80) is similar in pattern, but is much smaller and has all-dark bill. Common fall transient from late Aug to mid-Nov; rare in spring, in March and April (exceptionally rare in May and June). Occurs along both coasts, mainly in wet grassy fields, sometimes on mudflats. Call a low harsh *chrrrk!*

Stilt Sandpiper
Calidris himantopus

8 in (20 cm). In drab nonbreeding plumage, note combination of relatively **long, slightly drooping black bill** and **long yellowish green legs**. In breeding plumage, underparts that are heavily barred with black and rufous cheeks are distinctive. In flight, note **white rump and plain wings**. Both dowitchers are larger, have straight bills that are much longer, and have relatively shorter legs. Both yellowlegs (p. 74) are larger, have bright yellow legs, and lack distinct pale superciliary. See also Red Knot and Dunlin (p. 78). Uncommon transient, from Aug to Sept and March to April; a few records from other months. Mostly on shallow freshwater ponds, occasionally along coasts. Call a soft trilling *krreek*.

Buff-breasted Sandpiper
Tryngites subruficollis

8 in (20 cm). **Plain buffy face and breast** are distinctive; also note yellow legs. See Upland (p. 84), Pectoral, and Baird's (p. 80) Sandpipers, all of which occur in the same habitat as Buff-breasted. Uncommon fall transient (Aug to Oct); very rare in spring (March and April). Found on both coasts, in fields with short grass. Call a soft *grriit*.

Short-billed Dowitcher
Limnodromus griseus

10 in (25 cm). **Very long straight bill** distinguishes it from most other shorebirds. Nearly identical to Long-billed Dowitcher (see for distinctions); Wilson's Snipe (p. 84) also has long straight bill but is otherwise very different. In flight, shows **pale secondaries** and **white patch on rump that extends onto lower back** (pointed upward to form narrow triangle). Common transient and winter resident, from Aug to April; rare in summer. Occurs on both coasts, mainly on mudflats, but sometimes on shallow freshwater ponds near coast. Call (given mainly in flight) is a low *tududu* (more mellow than call of Long-billed).

Long-billed Dowitcher
Limnodromus scolopaceus

10 in (26 cm). Nearly identical to Short-billed Dowitcher, including pattern in flight; despite name, bill length overlaps with that of Short-billed and does not distinguish most individuals. Long-billed has light bands on tail that are usually much narrower than dark bands; on Short-billed, light bands are usually same width as (or wider than) dark bands. Immature Long-billed has plain tertials with pale edging; immature Short-billed has tertials with rufous edging and rufous lines or bars on the vane. Rare migrant (recorded from Oct to March); both status and distribution are uncertain due to difficulty of identification. Found mostly on shallow freshwater ponds and in wet grassy areas. Call a sharp *kik*, sometimes repeated in series. Long-billed often calls while feeding; Short-billed is usually silent when feeding (mainly calls in flight).

Pectoral
Sandpiper

nonbreeding
adult

breeding
adult

Stilt Sandpiper

breeding
adult

Buff-breasted
Sandpiper

nonbreeding
adult

Short-billed
Dowitcher

nonbreeding
adult

nonbreeding
adult

Long-billed
Dowitcher

Ruff
Philomachus pugnax

M 11 in (28 cm); F 9 in (23 cm). Most similar to the two yellowlegs species (p. 74), but plumper, with a small head and relatively short, slightly decurved bill. Color of legs varies: in immatures, greenish or brownish; in adults, pink, orange-red, or yellow. Pale edges on back feathers and scapulars produce scaled appearance. In flight, shows **large white ovals at sides of tail**, usually joined above tail to form U-shape. Breeding males develop elongated ruff around head, highly variable in color. Vagrant. Occurs on both coasts near Canal Area, in wet fields with short grass. **Not illustrated**.

Upland Sandpiper
Bartramia longicauda

10 in (25 cm). Shape is distinctive: note **small head, long neck, and relatively long tail**; mostly brown upperparts, short straight bill, large dark eyes, and yellow legs also aid in recognition. Transient: uncommon in fall (mid-Aug to late Dec); rare in spring (mid-March to late May). Occurs in lowlands on both slopes, in grassy areas.

Wilson's Snipe
Gallinago delicata

10.5 in (27 cm). **Very long straight bill** and **prominently striped head and back** are distinctive. In flight, note **back stripes, dark back and rump**, and **mostly orange-rufous tail**. Fairly common transient and winter resident, from Oct to April. Found throughout the country, to 4,300 ft (1,300 m); in wet grassy areas and marshes. Often difficult to see due to cryptic coloration; flies away erratically when flushed. Call a thin *scret!*

Wilson's Phalarope
Phalaropus tricolor

8.5 in (22 cm). In nonbreeding plumage, **thin needle-like black bill, white face**, and **pure white underparts** are distinctive. In flight, shows **white rump** and **plain wings**. See both yellowleg species (p. 74), Stilt Sandpiper (p. 82), and Red-necked Phalarope. Rare fall transient (Aug and Sept); very rare in spring (March). Found on shallow freshwater and saltwater ponds (or their margins); occasionally on mudflats. On land, dashes about actively in pursuit of prey; regularly swims, spinning about in tight circles as it picks insects from surface. Call a soft muffled *kek*.

Red-necked Phalarope
Phalaropus lobatus

8 in (20 cm). In nonbreeding plumage, similar to nonbreeding Wilson's Phalarope; distinguished by **black patch behind eye, white forehead, streaked back,** and **black legs**; when both species are together, also note slightly smaller size and shorter bill. Breeding male resembles breeding female but is duller. In flight, shows **dark center of rump** and **white wing stripe**. Common transient, from Aug to Nov and in April and May. In Panama, mainly pelagic, occurring on Pacific well offshore; flocks fly low and erratically over the water; very rare on shallow freshwater or saltwater ponds. Feeds while swimming, spinning about and picking small prey from the water. Call a hard *kett*.

Upland
Sandpiper

Wilson's
Snipe

breeding
female

Wilson's
Phalarope

nonbreeding
adult

breeding
male

nonbreeding
adult

breeding
female

Red-necked
Phalarope

nonbreeding
adult

nonbreeding
adult

LARIDAE. Members of this large group of waterbirds are found worldwide, in both marine and freshwater habitats. (Panama's species primarily occur along coasts.) They are strong and often graceful fliers. Gulls usually have a heavier build and a stouter bill than terns, and are often seen swimming (terns rarely swim); they mostly scavenge for food that they find either on shore or floating in water. Terns typically dive to catch fish and other animals, or simply pluck prey off the water's surface. The distinctive skimmers have odd, laterally compressed bills, with the lower mandible longer than the upper. They catch fish by flying low above the water and plowing its surface with the lower mandible. In Panama, most members of this family are migrants, and only three breed locally: Bridled Tern, Sooty Tern, and Brown Noddy.

Laughing Gull　　　　　　　　　　　　　　　*Leucophaeus atricilla*

15.5 in (40 cm); WS 41 in (103 cm). By far the most common gull. All plumages very similar to respective plumages of much rarer Franklin's Gull (see for comparisons). Nonbreeding adult distinguished from all other gulls (except Franklin's) by combination of **all-black bill** and **slate-gray back and wings**. Brownish immature differs from much rarer immature Ring-billed (p. 88) and Herring Gulls (p. 88) by more slender build and relatively longer and thinner bill. In breeding plumage (often seen in March and April), has black hood and red bill. In flight, adult distinguished from adult Franklin's by wing pattern (**black tips blend gradually with slate-gray wings**); immature set apart from immature Franklin's by **black terminal tail band that extends to outer edge of tail**. Very common to abundant transient and winter resident (most frequent from Oct to early April); some birds present in summer. Occurs on coasts and on larger lakes; sometimes found far offshore.

Franklin's Gull　　　　　　　　　　　　　　*Leucophaeus pipixcan*

14 in (36 cm); WS 35.5 in (90 cm). Slightly smaller and more slender than Laughing Gull (which is much more common); on nonbreeding adult and immature, note **more distinct partial hood**. In flight, adult differs from Laughing Gull by **white band separating black wing tips from rest of wing** (also note large white tips on outer primaries); immature distinguished from immature Laughing Gull by **black terminal tail band that does not extend to outer edge of tail** (outer tail feathers are white). Underparts are also whiter. In breeding plumage, has black hood and red bill; white crescents around eyes are wider than in Laughing Gull. Uncommon transient (in Nov and Dec, and April and May); rare in winter and summer. Occurs on coasts and larger lakes; sometimes found far offshore.

Sabine's Gull　　　　　　　　　　　　　　　　　*Xema sabini*

13.5 in (34 cm); WS 34.5 in (88 cm). In flight (all plumages), striking wing pattern is diagnostic; especially note **black wedge extending from wrist across outer primaries** and **white triangle on inner primaries and secondaries**. Tail is shallowly forked; on adult, tail is white; on immature, note narrow black tip. In breeding plumage, has slaty gray hood. Immature browner, with scaly pattern on back. Bill slender; in adult, **black with yellow tip**; in immature, all black. Uncommon transient, mainly Oct to Dec and March to June. Usually on Pacific; one record from Caribbean. Occurs on offshore waters (rarely seen from shore).

Lesser Black-backed Gull　　　　　　　　　　　*Larus fuscus*

22 in (56 cm); WS 49 in (125 cm). Similar to Herring Gull (p. 88), but adult is distinctly smaller and has **slaty gray back and wings** and **yellow legs**. Immature distinguished from immature Herring by more distinct streaking on breast. Vagrant; recorded in Panamá City area and on Caribbean side of Canal Area. Occurs on and near coast. **Not illustrated**.

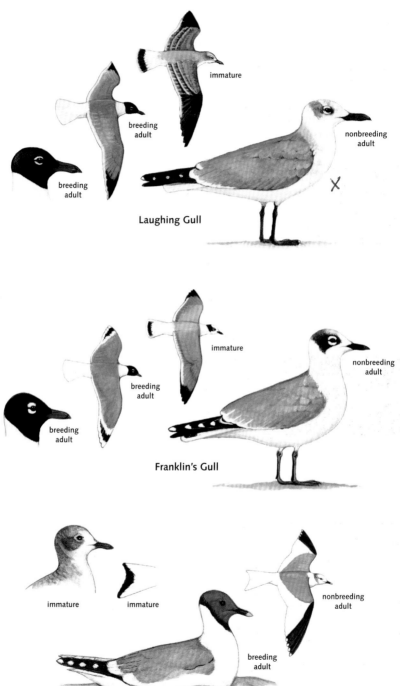

Laughing Gull

immature

breeding adult

breeding adult

nonbreeding adult

Franklin's Gull

immature

breeding adult

breeding adult

nonbreeding adult

Sabine's Gull

immature

immature

breeding adult

nonbreeding adult

Belcher's Gull
Larus belcheri

20 in (51 cm); WS 49 in (124 cm). Adult has **heavy yellow bill with black and red bands near tip, broad black subterminal tail band**, white underparts, slaty gray back and wings, and yellow legs. Breeding adult has white head; nonbreeding adult and older immatures have **brownish gray hood**; younger immatures are mostly brown, with unstreaked gray-brown head and breast. On all immatures, bill is a duller yellow, with a black tip. Vagrant; recorded on Pacific, in Panamá City and environs, both on and near the coast. Breeds in South America. **Not illustrated**.

Ring-billed Gull
Larus delawarensis

19.5 in (49 cm); WS 49 in (124 cm). On adult, **yellow bill with black band near tip** is distinctive; also note **yellowish legs** (but see much rarer Belcher's Gull). Has heavier build than Laughing Gull (p. 86), with paler back and wings; wing tips are black with white spots on outer primaries. Compare also with Herring Gull. Both immature Ring-billed and immature Herring Gull are brownish and have pink bill (with dark tip) and pink legs, but immature Ring-billed is smaller and paler. Rare winter resident, mostly Nov to April; a few present in summer. Recorded mostly from Canal Area and vicinity, on both coasts.

Herring Gull
Larus argentatus

24 in (61 cm); WS 55 in (140 cm). Much **larger** than Laughing (p. 86) or Ring-billed Gulls. On adult, **yellow bill with red spot near tip of lower mandible** is shared only with much rarer Lesser Black-backed (p. 86) and Kelp Gulls; differs from these by paler gray back and **pink legs**. Immature brownish, with pink legs and pink bill with dark tip (bill sometimes mostly dark with pink base); larger and darker than immature Ring-billed Gull. Rare winter resident, mainly Dec to April. Most records from Canal Area. Favors coasts.

Kelp Gull
Larus dominicanus

23 in (58 cm); WS 53 in (135 cm). Similar to Herring Gull; adult differs by **heavier bill, dark slaty gray back and wings**, and **dull greenish (or yellowish) legs**; in nonbreeding plumage, lacks streaking on hindneck that is present in nonbreeding Herring. Distinguished from Lesser Black-backed Gull (p. 86) by heavier bill, darker back and wings, and duller legs. Immature very similar to immature Lesser Black-backed but has heavier bill and darker tail. Vagrant; recorded in Panamá City area, on coast. Breeds in South America. **Not illustrated**.

Gray Gull
Leucophaeus modestus

18 in (46 cm); WS not recorded. Nonbreeding adult is almost **entirely dark lead gray**; immature mostly brownish gray. Breeding adult has whitish hood. In flight (all plumages), white tips on secondaries form **broad white trailing edge on inner wing**; also note **gray tail with black subterminal band and white tip**. Generally a vagrant but on rare occasions more numerous, including 1997–1998 El Niño event, when more than 100 were present near Panamá City. Recorded only on Pacific side of Panama, on coast and at sea. Breeds in South America.

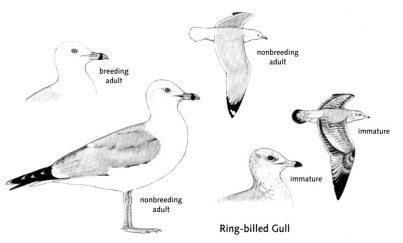

breeding adult

nonbreeding adult

immature

immature

nonbreeding adult

Ring-billed Gull

breeding adult

nonbreeding adult

immature

nonbreeding adult

Herring Gull

breeding adult

nonbreeding adult

immature

nonbreeding adult

Gray Gull

Bonaparte's Gull
Chroicocephalus philadelphia

13 in (34 cm); WS 32 in (82 cm). A small gull with a **thin, all-black bill**. In flight, adult shows **white wedge extending from wrist to outer primaries**, which have narrow black tipping; immature similar, but has **black along leading edge of outer wing**, and **diagonal dark band across wing above secondaries**, together forming an M-shape on the wings. Adult has all-white tail; that of immature shows black tip. Nonbreeding adult and immature have mostly white head with a black spot on ear coverts; breeding adult has black head. Vagrant, recorded only from Panamá City, and from near Caribbean coast of Canal Area. **Not illustrated**.

Gray-hooded Gull
Chroicocephalus cirrocephalus

17 in (42 cm); WS 40 in (102 cm). Adult has **red bill and legs** and **pale gray hood**; when not breeding, legs are duller and hood is less distinct. Also note **white eye**. In flight, shows **white wedge from wrist to outer primaries**; outer primaries are broadly tipped with black, with a white spot near wing tip. Immature similar to adult, but has dull yellowish bill and legs; dark smudge on ear coverts; black tail tip (tail entirely white in adult); and lacks white spot on primaries. Vagrant; all records from Panamá City area. Breeds in South America. **Not illustrated**.

Gull-billed Tern
Gelochelidon nilotica

15.5 in (39 cm); WS 37 in (94 cm). Distinguished from other terns by **heavy** (almost gull-like), **all-black bill**; also **paler** than other terns (appears whitish overall) except Sandwich (p. 92) and vagrant White (p. 96); tail only slightly forked. Nonbreeding adult and immature have **gray patch extending behind eye**, much less distinct than patch on Forster's Tern (p. 94). In breeding plumage, has black cap. Uncommon migrant; some present all year, with no pronounced peak in abundance, mostly along Pacific coast; rare on Caribbean.

Bridled Tern
Onychoprion anaethetus

14 in (36 cm); WS 30 in (76 cm). Darker gray coloration on back and wings distinguishes it from most other terns, except Sooty and Black (p. 94). Distinguished from Sooty by **whitish collar across back of neck** (can be difficult to detect when bird is observed at sea), **dark gray** (not black) **back**, and, at close range, **white forehead extending behind eye as a narrow superciliary**. Black Tern has only slightly notched tail and different head pattern. Mainly pelagic; rare far offshore in Gulf of Panamá and Gulf of Chiriquí. Breeds on small islets off south coast of Los Santos.

Sooty Tern
Onychoprion fuscatus

17.5 in (44 cm); WS 35.5 in (90 cm). Similar to Bridled Tern, but **back is black** instead of gray. Sooty lacks whitish collar of Bridled (however, on some nonbreeding birds, nape is paler than rest of back and can suggest a collar); **white forehead extends back only as far as eye**. Immature is mostly dark (whitish on belly); differs from other mostly dark terns by **long forked tail** and **white underwing coverts**. Mainly pelagic; rare offshore on Pacific side, in both Gulf of Panamá and Gulf of Chiriquí; one record (exact locality uncertain; not mapped) of a vagrant from Caribbean slope of Canal Area. Breeds on small islets off south coast of Los Santos.

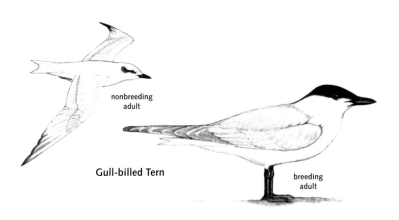

nonbreeding
adult

Gull-billed Tern

breeding
adult

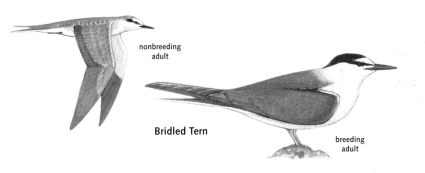

nonbreeding
adult

Bridled Tern

breeding
adult

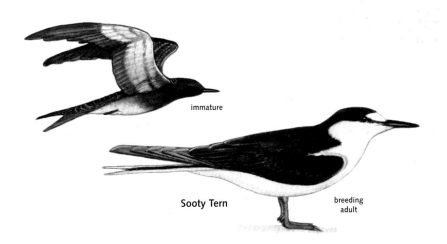

immature

Sooty Tern

breeding
adult

Caspian Tern
Hydroprogne caspia

21.5 in (54 cm); WS 52 in (134 cm). Distinguished from much more common Royal Tern by heavier, **deep red** (not reddish orange) **bill** with **dark tip** and, in flight, **primaries that are paler above, darker below**. In nonbreeding plumage, **black crown is streaked with white** (on nonbreeding Royal, forehead is entirely white). Rare winter resident from Nov to March; mainly on Caribbean coast; also recorded on Pacific coast, and inland on Lake Gatún and at Las Macanas Marsh in Herrera.

Royal Tern
Thalasseus maximus

19.5 in (50 cm); WS 43 in (109 cm). Most common of the large terns. Distinguished from most other terns by **stout reddish orange bill**. In nonbreeding plumage, forehead and most of top of crown are white. Compare much rarer Caspian and Elegant Terns. Very common winter resident; also common in summer. Found along both coasts (though more common on Pacific), sometimes far offshore; also on large bodies of fresh water.

Elegant Tern
Thalasseus elegans

16.5 in (42 cm); WS 31 in (78 cm). Slightly smaller than much more common Royal Tern; also distinguished by **more slender** (slightly down-curved) **bill**, which is usually yellow to yellow-orange (sometimes orange-red); often has pale tip. Crest longer and shaggier than Royal's; in nonbreeding plumage, black extends farther forward on crown and (usually) surrounds eye. Rare migrant on Pacific coast, with no pronounced peak in abundance.

Sandwich Tern
Thalasseus sandvicensis

16.5 in (42 cm); WS 36 in (92 cm). **Long, slender, black bill with pale (usually yellow) tip** is diagnostic in all plumages. (Note, however, that pale tip can be difficult to see at a distance.) Paler than all other terns except Gull-billed (p. 90) and vagrant White (p. 96). Common winter resident (most numerous Dec to April); some present in summer. Found along both coasts (though more common on Pacific), and on large bodies of fresh water.

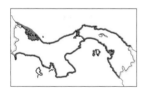

Common Tern
Sterna hirundo

14 in (35 cm); WS 31.5 in (80 cm). In breeding plumage, **red legs** distinguish it from all other terns except much rarer Forster's (see for distinctions, p. 94). In nonbreeding and immature plumages, note that leading edge of forewing is dark. On perched birds, this forms a **dark bar on shoulder** (shared only with immature Least Tern, p. 94, which is much smaller; rare Arctic Tern, p. 94, has much less distinct bar). In flight (all plumages), **dark outer edge of tail** (less distinct in immature) distinguishes it from all other terns except Arctic. Fairly common transient, mostly in Oct and Nov, and in April; uncommon in winter, rare in summer. Found along both coasts (though more common on Pacific) and on large bodies of fresh water.

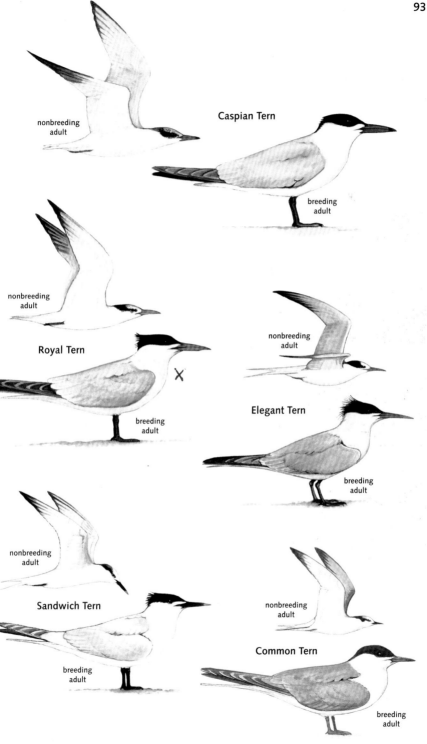

nonbreeding
adult

Caspian Tern

breeding
adult

nonbreeding
adult

Royal Tern

X

breeding
adult

nonbreeding
adult

Elegant Tern

breeding
adult

nonbreeding
adult

Sandwich Tern

breeding
adult

nonbreeding
adult

Common Tern

breeding
adult

Arctic Tern
Sterna paradisaea

14 in (36 cm); WS 31 in (80 cm). Very similar to Common Tern (p. 92) but much rarer; in all plumages, perched birds distinguished by shorter bill, more rounded head, and much shorter legs. In flight, **primaries and secondaries are almost uniformly pale gray**, with only narrow black tipping on trailing edge of primaries (dark tipping much more extensive in Common and Forster's Terns). Vagrant; recorded on Pacific coast at Panamá City; also off Darién (at sea). **Not illustrated**.

Forster's Tern
Sterna forsteri

15 in (38 cm); WS 31 in (78 cm). Very similar to Common Tern (p. 92) but much rarer. In nonbreeding plumage, distinguished by **dark patch behind eye (not extending around back of head)** and **lack of dark bar on forewing**. In flight, shows **gray tail with white outer edge**. Rare migrant; recorded mainly from Caribbean coast of Canal Area; a few records from Pacific coast, in Canal Area and Herrera. **Not illustrated**.

Least Tern
Sternula antillarum

9 in (23 cm); WS 20 in (51 cm). Smallest tern. In breeding plumage, distinguished from other small terns by **mostly yellow bill with black tip**; nonbreeding adult and immature have black bill. Black Tern (in both nonbreeding adult and immature plumages) is much darker and has only slightly notched tail. Uncommon transient, mainly Aug to Jan and April to May; a few present in summer; on both coasts.

Yellow-billed Tern
Sternula superciliaris

9 in (23 cm); WS not recorded. Very similar to Least Tern, but has larger and **all-yellow bill** (lacks black tip) and more extensive black on primaries. Immature has duller yellowish bill with dark tip. Vagrant; recorded near Pacific coast in Coclé and Herrera, and near Caribbean coast of Canal Area. Breeds in South America. **Not illustrated**.

Large-billed Tern
Phaetusa simplex

14.5 in (37 cm); WS 36 in (92 cm). Combination of **very large, all-yellow bill** and **distinctive wing pattern** makes this species unmistakable. Very rare migrant; recorded from both coasts of Canal Area, and from Pacific coast in eastern Panamá Province and Herrera.

Black Tern
Chlidonias niger

9 in (23 cm); WS 26 in (66 cm). In nonbreeding plumage, combination of small size, dark back and wings, head pattern, and only slightly forked tail is distinctive; particularly note **dark smudge on side** below shoulder. Breeding plumage (seen only briefly in Panama) is unmistakable. Fairly common transient and winter resident, mostly Oct to April; a few present in summer. Found along both coasts (though more common on Pacific) and on large bodies of fresh water; often seen far offshore.

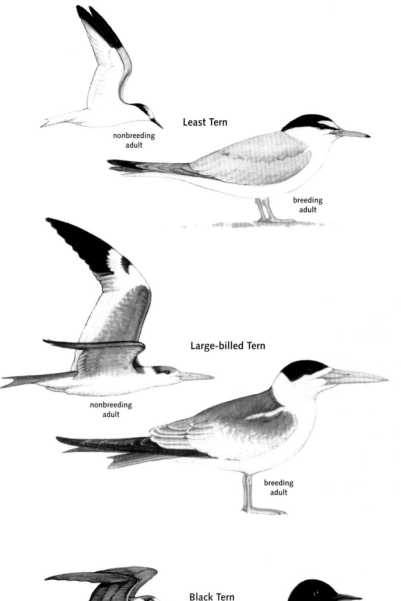

Least Tern

nonbreeding adult

breeding adult

Large-billed Tern

nonbreeding adult

breeding adult

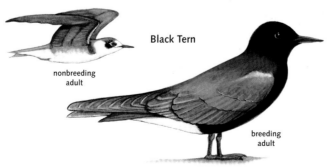

Black Tern

nonbreeding adult

breeding adult

White Tern
Gygis alba

12 in (30 cm) WS 31 in (78 cm). Adult is only **entirely white tern** (except for narrow black eye-ring, slender black bill, and blackish legs). Immature has dusky patch on nape, blackish patch on ear coverts, and brownish mottling on back. Breeds on oceanic islands; mainly pelagic when not breeding. Vagrant; only record is two birds seen off coast of eastern Panamá Province (1983). **Not illustrated.**

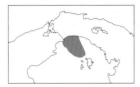

Inca Tern
Larosterna inca

16 in (41 cm); WS not recorded. **Long whitish plumes** curving back from corners of **heavy red bill** make adult unmistakable. Browner immature, with dark bill and much less prominent plumes, is still easy to identify. In flight, in any plumage, note **shallowly forked tail** and **whitish trailing edge of wing**. Large numbers invaded Gulf of Panamá from normal South American range during strong El Niño event of 1983. None seen since but could occur again if such conditions repeat.

Brown Noddy
Anous stolidus

16.5 in (42 cm); WS 32.5 in (82 cm). **Overall sooty brown coloration** and **double-rounded** (not forked) **tail** are distinctive. On adult, also note **pale crown** (grayish on Pacific birds, whitish on Caribbean birds). Immature darker and lacks pale crown. Mainly pelagic; rare offshore on Pacific side, in both Gulf of Panamá and Gulf of Chiriquí; very rare on Caribbean coast of Canal Area. Breeds on small islets off south coast of Los Santos.

Black Noddy
Anous minutus

15 in (37 cm); WS 27 in (69 cm). Very similar to Brown Noddy but mostly **blackish** rather than sooty brown, with a **whiter, more distinctly demarcated crown**; bill is thinner and straighter. Vagrant; one record off coast of Los Santos (1998). **Not illustrated**.

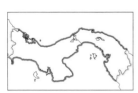

Black Skimmer
Rynchops niger

17.5 in (45 cm); WS 46 in (117 cm). **Very large black and red bill** (with lower mandible longer than upper) makes this species unmistakable. Two races occur in Panama: birds breeding in North America have mostly white tail with gray central feathers; those breeding in northern South America have mostly dark gray tail with outer feathers edged white. Uncommon migrant to both coasts, with no clear pattern of seasonality. Usually seen standing on sandbars or mudflats with other gulls and terns.

immature

Inca Tern

adult

Brown Noddy

adult
Caribbean race

North American
race

Black Skimmer

North American
race

STERCORARIIDAE. Members of this small family of gull-like birds breed in polar regions but are found as migrants worldwide. When not breeding, they are largely pelagic. Powerful fliers with strong hooked beaks, they often steal food from other seabirds. Identification can be difficult because of variation due to age, season, and color morph, and often depends on subtle clues from structure and plumage.

South Polar Skua
Stercorarius maccormicki

21 in (53 cm); WS 50 in (127 cm). Larger and more heavily built than Pomarine Jaeger. Three color morphs occur. Pale morph has pale brown head and underparts; intermediate morph is mostly dark brown, with a contrasting paler nape; dark morph is uniform dark blackish brown. All morphs have **prominent white patch across base of primaries on upper wing**, much more conspicuous than that of jaegers. Rare migrant to offshore waters on Pacific. **Not illustrated**.

Pomarine Jaeger
Stercorarius pomarinus

28.5 in (72 cm), including long tail plumes; WS 49 in (124 cm). Highly variable. Dark morphs are mostly sooty brown above and below but retain white patch in primaries; intermediates also occur. Very similar to respective plumages of Parasitic Jaeger; best distinguished by heavier build, proportionately larger head, and heavier bill; in flight, wings are broader, especially across base. Immature is more heavily and evenly barred below than immature Parasitic of equivalent age or morph; usually lacks pale nape shown by most immature Parasitics. Compare also with South Polar Skua. Breeding adult has diagnostic elongated and **twisted spoon-shaped tail feathers**, but is not often seen in Panama. Uncommon transient and winter resident, from Oct to April; some present in summer. Occurs on both coasts, mainly far offshore on Pacific; sometimes close to land on Caribbean in Bocas del Toro and Canal Area.

Parasitic Jaeger
Stercorarius parasiticus

22 in (56 cm), including long tail plumes; WS 41 in (105 cm). Highly variable; occurs in pale, dark, and intermediate morphs, as does very similar Pomarine Jaeger. Breeding adult, infrequently seen in Panama, has elongated and **pointed central tail feathers** (not as long as those of much rarer Long-tailed Jaeger). Uncommon transient and winter resident, from Oct to April; some present in summer. Occurs on both coasts, far offshore on Pacific; sometimes close to land on Caribbean in Bocas del Toro and Canal Area.

Long-tailed Jaeger
Stercorarius longicaudus

21 in (54 cm), including long tail plumes; WS 31 in (80 cm). Very similar to Parasitic Jaeger, but more slender and with narrower wings; in breeding plumage, has highly elongated and **pointed central tail feathers** (longer than those of Parasitic), but these are often broken or missing. In flight adults and older immatures show **distinct contrast between grayish upper wing coverts and dark primaries and trailing edge of secondaries** (no contrast in Parasitic or Pomarine) and **much less white in primaries** (inconspicuous from above, none showing from below) than other jaegers. Vagrant; recorded off Caribbean coast of Canal Area and, on Pacific, in Gulf of Panamá. **Not illustrated**.

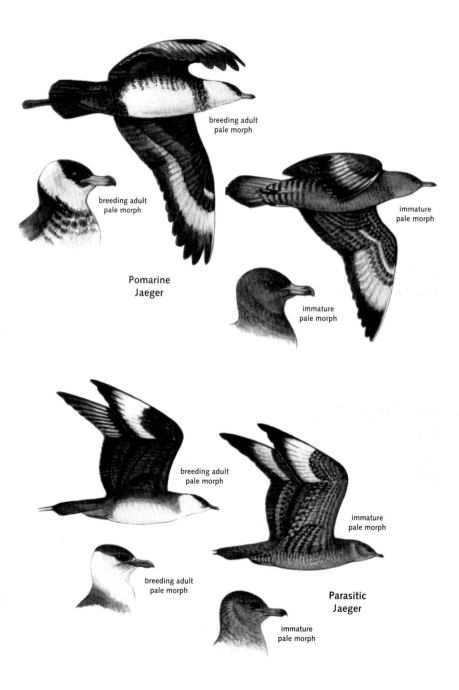

breeding adult
pale morph

breeding adult
pale morph

immature
pale morph

immature
pale morph

**Pomarine
Jaeger**

breeding adult
pale morph

immature
pale morph

breeding adult
pale morph

immature
pale morph

**Parasitic
Jaeger**

COLUMBIDAE. Members of this large cosmopolitan family typically have bulky bodies, small heads, thin soft bills, and short legs. They feed on fruits, seeds, and other vegetable matter, and fly strongly and swiftly. The large species of the genus *Patagioenas* (formerly placed in *Columba*) are mainly arboreal, while the remaining Panama species frequently walk and forage on the ground. Many pigeons and doves have far-carrying cooing or hooting calls, and are far more often heard than seen. Ground-dwelling species often perch higher when calling; this is especially true of the secretive and mainly forest-dwelling quail-doves (*Geotrygon*).

Rock Pigeon   *Columba livia*
12.5 in (32 cm). The familiar domestic pigeon. Birds that resemble the original wild form are mostly gray with white rump, but a wide variety of other color types occur, including white, reddish, brown, and blackish; plumage is often variegated. Feral or semidomesticated birds are common in cities and towns; sometimes also found around farms with livestock. They especially favor Panamá City's high-rise buildings, which provide roosts and nesting sites comparable to their original rocky-cliff habitat.

Plumbeous Pigeon   *Patagioenas plumbea*
13 in (33 cm). Very similar to more widespread Ruddy and Short-billed Pigeons; best distinguished by call. At close range, can be told from these by **whitish** (not reddish) **eye**; in addition, paler head and underparts contrast more noticeably with dark back and wings (this character may be difficult to see depending on lighting). Very rare Dusky Pigeon shares whitish eye but has brownish belly. Fairly common in southeastern Darién, to at least 5,000 ft (1,500 m); in middle and upper levels of forest. Call a three-note *coo, whit-COO* (accented on last note). Ruddy and Short-billed typically have four-note calls; Dusky has a three-note call, but last two notes are evenly accented.

Ruddy Pigeon   *Patagioenas subvinacea*
12 in (30 cm). Has slighty more rufous back than very similar Short-billed Pigeon; best distinguished by call. In eastern Darién, also compare with Plumbeous Pigeon. Fairly common in western highlands, above 4,000 ft (1,200 m) in Chiriquí, somewhat lower in Veraguas. Also fairly common on Pacific slope from eastern Panamá Province eastward, and on Caribbean slope in eastern Kuna Yala; in lowlands and foothills, to about 3,000 ft (900 m). Found in middle and upper levels of forest; when perched high in trees, can be difficult to see (like Short-billed). Call a *coo, who-CO-coo* (accented on third note).

Short-billed Pigeon   *Patagioenas nigrirostris*
11 in (28 cm). More uniformly colored than other large arboreal pigeons except Ruddy; back is somewhat more olive-brown (contrasting more with head and neck) than in that species, but best distinguished by call. Often difficult to see as it perches in foliage high in trees. Common in middle and upper levels of forest on entire Caribbean slope and on Pacific slope from eastern Panamá Province eastward; local on western Pacific slope, mainly in foothills and lower highlands (to 4,800 ft [1,450 m]). Call a *coo, WHIT-co-COO* (accented on second and fourth notes).

Dusky Pigeon   *Patagioenas goodsoni*
9 in (23 cm). Smaller than Short-billed, Ruddy, and Plumbeous Pigeons; note **brownish belly** that contrasts with **mostly gray head and breast**. Has whitish eye (shared with Plumbeous). Very rare, with just two records from forest in eastern Darién. Call a *coo, cuh-coo* (last two notes evenly accented). **EL**

wild form

white form

Rock Pigeon

variegated form

Plumbeous Pigeon

Ruddy Pigeon

Short-billed Pigeon

Dusky Pigeon

Pale-vented Pigeon
Patagioenas cayennensis

12.5 in (32 cm). **Multicolored upperparts** (including rufous back contrasting with gray rump) are distinctive among large arboreal pigeons; also note **whitish belly and vent**. Common in lowlands, in upper levels of woodland, mangroves, and forest edge, and in open areas, parks, and residential areas with large trees; uncommon in foothills; to 4,000 ft (1,200 m). Call a mournful *WHOO! cuk-tu-COO! cuk-tu-COO! cuk-tu-COO!*

Scaled Pigeon
Patagioenas speciosa

12.5 in (32 cm). **Scaled neck and underparts** are diagnostic; also note mostly **red bill**. Common in upper levels of woodland and forest edge, and in shrubby areas; to 4,100 ft (1,250 m). Call a very low-pitched *whooo! whut-whooo! whut-whoooo!*

White-crowned Pigeon
Patagioenas leucocephala

13.5 in (34 cm). Combination of **mostly dark, slaty gray plumage** and **white crown** is diagnostic (crown can be hard to see in flight). Immature has only small amount of white on front of crown. **Bill red with pale tip**. Occurs on Caribbean coast and on offshore islands. Uncommon in Bocas del Toro and Ngöbe-Buglé; rare in Kuna Yala. Found in upper levels of mangroves and in forest edge. Call a low *coooo, cuk-coooo, cuk-coooo.*

Band-tailed Pigeon
Patagioenas fasciata

13.5 in (34 cm). **Two-tone tail** is diagnostic, as is prominent **white band on nape**; also note **yellow bill**. Common in western highlands, eastward to Coclé; mostly above 5,300 ft (1,600 m), but sometimes down to 4,000 ft (1,200 m). Found in forest and in nearby clearings with tall trees, in upper levels. Call a deep *whoo!* or *whoo-ah!*

White-winged Dove
Zenaida asiatica

11 in (28 cm). Most similar to Mourning Dove; distinguished by **white patch on wing** (visible on perched birds, but especially prominent in flight) and shorter, **square tail with conspicuous white corners**. Uncommon in Coclé and Herrera; found on ground in mangroves and adjacent scrub and open areas. Call a mournful, somewhat raspy *cuh-cuk-tu-coooo* (often transliterated as *who-cooks-for-you*).

Eared Dove
Zenaida auriculata

10 in (25 cm). Smaller than Mourning Dove, and with **rounded** (not pointed) **tail**. Vagrant; recorded from Caribbean side of Canal Area, and from Tocumen Marsh in eastern Panamá Province. **Not illustrated**.

Mourning Dove
Zenaida macroura

11 in (28 cm). **Long pointed tail (edged with white)** is diagnostic. Uncommon on Pacific slope, eastward to western Panamá Province; local breeding population supplemented by migrants in winter. Forages on ground in open areas. Call a mournful, hollow *whooo, who, who, who.*

Pale-vented Pigeon

Scaled Pigeon

adult

immature

White-crowned Pigeon

Band-tailed Pigeon

tail

wing

White-winged Dove

Mourning Dove

Common Ground-Dove

Columbina passerina

6 in (15 cm). Combination of **bill with reddish or yellow base** and **scaly pattern on rear crown, neck, and upper breast** distinguishes it from other small doves. Found near coast, foraging on ground in open areas. Uncommon; occurs in southern Coclé and in Herrera and Los Santos. Call a long series of coos, given about once per second and rising at the end: *hoooip . . . hoooip . . . hoooip . . . hoooip.*

Plain-breasted Ground-Dove

Columbina minuta

6 in (15 cm). **Grayer back** and **white tail corners** distinguish it from larger (and more widespread) female Ruddy Ground-Dove. The Common Ground-Dove (very limited range) shares white tail corners. Forages on ground in relatively dry, open areas. Common on Pacific slope, eastward to Darién; rare on Caribbean slope in Canal Area; in lowlands. Call a long series of short coos, each repeated every second or less: *hoop . . . hoop . . . hoop . . . hoop.*

Ruddy Ground-Dove

Columbina talpacoti

6.5 in (17 cm). On male, **bright rufous back contrasting with gray head** is diagnostic. Female distinguished from Plain-breasted Ground-Dove by browner back and lack of white in tail. Female distinguished from female Blue Ground-Dove by **black** (not chestnut) **markings on wings** and brown (not chestnut) rump that does not contrast strongly with rest of back. Occurs in open and shrubby areas and in cities and towns; forages on ground. Very common in almost the entire country, to 5,300 ft (1,600 m). Call a long series of two-syllable coos, repeated about once per second: *hu-ooop . . . hu-ooop . . . hu-ooop . . . hu-ooop.*

Blue Ground-Dove

Claravis pretiosa

8 in (20 cm). **Mostly bluish gray** male is unmistakable. Female distinguished from female Ruddy Ground-Dove by **chestnut** (not black) **markings on wings** and **chestnut** (not brown) **rump and tail** that contrast with brownish back; larger female Maroon-chested Ground-Dove has white in tail and brownish rump. Fairly common in almost the entire country, to 5,300 ft (1,600 m). Found in forest edge, woodland, and shrubby areas. Call a series of deep resonant coos, repeated about once per second: *HOOP . . . HOOP . . . HOOP . . . HOOP . . . .* (Coos are sometimes given singly rather than in series.)

Maroon-chested Ground-Dove

Claravis mondetoura

8.5 in (22 cm). On male, combination of **reddish-maroon breast** and **tail with white outer edges** (the latter conspicuous in flight) makes it unmistakable; also note **dark violet wing-bars**. Female distinguished from smaller female Ruddy and Blue Ground-Doves by **purplish wing-bars** and **white tail corners**. Very rare in highlands of western Chiriquí, mostly above 5,000 ft (1,500 m); one old record from Cerro Campana in western Panamá Province. Found on ground in forest, especially forest with bamboo understory; most likely encountered when bamboo is seeding. Call a series of deep resonant two-syllable coos, each repeated about once per second: *hu-WHOOP . . . hu-WHOOP . . . hu-WHOOP . . . hu-WHOOP.*

Common Ground-Dove

Plain-breasted Ground-Dove

male

female

male

female

Ruddy Ground-Dove

male

female

Blue Ground-Dove

male

female

Maroon-chested Ground-Dove

White-tipped Dove
Leptotila verreauxi

10 in (26 cm). Distinguished from other *Leptotila* doves and all quail-doves by **light blue orbital and loral skin**; white on tail tip is more extensive than on other *Leptotila* species. Very common on Pacific slope and on central Caribbean slope; rare in Bocas del Toro; to 6,000 ft (1,800 m). Found on ground in forest edge, shrubby areas, second growth, urban parks, and suburbs. Call a deep hollow-sounding *hu-huuu* (usually double-noted, occasionally single).

Gray-headed Dove
Leptotila plumbeiceps

10 in (25 cm). Distinguished from White-tipped and Gray-chested Doves by **bluish gray crown** that contrasts strongly with **buffy cheeks**; no range overlap with Brown-backed Dove. Rare in lowlands of Bocas del Toro; found on ground in forest. Call a single, soft *whooo* (higher pitched than that of Gray-chested Dove).

Brown-backed Dove
Leptotila battyi

9.5 in (24 cm). Brighter rufous-brown on back and more pinkish below than Gray-headed Dove (no range overlap); distinguished from White-tipped and Gray-chested Doves by **bluish gray crown** that contrasts strongly with **buffy cheeks**. Fairly common on Coiba Island; uncommon on Cébaco Island and in southwestern Azuero Peninsula. Found on ground in forest. Call a deep *whooooo* (usually single note, sometimes double) that resembles that of White-tipped Dove (whose call is usually double-noted). Considered a subspecies of Gray-headed Dove by AOU. **PL***

Gray-chested Dove
Leptotila cassini

10 in (25 cm). Distinguished from White-tipped Dove by **reddish orbital and loral skin**, **grayer breast**, and less extensive white on tail tip; unlike that species, found mostly inside forest. In their limited ranges, compare also Gray-headed and Brown-backed Doves. Race found in western Chiriquí has rufous nape. Fairly common on Caribbean slope, and on Pacific slope from Canal Area eastward; in lowlands, mostly below 2,000 ft (600 m); uncommon and local on Pacific slope in western Chiriquí and Veraguas; to 3,200 ft (1,300 m). Found on ground in forest. Call a low, single-note *whooooh*, rising slightly and then falling.

Olive-backed Quail-Dove
Geotrygon veraguensis

9 in (23 cm). White forehead and **prominent white cheek stripe** that contrasts strongly with mostly dark head and body are distinctive. Rare on Caribbean slope, and on Pacific slope from eastern Panamá Province eastward; to 3,000 ft (900 m). Found on ground in forest. Call a deep resonant *woOOOuuu* (similar to that of Ruddy Quail-Dove, p. 108).

Chiriqui Quail-Dove
Geotrygon chiriquensis

11 in (28 cm). Combination of **dark gray crown and nape** and **cinnamon-rufous breast** is diagnostic. Uncommon in western highlands, eastward to Coclé; mainly 4,000 to 6,500 ft (1,200 to 2,000 m); on ground in forest. Call a deep resonant *whoooooh*. **WH**

White-tipped Dove

Gray-headed Dove

Brown-backed Dove

Gray-chested Dove

western
Chiriqui race

Olive-backed
Quail-Dove

Chiriqui Quail-Dove

Purplish-backed Quail-Dove *Geotrygon lawrencii*

10 in (26 cm). Note **black moustachial stripe** that contrasts strongly with **whitish face**. Buff-fronted Quail-Dove (mainly at higher elevations) is similar in general pattern but has buff forehead, greenish nape, and mostly chestnut back and wings. Rare in foothills (both slopes); mainly 1,500 to 3,500 ft (450 to 1,050 m) but sometimes to 4,800 ft (1,450 m). Found on ground in forest. Call a nasal, hollow, froglike *cowh*, repeated at 3-second intervals. **CL, EL**

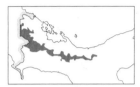

Buff-fronted Quail-Dove *Geotrygon costaricensis*

10 in (26 cm). **Buff forehead** and **greenish nape** are diagnostic. Chiriqui Quail-Dove (p. 106), found in same habitat, has cinnamon-rufous (not gray) breast. Uncommon in western highlands, eastward to Veraguas; 4,000 to 10,000 ft (1,200 to 3,000 m). Found on ground in forest. Call a high-pitched *cwa*, repeated at 1-second intervals. **WH**

Russet-crowned Quail-Dove *Geotrygon goldmani*

11 in (28 cm). Combination of **rufous crown and nape** and **gray chest** is diagnostic. Uncommon in foothills of eastern Panama, from 2,500 to 5,300 ft (750 to 1,600 m). Found on ground in forest. Call a very low-pitched, descending *whoooaah*, repeated at 5-second intervals. **EH**

Violaceous Quail-Dove *Geotrygon violacea*

9 in (23 cm). Only quail-dove that lacks a strong facial pattern. Distinguished from *Leptoptila* doves (p. 106) by **violet back, lack of white in tail**, and **chestnut wings** (Brown-backed Dove has brown wings but does not overlap in range). Rare and local in eastern Panama, to 5,000 ft (1,500 m); on ground in forest. Like other quail-doves, Violaceous makes no wing noises when flushed (*Leptotila* doves typically make a whirring sound with wings when they take off). Call a hollow *whooah*, repeated at about 5-second intervals (higher pitched than that of Ruddy Quail-Dove).

Ruddy Quail-Dove *Geotrygon montana*

8.5 in (22 cm). Only quail-dove with **brown** (not black) **moustachial stripe**. Male, mostly rufous with **buffy facial stripe**, is distinctive; duller female also has **buffy facial stripe**. Fairly common throughout the country, to 4,000 ft (1,200 m); found on ground in forest. Call a low soft *whoooah*, given at 3- to 5-second intervals (shorter and lower pitched than that of Gray-chested Dove, p. 106).

Purplish-backed
Quail-Dove

Buff-fronted
Quail-Dove

Russet-crowned
Quail-Dove

Violaceous
Quail-Dove

female

male

Ruddy
Quail-Dove

PSITTACIDAE. Members of this large family occur mainly in the tropics and subtropics. Parrots use their strong stout bills to feed on fruits and nuts, often holding and manipulating food with their feet. Most are gregarious, occurring in noisy flocks of a few pairs up to a hundred or more. Except for some macaws, most Panama species are mainly green and can be surprisingly difficult to see when they are feeding quietly amid foliage. Some species, especially macaws, are threatened owing to capture for the pet trade, and have disappeared from much of their former ranges.

Azuero Parakeet   *Pyrrhura eisenmanni*

9 in (23 cm). **Bold scalloping on neck and chest** is diagnostic; also note dark head with **pale cheek patch** and **maroon patch on belly**. Uncommon in its very limited range in the southwestern Azuero Peninsula; found in middle and upper levels of forest. Considered a subspecies of Painted Parakeet (*Pyrrhura picta*) by AOU. **PL***

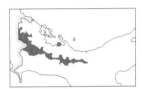

Sulphur-winged Parakeet   *Pyrrhura hoffmanni*

9.5 in (24 cm). Distinguished from larger Crimson-fronted Parakeet by **red ear patch** and lack of red on forehead; in flight (from above), distinguished by **yellow patches on wing**, and (from below) by lack of red on wings. Common in western highlands, eastward to Veraguas; mostly above 4,000 ft (1,200 m). Found in upper levels of forest and in open areas with some trees. Flight call a high-pitched squeaky chattering *kree kree kree* or *kre-yik kreyik*. **WH**

Crimson-fronted Parakeet   *Aratinga finschi*

10 in (26 cm). Largest parakeet. Note **red forehead** and, in flight from below, **red patch on forewing** (bordered behind by yellow). Common or Caribbean slope in Bocas del Toro and Ngöbe-Buglé; common on Pacific slope, eastward to western side of Azuero Peninsula; to 5,500 ft (1,650 m). Found in upper levels of forest and in open areas with some trees. Call a loud raucous screeching *KEE-KEE-KEE-KEE-KI-KRIK*.

Olive-throated Parakeet   *Aratinga nana*

9.5 in (24 cm). Note **brownish olive throat and chest** (no range overlap with Brown-throated Parakeet). Lacks red, orange, or yellow in plumage. Common in lowlands of Bocas del Toro, in upper levels of forest edge and in open areas with some trees. Call a sharp, grating *krik-krik-krik-krik*.

Brown-throated Parakeet   *Aratinga pertinax*

9 in (23 cm). Note **brown throat and chest** (no overlap with Olive-throated Parakeet) and **orange patch below eye**; lacks red or yellow in plumage. Common on Pacific slope eastward to Panamá City area; rare on Caribbean slope in Canal Area. Found in lowlands, in open and scrubby areas with scattered trees. Calls include a sharp metallic chattering *skreeik skreeik skreeik*.

Barred Parakeet   *Bolborhynchus lineola*

6.5 in (16 cm). **Fine black barring** is diagnostic but difficult to see unless lighting conditions are ideal. Usually occurs at higher elevations than Orange-chinned Parakeet (p. 114); distinguished from Red-fronted Parrotlet (p. 114) by **pointed tail** and lack of red or yellow in plumage. Rare in western highlands; can become common when bamboo is seeding; usually above 5,000 ft (1,500 m), but sometimes down to 2,000 ft (600 m). Found in upper levels of forest. Call a soft, high-pitched musical chattering.

Azuero
Parakeet

Sulphur-winged
Parakeet

Crimson-fronted
Parakeet

Olive-throated
Parakeet

Brown-throated
Parakeet

Barred Parakeet

Scarlet Macaw
Ara macao

34.5 in (88 cm). Distinguished from Red-and-green Macaw (no range overlap) by **yellow** (not green) **wing coverts**. Fairly common on Coiba Island; very rare in southwestern Azuero Peninsula. Found in upper levels of forest and adjacent open and scrubby areas with tall trees. Calls include very loud screeches and squawks.

Red-and-green Macaw
Ara chloropterus

33 in (84 cm). Distinguished from Scarlet Macaw (no range overlap) by **green** (not yellow) **wing coverts**. Uncommon in Darién and eastern Kuna Yala; to 3,000 ft (900 m). Found in upper levels of forest and adjacent open areas with tall trees. Favors hilly areas. Calls include very loud screeches and squawks.

Chestnut-fronted Macaw
Ara severus

17.5 in (44 cm). Much smaller than Great Green Macaw, with proportionately smaller head and bill and **dull chestnut** (not red) **forehead**. In flight, **reddish undersides of wings and tail** are diagnostic. Common in Darién, to 2,000 ft (600 m). Found in upper levels of forest edge and in open areas with scattered trees, especially along rivers and in swampy areas. Calls include various loud screeches and squawks, somewhat higher pitched than those of larger macaws.

Great Green Macaw
Ara ambiguus

29 in (74 cm). Much larger than Chestnut-fronted Macaw, with **red** (not dull chestnut) **forehead** and proportionately larger head and bill. In flight, **undersides of wings and tail are dull yellowish**. Common in remoter areas of Darién; rare in Bocas del Toro, northern Veraguas, southern Azuero Peninsula, eastern Panamá Province, and Kuna Yala; to 5,000 ft (1,500 m). Found in upper levels of forest and in adjacent open areas with tall trees. Favors hilly areas. Calls include very loud screeches and squawks.

Blue-and-yellow Macaw
Ara ararauna

31 in (79 cm). Unmistakable. Uncommon in eastern Panamá Province and Darién; to 2,000 ft (600 m). Found in upper levels of forest and in adjacent open areas with large trees. Favors swampy areas. Calls include loud screeches and squawks, often with a wavering quality.

Scarlet Macaw

Red-and-green Macaw

Chestnut-fronted
Macaw

Great Green Macaw

Blue-and-yellow
Macaw

Spectacled Parrotlet
Forpus conspicillatus

4.5 in (12 cm). In all plumages, distinguished from Orange-chinned Parakeet by lack of brown shoulder patch; also smaller and with a relatively shorter tail than that species. On male, combination of **blue rump, wing patch**, and **patch around eye** is diagnostic. Female lacks blue in plumage. Uncommon in lowlands of eastern Panamá Province and Darién. Found in open areas with scattered trees, woodland, and forest edge. Call a sharp high-pitched chittering that includes buzzy *ziit* notes (softer than calls of Orange-chinned Parakeet).

Orange-chinned Parakeet
Brotogeris jugularis

6.5 in (17 cm). **Brown shoulders** are diagnostic; orange chin is usually hard to see. In flight, note yellow wing-linings. **Pointed tail** distinguishes it from all other small parakeets except Barred (p. 110). Smaller and with a shorter tail than *Aratinga* parakeets (p. 110). By far the most common and widespread small parrot in Panama; often in large noisy flocks. In lowlands, very common in open areas with some trees, second growth, and urban areas; fairly common in upper levels of forest and woodland. Less common in foothills. Very rare in Bocas del Toro. Calls include loud harsh chattering and sharp *zhreet!* notes.

Red-fronted Parrotlet
Touit costaricensis

6 in (15 cm). This and Blue-fronted Parrotlet (similar but no range overlap) are only small parrots with **square tails**. Note **red on head and forewing** and, in flight from below, yellow pattern on wings. Female has less red on wing. Rare. Occurs in foothills of western Panama, mainly on Caribbean slope; occasionally on Pacific slope, in Chiriquí; from 2,500 to 4,000 ft (750 to 1,200 m); a few records from lowlands in Bocas del Toro and Ngöbe-Buglé. Found in upper levels of forest. Call a high soft *che-wet*. **WH**

Blue-fronted Parrotlet
Touit dilectissimus

6 in (15 cm). Very similar to Red-fronted Parrotlet (no range overlap); male distinguished from male Red-fronted by **blue** (not red) **forecrown** and less red around eye. Female has less red on wing than male. Rare in foothills and lower highlands of eastern Panama; recorded from 2,000 to 5,300 ft (600 to 1,600 m). Occurs in forest. Call a soft sharp *cheee-che-chew*.

Saffron-headed Parrot
Pyrilia pyrilia

8.5 in (22 cm). **All-yellow head** is diagnostic. In flight, note **red underwing coverts and axillars** (on Brown-hooded Parrot, red is restricted to axillars). Rare in eastern Darién, to 2,300 ft (700 m); found in upper levels of forest. Call a high-pitched *chi-weeek!* (similar to that of Brown-hooded Parrot).

Brown-hooded Parrot
Pyrilia haematotus

8.5 in (22 cm). Mostly **brown head**, with red ear patch and white around eye, is distinctive. In flight, note **red axillars**. The race that occurs from Canal Area eastward has red band across foreneck (less conspicuous in female). Fairly common in most of the country but somewhat more common in eastern Panama; to 6,300 ft (1,900 m). Found in upper levels of forest. Relatively high-pitched calls include a *chewek!* and a trilling *zhreeee!*

male

Spectacled Parrotlet

male

Orange-chinned Parakeet

male

Red-fronted Parrotlet

male

male

Blue-fronted Parrotlet

male

Saffron-headed Parrot

male eastern race

male western race

Brown-hooded Parrot

male western race

Blue-headed Parrot
Pionus menstruus

9.5 in (24 cm). **Blue head** is diagnostic. Also note **red undertail coverts** (shared only with White-crowned Parrot). Flies with much **deeper wing-strokes** than *Amazona* parrots. Common throughout the country, to 4,000 ft (1,200 m). Found in upper levels of forest, woodland, and adjacent areas with scattered trees. Call a shrill, high-pitched *zher-renk!* (typically double notes).

White-crowned Parrot
Pionus senilis

9.5 in (24 cm). Combination of conspicuous **white crown and throat** is diagnostic. Like Blue-headed Parrot, flies with very **deep wing-strokes**. Uncommon in western Chiriquí and Bocas del Toro; to 5,900 ft (1,800 m). Found in upper levels of forest edge and open areas with scattered trees. Call a high-pitched *zhrrek!*

Red-lored Parrot
Amazona autumnalis

13 in (33 cm). **Red forehead and lores** distinguish it from other *Amazona* parrots, but these can be difficult to see at a distance. Smaller than Mealy Parrot, with less prominent eye-ring and yellower cheeks. Like other *Amazona* parrots, flies with very **shallow stiff wing-strokes** and shows **red patch in secondaries**. Common on both slopes to 3,000 ft (900 m). Found in upper levels of forest and adjacent areas with some trees. Unlike Mealy, capable of persisting in deforested areas as long as some trees remain (as in gallery forest). In Canal Area, calls include a distinctive *krack-co-rak* (not heard in some other areas); other calls are similar to those of Mealy, but higher pitched.

Mealy Parrot
Amazona farinosa

15 in (38 cm). Larger than other *Amazona* parrots, and further distinguished from them by a more **prominent white eye-ring** and by lack of red or yellow on head. Like other *Amazona* parrots, flies with very **shallow stiff wing-strokes** and shows **red patch in secondaries**. Fairly common on both slopes to 5,000 ft (1,500 m). Found in upper levels of forest. Loud calls are mostly similar to those of Red-lored Parrot (although deeper), but also include a distinctive *chop-chop* or *cheeyup-cheeyup*.

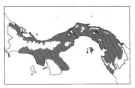

Yellow-crowned Parrot
Amazona ochrocephala

12 in (30 cm). **Yellow forecrown** diagnostic, but can be hard to see at a distance. Like other *Amazona* species, flies with very **shallow stiff wing-strokes** and shows **red patch in secondaries**. Fairly common in open areas with scattered trees, gallery woodland, and in and near mangroves; also fairly common in and around parks in Panamá City. Occurs in lowlands. Calls (which include a guttural *cuh-RAO!*) are deeper and hoarser than those of other *Amazona* parrots.

Blue-headed
Parrot

White-crowned
Parrot

Red-lored
Parrot

Mealy
Parrot

Yellow-crowned
Parrot

CUCULIDAE. These mainly insectivorous birds occur in temperate and tropical regions throughout much of the world. Panama's species are slender and have long tails; with the exception of the anis, they are furtive and inconspicuous—and far more often heard than seen. Many Old World cuckoos are nest parasites, laying their eggs in the nests of other species and thereby delegating the raising of their young to them, but among Panama species only the Striped and Pheasant Cuckoos have this habit. The three species of anis are communal breeders; a group of birds lay their eggs together in a large bulky nest and share in raising the young.

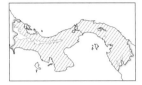

Yellow-billed Cuckoo   *Coccyzus americanus*

11 in (28 cm). Distinguished from Black-billed and Mangrove Cuckoos by extensive **rufous in primaries**; whiter below than Mangrove Cuckoo. Also note **mostly yellow bill** (dark culmen and tip) and **large white spots on underside of tail**. Uncommon transient, mainly in fall, from mid-Sept to early Dec; rare in spring (mainly April). Occurs in lowlands, usually in scrubby areas and forest edge. Mostly silent in migration.

Black-billed Cuckoo   *Coccyzus erythropthalmus*

11 in (28 cm). Distinguished from Yellow-billed and Mangrove Cuckoos by **all-black bill** (immature may have some yellow at base), **narrow red orbital ring** (greenish in immature), and, seen from below, **narrow white tips to tail feathers** (reduced to pale edging in immature); from below, both Yellow-billed and Mangrove show large white spots on tail. Yellow-billed has extensive rufous in primaries. Rare transient, mainly in fall, from late Sept to early Nov; very rare in spring (April). Can occur in almost any habitat, but most often found in forest edge, scrub, and open areas with scattered bushes and trees. Usually in lowlands; one record from Chiriquí highlands. Mostly silent in migration.

Mangrove Cuckoo   *Coccyzus minor*

12 in (30 cm). Distinguished from Black-billed and Yellow-billed Cuckoos by **distinct black mask** and **buffy underparts** (coloration varies in intensity); note that immature Black-billed may be pale buffy below but lacks prominent white spots on underside of tail. Status uncertain; most often reported in winter (Jan to March), suggesting that these records pertain to migrants from the north, but may breed in Panama. Rare; mainly near Pacific coast, in lowlands; to 2,000 ft (600 m). Found in scrubby areas and forest edge (not restricted to mangroves). Call a low hoarse croaking *gwa-gwa-gwa-gwa-gwa* (not yet reported to call in Panama).

Dwarf Cuckoo   *Coccycua pumila*

8 in (20 cm). Smaller than *Coccyzus* cuckoos, with a **much shorter tail** and with **rufous throat and chest**. Crown gray, rest of upperparts grayish brown; lower underparts creamy white; tail black with small white tipping; bill black. Immature has pale gray throat. Vagrant; one record from Tocumen Marsh, in eastern Panamá Province (1979). Inhabits woodland and shrubby areas.

Gray-capped Cuckoo   *Coccyzus lansbergi*

10 in (25 cm). Darker than other *Coccyzus* cuckoos. Has **dark gray cap** that extends to below eyes; rest of **upperparts rich rufous brown**; **deep rufous buff underparts**; black tail with large white spots; and black bill. Vagrant; recorded from Tocumen Marsh in eastern Panamá Province and from Cana in Darién. Inhabits woodland and shrubby areas.

Yellow-billed
Cuckoo

adult

Black-billed
Cuckoo

Mangrove
Cuckoo

Dwarf
Cuckoo

Gray-capped
Cuckoo

Dark-billed Cuckoo *Coccyzus melacoryphus*

10 in (25 cm). Resembles Mangrove Cuckoo (p. 118) but has **all-black bill** and a **narrow pale gray band that extends from lower cheeks to side of neck**. Vagrant; one record from Tocumen Marsh, in eastern Panamá Province (1980). Found in woodland and shrubby areas. **Not illustrated**.

Squirrel Cuckoo *Piaya cayana*

17 in (43 cm). Easily recognized by **bright rufous upperparts** and **exceptionally long tail**. Distinguished from Little Cuckoo by much larger size, **yellowish green** (not red) **orbital skin**, and **strong contrast between rufous chest and gray lower breast and belly**. Common in open country, to over 6,600 ft (2,000 m). Occurs at all levels in forest, woodland, and scrubby areas with some trees; sometimes even found in fencerows. Often scrambles in squirrel-like fashion through vegetation. Has a wide variety of calls, notably a loud *chick-KAW* with the cadence of a wolf-whistle; a hoarse *yee-how*; and a prolonged series of sharp *pik* notes.

Little Cuckoo *Coccycua minuta*

10.5 in (26 cm). Similar to Squirrel Cuckoo, but much smaller and with proportionately **shorter tail, red** (not yellowish green) **orbital skin**, and **less contrast on underparts**. Uncommon; from Canal Area eastward, to 2,500 ft (750 m). Found in lower levels of forest edge and woodland, especially in thick tangles of vegetation; usually near water. Call a soft piping *whuuur! wiwiwiwih*.

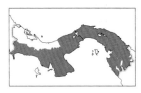

Striped Cuckoo *Tapera naevia*

11 in (28 cm). Note short bushy crest and long graduated tail. Distinguished from much rarer Pheasant Cuckoo by smaller size, **striped back, unspotted breast**, and narrower tail. Usually secretive, keeping to dense undergrowth; difficult to see except when calling from the top of a shrub or fence post. Common on entire Pacific slope, and on Caribbean from northern Coclé eastward; to 5,000 ft (1,800 m). Found in shrubby patches and thickets in open areas. Frequently heard call consists of two sharp, clear, whistled notes, with the second slightly higher; also a more prolonged *wheet-wheet-wheet-wheet-WHEdup*.

Pheasant Cuckoo *Dromococcyx phasianellus*

14 in (36 cm). Note **exceptionally broad tail feathers**; further distinguished from Striped Cuckoo by larger size, **spotted breast**, and **scaled** (not striped) **back**. Looks small-headed. Rare and local (recorded from various parts of the country, but true distribution is not well known due to secretive habits); to at least 4,000 ft (1,200 m). Found on ground in dense undergrowth of both forest edge and woodland. Very furtive, and difficult to see. Call similar to the two-note call of Striped Cuckoo but with additional notes, including either a quavering third note or a rapid sequence of two or three short notes.

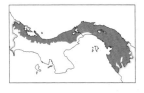

Rufous-vented Ground-Cuckoo *Neomorphus geoffroyi*

19.5 in (50 cm). This large, long-tailed, terrestrial species is virtually unmistakable; note **crest, blue orbital skin**, and **heavy yellow bill**. Young immature is mainly blackish. Rare on entire Caribbean slope and on Pacific from eastern Panamá Province eastward; to at least 5,000 ft (1,450 m). Found on ground in forest. Rarely found away from army ants (especially larger swarms), which it follows to catch the prey they stir up. Very shy and wary. Mostly silent; clacks bill loudly in alarm; also gives a deep moaning *huuuuuua*.

Little
Cuckoo

Squirrel
Cuckoo

Pheasant
Cuckoo

Striped
Cuckoo

adult

Rufous-vented
Ground-Cuckoo

Greater Ani
Crotophaga major

17.5 in (44 cm). Larger than other two anis; note **whitish eye, upper mandible arched for basal two-thirds only** (giving "broken-nose" appearance), **plumage that is blue-black** (rather than dull black), and **sleeker and glossier** appearance. Immature is dull black and lacks arch on culmen. Common on Caribbean slope from western Colón Province eastward, and on Pacific from Canal Area eastward. Found in lowlands, in dense vegetation bordering rivers and streams and in swamps and marshes. Occurs in groups of about 12 individuals (occasionally as many as 30). Calls include a clucking *gw'uh-gw'uh-gw'uh* (groups may jointly give a loud, prolonged growling).

Smooth-billed Ani
Crotophaga ani

13 in (33 cm). Very similar to slightly smaller Groove-billed Ani; best distinguished by call. On adults, bill usually has **high-arched culmen**; note distinct notch at base. In all plumages, **bill is smooth** (sometimes with just faint grooving at base). Immature has bill similar in shape to that of Groove-billed; note that immature Groove-billed also has smooth bill. See also Greater Ani. Common on both slopes, to 4,000 ft (1,500 m); absent from Bocas del Toro and Caribbean slope of Ngöbe-Buglé and Veraguas. Found in fields, pastures, scrub, and other open areas. Occurs in small groups, often following cattle. Flight awkward and floppy; frequently looks disheveled. Call a shrill whining *ooooo-ik!*, rising at the end.

Groove-billed Ani
Crotophaga sulcirostris

12 in (31 cm). Very similar to slightly larger Smooth-billed Ani; best distinguished by call. Adult has **grooves on upper mandible,** but these can be difficult to see at a distance or in poor light; immature has smooth bill. Culmen less arched than in most adult Smooth-billed. See also Greater Ani. Common on most of Pacific slope and on Caribbean in Bocas del Toro; rare on Caribbean slope of Canal Area and in Darién. Occurs in lowlands, in fields, pastures, scrub, and other open areas. Similar in habits to Smooth-billed. Call a sharp dry *chu-irr!*

Barn Owls

TYTONIDAE. Barn owls, found through much of the world, are similar to typical owls but differ in details of anatomy. They are distinguished externally by heart-shaped facial disks and long legs. Their diet consists mainly of rodents, which they capture using their excellent night vision and acute hearing.

Barn Owl
Tyto alba

14 in (36 cm). **Heart-shaped pale facial disk outlined in black** is diagnostic. Palest owl (ranging from whitish to buffy on face and underparts); lacks any heavy markings. Appears ghostly in flight. Fairly common on Pacific slope and on Caribbean in Bocas del Toro and Canal Area; to at least 5,100 ft (1,550 m). Found in open areas, especially around human habitations. Mostly nocturnal; sometimes active in early morning or late afternoon. Call a loud grating shriek.

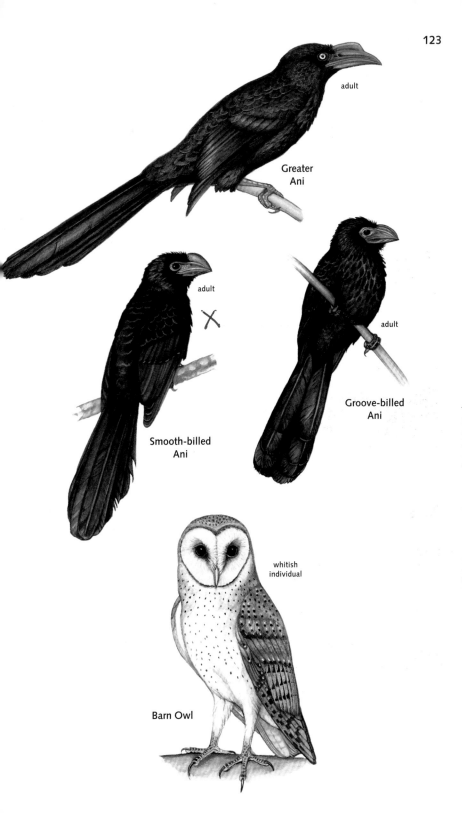

Greater
Ani

adult

adult

Smooth-billed
Ani

Groove-billed
Ani

adult

whitish
individual

Barn Owl

STRIGIDAE. Members of this family of mainly nocturnal birds of prey occur nearly throughout the world. Large, forward-facing eyes give them a distinctive appearance. While they see very well at night, their hearing is so keen that they can zero in and capture prey by sound alone, even in absolute darkness. Owls feed on a wide variety of animals, including mammals, birds, and, in the case of the smaller species, large insects. Unlike most other owls, the pygmy owls (*Glaucidium*) often hunt by day. Several Panama species are variable in color, with gray, brown, or rufous morphs. Because owls are active mainly at night, vocalizations are particularly important for finding and identifying them. During the day, they can also be found at roosts in dense vegetation.

Crested Owl
Lophostrix cristata

15 in (38 cm). On both dark and pale morphs, **long white or buffy superciliaries** (that extend in unbroken line from bill to long ear tufts) are diagnostic; also note unstreaked underparts and whitish spots on wings. Rare on both slopes, to 3,000 ft (900 m); in lower and middle levels of forest. Call a deep, resonant *bwooorr*.

Spectacled Owl
Pulsatrix perspicillata

18.5 in (48 cm). **White crescents** ("spectacles") framing eyes on dark face are distinctive. Also note lack of ear tufts and **contrast between dark chest band and pale lower breast and belly**. Young immature mostly buffy white with blackish face and brown wings. Uncommon on both slopes, to 4,000 ft (1,200 m). Inhabits forest. Call is a rapid series of short notes that become softer toward the end (sounds like muffled knocking on wood): *bubububububububuhbuhbuh*.

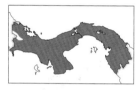

Mottled Owl
Ciccaba virgata

12 in (31 cm). Combination of **lack of ear tufts** and **streaked lower breast and belly** is distinctive among medium-sized owls. Much larger than pygmy-owls (p. 126), and differs in lacking spots or streaks on crown; also note **brown eyes**. A paler morph also occurs. Common on both slopes, to 7,000 ft (2,100 m). Found at lower and middle levels of forest and woodland. Gives a variety of calls, including a muffled *hWHOO*, often repeated two or more times, and a catlike screeching *keeayow*.

Black-and-white Owl
Ciccaba nigrolineata

15 in (38 cm). **Fine black-and-white barring on underparts** is unique. Uncommon on both slopes, to 7,000 ft (2,100 m). Occurs in lower and middle levels of forest. Call an accelerating series of deep notes, accented on last or next-to-last syllable: *buh-buh-bu-bu-bu-BWA!* or *buh-buh-bu-bu-bu-BWA!-bu*.

Striped Owl
Pseudoscops clamator

14 in (35 cm). Only medium-sized owl with combination of **ear tufts** and **streaked underparts**; much larger than screech-owls (p. 126). Uncommon on Pacific slope eastward to eastern Panamá Province; rare on Caribbean, in Canal Area and eastern Colón Province; to 3,500 ft (1,050 m). Found in open grassy or scrubby areas. Call a shrill, high-pitched *heeAH!*

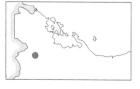

Unspotted Saw-whet Owl
Aegolius ridgwayi

7.5 in (19 cm). **Only small owl without streaking or barring on underparts**. Very rare; one record in 1965 at 7,600 ft (2,300 m) on Volcán Barú, Chiriquí. Call a series of evenly spaced whistles, similar to that of pygmy-owls (p. 126).

Crested
Owl

pale morph

dark morph

adult

Spectacled
Owl

Black-and-white
Owl

Striped
Owl

dark morph

Mottled Owl

Unspotted Saw-whet
Owl

Tropical Screech-Owl
Megascops choliba

8.5 in (22 cm). Screech-owls are the only small owls with ear tufts. This species is distinguished from other screech-owls by **distinct black rim to facial disk**; also note **pale superciliaries**. Has stronger vertical streaking below than Vermiculated. Rare rufous morph has similar markings. Fairly common on entire Pacific slope and on Caribbean in northern Coclé, the Canal Area, and eastern Kuna Yala; to 4,000 ft (1,200 m). Found in open areas with scattered trees, woodland, and towns and suburban areas. Call a burry trill, usually terminating in a loud final note: *kukukukukuKU!* The final note is sometimes doubled: *kukukukukuKUH-koo!* (or occasionally tripled).

Vermiculated Screech-Owl
Megascops guatemalae

8.5 in (22 cm). Both gray and rufous morphs are distinguished from Tropical Screech-Owl by **lack of distinct rim to facial disk, lack of prominent pale superciliaries**, and **underparts with mainly horizontal vermiculated pattern** (instead of vertical streaking). See also Bare-shanked Screech-Owl (mainly higher elevations). Uncommon on Caribbean slope eastward to Canal Area; uncommon on Pacific slope, both from Canal Area eastward and, locally, in western foothills; to 3,600 ft (1,100 m). Occurs in lower and middle levels of forest. Call a descending froglike churr: *kurrrooooh.*

Bare-shanked Screech-Owl
Megascops clarkii

9.5 in (24 cm). Combination of **tawny facial disk without a distinct rim** and **whitish spotting below** distinguishes it from other screech-owls. Occurs in rufous and brown morphs. Rare in highlands of western Panama eastward to Veraguas; also rare in highlands of eastern Darién; from 3,600 to 7,000 ft (1,060 to 2,100 m). Found in lower and middle levels of forest. Call a series of low *whoo* notes that are variously spaced and accented. **WH, EH**

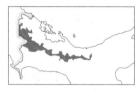

Costa Rican Pygmy-Owl
Glaucidium costaricanum

6 in (15 cm). Occurs in brown and rufous morphs. In both, **barring on sides of breast and on flanks** distinguishes it from other pygmy-owls (no known range overlap). Differs from Ferruginous Pygmy-Owl in having **small pale spots on crown** (not streaks); in immature, crown spots are reduced or lacking. Occurs at higher elevations than other pygmy-owls. Rare in western highlands eastward to Veraguas; mostly above 5,000 ft (1,500 m). Found at lower and middle levels of forest. Call a long series of even, usually doubled, notes: *poop-poop, poop-poop, poop-poop.* **WH**

Central American Pygmy-Owl
Glaucidium griseiceps

5.5 in (14 cm). Distinguished from Ferruginous Pygmy-Owl by **small pale spots on grayish crown** rather than streaks; from Costa Rican Pygmy-Owl by **lack of barring on sides**; no known range overlap with either. Immature lacks crown spots. Rare on Pacific slope, from eastern Panamá Province eastward; rare on Caribbean in Bocas del Toro, Canal Area, eastern Panamá Province, and eastern Kuna Yala; to at least 3,300 ft (1,000 m). Found at lower and middle levels of forest. Call a series of evenly spaced whistled notes that varies from 2 to 18 notes: *pew pew pew pew* (usually slower than call of Ferruginous Pygmy-Owl).

Ferruginous Pygmy-Owl
Glaucidium brasilianum

6.5 in (16 cm). Occurs in brown and rufous morphs. **Small pale streaks on crown** (rather than spots) distinguish it from other pygmy-owls (no known range overlap); further distinguished from Costa Rican Pygmy-Owl by **lack of barring on sides**. Immature mostly lacks streaks on crown. Uncommon on Pacific slope eastward to western Panamá Province. Found in lowlands, in scrub and thickets in open areas. Call a series of evenly spaced whistled notes: *piw-piw-piw-piw-piw* (somewhat sharper and usually faster than call of Central American Pygmy-Owl).

Tropical
Screech-Owl

gray morph

Vermiculated
Screech-Owl

rufous morph

gray morph

Bare-shanked
Screech-Owl

rufous
morph

adult rufous
morph

Costa Rican
Pygmy-Owl

adult brown
morph

Central American
Pygmy-Owl

adult

Ferruginous
Pygmy-Owl

adult brown
morph

CAPRIMULGIDAE. Members of this family occur nearly worldwide. All are insectivorous, and the majority are principally nocturnal (the nighthawks are often also active at dusk and dawn). Nightjars have short but very wide bills, flanked by bristles that allow them to scoop insects out of the air while on the wing. The nighthawks forage for insects in continuous flight, while other members of the family mainly rest on the ground or on low perches and fly up to catch insects as they pass by. The cryptic coloration of nightjars makes them difficult to find and identify. Some species can be located by driving back roads and looking for their red eyeshine as they rest on the surface of the road. Vocalizations are important for identification, as are the position and size of markings on wings and tail.

Short-tailed Nighthawk
Lurocalis semitorquatus

8 in (20 cm). Overall **very dark; lacks white in wings and tail**. Note **very short, square tail**. Uncommon to rare. Widespread on Caribbean slope and on Pacific slope in eastern Panamá Province and Darién; local elsewhere on Pacific; to 5,000 ft (1,450 m). Best recognized by **erratic, batlike flight** as it forages over forest canopy or clearings at dusk or dawn. Perches by day lengthwise along higher branches; on perched birds, wings project well beyond end of tail. Flight call is a sharp *chwit!*

Lesser Nighthawk
Chordeiles acutipennis

8 in (20 cm). Very similar to Common Nighthawk; in flight, distinguished by location of **pale** (white in male, pale buff in female) **wing band, closer to tip than to wrist**; also has less sharply pointed wings and tends to fly lower. Female has pale buff throat and lacks white in tail. When resting, wing tips do not exceed tip of tail. Fairly common on Pacific slope; local breeding population is supplemented by migrants from north from July to April (when it may also occur on Caribbean slope). Occurs from lowlands to lower highlands, in open areas (often near mangroves or swampy areas). Calls include an evenly pitched froglike trill and a bleating whinny.

Common Nighthawk
Chordeiles minor

9 in (23 cm). Very similar to Lesser Nighthawk; in flight, distinguished by location of **pale** (white in both sexes) **wing band, near midpoint between tip and wrist**; also has more sharply pointed wings and tends to fly higher. Female has pale buff throat and lacks white in tail. When resting, wing tips extend beyond tip of tail. Fairly common on Pacific slope, eastward to eastern Panamá Province. Migrants from north occur as transients (recorded in Sept and Oct; period of spring passage not known) on both slopes, but especially along the Caribbean coast; Panama breeding population migrates to South America between late Nov and early March. Occurs in lowlands and foothills, in open areas. Flight call (frequently given) is a nasal buzzy *peent!* or *beezhnt!*; during courtship, males in dive display produce a whooshing or booming sound with wings.

Common Pauraque
Nyctidromus albicollis

9.5 in (24 cm). Variable; individuals range from rufous brown to gray. Resting birds distinguished from White-tailed Nightjar (p. 130) by **lack of nuchal collar**; from nighthawks by **wings extending only half the length of tail**; from Chuck-will's-widow and Rufous Nightjar (p. 130) by **more conspicuous buff spotting on wings**. In flight, male shows broad white band across primaries (narrower in female) and extensive white in tail (reduced to white tail corners in female); compared to White-tailed Nightjar, note rounded rather than nearly square, slightly notched tail. Common in lowlands and foothills. Found in open and scrubby areas, clearings, forest edge, and woodland. Call a buzzy whistling *woHEERrr!*, sometimes preceded by several sharp notes: *wik-wik-wik-wHEERrr!*

Short-tailed
Nighthawk

male

Lesser Nighthawk

male

male

Common Nighthawk

male

male
gray individual

Common Pauraque

male
gray individual

Chuck-will's-widow
Caprimulgus carolinensis

11 in (28 cm). Variable in coloration, ranging from rufous to gray. Almost identical to Rufous Nightjar (see that species for comparisons). Rare winter resident, from Oct to April; most numerous in western Panama and, generally, in lowlands; to 5,300 ft (1,600 m). Occurs in forest and woodland. Usually silent in Panama.

Rufous Nightjar
Caprimulgus rufus

10 in (26 cm). In flight, lacks white or buff band on primaries. Very similar to Chuck-will's-widow, but somewhat smaller; averages more rufous but coloration overlaps and often the two species cannot be reliably distinguished in the field on this basis. On male, the terminal quarter of the inner web of the three outer tail feathers is white, and the outer web is tawny and unmarked; on male Chuck-will's-widow, the inner web of the three outer tail feathers is white for most of its length, and the outer web is tawny with dark markings. Females of both species lack white in tail. Fairly common on Pacific slope in Canal Area, eastern Panamá Province, and on Coiba Island; apparently rare and local elsewhere on Pacific slope and on Caribbean in Bocas del Toro, Canal Area, and Kuna Yala. Occurs in lowlands and foothills, in forest edge and woodland. Call a rapid, high-pitched *chuck, wik-wik-WHEeoh!*, similar to that of Chuck-will's-widow but faster and higher pitched; calling birds are almost certainly this species.

Whip-poor-will
Caprimulgus vociferus

9.5 in (24 cm). Variable in coloration, ranging from rufous to gray. Note **dark median line on crown** and **distinct pale gray stripe along side of back**. Tail corners large and white in male, small and buffy in female. In flight, lacks white or buff band on primaries. Vagrant, with two records from highlands of western Chiriquí, from 4,300 to 6,500 ft (1,300 to 1,950 m). Usually found in forest edge. Unlikely to call in Panama.

Dusky Nightjar
Caprimulgus saturatus

8.5 in (22 cm). **Darker** and **plainer** than other members of the family, and occurs at higher elevations than most. Tail corners white in male, buffy in female. In flight, lacks white or buff band on primaries. Uncommon in western highlands, eastward to eastern Chiriquí, mostly above 5,000 ft (1,500 m). Found in forest and adjacent open areas. Call a burry whistled *FEE-pur-WHEE!* **WH**

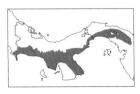

White-tailed Nightjar
Caprimulgus cayennensis

8.5 in (21 cm). Prominent **cinnamon collar** (paler in female) across hindneck is distinctive. Female is darker above and buffier below, with buffy throat. In flight, male shows white band across middle of primaries and extensive white along sides of tail (entire underside of tail is white); female lacks white in wings or tail. Tail is nearly square, with a slight notch. Rare; occurs on Pacific slope, eastward to western Darién. Found in lowlands, in dry grassy open areas. Call consists of a short introductory note followed by a thin high-pitched whistle that rises and then falls, *chik-fWHEeee*.

Ocellated Poorwill
Nyctiphrynus ocellatus

8.5 in (22 cm). Mostly **dark grayish brown**, with **dark spots (bordered with buff or rufous) on scapulars and wing coverts**. Note white band or throat; usually has **two white spots on wing coverts**. Underparts have small white spots; tail narrowly tipped white. Inhabits forest. Vagrant; one record from western Colón Province near Canal Area (1978). **Not illustrated**.

Chuck-will's-widow

male rufous
individual

Rufous Nightjar

male rufous
individual

Whip-poor-will

male rufous
individual

Dusky Nightjar

male

White-tailed Nightjar

male

NYCTIBIIDAE. Members of this small family occur only in the neotropics. These nocturnal, nightjar-like birds have large eyes and short, very wide bills. During the day, potoos normally sit motionless on branches or stumps, with the bill facing forward. However, if a bird detects the presence of an observer, it will slowly stretch its body and point the bill upward, enhancing even more its resemblance to a dead snag. Potoos are more easily seen at night, when they often sit on exposed perches to sally out for insects, and can then be located by their bright eyeshine and loud calls.

Great Potoo
Nyctibius grandis

19 in (48 cm). Much larger than Common Potoo, with a proportionately larger head; overall paler, **lacking pale cheek stripe and dark malar stripe** of Common. **Eyes brown**, reflecting yellow-orange at night. Uncommon on entire Caribbean slope and on Pacific slope from eastern Panamá Province eastward. Found in lowlands, in upper levels of forest and adjacent clearings with trees. Call a loud, explosive roar: *bWARRRR!*

Common Potoo
Nyctibius griseus

14 in (36 cm). Occurs in brown morph (not illustrated) and gray morph. Smaller and more slender than Great Potoo; generally darker, with **pale cheek stripe bordered below by dark malar stripe**. **Eyes yellow**, reflecting yellow-orange at night. Fairly common on both slopes, to 4,000 ft (1,200 m). Found in middle levels of forest edge, woodland, second growth, and clearings. Call a haunting, melancholy series of wailing notes, loud at first, becoming gradually softer and falling in pitch: *WHEEUU, whu, hu, hu, hu.*

Oilbird

STEATORNITHIDAE. The sole member of its family, the Oilbird is the only nocturnal fruit-eating bird; it plucks oily fruits from palms and other trees in flight. It resembles a large nightjar but has a stout hawklike hooked beak. Oilbirds nest colonially in caves or dark narrow ravines, finding their way by listening for the echoes of audible clicks they make with their bills. During the nonbreeding season, they disperse away from the nesting caves, and then occasionally can be found during the day perched horizontally on branches in the forest understory.

Oilbird
Steatornis caripensis

17.5 in (44 cm). **Bright rufous coloration** and **white spots on wings, tail, and head** make it unmistakable. Eyeshine bright red. Rare but regular in and near the Canal Area (occasionally found in Panamá City, in parks or on buildings, where evidently attracted by street lights); recorded also from Cerro Azul; one record from Darién. A breeding colony probably exists somewhere in the Chagres River Basin. Makes bill clicks in flight; at breeding colony, gives loud screeches and growls.

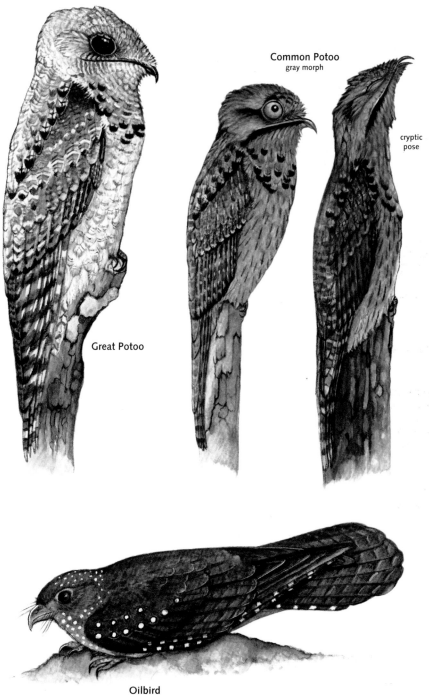

Common Potoo
gray morph

cryptic
pose

Great Potoo

Oilbird

APODIDAE. Swifts, nearly cosmopolitan in distribution, are the most aerial of all birds. They feed on small insects caught on the wing and are unable to perch normally—they rest by clinging to vertical surfaces with their tiny sharp-clawed feet. Some species even copulate or sleep in flight. Swifts resemble swallows, and are often seen feeding with them, but have a more erratic, stiff-winged flight. Most species may be found over almost any type of habitat, from open areas to forest. Identification can be difficult, since field marks are often subtle (for example, the degree of contrast between the throat and the rest of the body). If possible, try to view flocks against a dark background rather than a bright sky.

Black Swift
Cypseloides niger

6 in (15 cm). A **large,** almost entirely **dark swift** with a relatively **long, broad tail** (slightly notched in adult male); has inconspicuous whitish frosting on forehead. Immature has vague whitish barring below. Very rare, with scattered records from Chiriquí and Bocas del Toro eastward to Darién; status uncertain, probably a migrant from north but may breed in Panama.

White-chinned Swift
Cypseloides cryptus

5.5 in (14 cm). Small white chin spot is diagnostic but not normally visible in the field (and is lacking in some individuals). Distinguished from Black and Chestnut-collared Swifts by relatively **shorter, square tail**; blacker than female or immature Chestnut-collared. Very rare vagrant; recorded from eastern Kuna Yala (1932) and Coiba Island, Veraguas (1957).

Chestnut-collared Swift
Streptoprocne rutila

5 in (13 cm). **Chestnut collar** of adult male (reduced or absent in female and immature) is diagnostic but can be difficult to see in poor light. Rare in foothills and highlands eastward to Cerro Azul in eastern Panamá Province; very rare in lowlands on Caribbean slope and on western Pacific slope.

White-collared Swift
Streptoprocne zonaris

8 in (20 cm). Largest swift. Conspicuous **white collar** is diagnostic (on immature, white collar is reduced or, in rare cases, absent); also note forked tail. Fairly common throughout most of the country in foothills and highlands; uncommon in Caribbean lowlands; rare in Pacific lowlands.

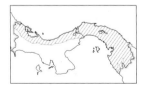

Chimney Swift
Chaetura pelagica

5 in (13 cm). Larger and **more uniformly colored** than all other *Chaetura* swifts except Chapman's (see for distinctions, p. 136). Throat paler than rest of underparts, but does not contrast as much as in Vaux's Swift; rump is only slightly paler than rest of upperparts and contrasts less than it does in lowland race of Vaux's. Uncommon transient from Oct to Nov and March to May. Occurs on entire Caribbean slope, and on Pacific slope from eastern Panamá Province eastward. Steady directional flight of migrating flocks or scattered individuals can help pick them out from resident swifts.

Vaux's Swift
Chaetura vauxi

4.5 in (11 cm). **Pale throat contrasts distinctly with rest of underparts**. On lowland race, pale rump contrasts with rest of upperparts (though less so than in Band-rumped or Costa Rican Swifts, p. 136); highland race shows little contrast. Highland race common in highlands of Chiriquí and Bocas del Toro, where it is usually the only *Chaetura* swift. Lowland race uncommon to rare in lowlands of Pacific slope, eastward to Canal Area; rare on Caribbean slope of Canal Area; uncommon on Coiba Island and in Pearl Islands.

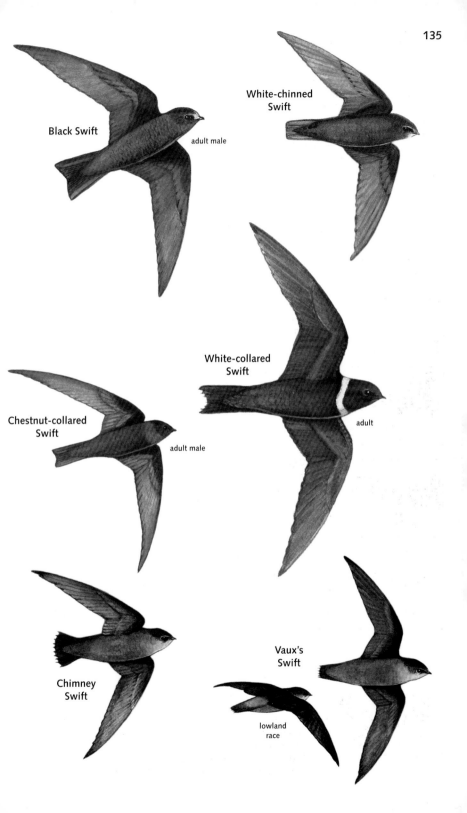

Black Swift
adult male

White-chinned
Swift

White-collared
Swift
adult

Chestnut-collared
Swift
adult male

Chimney
Swift

Vaux's
Swift

lowland
race

Chapman's Swift
Chaetura chapmani

4.5 in (12 cm). Most similar to Chimney Swift (p. 134). Distinguished by blacker crown, nape, and upper back, all with glossy bluish sheen that is absent on Chimney; paler lower back and rump contrast with rest of back; throat is only slightly paler than rest of underparts, with less contrast than on Chimney. Very rare, with scattered records from Canal Area eastward to Darién. Status uncertain; probably a vagrant from South America but may breed in Panama.

Short-tailed Swift
Chaetura brachyura

4.5 in (11 cm). **Nearly tailless appearance** makes this species relatively easy to recognize; also note **pale rump and undertail coverts that contrast strongly with rest of plumage**. Throat is only slightly paler than rest of underparts, showing little contrast. Fairly common from Canal Area eastward to Darién; rare in southern Coclé. Occurs in lowlands, over open areas.

Ashy-tailed Swift
Chaetura andrei

4.5 in (12 cm). Mainly dark sooty brown, with contrasting paler grayish brown rump and pale gray throat; tail short, mostly concealed by uppertail coverts. Chimney Swift (p. 134) has longer tail and less contrasting rump; Short-tailed Swift has less contrasting throat than Ashy-tailed and even shorter tail; Vaux's Swift (p. 134) is smaller and has longer tail; also, its rump is darker and browner than on Ashy-tailed and shows less contrast with upperparts. Vagrant, with two records, from eastern Panamá Province (1923) and southern Coclé (1975). **Not illustrated**.

Band-rumped Swift
Chaetura spinicaudus

4.5 (11 cm). **Narrow whitish band across lower back** is distinctive (shared only with Costa Rican Swift; no range overlap). Also note pale throat. Gray-rumped Swift (no range overlap) has much wider grayish rump patch. Common in lowlands and foothills from northern Veraguas eastward.

Costa Rican Swift
Chaetura fumosa

4.5 in (11 cm). Nearly identical to Band-rumped Swift (no range overlap); has **wider, grayer band across lower back**. Rare in western Chiriquí; from lowlands to lower highlands. **PL**

Gray-rumped Swift
Chaetura cinereiventris

4.5 in (11 cm). **Large triangular pale gray rump patch** is distinctive; Band-rumped and Costa Rican Swifts (no range overlap) have narrower, paler bands on back. Fairly common in western Bocas del Toro, in lowlands and foothills.

Lesser Swallow-tailed Swift
Panyptila cayennensis

5 in (13 cm). Striking **black-and-white pattern** and **long forked tail** (usually held closed, so that it appears pointed) make this species unmistakable. Fairly common nearly throughout the country, from lowlands to lower highlands.

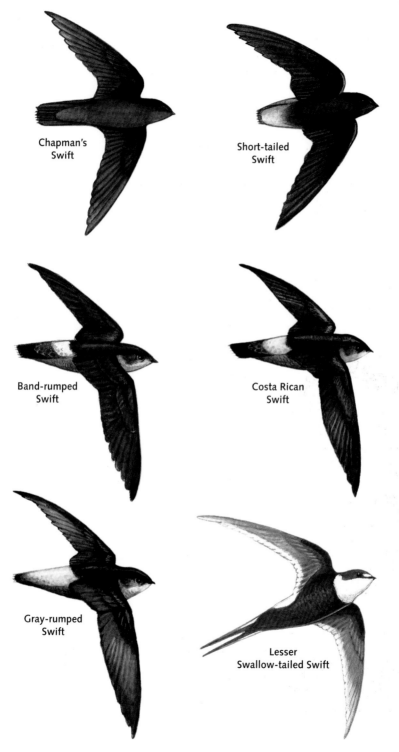

Chapman's Swift

Short-tailed Swift

Band-rumped Swift

Costa Rican Swift

Gray-rumped Swift

Lesser Swallow-tailed Swift

TROCHILIDAE. Hummingbirds, the world's smallest birds, occur only in the Americas, reaching their greatest diversity at middle elevations in the tropics. Their long, thin bills and acrobatic flight are adaptations for feeding on flower nectar, which they supplement with insects and other small invertebrates. They can hover in place and even fly backward, the only birds able to do so. The brilliant iridescent colors of many species are produced by feather structure rather than pigment, and so are only apparent in the right light; otherwise the colors look blackish. Females are often drab and difficult to distinguish; tail shape, tail coloration, and face pattern provide important clues. Hermits are a distinctive group of mainly dull-colored hummingbirds that have exceptionally long, curved bills. Male hummingbirds, which play no part in raising the young, have a variety of courtship displays. In some species, males sing their squeaky songs in loose groups known as leks; in others males sing alone. In yet other species, in particular those of the genus *Selasphorus*, males perform spectacular diving displays.

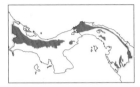

Green Hermit
Phaethornis guy

6 in (15 cm). Similar in size and shape to Long-billed Hermit, but note **dark metallic green upperparts** and **red lower mandible**. Male mostly dark green below; female mostly grayish below, with more prominent buffy stripes on face and throat. Common in foothills and lower highlands on both slopes; mainly 2,000 to 5,500 ft (600 to 1,650 m); rare in lowlands on Caribbean slope. Found in lower levels of forest. Males sing in leks in forest undergrowth; call a sharp *wheenk!*, repeated about once every 2 seconds (lower pitched than that of Long-billed Hermit).

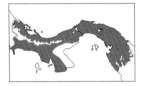

Long-billed Hermit
Phaethornis longirostris

6 in (15 cm). **Mostly brown upperparts** (rump is cinnamon) distinguish it from other hermits of similar size that have long tails; Stripe-throated Hermit (p. 140) is much smaller. Common on both slopes, to 3,000 ft (900 m). Found in lower levels of forest. Males sing in leks in forest understory; call a sharp *whik*, repeated at about 1-second intervals.

White-whiskered Hermit
Phaethornis yaruqui

5 in (13 cm). Similar to Green Hermit, but **central stripe on throat is whitish or grayish** rather than buffy; **crown bronzy**; bill somewhat straighter. Probably a rare resident, with one record from easternmost Darién (1996).

Pale-bellied Hermit
Phaethornis anthophilus

5 in (13 cm). Most similar to Long-billed Hermit; distinguished by **bronzy green** (not brownish) **upperparts, whitish** (not pale buffy) **underparts**, and **lack of central pale stripe on throat**. Occurs in more open areas than other long-tailed hermits. Common on the larger Pearl Islands; rare in lowlands on Pacific slope from eastern Panamá Province eastward, and in lowlands on Caribbean slope in eastern Kuna Yala. Found in lower levels of forest in the Pearl Islands, and in forest edge, woodland, and thickets on the mainland.

female

male

Green
Hermit

Long-billed
Hermit

White-whiskered
Hermit

Pale-bellied
Hermit

Rufous-breasted Hermit
Glaucis hirsutus

4.5 in (12 cm). Combination of **rounded, mostly chestnut tail** and **mostly rufous underparts** distinguishes it from all other hermits except Bronzy (little range overlap; see for distinctions). Fairly common in lowlands; occurs on Caribbean slope, from Bocas del Toro eastward; and on Pacific slope, from western Panamá Province eastward. Found in forest edge and in clearings in forest, especially around patches of *Heliconia*, bananas, and other large flowering herbs.

Bronzy Hermit
Glaucis aeneus

4.5 in (11 cm). Very similar to Rufous-breasted Hermit; distinguished by **bronzy cast on upperparts, darker lower mandible** (lower mandible yellow in Rufous-breasted), and **rufous undertail coverts** (like rest of underparts; undertail coverts are grayish or buffy in Rufous-breasted). Note that Bronzy and Rufous-breasted overlap only in the small area between the town of Chiriquí Grande (in Bocas del Toro) and the Valiente Peninsula (in Ngöbe-Buglé). Fairly common in lowlands; occurs on Caribbean slope in Bocas del Toro and Ngöbe-Buglé, and on western Pacific slope, eastward to Veraguas. Found in forest edge and clearings in forest. Habits similar to those of Rufous-breasted Hermit.

Band-tailed Barbthroat
Threnetes ruckeri

4.5 in (12 cm). Distinguished from other hermits by **black throat that contrasts strongly with rufous chest** and by **black-and-white banded tail** (conspicuous when spread in flight). Uncommon in lowlands and foothills on entire Caribbean slope; also uncommon in lowlands and foothills on Pacific slope in western Chiriquí (elsewhere on western Pacific slope, occurs only in foothills), and from Canal Area eastward. Found in forest edge and clearings in forest, especially around *Heliconia* and other large flowering herbs.

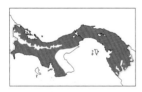

Stripe-throated Hermit
Phaethornis striigularis

3.5 in (9 cm). Combination of **tiny size, bright cinnamon underparts**, and **chestnut rump** is unique; Long-billed Hermit (p. 138) is much larger and is duller pale buff below. Tail pointed but lacks elongated white tips of other long-tailed hermits. Common on both slopes, to 4,300 ft (1,300 m). Found in lower levels of forest and in forest clearings. Males sing in leks in forest understory; call a thin sharp *tsip!*, repeated about twice per second (higher pitched than call of Long-billed Hermit).

White-tipped Sicklebill
Eutoxeres aquila

4.5 in (12 cm). **Extremely decurved bill**, bent almost in a half circle, makes this species unmistakable; also note **heavily streaked underparts** and **graduated, white-tipped tail**. Uncommon in foothills on both slopes; mostly 1,000 to 5,000 ft (300 to 1,500 m); a few records from lowlands on Caribbean slope. Occurs in lower levels of forest; especially fond of wet ravines and *Heliconia* thickets.

Tooth-billed Hummingbird
Androdon aequatorialis

5.5 in (14 cm). Combination of **extremely long straight bill** and **heavily streaked underparts** is diagnostic; also note conspicuous **white band on rump** (sometimes broken in middle). This species's common name refers to tiny serrations on the bill (not visible in the field). Uncommon in foothills and highlands in eastern Darién, from 2,000 to 5,300 ft (600 to 1,600 m). Found in lower and middle levels of forest, where it favors long-tubed flowers of epiphytes.

Rufous-breasted Hermit

Bronzy Hermit

Band-tailed Barbthroat

Stripe-throated Hermit

White-tipped Sicklebill

Tooth-billed Hummingbird

Scaly-breasted Hummingbird
Phaeochroa cuvierii

4.5 in (12 cm). The best field mark on this large, rather nondescript species is the **large white spots on corners of tail**; also note **small pale spot behind eye, pinkish base to lower mandible**, and inconspicuous scaling on breast. Most similar to female White-necked Jacobin (see for distinctions); also compare female plumeleteers (p. 152), female Blue-chested Hummingbird (p. 150), and female Charming Hummingbird (p. 150). Uncommon in lowlands on Pacific slope; rare in lowlands on Caribbean slope from Canal Area eastward. Occurs in open areas, scrub, second growth, and mangroves. Males sing persistently from exposed perches (either alone or in small groups), giving a variety of high chipping notes.

Violet Sabrewing
Campylopterus hemileucurus

6 in (15 cm). Spectacular male is unmistakable due to **glittering violet plumage** and conspicuous **white tail corners**. Female also distinctive; note large size, **curved all-dark bill, violet throat**, and **white tail corners**. Fairly common in foothills and highlands of western Panama, eastward to Coclé; mainly from 3,000 to 5,500 ft (900 to 1,650 m), but occasionally lower. Found in lower and middle levels of forest and adjacent clearings.

White-necked Jacobin
Florisuga mellivora

4.5 in (11 cm). Male is unique, with **all-blue head, white lower breast and belly**, and **mostly white tail**. Typical female somewhat resembles Scaly-breasted Hummingbird but is more conspicuously **scaled on breast** and whiter on belly, lacks spot behind eye, and has **all-dark bill**; female Green-crowned Brilliant (p. 154) has white malar stripe and white spot behind eye. Many females show varying degrees of male-type plumage, especially blue head and white tail. Some females have buffy facial stripes. Common on both slopes, to about 5,000 ft (1,500 m). Found in forest edge and adjacent clearings, and in canopy of forest. Frequently feeds in flowering trees; also catches small insects in flight. Male has a swooping territorial display (often given at treetop level) in which he fans open his white tail.

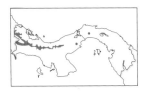

Brown Violet-ear
Colibri delphinae

4.5 in (12 cm). This drab species is best distinguished by **pale malar stripe that borders dark throat** (throat has green-to-violet sheen in good light); also note **violet ear patch** (difficult to see in poor light) and relatively **short straight bill**. Rare and local in foothills and lower highlands, from 3,000 to 4,500 ft (900 to 1,350 m). Found in lower and middle levels of forest and adjacent clearings.

Green Violet-ear
Colibri thalassinus

4.5 in (11 cm). Best recognized by **violet ear patch**, shared only with Brown Violet-ear (which is otherwise very different). Also note relatively short straight bill and **tail with blue tip and blackish subterminal band**; more uniformly green than most other hummingbirds. Very common in western highlands, eastward to Veraguas and Azuero Peninsula; mostly above 5,000 ft (1,500 m), sometimes down to 3,000 ft (900 m). Found in forest edge and adjacent clearings. Males sing persistently throughout much of the day, often from an inconspicuous high perch; call a high, two-note *chup-chit*.

Green-fronted Lancebill
Doryfera ludovicae

4.5 in (11 cm). Combination of **extremely long straight bill** and **overall dark appearance** should prevent confusion; also note small white spot behind eye, coppery crown, bluish rump, and, in good light, glittering green patch on forehead. Rare and local in foothills and highlands, from 900 to 7,600 ft (900 to 2,300 m). Found in lower and middle levels of forest; favors wet ravines.

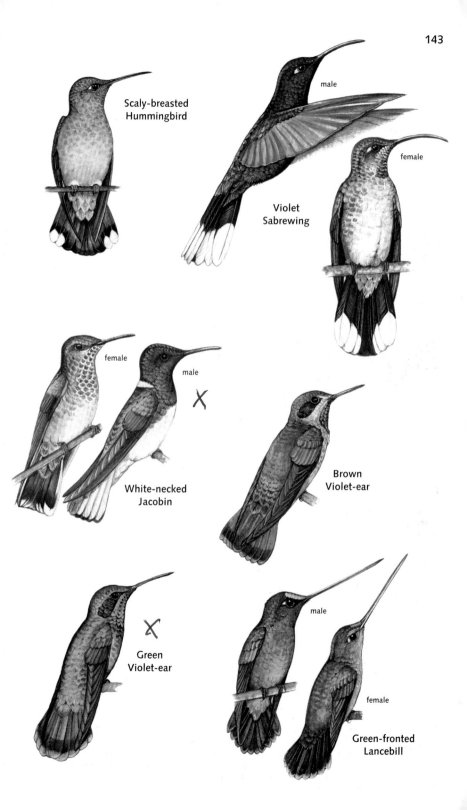

Scaly-breasted
Hummingbird

male

female

Violet
Sabrewing

female

male

X

White-necked
Jacobin

Brown
Violet-ear

X

Green
Violet-ear

male

female

Green-fronted
Lancebill

Veraguan Mango   *Anthracothorax veraguensis*
4.5 in (12 cm). Male is distinguished by **mainly green underparts**, with **deeper greenish blue stripe** (lacking any black) **on center of throat, breast, and belly** and **broad maroon tail**; also note slightly curved, all-black bill. Female, which also has **maroon tail**, has **white underparts with greenish blue** stripe (sometimes blackish on foreneck) down center. On female Green-breasted Mango, central stripe is mostly black (mixed with some green); on female Black-throated Mango, central stripe is entirely black. Immature similar to female but shows rufous along sides of neck and upper breast. Uncommon in lowlands; occurs from Chiriquí eastward to southern Coclé; a few records from Caribbean slope, in Ngöbe-Buglé (on the Valiente Peninsula), western Colón Province, and Canal Area. Found in open areas and scrub. Often seen in flowering trees. **PL**

Green-breasted Mango   *Anthracothorax prevostii*
4.5 in (12 cm). Both sexes similar to respective plumages of Veraguan Mango. Male has **black stripe extending from throat to lower breast**; on female, **breast stripe mostly black** (mixed with some green). In both sexes, note **maroon tail**. Uncommon in lowlands on Caribbean slope in Bocas del Toro (including Bastimentos and Colón Islands) and Ngöbe-Buglé; rare in lowlands on Pacific slope in Chiriquí. Found in open and shrubby areas. Frequents flowering trees.

Black-throated Mango   *Anthracothorax nigricollis*
4.5 in (12 cm). Male distinguished by **black stripe (bordered with blue) that runs down center of green breast (from throat to belly)** and by **maroon tail**. Male Veraguan Mango lacks black in breast stripe. Female shares **maroon tail**; **black stripe extends down center of white underparts**; very similar female Veraguan Mango has mainly greenish stripe. Immature similar to female, but has rufous along sides of neck and upper breast. Common in lowlands; found on Pacific slope, from southern Veraguas eastward; and on Caribbean slope, from western Colón Province eastward. Inhabits open and scrubby areas. Often feeds in flowering trees.

Ruby-topaz Hummingbird   *Chrysolampis mosquitus*
3.5 in (9 cm). Male unmistakable; **crown and nape a glowing ruby red, throat and breast glittering orange-yellow**, body mostly brown, **tail and undertail coverts chestnut**. (Male may look mainly blackish in poor light, however.) Female is bronzy or coppery green above, grayish white below, and has tail with **outer feathers mostly chestnut** (central feathers bronzy green), a dusky subterminal band, and white tipping. Vagrant, with two records, from El Real, Darién (1985, 2008). Occurs in forest edge and scrubby areas. **Not illustrated**.

Garden Emerald   *Chlorostilbon assimilis*
3 in (8 cm). Male is best recognized by combination of **small size, almost entirely green plumage**, and **distinctly forked blue-black tail**. Female is only small hummingbird with a **distinct dark mask bordered behind eye by white superciliary**; female Magnificent Hummingbird (p. 154) has similar facial pattern but is much larger. In both sexes, also note relatively **short, all-black bill**. Fairly common in lowlands of both coasts; less common in foothills; to at least 4,000 ft (1,200 m). Found in open areas, scrubby areas, and gardens.

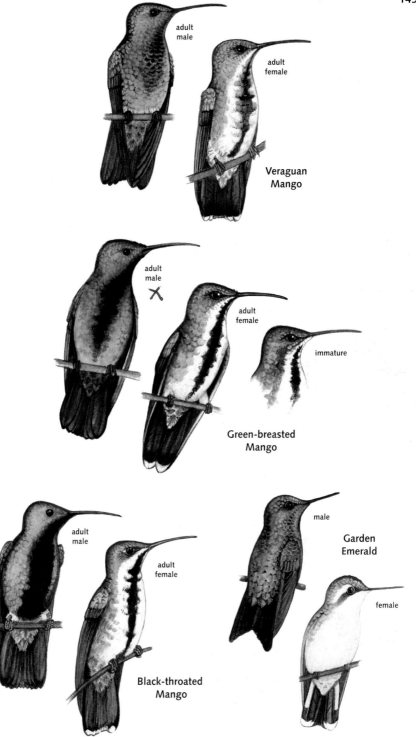

adult
male

adult female

Veraguan
Mango

adult
male

adult
female

immature

Green-breasted
Mango

adult
male

adult
female

male

Garden
Emerald

female

Black-throated
Mango

Violet-headed Hummingbird
Klais guimeti

3 in (8 cm). No other small hummingbird has such a conspicuous **small white spot behind eye**. On male, combination of **violet crown and throat** is distinctive; on female, **bluish crown** is distinctive. Fairly common in foothills of both slopes; mainly 1,000 to 4,000 ft (300 to 1,200 m); rare in lowlands. Occurs in lower and middle levels of forest.

Rufous-crested Coquette
Lophornis delattrei

3 in (7 cm). On male, **elongated rufous crest** is unmistakable. Female best distinguished by tiny size, **rufous forecrown**, and conspicuous **pale band across rump**. Rare and local in lowlands of both slopes; somewhat more numerous in foothills on Caribbean slope, from Ngöbe-Buglé eastward; to 3,000 ft (900 m). Found in forest edge and adjacent clearings.

White-crested Coquette
Lophornis adorabilis

3 in (7 cm). Male's **elongated white crest** makes it unmistakable. Female distinguished by tiny size, **white throat and upper breast** (flecked with bronze on throat), **rufous lower underparts**, and conspicuous **pale band across rump**. Rare and local in western Chiriquí, to 4,000 ft (1,200 m). Occurs in forest edge and adjacent clearings, and in gardens. **PL**

Green Thorntail
Discosura conversii

M 4.5 in (11 cm), including long tail; F 3 in (7 cm). Male's **long, very deeply forked tail with pointed feathers** is unique; also note conspicuous **white rump band**. Female also distinctive, with conspicuous **white malar stripe, white patch on flanks,** and **white rump band**. Rare in foothills of both slopes; mostly 2,000 to 4,000 ft (600 to 1,200 m). Found in forest edge and adjacent clearings.

Violet-crowned Woodnymph
Thalurania colombica

M 4.5 in (11 cm); F 3.5 in (9 cm). On male, combination of **green throat, glittering violet crown, violet shoulders and lower underparts, and forked tail** is distinctive. Male Green-crowned Woodnymph has green (not violet) crown (little if any range overlap). Male Violet-bellied Hummingbird (p. 148) is smaller, lacks violet on crown and back, and has rounded tail and reddish lower mandible. Female best recognized by distinctly two-tone underparts, with **pale gray throat and chest contrasting with darker lower breast and belly**; also note **fairly long, slightly curved all-black bill**; probably not distinguishable in field from female Green-crowned Woodnymph. Common in lowlands, less common in foothills; occurs on both slopes, eastward on Pacific to eastern Panamá Province, and eastward on Caribbean to western Kuna Yala; to 4,300 ft (1,300 m). Found in lower levels of forest and in adjacent clearings. Favors *Heliconia* patches.

Green-crowned Woodnymph
Thalurania fannyi

M 4.5 in (11 cm); F 3.5 in (9 cm). Very similar to Violet-crowned Woodnymph (little if any range overlap); male differs from male of that species in **glittering green crown**; females probably not distinguishable. Common in lowlands, less common in foothills; occurs on Pacific slope from eastern Panamá Province eastward, and on Caribbean slope in Kuna Yala; to 3,300 ft (1,000 m). Found in lower levels of forest and in adjacent clearings.

male

female

Violet-headed Hummingbird

male

female

Rufous-crested Coquette

female

male

White-crested Coquette

male

female

Green Thorntail

male

female

Violet-crowned Woodnymph

male

Green-crowned Woodnymph

Fiery-throated Hummingbird
Panterpe insignis

4.5 in (11 cm). **Glittering blue crown** and **orange-to-red throat** make this species unmistakable (but these can be difficult to see except in good light). **Bluish iridescence on rump** is distinctive; also note **medium-length straight bill with pink lower mandible** and **blue-black tail**. Uncommon in highlands of western Chiriquí and Bocas del Toro, mostly above 5,900 ft (1,800 m). Found in forest edge and adjacent clearings. **WH**

Violet-bellied Hummingbird
Damophila julie

3.5 in (9 cm). Male distinguished from larger male woodnymphs (p. 146) by **rounded tail, reddish lower mandible**, and **lack of glittering crown**. Female distinguished from female woodnymphs by **reddish lower mandible, more uniformly gray underparts,** and **green on side of head that extends below eye**. Female Sapphire-throated Hummingbird has whiter underparts, distinct green spotting along sides of breast, and forked tail. Fairly common on Pacific slope from western Panamá Province eastward, and on Caribbean from northern Coclé eastward; to 2,800 ft (850 m). Found in lower levels of forest and in adjacent clearings. Males (often in small loose groups) sing persistently from perches a few yards above the ground, giving a descending buzzy *whiiirrrr*.

Humboldt's Sapphire
Hylocharis humboldtii

4 in (10 cm). On male, combination of **blue crown and chin** and **bright red bill with black tip** is unique; male Blue-throated Goldentail has green crown and greenish gold tail. Female most resembles female Sapphire-throated Hummingbird but has **more extensive green spotting on underparts** and **less distinctly forked tail**. Uncommon in eastern Darién, in mangroves and scrub along coast; not known to occur inland.

Blue-throated Goldentail
Hylocharis eliciae

3.5 in (9 cm). **Metallic greenish gold tail** is unique; also note relatively **short, stout, bright red bill with black tip**. Rufous-tailed Hummingbird (p. 150) can appear bluish on throat, but tail is a nonmetallic rufous and bill is not as bright red. Uncommon on Pacific slope, to 3,000 ft (900 m). Found in lower levels of forest and adjacent clearings. Males sing in loose groups from perches in understory; call a variable series of sharp notes beginning with a sharp *tseee* (some notes doubled).

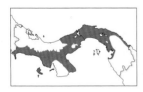

Sapphire-throated Hummingbird
Lepidopyga coeruleogularis

3.5 in (9 cm). On male, combination of **violet-blue throat** and **distinctly forked tail** is unique; on male Blue-chested Hummingbird (p. 150) and male Charming Hummingbird (p. 150) blue is restricted to chest, and tail is only slightly forked. Female distinguished from female woodnymphs (p. 146) and female Violet-bellied Hummingbirds by **pure white underparts, green spotting along sides of breast,** and **distinctly forked tail**. Fairly common on Pacific slope from Chiriquí to Darién, and on Caribbean slope from northern Coclé eastward; mainly near coast but occasionally well inland. Found in scrub, woodland, and mangroves.

Violet-capped Hummingbird
Goldmania violiceps

3.5 in (9 cm). On male, combination of **violet crown** and **forked chestnut tail** is unique. Female is only hummingbird with combination of **mostly white underparts** and **chestnut tail**. Fairly common in foothills on both slopes, from eastern Colón and eastern Panamá Province eastward (but absent from southeastern Darién); mainly 2,000 to 4,000 ft (600 to 1,200 m). Found in lower levels of forest (especially cloud forest). **EH**

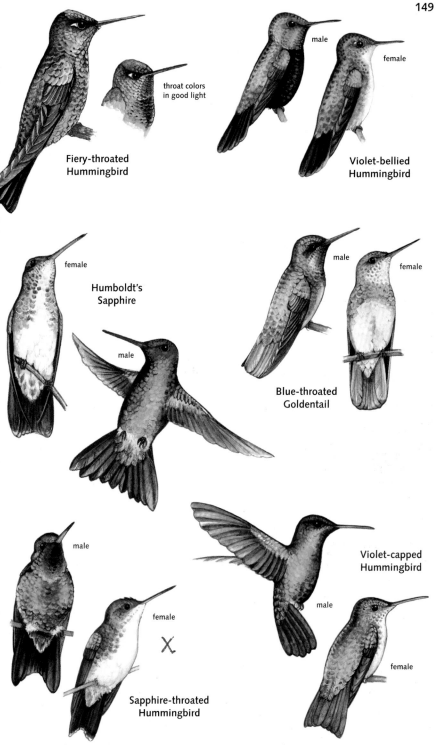

Fiery-throated Hummingbird

throat colors in good light

Violet-bellied Hummingbird

male

female

Humboldt's Sapphire

female

male

Blue-throated Goldentail

male

female

Sapphire-throated Hummingbird

male

female

Violet-capped Hummingbird

male

female

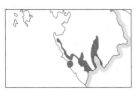

Pirre Hummingbird
Goethalsia bella

3.5 in (9 cm). Mostly **bright cinnamon-buff tail** makes both sexes unmistakable (within the very limited range of this species); also note male's **chestnut forehead and lores** and female's **cinnamon-buff underparts**. Common in southeastern Darién; mostly above 3,300 ft (1,000 m), but occasionally down to 2,000 ft (600 m); one record near sea level. Occurs in lower levels of forest. Formerly known as Rufous-cheeked Hummingbird. **EH**

Snowy-bellied Hummingbird
Amazilia edward

4 in (10 cm). Distinguished from Rufous-tailed Hummingbird by **sharp demarcation between green chest and pure white lower breast and belly. Lower back and rump are coppery**; tail is also coppery on birds in most of Panama (birds from Chiriquí eastward to southern Coclé have blue-black tail). Common on Pacific slope; on Caribbean slope, common from northern Coclé to eastern Colón Province, rare in Bocas del Toro; to over 6,000 ft (1,800 m). Found in open areas, scrub, and gardens.

Rufous-tailed Hummingbird
Amazilia tzacatl

4 in (10 cm). The most common and widespread hummingbird in Panama. Distinguished from Blue-throated Goldentail (p. 148) by **rufous tail** that is not metallic (Goldentail has metallic greenish gold tail); bill is longer and not as bright red. Snowy-bellied Hummingbird shows distinct demarcation between green chest and white lower breast and belly. Very common on both slopes, to 5,300 ft (1,600 m). Found in open areas, scrub, clearings, and gardens.

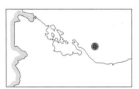

Escudo Hummingbird
Amazilia handleyi

4.5 in (12 cm). Very similar to Rufous-tailed Hummingbird (no range overlap) but distinctly larger. Restricted to Escudo de Veraguas Island off the coast of Ngöbe-Buglé, where it is abundant in forest and coastal vegetation. Considered a subspecies of Rufous-tailed Hummingbird by AOU. **Not illustrated. EV***

Blue-chested Hummingbird
Amazilia amabilis

4 in (10 cm). Nearly identical to Charming Hummingbird (no range overlap). Male relatively nondescript, but in good light, note **glittering bluish green crown, glittering violet-blue patch on upper chest,** and **blackish, slightly forked tail**. Female distinguished from similar hummingbirds by **conspicuous spotting on throat and upper breast** and a **bluish sheen on chest**; also note pinkish base to lower mandible; female White-necked Jacobin (p. 142) is larger and has all-dark bill; Scaly-breasted Hummingbird (p. 142) has conspicuous white tail corners. Fairly common in lowlands; occurs on entire Caribbean slope and on Pacific slope from Canal Area eastward; to 2,000 ft (600 m). Found in lower levels of forest and in adjacent clearings.

Charming Hummingbird
Amazilia decora

3.5 in (9 cm). Very similar to Blue-chested Hummingbird (no range overlap) but has longer bill; male has larger glittering crown patch, female has brighter bluish green crown; see that species for distinctions from other hummingbirds. Fairly common but local in western Chiriquí; to 4,000 ft (1,200 m). Inhabits lower levels of forest and adjacent clearings. **PL**

Pirre
Hummingbird

female

male

Snowy-bellied
Hummingbird

western
race

eastern
race

Rufous-tailed
Hummingbird

Charming
Hummingbird

female

male

Blue-chested
Hummingbird

female

male

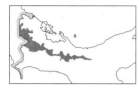

Stripe-tailed Hummingbird
Eupherusa eximia

4 in (10 cm). Male can be recognized by combination of **mainly green underparts, extensive white in tail**, and conspicuous **cinnamon wing patch** (visible at rest and in flight). Female very similar to smaller female Black-bellied Hummingbird, but has more prominent cinnamon wing patch and **two white outer tail feathers with black tips and outer edges** (in female Black-bellied, outer three tail feathers are mostly white). White-tailed Emerald lacks wing patch; female is whiter below and has black subterminal tail band. Uncommon in western highlands eastward to Veraguas; in western Chiriquí, mainly above 5,000 ft (1,500 m); in Veraguas, down to about 2,600 ft (800 m). Found in lower levels of forest and in adjacent clearings.

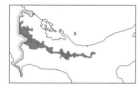

Black-bellied Hummingbird
Eupherusa nigriventris

3 in (8 cm). Male's **black face and underparts** make it unmistakable; also note **extensive white in tail** and **cinnamon wing patch**. Female very similar to larger female Stripe-tailed Hummingbird, but cinnamon wing patch is less conspicuous (sometimes not visible), and **outer three tail feathers are mostly white** (in female Stripe-tailed, outer two tail feathers are white with black tips and black outer edges). Female White-tailed Emerald is whiter below and has black subterminal tail band. Uncommon in western highlands, mainly on Caribbean slope; from 3,000 to 6,000 ft (900 to 1,800 m). Occurs in lower levels of forest and in adjacent clearings; prefers wetter forest. **WH**

White-tailed Emerald
Elvira chionura

3 in (8 cm). Smaller and has shorter bill than similar Stripe-tailed Hummingbird. Male distinguished from male of that species by **lack of cinnamon wing patch**. Female distinguished from female Stripe-tailed and female Black-bellied by **lack of cinnamon wing patch**; also has whiter underparts and **black subterminal tail band**. Uncommon in upper foothills and highlands in western Panama, above 3,300 ft (1,000 m). Found in lower levels of forest and in adjacent clearings. **WH**

White-vented Plumeleteer
Chalybura buffonii

4.5 in (12 cm). Conspicuous **enlarged white undertail coverts** are shared only with Bronze-tailed Plumeleteer; distinguished from that species by **black** (not pink) **feet** and **all-black bill**. Also distinguished by blue-black tail in most of its Panama range (race of Bronzed-tailed Plumeleteer in southeastern Darién also has a bluish tail). In comparison with other similar species, note relatively large size and long, slightly curved bill; female is evenly gray below, lacking scaling of similarly sized Scaly-breasted Hummingbird (p. 142) and female White-necked Jacobin (p. 142). Fairly common on Pacific slope from western Panamá Province eastward, and on Caribbean slope from northern Coclé to Canal Area; to 2,000 ft (600 m). Found in lower levels of forest.

Bronze-tailed Plumeleteer
Chalybura urochrysia

4.5 in (12 cm). Similar to White-vented Plumeleteer, but **enlarged white undertail coverts** are somewhat less prominent. Distinguished from that species by **bright pink feet** (often conspicuous), **reddish base to lower mandible**, and bronzy tail (note that race found in southeastern Darién has blue tail with only a faint bronze cast). See White-vented Plumeleteer for comparisons with other species. Uncommon in lowlands on Caribbean slope; somewhat more common in foothills of Caribbean slope and in foothills on Pacific slope (where it is local); to 3,000 ft (900 m). Found in lower levels of forest.

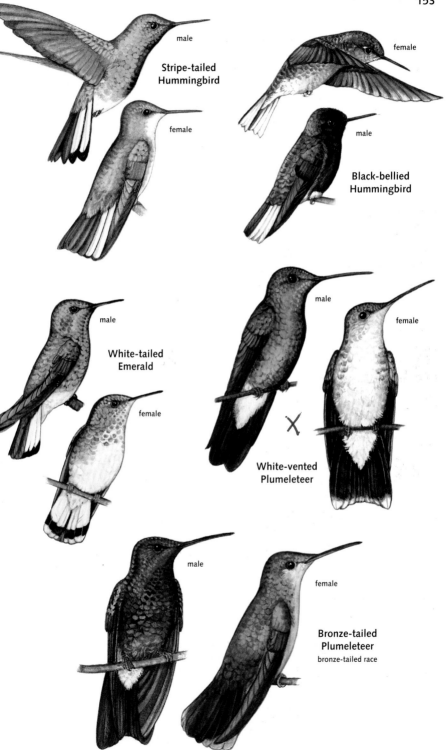

male

Stripe-tailed
Hummingbird

female

female

male

Black-bellied
Hummingbird

male

White-tailed
Emerald

female

male

female

X

White-vented
Plumeleteer

male

female

Bronze-tailed
Plumeleteer
bronze-tailed race

White-bellied Mountain-gem
Lampornis hemileucus

4 in (10 cm). Combination of **long white postocular stripe** and **white breast and belly** is distinctive; much smaller female Garden Emerald (p. 144) has distinct blackish mask; much larger female Magnificent Hummingbird has less prominent postocular stripe, is darker below, and has longer bill. Uncommon in foothills of western Panama; mainly on Caribbean slope, but occurs locally on Pacific slope; 2,500 to 3,500 ft (750 to 1,050 m). Found in lower levels of wetter forest and in adjacent clearings. **WH**

Purple-throated Mountain-gem
Lampornis calolaemus

4.5 in (11 cm). On both male and female, note **long white postocular stripe**; male has **purple gorget**; female has **mainly rufous underparts**. Male differs from male White-throated Mountain-gem in gorget color; from male White-bellied Mountain-gem in dark underparts. Female is slightly darker than female White-throated, but this is unlikely to be evident in the field. Common in foothills and highlands from central Chiriquí (Fortuna area) eastward to Coclé; 2,000 to 5,000 ft (600 to 1,500 m). Purple-throated males have occasionally been reported from western Chiriquí, in the Boquete and Cerro Punta areas, where White-throated males predominate. Found in lower levels of forest and adjacent clearings.

White-throated Mountain-gem
Lampornis castaneoventris

4.5 in (11 cm). Very similar to Purple-throated Mountain-gem, but male has **white gorget**; female is slightly paler than female of that species but probably is not distinguishable in the field. Common in highlands, from Costa Rican border to western Chiriquí (Boquete area); mostly above 5,000 ft (1,500 m). Found in lower levels of forest and in adjacent clearings. **WH**

Green-crowned Brilliant
Heliodoxa jacula

5 in (13 cm). Male is best identified by combination of large size, **mostly green coloration**, and **large, forked blue-black tail** (central tail feathers bronzy in eastern Darién); at close range note **small glittering violet spot on lower throat**. Female is distinguished by combination of **prominent green spotting on white underparts** and **thin white line below eye**. Immature resembles female but has variable amount of **cinnamon on chin and sides of throat**. Uncommon in foothills and highlands on both slopes; 1,700 to 7,000 ft (500 to 2,100 m). Occurs in lower levels of forest and in adjacent clearings.

Magnificent Hummingbird
Eugenes fulgens

6 in (15 cm). In good light, male's **violet crown** and **bluish green gorget** are distinctive among highland hummingbirds (much smaller Violet-crowned Woodnymph, p.146, is confined to lower elevations); in poor light, male can appear mostly blackish; then note large size and **long straight black bill**. Female is distinguished by combination of large size, **long straight black bill**, **white postocular stripe**, and **gray underparts**. Fairly common in highlands of western Chiriquí, mostly above 5,300 ft (1,600 m). Found in lower and middle levels of forest and in adjacent clearings.

Greenish Puffleg
Haplophaedia aureliae

4.5 in (11 cm). Distinctive **puffy white leg-tufts** are usually conspicuous but occasionally concealed; also note **scaly effect on underparts** and **coppery crown and rump**. Common in foothills and highlands of eastern Darién; mostly above 3,000 ft (900 m); sometimes down to 1,700 ft (500 m). Occurs in lower levels of forest.

White-bellied
Mountain-gem

male

female

Purple-throated
Mountain-gem

male

female

White-throated
Mountain-gem

male

adult
male

immature

adult
female

Green-crowned
Brilliant

Magnificent
Hummingbird

male

female

Greenish
Puffleg

Snowcap
Microchera albocoronata

2.5 in (6 cm). Spectacular male is **dark purple**, with **white cap** and **mostly white tail**, making it easy to identify. Female best recognized by **tiny size, short bill**, and **extensive white in tail**; differs from female White-tailed Emerald (p. 152) in **lack of green spotting on underparts**. Rare in western Panama, mainly on Caribbean slope, in foothills and lower highlands; 2,000 to 5,500 ft (600 to 1,650 m). Found in forest edge and in adjacent clearings.

Purple-crowned Fairy
Heliothryx barroti

5 in (13 cm). **Pure white underparts,** cleanly demarcated from green upperparts, are distinctive; also note short bill, black mask, and **long tapering tail with extensive white on sides**. Fairly common in lowlands and foothills on both slopes, to 4,000 ft (1,200 m); rare in highlands, to 6,000 ft (1,800 m). Has exceptionally graceful swooping and pirouetting flight, during which it often fans tail. Forages in middle and upper levels of forest but sometimes comes lower.

Long-billed Starthroat
Heliomaster longirostris

4.5 in (11 cm). Combination of **exceptionally long straight bill** and prominent **whitish malar stripe** is distinctive. Also note whitish streak down center of lower back and rump (sometimes concealed). Rare on Pacific slope and on Caribbean slope in Bocas del Toro, Canal Area, and eastern Kuna Yala; to 5,000 ft (1,500 m). Found in forest edge, scrub, and gardens.

Magenta-throated Woodstar
Calliphlox bryantae

3 in (8 cm). Similar to Purple-throated Woodstar but no range overlap. On male, combination of **long forked tail** (usually held closed) and **magenta gorget** is distinctive; also note **whitish spots on sides of rump**. Male Ruby-throated Hummingbird (p. 158) has red gorget, only slightly forked tail, and lacks rump spots. Female's **whitish spots on side of rump** and lack of spotting on throat distinguish it from female Volcano, Scintillant, and Glow-throated Hummingbirds (p. 158). Rare in upper foothills and lower highlands in Chiriquí and Veraguas; 3,000 to 5,800 ft (900 to 1,750 m). Found in forest edge and adjacent clearings. **WH**

Purple-throated Woodstar
Calliphlox mitchellii

3 in (7 cm). Similar to Magenta-throated Woodstar but no range overlap. On male, combination of **long forked tail** and **violet gorget** is unique in its range; also note **whitish spots on side of rump** and **broad whitish band across chest** (below gorget). On female, combination of **whitish band on chest, mainly rufous lower underparts**, and **whitish spots on side of rump** is distinctive in its range; female Rufous-crested Coquette (p. 146) has rufous on face and complete pale band on rump. Uncommon; recorded only from eastern Darién, both in vicinity of Cana and, above it, on Cerro Pirre; above 1,700 ft (500 m). Found in lower levels of forest and in adjacent clearings.

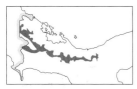

Snowcap

female

male

Purple-crowned
Fairy

female

male

Long-billed
Starthroat

Magenta-throated
Woodstar

male

female

Purple-throated
Woodstar

male

female

Ruby-throated Hummingbird *Archilochus colubris*

3 in (8 cm). On male, combination of **red gorget** and **black forked tail** is distinctive in its normal range in western Pacific lowlands; in western Pacific highlands, compare male Magenta-throated Woodstar (p. 156). Female distinguished by combination of **small white postocular spot** and **white tips to outer tail feathers**; most like female Garden Emerald (p. 144), but that species has long white postocular stripe (not just postocular spot) and distinct black mask. Immature male similar to female but has a few red flecks on throat. Very rare migrant (probably winter resident) in western Pacific lowlands (sometimes extends to highlands); most records from western Chiriquí. Inhabits open and scrubby areas.

Volcano Hummingbird *Selasphorus flammula*

3 in (8 cm). On male, **grayish purple to grayish green gorget** is unique; also note **mostly black tail** (feathers have some rufous edging). Male Scintillant Hummingbird has orange-red gorget and much more rufous in tail; no range overlap with Glow-throated Hummingbird. Female very similar to female Scintillant, but is less rufous below and has less rufous in tail (four central tail feathers are mostly green). See also Magenta-throated Woodstar (p. 156). Fairly common in Chiriquí highlands, mostly above 6,500 ft (1,950 m); generally occurs at higher elevations than Scintillant. Found in shrubby areas and forest clearings. **WH**

Scintillant Hummingbird *Selasphorus scintilla*

3 in (8 cm). Very similar to Glow-throated Hummingbird (little range overlap; see that species for distinctions). Male distinguished from male Volcano Hummingbird by **orange-red gorget** and **mostly rufous tail** (mostly black in Volcano). Female differs from female Volcano Hummingbird in having more rufous underparts and more rufous in tail. Fairly common in highlands of western Chiriquí; mostly 4,000 to 7,000 ft (1,200 to 2,100 m), occasionally to 9,900 ft (3,000 m); two specimen records from Ngöbe-Buglé, within range of Glow-throated. Found in shrubby areas, forest clearings, and gardens. **WH**

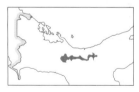

Glow-throated Hummingbird *Selasphorus ardens*

3 in (7 cm). Male distinguished from male Scintillant Hummingbird by **rose-red or purplish red** (not orange-red) **gorget** and **mostly black tail** (feathers have some rufous edging). Female very similar to female Scintillant, but has somewhat less rufous in tail (probably not reliably distinguishable in the field). Uncommon in highlands of Ngöbe-Buglé and Veraguas, mostly above 4,000 ft (1,200 m). Found in shrubby areas and forest edge. **WH***

Ruby-throated
Hummingbird

adult
male

female

Volcano
Hummingbird

male

female

Scintillant
Hummingbird

male

female

Glow-throated
Hummingbird

male

female

TROGONIDAE. Trogons are widely distributed in tropical areas of the world but reach their greatest diversity in the Americas. Often brightly colored, they have a distinctive chunky shape; large heads; short, stout bills; and, usually, squared-off tails (quetzals have tapering tail plumes). Trogons are generally lethargic, sitting quietly for long periods before sallying out to pluck fruit or glean large insects from vegetation. This behavior can make them surprisingly difficult to see, even when they are giving their loud, distinctive calls. Trogons nest in cavities they excavate in rotting wood or hollow out in termite or wasp nests. Some Panama species are quite similar; colors of underparts, orbital ring, and bill, and pattern on undertail are often keys to identification.

White-tailed Trogon
Trogon viridis

10.5 in (27 cm). **Mostly white underside of tail** distinguishes both sexes from all other trogons except male Baird's Trogon (no range overlap); note that female has some black barring on inner feather webs. In comparison to smaller Violaceous Trogon, note **blue orbital ring**; on female White-tailed, gray chest extends lower than on female Violaceous; female White-tailed also **lacks white band** separating chest from yellow belly. Fairly common on Caribbean slope from eastern Bocas del Toro eastward, and on Pacific from eastern Panamá Province eastward; to 1,800 ft (550 m). Found in lower and middle levels of forest. Typical call is a series of resonant *auwp* notes that first accelerate in tempo and at the same time increase in volume, and then decelerate.

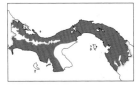

Violaceous Trogon
Trogon violaceus

9 in (23 cm). Male is only trogon with **yellow orbital ring**; further distinguished from male White-tailed Trogon by **barring on underside of tail** and **vermiculated pattern on wing**; from male Black-throated by **blue head and chest**. Female distinguished from female White-tailed by **barring on underside of tail** and **whitish orbital skin in front of and behind eye**; also, gray chest does not extend as low and is separated from belly by **white band**. Female Black-throated is brown above. Fairly common on both slopes, to 4,300 ft (1,300 m). Found in lower levels of forest edge and woodland. Call a series of evenly spaced high *hwilk* notes, all on the same pitch (less resonant than call of Slaty-tailed, p.162).

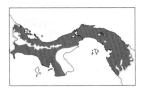

Black-throated Trogon
Trogon rufus

10 in (25 cm). On male, combination of **yellow belly** and **green head and chest** is unique; male further distinguished from male Violaceous Trogon by **blue orbital ring** and **yellow bill**. On female, combination of **yellow belly** and **brown upperparts** is unique. Fairly common on both slopes, to 3,000 ft (900 m). Found in lower levels of forest. Call a descending series of two to five *caow* notes, with noticeable spacing between each note.

Baird's Trogon
Trogon bairdii

11.5 in (29 cm). On male, combination of **white underside of tail** and **orange-red belly** distinguishes it from all other trogons. Female distinguished from larger Slaty-tailed Trogon (p. 162) by more orange (not as red) belly, **all-dark bill**, and **barring on underside of tail**; no range overlap with other red-bellied trogons. Uncommon and local in westernmost Chiriquí, mainly on Burica Peninsula; to 4,000 ft (1,200 m). Found at lower and middle levels, in remaining forest patches and in gallery forest. Call similar to that of White-tailed Trogon (but no range overlap). **PL**

White-tailed
Trogon

male

female

Violaceous
Trogon

male

female

Black-throated
Trogon

male

female

Baird's
Trogon

male

female

Collared Trogon
Trogon collaris

10 in (26 cm). Except for **red belly**, both sexes virtually identical to respective sexes of Orange-bellied Trogon. Male somewhat similar to male Lattice-tailed Trogon but distinguished by **dark eye, white breast band**, and broader white barring on tail. Males of races found in eastern Panama have wider white terminal tail band than those in west. Fairly common in highlands of western Chiriquí and Bocas del Toro; mostly from 4,000 to 8,000 ft (1,200 to 2,400 m), occasionally higher or lower; also fairly common in highlands of Darién, above 2,500 ft (750 m). Found in lower and middle levels of forest. Call a high-pitched descending *cow*, often doubled or tripled (sometimes notes are given in a longer series).

Orange-bellied Trogon
Trogon aurantiiventris

10 in (26 cm). Differs from Collared Trogon in **orange belly**; the two species overlap only in western Chiriquí. Fairly common; occurs in western foothills and highlands eastward to Cerro Campana (western Panamá Province); 2,000 to 6,000 ft (600 to 1,800 m). Found in lower and middle levels of forest. Call identical to that of Collared Trogon. **WH**

Black-tailed Trogon
Trogon melanurus

12 in (31 cm). **Yellow bill** (upper mandible mostly blackish in female) distinguishes both sexes from Slaty-tailed Trogon; male also has **white band separating green chest from red lower breast and belly**. No range overlap with Lattice-tailed Trogon. Fairly common from Canal Area eastward; to 1,800 ft (550 m). Found in lower and middle levels of forest and (sometimes) in mangroves. Call a series of evenly spaced, loud yelping *kwow* notes (higher pitched, faster, and more resonant than that of Slaty-tailed).

Slaty-tailed Trogon
Trogon massena

12.5 in (32 cm). Only trogon with **orangish red bill** (upper mandible mostly blackish in female). Lattice-tailed Trogon has pale eye and narrow barring on underside of tail. Both sexes of Black-tailed Trogon have yellow bill (only on base in female); male Black-tailed has white band separating green chest from red lower breast and belly. Common on both slopes, to 4,600 ft (1,400 m). Found in lower and middle levels of forest and (sometimes) in mangroves. Call a series of deliberate clucking *cuh* notes that sometimes accelerate at the beginning.

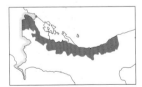

Lattice-tailed Trogon
Trogon clathratus

12 in (30 cm). Only trogon with **pale eye**. Further differs from Slaty-tailed Trogon in **yellow bill** (upper mandible mostly blackish in female) and **inconspicuous narrow white barring on underside of tail**. Male somewhat similar to male Collared Trogon but lacks white breast band and prominent white tail barring. Rare on western Caribbean slope; also extends into foothills on western Pacific slope; to 3,500 ft (1,050 m). Found in lower and middle levels of forest. Call a series of *cuh* notes, first becoming louder and then abruptly tapering off. **CL**

Collared Trogon
male western race
female

Orange-bellied Trogon
male
female

Black-tailed Trogon
male
female

Slaty-tailed Trogon
male
female

Lattice-tailed Trogon
male
female

Resplendent Quetzal
Pharomachrus mocinno

14 in (35 cm); male's plumes add up to 30 in (76 cm). Spectacular male, one of the most beautiful birds in the world, is unmistakable; extremely long **trailing plumes** are actually elongated uppertail coverts rather than tail feathers. Female, much larger than other trogons in range, is only one with combination of **green chest, gray lower breast and belly**, and **red vent**. Fairly common in western highlands, eastward to Veraguas; mostly above 5,000 ft (1,500 m); migrates between elevations in response to availability of fruiting trees. Found in middle and upper levels of forest, woodland, and adjacent clearings with tall trees. Call a series of resonant yelping *hwow* notes.

Golden-headed Quetzal
Pharomachrus auriceps

13.5 in (34 cm). On male, **golden green head** and **elongated green plumes extending past tip of tail** should preclude confusion. On female, combination of **bronzy brown head and chest** and **green back** is distinctive; all other green-backed trogons in range have vermiculated pattern on wing. Rare on Cerro Pirre in eastern Darién, above 4,000 ft (1,200 m). Found in middle and upper levels of forest. Call a distinctive whistled *whi-wheuu*, repeated six to eight times in rapid succession.

male

female

Resplendent
Quetzal

Golden-headed
Quetzal

male

female

MOMOTIDAE. This small family occurs in much of the neotropics but is most diverse in Central America. Motmots generally capture prey by sallying out from a perch; they eat insects, small vertebrates, and fruit. Panama's three largest species have racquet-tipped tails, which they often flick from side to side like a pendulum. Because motmots may sit quietly for long periods, they are less conspicuous than their size and coloration would suggest. Their loud hooting calls, heard most frequently near dawn, are often the best indicator of their presence. Motmots nest in long burrows they excavate in steep banks.

Rufous Motmot
Baryphthengus martii

17.5 in (44 cm). Distinguished from Broad-billed Motmot by **much larger size** and by **rufous on underparts that extends down to belly** (not just on chest); also note **violet** (not blackish) **primaries.** Common in lowlands and foothills on Caribbean slope, and on Pacific slope from western Panamá Province eastward; uncommon in foothills on Pacific slope of Veraguas and Coclé; to 4,300 ft (1,300 m). Found in lower levels of forest. Call a deep resonant rapid *boo-bup-bup* (usually three notes, sometimes two or just one).

Broad-billed Motmot
Electron platyrhynchum

12.5 in (32 cm). Similar to Rufous Motmot, but much **smaller; rufous on underparts confined to chest** rather than extending to belly. Also note **blue chin** (not always easy to see). Common on entire Caribbean slope and on Pacific slope from eastern Panamá Province eastward; rare on western Pacific slope (where it occurs locally in foothills); to 4,800 ft (1,450 m). Found in lower levels of forest. Call a hoarse *awwnnk!,* suggesting a whistle on a toy train.

Tody Motmot
Hylomanes momotula

7 in (18 cm). Easily distinguished from other motmots by **small size,** relatively **short tail,** and **prominent whitish stripes on face and throat;** also note short blue superciliary. Rare from Veraguas eastward, in foothills; also rare in Darién, where it occurs in both lowlands and foothills; to 4,000 ft (1,200 m). Found in lower levels of forest. Call a loud, yelping *gwa-gwa-gwa-gwa-gwa* (given more rapidly when excited).

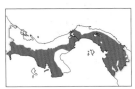

Blue-crowned Motmot
Momotus momota

15.5 in (39 cm). **Broad bright blue band on crown** makes this species easy to recognize. Race in western Panama is greenish on throat and lower belly, and dull rufous on breast and upper belly (a few birds are mostly rufous below); race in eastern Panama is mainly rufous brown below, sometimes with olive wash on throat and lower belly. Fairly common on Pacific slope; uncommon on Caribbean slope in Canal Area and eastern Kuna Yala; to 6,000 ft (1,800 m). Found in forest edge, gallery forest, and thickets and hedgerows in open areas. Usual call in western Panama is a hooting, two-noted *hoop, hoop,* with a distinct pause between notes; call is similar to that of Rufous Motmot but less resonant and with a longer gap between notes. In eastern Panama usually gives a single *whoop* (sometimes gives a two-noted *whoop-up,* with only a brief pause between notes). Plumage and vocal differences suggest western and eastern races may represent separate species.

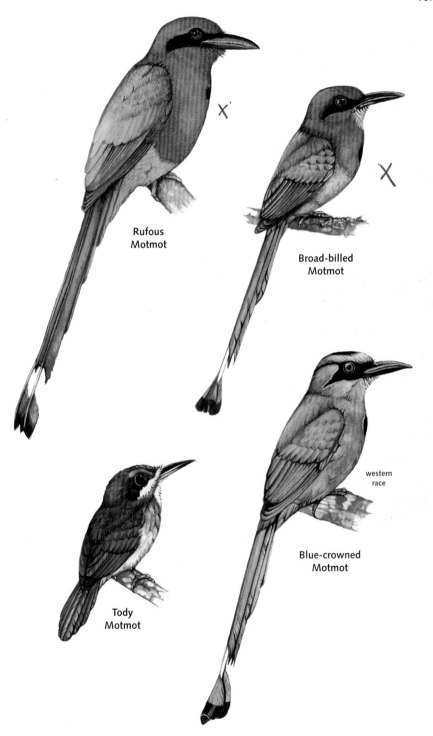

Rufous
Motmot

Broad-billed
Motmot

Tody
Motmot

western
race

Blue-crowned
Motmot

ALCEDINIDAE. This nearly cosmopolitan family reaches its greatest diversity in the tropics of the Old World. Only six species are found in the Americas, all of which occur in Panama. Although many kingfishers eat a wide variety of animals, the species found in Panama feed mainly on fish, usually caught by plunge-diving from a streamside perch. New World kingfishers nest in burrows excavated in steep banks. Similar species can be distinguished by size and the pattern of the underparts. Except for the Belted Kingfisher, males are more extensively rufous below than females.

Ringed Kingfisher
Megaceryle torquata

15.5 in (40 cm). By far the **largest** kingfisher. Distinguished from all but Belted Kingfisher by **blue-gray upperparts**; differs from that species by **mostly rufous underparts** (although female Ringed has wide blue band and narrow white band on breast). Common along coasts and on lakes, rivers, and larger streams; to 4,300 ft (1,300 m).

Belted Kingfisher
Megaceryle alcyon

12 in (30 cm). Distinguished from all but much larger Ringed Kingfisher by **blue-gray upperparts**; set apart from that species by **mainly white underparts with blue breast band** (on female, note narrow rufous breast band). Uncommon winter resident, from Sept to April (occasionally in May and June); mostly in lowlands but occasionally to lower highlands. Usually along coasts but sometimes found on lakes and larger rivers.

Amazon Kingfisher
Chloroceryle amazona

12 in (30 cm). Much larger than Green Kingfisher, with proportionately **larger, heavier bill**; further distinguished from that species by **lack of white spots on wings** and much less white in tail; on female, **single green breast band is broken in the middle**. Green-and-rufous Kingfisher is extensively rufous below. Fairly common on lakes, rivers, and larger streams; to 2,000 ft (600 m).

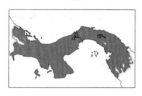

Green Kingfisher
Chloroceryle americana

7 in (18 cm). Differs from much larger Amazon Kingfisher by **white spotting on wings** and **extensive white in tail** (conspicuous in flight). Female has **one or two green breast bands: upper band is complete**; lower band, if present, may be complete or only partial. Green-and-rufous Kingfisher is extensively rufous below. Common on lakes, rivers, and streams; uncommon in mangroves and along coasts; to 5,300 ft (1,600 m).

Green-and-rufous Kingfisher
Chloroceryle inda

8.5 in (21 cm). More **extensively rufous below** than any other green-backed kingfisher; much smaller American Pygmy Kingfisher has white belly and vent. Rare on Caribbean slope and on Pacific slope from eastern Panamá Province eastward. Occurs in lowlands; found on small forest streams, and in freshwater swamps and mangroves.

American Pygmy Kingfisher
Chloroceryle aenea

5 in (13 cm). **Smallest** kingfisher; distinguished from Green-and-rufous Kingfisher by **white belly and vent**. Uncommon in lowlands on both slopes. Found on small streams in forest; also at edges of lakes and rivers with forested shores and in mangroves.

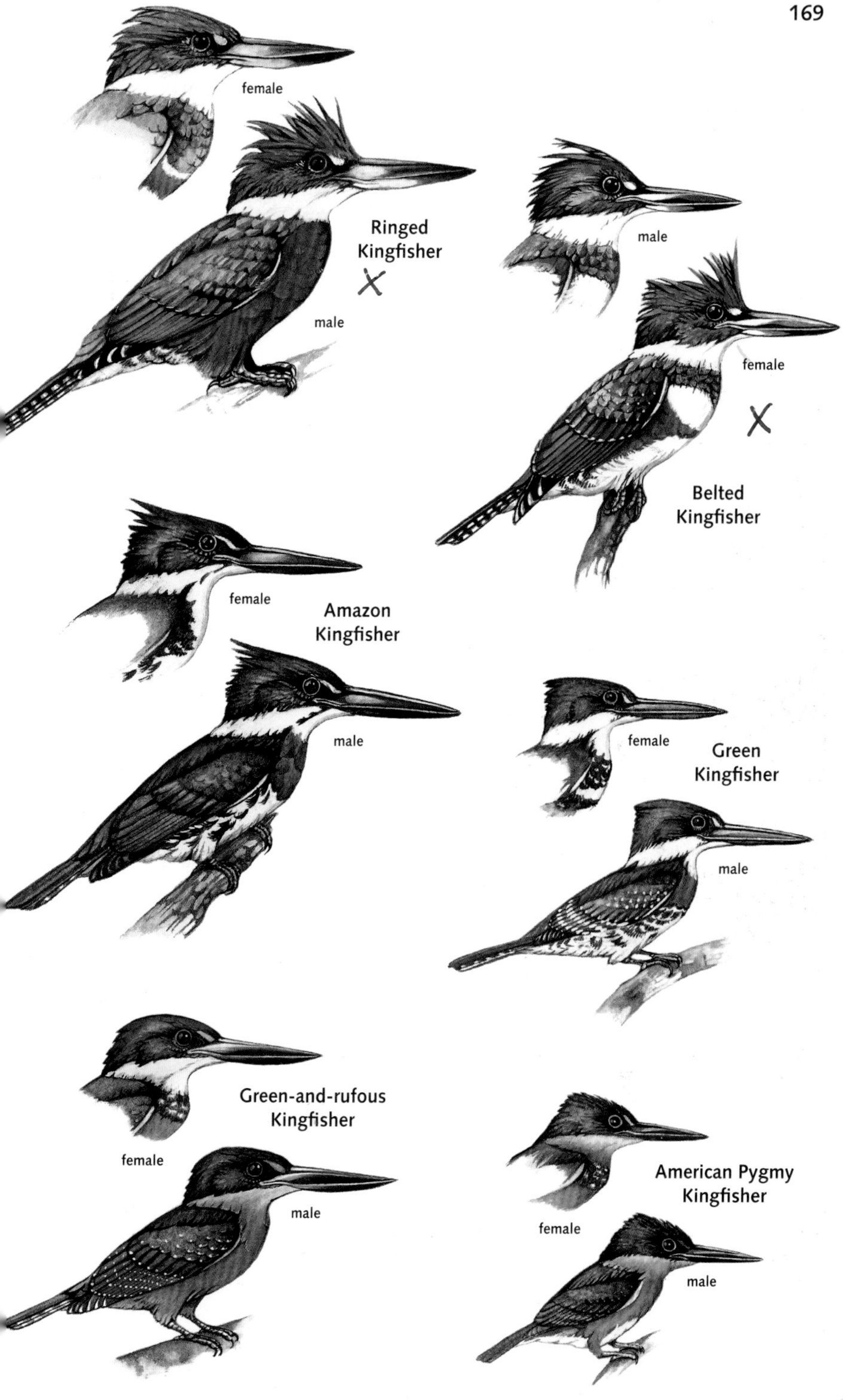

female

Ringed
Kingfisher

X

male

male

female

X

Belted
Kingfisher

female

Amazon
Kingfisher

male

female

Green
Kingfisher

male

Green-and-rufous
Kingfisher

female

male

American Pygmy
Kingfisher

female

male

BUCCONIDAE. Members of this family occur exclusively in the neotropics. Puffbirds generally have large heads and short tails and are clad mainly in black, white, and brown. They perch quietly for long periods, sallying out to catch large insects or sometimes small vertebrates. Puffbirds nest in holes they excavate in termite nests or in burrows they dig in the forest floor.

Barred Puffbird
Nystalus radiatus

8.5 in (21 cm). Extensive **narrow black barring above and below** and **broad buff collar** should preclude confusion; also note large heavy bill and upright posture. Female Fasciated Antshrike (p. 202) is much smaller, shows chestnut cap, lacks collar, and has more horizontal stance. Uncommon on Caribbean slope in northern Coclé, western Colón Province, and eastern Kuna Yala (one recent record from Canal Area); also uncommon on Pacific slope in Darién; to 2,000 ft (600 m). Found in lower and middle levels of forest and adjacent clearings with trees. Call a long, drawn-out "wolf-whistle," with a pause between notes: *wheeeet . . . wheeeeeeoooh.*

White-necked Puffbird
Notharchus hyperrhynchus

9.5 in (24 cm). Distinguished from Black-breasted and Pied Puffbirds by **white forehead** and much more extensive white on throat and chest. Fairly common in lowlands on both slopes. Inhabits forest canopy. Generally silent; call a high-pitched whickering.

Black-breasted Puffbird
Notharchus pectoralis

8.5 in (22 cm). In comparison to White-necked and Pied Puffbirds, note **large white ear patch** and **more extensive black on chest**. Fairly common in lowlands; found on Caribbean slope in Canal Area, eastern Colón Province, and western Kuna Yala, and on Pacific from Canal Area eastward. Inhabits forest canopy. Call a prolonged series of whistled *whik* notes, ending in a series of descending couplets: *whik-kooo, whik-koo, whik-ku.*

Pied Puffbird
Notharchus tectus

6 in (15 cm). Smallest black-and-white puffbird; distinguished from White-necked and Black-breasted Puffbirds by **narrow black breast band, narrow white superciliary, white patch on scapulars**, and **white tipping on tail**. Uncommon in lowlands; found on Caribbean slope in Bocas del Toro and from the Canal Area eastward, and on Pacific slope from eastern Panamá Province eastward. Occurs in canopy of forest and in adjacent clearings with trees. Call a series of high, thin, reedy two-syllable whistles, often slowing down at the end.

White-whiskered Puffbird
Malacoptila panamensis

7.5 in (19 cm). Readily identified by squat, "puffy" appearance, **streaked underparts**, and **conspicuous white "whiskers"** at sides of bill. Fairly common in lowlands, uncommon in foothills; to 4,000 ft (1,200 m). Found in lower levels of forest. Generally silent; call a high, thin, hissing whistle: *tseeuuu.*

Lanceolated Monklet
Micromonacha lanceolata

5 in (13 cm). **Heavy black streaking on pure white underparts** is distinctive; much more boldly patterned below than larger White-whiskered Puffbird, and **lacks pale spotting on upperparts**. Very rare on western Caribbean slope, from Bocas del Toro to Veraguas; on Pacific slope, occurs very marginally above Santa Fe (Veraguas); one record from eastern Darién; recorded from 1,600 to 2,300 ft (500 to 700 m). Found in lower levels of wet forest. Call a series of thin ascending whistles: *tseeeup, tseeeup, tseeeup.*

Barred Puffbird

White-necked
Puffbird

Black-breasted
Puffbird

Pied Puffbird

male

White-whiskered
Puffbird

female

Lanceolated
Monklet

Gray-cheeked Nunlet
Nonnula frontalis

5.5 in (14 cm). Combination of **gray sides of head** and **bright cinnamon throat and breast** is distinctive; also note narrow red orbital ring. Uncommon in lowlands; found on Caribbean slope, in northern Coclé and western Colón Province, and on Pacific slope, from eastern Panamá Province eastward. Formerly occurred on Caribbean slope in Canal Area, but no recent records. Found in lower levels of forest edge and woodland, often within dense vegetation or vine tangles. Sometimes joins mixed flocks. Call a long series of plaintive notes: *wheeip, wheeip, wheeip.*

White-fronted Nunbird
Monasa morphoeus

11 in (28 cm). Combination of **long bright red bill** and **mostly slate-gray plumage** makes this species unmistakable; also note white forehead. Race found in western Panama has white chin (also found in some individuals eastward to Canal Area); on races in eastern Panama, black on head extends onto chest. Uncommon on Caribbean slope in western Panama and on both slopes from eastern Colón and eastern Panamá Province eastward; to about 2,000 ft (600 m), rarely to 3,000 ft (900 m). Found in middle and upper levels of forest; often in small groups. Has a variety of loud whistled and whinnying notes; groups gather together to chorus raucously with bills pointed upward.

Jacamars

GALBULIDAE. The jacamars are slender, long-billed birds found only in the neotropics. They feed primarily on butterflies, perching on a branch with their bill angled upward until one passes by, then sallying out to catch it in flight. Jacamars nest mainly in burrows in banks.

Dusky-backed Jacamar
Brachygalba salmoni

6.5 in (17 cm). Distinguished from Rufous-tailed Jacamar by **much darker blackish green upperparts and chest band** and **black underside of tail**. Uncommon in lowlands of eastern Darién; to about 2,000 ft (600 m). Found in middle and upper levels of forest edge and in clearings with trees. Call a high thin rising *psee*, sometimes repeated in a long series.

Great Jacamar
Jacamerops aureus

11 in (28 cm). **Larger** with **much heavier bill** than the other two jacamars, and **lacks green chest band**. Female lacks white patch on lower throat. Uncommon on entire Caribbean slope and on Pacific slope from Canal Area eastward; to 2,000 ft (600 m). Found in lower and middle levels of forest. Call a piercing high-pitched whistle, slurred and fading away at the end: *keEEEEEaaahhh* (reminiscent of some hawks).

Rufous-tailed Jacamar
Galbula ruficauda

9 in (23 cm). Distinguished from Dusky-backed Jacamar by **rufous underside of tail** and **brighter green upperparts and chest band**. Race in eastern Panama lacks black on chin, and only the central pair of tail feathers is green (not two central pairs, as in western race). Great Jacamar is larger and lacks chest band. Uncommon in lowlands and foothills of western Chiriquí, Bocas del Toro, and Caribbean slope of Ngöbe-Buglé, to 4,000 ft (1,200 m); also uncommon in lowlands of eastern Darién, to 2,000 ft (600 m); two records from eastern Panamá Province. Found in lower and middle levels of forest edge and woodland and in clearings with trees. Call a sharp rising *wheeik!* (also gives a long series of similar notes that accelerate at the end).

Gray-cheeked
Nunlet

White-fronted
Nunbird

western
race

eastern race

Dusky-backed
Jacamar

male

Rufous-tailed
Jacamar

male
western race

Great
Jacamar

male

female
western race

RAMPHASTIDAE. The barbets are stocky, stout-billed birds that occur in tropical regions throughout the world. The toucans, exclusive to the neotropics, are famous for their outsize bills; they were formerly considered a separate family. Barbets and toucans feed mainly on fruit, supplemented by insects and other arthropods; the toucans also take lizards and other small vertebrates and raid the nests of other birds. All members of the family nest in holes in trees.

Spot-crowned Barbet *Capito maculicoronatus*

6.5 in (17 cm). Easily recognized by combination of **stout gray bill, black upperparts**, and **white lower underparts with bold black streaking on flanks**. Flank patch is orange in most of Panama range, bright red in Darién and Kuna Yala. Uncommon on Caribbean slope from northern Veraguas eastward and on Pacific from eastern Panamá Province eastward; to 3,000 ft (900 m). Found in middle and upper levels of forest. Often with mixed-species flocks. Call a series of harsh *kkaaak* notes.

Red-headed Barbet *Eubucco bourcierii*

6 in (15 cm). Male is the only Panama bird with combination of **red head** and **yellow bill**. Female also easily recognized by **black mask, blue-gray cheeks**, and **green back**. Uncommon from Chiriquí eastward to Coclé and in eastern Darién; mostly 3,000 to 6,000 ft (900 to 1,800 m); locally down to 2,000 ft (600 m). Found in all levels of forest. Often with mixed-species flocks. Generally silent; sometimes gives a fast series of hollow motmot-like notes: *who-ho-ho-ho-ho-ho-ho*.

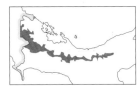

Prong-billed Barbet *Semnornis frantzii*

7 in (18 cm). Combination of **stout, blue-gray bill** and **tawny head and breast** is distinctive. Usually in small groups. Uncommon in all levels of forest in western highlands, mostly 5,000 to 7,500 ft (1,500 to 2,250 m); locally down to 3,300 ft (1,000 m). Call, often given in a long series, is a deep resonant *gwa-gwa-gwa-gwa-gwa* (sometimes performed as a duet or a group chorus). **WH**

Blue-throated Toucanet *Aulacorhynchus caeruleogularis*

12 in (30 cm). The only **mostly green** toucan. Birds in western Chiriquí have red spot on base of culmen (absent on birds from Ngöbe-Buglé eastward). Common in foothills and highlands of western Panama eastward to Coclé, and in eastern Darién; rare in foothills and highlands in western Panamá Province and western Kuna Yala; from 2,000 to 8,000 ft (600 to 2,400 m). Found in all levels of forest. Has variety of croaking or barking calls; sometimes gives hoarse *krrrik* in prolonged series. Considered by AOU to be included in Emerald Toucanet (*Aulacorhynchus prasinus*). **WH**

Yellow-eared Toucanet *Selenidera spectabilis*

15 in (38 cm). Only toucan with **almost entirely black underparts** (with exception of chestnut thighs and red vent). Also note male's conspicuous **yellow ear patch** and female's **chestnut crown and nape**. Uncommon in foothills on both slopes, mostly 1,500 to 3,500 ft (450 to 1,050 m), occasionally to 4,800 ft (1,450 m); rare in lowlands on Caribbean slope. Found in all levels of forest. Call a dry clacking croak, *kk-rrt*, similar to that of Keel-billed Toucan but lower and more grating.

female
eastern race

Red-headed
Barbet

male

female

Spot-crowned
Barbet

male
eastern race

western form

eastern form

Blue-throated
Toucanet

Prong-billed
Barbet

female

male

Yellow-eared
Toucanet

Collared Aracari
Pteroglossus torquatus

16.5 in (42 cm). Smallest toucan in most lowland areas; note **mostly whitish upper mandible** and **blackish band across yellow underparts**; Fiery-billed Aracari (no range overlap) has mostly orange upper mandible and red belly band. Race found in easternmost Darién has black stripe on side of upper mandible and lacks chestnut collar on hindneck. Common on entire Caribbean slope and on Pacific slope from western Panamá Province eastward; to 3,000 ft (900 m). Found in middle and upper levels of forest, usually in small groups of up to about a dozen. Call a high-pitched wheezy *khwhilk!*

Fiery-billed Aracari
Pteroglossus frantzii

16.5 in (42 cm). **Mostly reddish orange upper mandible** is diagnostic; also note red band on yellow underparts; no range overlap with similar Collared Aracari. Uncommon in Chiriquí and southern Veraguas; to 4,000 ft (1,200 m), rarely to 7,300 ft (2,200 m). Found in middle and upper levels of forest, usually in small groups of up to about a dozen. Call similar to that of Collared Aracari. **PL**

Keel-billed Toucan
Ramphastos sulfuratus

19 in (48 cm). **Gaudy, multicolored bill** makes this species unmistakable. Common on both slopes but more local on Pacific; to 3,000 ft (900 m). Found in upper levels of forest and woodland and in adjacent cleared areas with tall trees; less restricted to forest than Chestnut-mandibled Toucan, and sometimes even found in city parks and other urban areas where there are trees. Call a froglike, croaking *krre-ek*, often repeated for long intervals.

Chestnut-mandibled Toucan
Ramphastos swainsonii

21 in (53 cm). Largest toucan. Distinguished from Keel-billed Toucan by **chestnut and yellow bill**; in easternmost Darién, see Choco Toucan. Fairly common on entire Caribbean slope; also fairly common on Pacific slope, in both western Chiriquí and from western Panamá Province eastward; to 5,500 ft (1,650 m). Found in upper levels of forest. Call a loud, yelping *keeYOO, kedek, kedek* (sounds almost gull-like).

Choco Toucan
Ramphastos brevis

18.5 in (47 cm). Very similar to Chestnut-mandibled Toucan but smaller (about the size of Keel-billed); **dark areas of bill are blackish instead of chestnut**. Recorded in Panama only from vicinity of Cana in Darién. Found in forest. Best distinguished from Chestnut-mandibled by call, which is similar to that of Keel-billed but shorter and not as harsh. **EL**

Collared Aracari

chestnut-collared
race

Fiery-billed
Aracari

Keel-billed
Toucan

Chestnut-mandibled
Toucan

Choco Toucan

PICIDAE. The woodpeckers are a familiar group, found throughout much of the world (although not in Australasia). They are well adapted for drilling in wood, with strong, straight, chisel-like bills, grasping feet, and (except for the piculets) stiffened tail feathers that serve as props for hitching up trunks and branches. Woodpeckers feed mainly on wood-boring insects, but some may also take ants from the ground or pick off flying insects; they also consume some fruit (or nuts in the case of the Acorn Woodpecker). They can often be located by the tapping noise they make as they search for food; some also drum loudly as a territorial announcement. Most Panama species are strongly patterned in black and white, although some are mainly brown; males typically have more red on the head than females. Woodpeckers nest in tree holes they excavate; these are often later used by other species of hole-nesting birds.

Acorn Woodpecker
Melanerpes formicivorus

8 in (20 cm). **Striking facial pattern** makes this species virtually unmistakable; also the only woodpecker with **strongly streaked underparts**. In flight, **large white patch at base of primaries** and **white rump** are conspicuous. Common in western highlands, mainly above 4,000 ft (1,200 m). Found in upper levels of forest and in clearings with large trees. As its name implies, this species is partial to acorns; sometimes sallies from perch for insects. Has a variety of raucous calls, including a chuckling *k-k-k-RA-ha!* and a loud *AWWK-kruk*.

Golden-naped Woodpecker
Melanerpes chrysauchen

7 in (18 cm). Similar to Black-cheeked Woodpecker but has **yellow nape** and **broad white stripe down center of back** (back is barred in Black-cheeked); no range overlap. Hairy Woodpecker (p. 180) is also white on back but differs in head pattern. Rare in western Chiriquí, now mostly on Burica Peninsula; formerly eastward to southern Veraguas, but no recent records; to 4,300 ft (1,300 m). Found in middle levels of forest. Call a descending *whikaka*, similar to that of Black-cheeked Woodpecker.

Black-cheeked Woodpecker
Melanerpes pucherani

7 in (18 cm). Distinguished from Red-crowned Woodpecker by **black cheeks** and **black barring on lower underparts**; differs from Golden-naped Woodpecker in red nape and barred back (no range overlap). Common on entire Caribbean slope, ranging into more open areas in Bocas del Toro, where Red-crowned Woodpecker is absent; also common on Pacific slope, from Canal Area eastward (local on Pacific slope in western Panama); to 3,500 ft (1,050 m). Inhabits middle and upper levels of forest. Calls include a *churrr* and a *whika-ka*, similar to those of Red-crowned Woodpecker but not as harsh.

Red-crowned Woodpecker
Melanerpes rubricapillus

6.5 in (17 cm). Combination of **heavily barred back and wings** and **lack of strong barring on underparts** (flanks are faintly barred) is distinctive; Black-cheeked and Golden-naped Woodpeckers have black cheeks and distinct barring on lower underparts. Very common on Pacific slope eastward to Darién, and on Caribbean slope from northern Coclé eastward; mostly below 4,000 ft (1,200 m), occasionally to 6,000 ft (1,800 m). Found in open areas with scattered trees, tall scrub, mangroves, and urban areas. Call a loud harsh *churr-r-r-r*; also a rapid *whicka-whicka-whicka*.

female

male

**Acorn
Woodpecker**

male

**Golden-naped
Woodpecker**

female

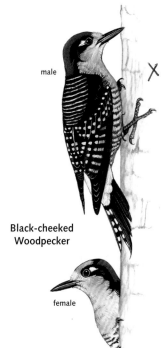

male

**Black-cheeked
Woodpecker**

female

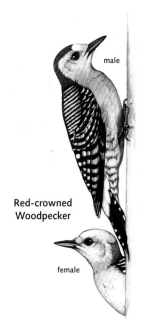

male

**Red-crowned
Woodpecker**

female

Olivaceous Piculet

Picumnus olivaceus

3.5 in (9 cm). Much **smaller** than other woodpeckers; note **dark cap with tiny speckles**. Best told from other small birds by distinctive foraging behavior: they creep on trunks and branches (not using tail for support) and cling acrobatically to small branches and twigs while pecking at them. The two xenops (p. 192) are similar in behavior but differ in color and pattern. Uncommon on Pacific slope and on Caribbean slope from Canal Area eastward; mainly below 4,000 ft (1,200 m), rarely to 5,400 ft (1,600 m). Found in lower and middle levels of forest edge, woodland, and scrub. Call a high, thin twittering.

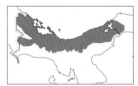

Yellow-bellied Sapsucker

Sphyrapicus varius

7.5 in (19 cm). In all plumages, **elongated white wing patch** is diagnostic. Female lacks red on throat. Hairy Woodpecker has similar head pattern but lacks wing patch and has white back. Most individuals seen in Panama are wearing dull immature plumage. Rare winter resident, recorded Nov to March. Occurs eastward to eastern Panamá Province; found most frequently in lowlands of Caribbean slope and in foothills and highlands on both slopes. Inhabits open areas with scattered trees, forest edge, and woodland. Usually silent in migration; sometimes gives a nasal *weee-unh*.

Hairy Woodpecker

Picoides villosus

6.5 in (17 cm). Combination of **striped head pattern, white back,** and **unmarked grayish brown underparts** is distinctive; Panama race is smaller and browner than those found in the United States and Canada. Common in western highlands, eastward to Ngöbe-Buglé; mostly above 5,000 ft (1,500 m), sometimes down to 4,000 ft (1,200 m). Found in forest (at all levels) and in adjacent clearings with trees. Call a sharp *wheek!*

Smoky-brown Woodpecker

Veniliornis fumigatus

6.5 in (16 cm). Only woodpecker that is so **uniformly brown** (though note red cap on male). Somewhat similar Red-rumped Woodpecker has barred underparts and red rump. Uncommon in foothills and highlands in western Panama eastward to Veraguas, and in eastern Darién; mostly 2,000 to 6,900 ft (600 to 2,100 m), occasionally down to sea level on Caribbean slope. Found in lower and middle levels of forest. Not very vocal; call a sharp *peek!*, softer than that of Hairy Woodpecker; also makes a churring *duwee-duwee-duwee*.

Red-rumped Woodpecker

Veniliornis kirkii

6.5 in (16 cm). Only small woodpecker with **red rump**, although this is often concealed by wings; in comparison to Smoky-brown Woodpecker, note **barred underparts**. Uncommon on Pacific slope in western Chiriquí and from eastern Panamá Province eastward; to at least 3,000 ft (900 m); fairly common on Coiba Island; formerly recorded from Veraguas foothills but no recent records. Found in lower and middle levels of forest. Not very vocal; call a thin *whik!*

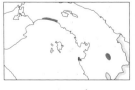

Spot-breasted Woodpecker

Colaptes punctigula

8.5 in (21 cm). Combination of **black crown** and **yellowish underparts with small black dots** is diagnostic. Rare and local in lowlands on Pacific slope in eastern Panamá Province and Darién. Occurs in middle and upper levels of mangroves, woodland, and open areas with scattered trees. Call a series of high, thin notes *pi-pi-pi-pi-pi-pi*.

female

male

Olivaceous Piculet

immature

male

Yellow-bellied Sapsucker

male

female

Hairy Woodpecker

male

female

male

Smoky-brown Woodpecker

female

male

Red-rumped Woodpecker

male

female

Spot-breasted Woodpecker

Golden-olive Woodpecker
Colaptes rubiginosus

8.5 in (21 cm). Distinguished from smaller Rufous-winged Woodpecker by **grayish white sides of head** and **dark gray crown**. Fairly common in foothills and highlands in western Panama, eastward to Coclé; mostly 1,600 to 5,600 ft (500 to 1,700 m). Found in middle and upper levels of forest, woodland, and clearings with trees. Calls include a churring trill and a sharp *wheenk!*

Rufous-winged Woodpecker
Piculus simplex

7 in (18 cm). Distinguished from larger Golden-olive Woodpecker by **olive-brown sides of head** and **spotting on chest**; rufous on wings is inconspicuous. Also note **pale eye**. Stripe-cheeked Woodpecker has whitish cheek stripe and small whitish spots on throat (no known range overlap). Rare in western Panama, eastward to Veraguas; to 4,000 ft (1,200 m). Found in lower and middle levels of forest. Call a loud, sharp, nasal *deeeah*; also a series of jaylike notes slurring downward: *heew heew heew heew.*

Stripe-cheeked Woodpecker
Piculus callopterus

6.5 in (17 cm). Distinguished from larger Golden-green Woodpecker by **whitish** (not yellow) **cheek stripe** and **whitish spotting on throat and chest**. Rufous-winged Woodpecker lacks whitish cheek stripe and has unspotted throat (no known range overlap). Uncommon in foothills on Pacific slope, from Coclé eastward, mostly from 1,000 to 3,300 ft (300 to 1,000 m); very rare in lowlands on Caribbean slope of eastern Panama. Found in lower and middle levels of forest. Usually quiet; call not described. **EL***

Golden-green Woodpecker
Piculus chrysochloros

8.5 in (22 cm). Distinguished from smaller Stripe-cheeked Woodpecker by **yellow** (not whitish) **cheek stripe, yellow throat**, and **barred** rather than spotted **chest**; female's **yellow crown** is unique. Rare in lowlands of eastern Panamá Province and Darién. One record from foothills above Cana, at 2,600 ft (800 m). Found in middle and upper levels of forest. Call a hoarse *wheerr.*

Cinnamon Woodpecker
Celeus loricatus

8 in (20 cm). Easily recognized by short crest and **mostly cinnamon-rufous upperparts**; in western Bocas del Toro, compare with Chestnut-colored Woodpecker. Fairly common on Caribbean slope, and on Pacific slope from Canal Area eastward; mostly below 1,600 ft (500 m). Found in upper levels of forest. Call a series of sharp descending whistles with a distinctive cadence: *wheee, wheee, whe-wit* (similar to call of Black-striped Woodcreeper, p. 198, but slower).

Chestnut-colored Woodpecker
Celeus castaneus

9.5 in (24 cm). Distinguished from Cinnamon Woodpecker by **uniformly rufous body** (on Cinnamon, underparts are distinctly paler than upperparts) and **contrast between body and paler head**. Uncommon in lowlands of Bocas del Toro and northern Ngöbe-Buglé, to 1,200 ft (350 m). Found in middle and upper levels of forest. Call a loud nasal *spYUrr*, sometimes followed by one or more *kek* notes.

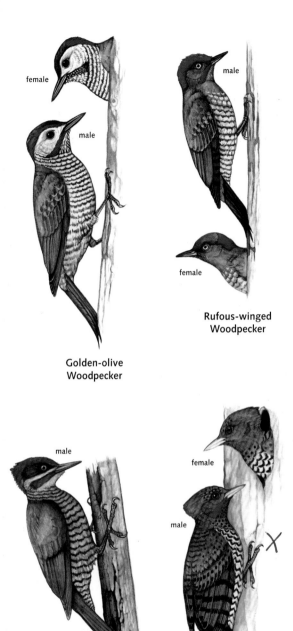

**Golden-olive
Woodpecker**

**Rufous-winged
Woodpecker**

**Stripe-cheeked
Woodpecker**

**Golden-green
Woodpecker**

**Cinnamon
Woodpecker**

**Chestnut-colored
Woodpecker**

Lineated Woodpecker

Dryocopus lineatus

12.5 in (32 cm). Similar in size to Crimson-crested and Pale-billed Woodpeckers; distinguished by **black patch around and behind eye** and by **white lines on back that are nearly parallel** (rather than converging in a V). Common on both slopes in lowlands; uncommon in foothills; to over 4,000 ft (1,200 m). Found at all levels in forest edge, woodland, and clearings with large trees. Call a loud *whikawhikawhikawhika*; also gives a rattling *ke-YUrrrr!* Drumming consists of several slow taps followed by an accelerating roll.

Crimson-crested Woodpecker

Campephilus melanoleucos

13.5 in (34 cm). Differs from Lineated Woodpecker in **lacking black patch around and behind eye; white lines on back converge in a V** (rather than being parallel). Very similar to Pale-billed Woodpecker (though no known range overlap); distinguished by **dark bill**; male further distinguished by white around base of bill and black-and-white ear patch, female by conspicuous white line on face. Fairly common from northern Ngöbe-Buglé and eastern Chiriquí eastward; to 3,000 ft (900 m). Found at all levels of forest and in clearings with large trees. Call a loud staccato *kehkekekekek*. Drumming consists of a series of three to five taps, the first loudest.

Pale-billed Woodpecker

Campephilus guatemalensis

12.5 in (32 cm). Distinguished from Crimson-crested (no known range overlap) and Lineated Woodpeckers by **pale whitish bill** and **lack of any white or black markings on sides of head** (female has black throat and black on front of crest). On Lineated, also note that white lines on back are almost parallel rather than converging in a V. Uncommon in lowlands of Bocas del Toro, northern Ngöbe-Buglé, and western Chiriquí; rare in foothills of western Chiriquí; to 5,300 ft (1,600 m). Found at all levels in forest and in clearings with large trees. Call a loud *kuh-kukehkek*. Drumming consists of two taps, the first louder.

Crimson-bellied Woodpecker

Campephilus haematogaster

12.5 in (32 cm). **Mostly red underparts and rump** are diagnostic. Also differs from other large woodpeckers in **buff** (rather than white) **facial stripe** and **lack of white stripes on back**. Rows of buff spots on flight feathers are conspicuous in flight (appearing as stripes) and may also show on closed wing. Rare on entire Caribbean slope and on Pacific slope in Darién (also occurs locally on Pacific slope in foothills of eastern Panamá Province); to 5,300 ft (1,600 m). Found in lower and middle levels of forest. Call a descending *kukukukrrrr*; also gives a series of sharp *pik!* notes. Drumming consists of two taps, the first louder.

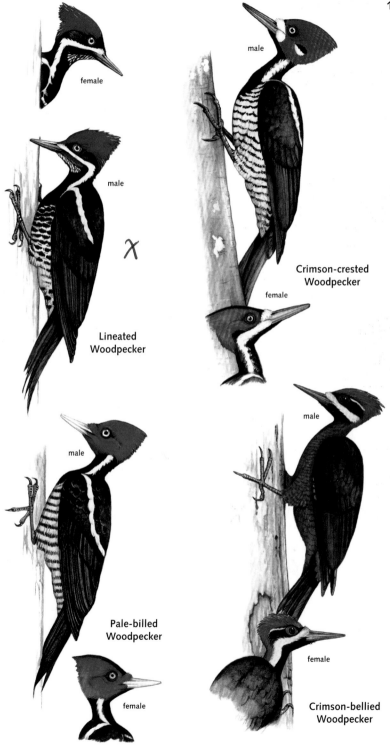

female

male

male

female

**Crimson-crested
Woodpecker**

χ

**Lineated
Woodpecker**

male

male

**Pale-billed
Woodpecker**

female

female

**Crimson-bellied
Woodpecker**

FURNARIIDAE. This large and very diverse family, known collectively as furnariids, occurs only in the neotropics. They are mainly insectivorous, and most are drab in coloration, often either brown or rufous, marked with paler streaks or spots. The ovenbirds, named for a South American species that makes a mud nest shaped like an earth-oven, comprise a wide variety of adaptive types, including species that recall titmice, creepers, wrens, thrushes, and other groups. The woodcreepers, until recently considered a separate family, are somewhat woodpecker-like, hitching themselves up trunks and branches with the aid of stiffened tail feathers; woodcreepers, however, glean insects from bark rather than drill into wood. Many furnariids are quite similar in appearance and are best distinguished by the pattern of streaks and spots on the head, back, or underparts. In Panama, ovenbirds reach their greatest diversity in foothills and highlands, while most woodcreepers occur in lowlands.

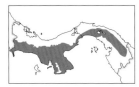

Pale-breasted Spinetail
Synallaxis albescens

6 in (15 cm). Combination of **long graduated tail, rufous crown and wing coverts**, and **pale underparts** is distinctive. Slaty Spinetail is much darker below; Wedge-tailed Grass-Finch (p. 358) is streaked on back and lacks rufous. Common on Pacific slope eastward to Darién; to 4,100 ft (1,250 m). Found in thickets and scrub in pastures and other open areas. Skulking; usually remains hidden in dense vegetation but sometimes sings from the top of shrubs or other exposed perch. Song, given frequently, is sharp sneezing *fwee-BEK*.

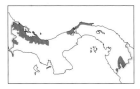

Slaty Spinetail
Synallaxis brachyura

6 in (15 cm). Shares **long graduated tail** and **rufous crown and wing coverts** with Pale-breasted Spinetail, but rest of plumage is mostly **dark slaty gray**. Uncommon locally on both slopes, mostly in lowlands and lower foothills; in western Chiriquí mainly between 2,000 and 4,500 ft (600 and 1,350 m). Found in shrubs and thick vegetation in clearings or forest edge. Secretive, usually remaining in dense cover; detected mostly by voice, a hoarse, descending *ch-ch-churrrrrr*.

Red-faced Spinetail
Cranioleuca erythrops

6 in (15 cm). Combination of **rufous cheeks and crown** and contrasting **olive-brown nape and back** is distinctive. More slender than any foliage-gleaner (pp. 190-193). Fairly common in western highlands eastward to Coclé and in highlands of eastern Darién; from 3,000 to 7,000 ft (900 to 2,100 m). Found in middle levels of forest. Differs in habits and habitat from other mainland spinetails; forages acrobatically in epiphytes, dead-leaf clusters, and on twigs. Often with mixed-species flocks. Song a series of very high-pitched trilling notes, accelerating at the end.

Coiba Spinetail
Cranioleuca dissita

5.5 in (14 cm). No similar species is found within its limited range on Coiba Island; note **rufous upperparts** and **buffy superciliary**. Fairly common in middle levels of forest and woodland, where it forages actively on trunks and branches and in foliage and vine tangles. Song similar to that of Red-faced Spinetail, but slower and not as high pitched: *che-che-che-chupchupchupchup*. Considered a subspecies of Rusty-backed Spinetail (*Cranioleuca vulpina*) by AOU. **PL***

Double-banded Graytail
Xenerpestes minlosi

4.5 in (12 cm). Only furnariid with **mostly gray upperparts** (darker on crown); also note **prominent whitish superciliary, two white wing-bars, and graduated tail**. Somewhat similar to some migrant warblers, but has longer, heavier bill and different foraging behavior. Forages acrobatically, especially in vine tangles; often hangs upside down. Uncommon in eastern Panamá Province and in Darién; to 3,300 ft (1,000 m). Found at middle levels of forest and woodland. Song is a long, dry, extremely rapid chattering trill, constant in pitch but increasing in volume.

Pale-breasted
Spinetail

adult

immature

Slaty
Spinetail

adult

immature

Red-faced
Spinetail

Coiba
Spinetail

Double-banded
Graytail

Spotted Barbtail
Premnoplex brunnescens

5.5 in (14 cm). No other furnariid shows combination of **dark brown plumage** with **large buff spots below**. Both treerunners have white rather than buffy throats; Wedge-billed Woodcreeper (p. 200) is streaked rather than spotted below and has rufous tail. Common in foothills and highlands; occurs from 2,000 to 7,500 ft (600 to 2,250 m). Found in lower and middle levels of moist forest. Creeps along trunks and branches, sometimes hanging upside down. Often accompanies mixed-species flocks. Song a rapid high-pitched buzzy trill; call a high sharp *tseep!*

Beautiful Treerunner
Margarornis bellulus

5.5 in (14 cm). Combination of **narrow white eye-ring, white throat**, and **conspicuous whitish spots on breast** should preclude confusion in its very limited range. Spotted Barbtail has buffy throat and buffy spotting below; Lineated Foliage-gleaner (p. 190) has narrow buff streaking below. Behavior similar to that of Ruddy Treerunner. Rare in highlands of eastern Panama, mostly above 3,300 ft (1,100 m). Found in middle and upper levels of forest. Call a high sharp *tsip!* **EH***

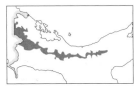

Ruddy Treerunner
Margarornis rubiginosus

6.5 in (16 cm). No other furnariid has combination of nearly **uniform bright rufous plumage** with **white superciliary and throat**. Uncommon in western highlands eastward to Coclé; in Chiriquí, mostly above 6,000 ft (1,800 m); in eastern part of range, down to 4,000 ft (1,200 m). Found at all levels in forest. Like a woodcreeper, it hitches up branches and trunks using its tail for support; sometimes hangs upside down and sometimes gleans in dead-leaf clusters. Often with mixed-species flocks. Call a variety of sharp high twittering notes. **WH**

Striped Woodhaunter
Hyloctistes subulatus

6.5 in (17 cm). Distinguished from other lowland furnariids by **indistinct buffy streaking on breast**. Western Panama race also has buffy streaks on back (absent in eastern Panama race). On Lineated Foliage-gleaner (p. 190), fine buffy streaking below is much more distinct. Similar in pattern to some woodcreepers (pp. 194-201), but unlike them, does not climb on trunks. Rare and local on both slopes, to 5,000 ft (1,500 m). Found in lower levels of forest. Unobtrusive; typically forages in dense vines and in epiphytes. Sometimes accompanies mixed-species flocks. Song a series of five to seven sharp, evenly spaced notes: *kip-kip-kip-kip-kip*; also gives a harsh *swirk!*

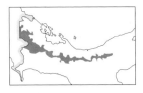

Streak-breasted Treehunter
Thripadectes rufobrunneus

8.5 in (21 cm). Large size, **tawny streaking on throat and chest**, and **lack of streaking on back** distinguish it from other furnariids. Ruddy Foliage-gleaner (p. 192) lacks chest streaking; immature Lineated Foliage-gleaner (p. 190) has tawny superciliary and streaks on nape. Uncommon in western highlands, eastward to Coclé; mostly 4,000 to 8,000 ft (1,200 to 2,400 m), occasionally as low as 2,500 ft (750 m). Found in lower levels of forest; often near streams. Song a grating *ki-krruuk!*, call a short sharp *chert!* **WH**

Spotted
Barbtail

Beautiful
Treerunner

Ruddy
Treerunner

western
race

Striped
Woodhaunter

Streak-breasted
Treehunter

Lineated Foliage-gleaner
Syndactyla subalaris

7 in (18 cm). Adult distinguished by **distinct buffy streaking on both underparts and upperparts** (especially nape). On Striped Woodhaunter (p. 188), streaking is much blurrier. Immature distinctive, with **bright tawny throat, superciliary (behind eye), and streaks on nape**; Streak-breasted Treehunter (p. 188) lacks superciliary and streaking above. Fairly common in foothills and highlands; mostly above 5,000 ft (1,500 m) in western Chiriquí, sometimes down to 2,500 ft (750 m) in eastern part of range. Found in lower and middle levels of forest. Gleans in dead-leaf clusters and epiphytes; occasionally accompanies mixed-species flocks. Call a series of sharp *chit* notes, starting off slowly, accelerating, then falling off at the end.

Scaly-throated Foliage-gleaner
Anabacerthia variegaticeps

6 in (15 cm). **Conspicuous ochraceous eye-ring and superciliary (behind eye)** are distinctive; also note grayish olive crown contrasting with brown back. Buff-throated Foliage-gleaner has buff eye-ring and superciliary; immature Lineated Foliage-gleaner has tawny throat. Uncommon in western highlands eastward to Ngöbe-Buglé; usually 4,000 to 6,000 ft (1,200 to 1,800 m), sometimes down to 3,500 ft (1,050 m). Found in middle levels of forest. Forages along branches and in leaf clusters and epiphytes. Often with mixed-species flocks. Call a dry, sharp *whik!*

Slaty-winged Foliage-gleaner
Philydor fuscipenne

6.5 in (17 cm). **Dusky wings contrasting strongly with chestnut back** distinguish it from other furnariids and Russet Antshrike (p. 204); also note **conspicuous tawny superciliary**. Uncommon in foothills, rare in lowlands; occurs locally on Caribbean slope from Veraguas eastward, and on Pacific in Darién; also found locally on Pacific slope in Veraguas and eastern Panamá Province but only in foothills; to at least 3,500 ft (1,050 m). Found in lower levels of forest, frequently with mixed-species flocks. Call a thin *chit!*

Buff-fronted Foliage-gleaner
Philydor rufum

7.5 in (19 cm). **Cinnamon-buff forehead, superciliary, and underparts** are distinctive. Buff-throated Foliage-gleaner (mostly at lower elevations) lacks buff on forehead. Very rare in highlands of western Chiriquí and Bocas del Toro; 4,000 to 7,000 ft (1,200 to 2,100 m). Found in upper levels of forest. Sometimes accompanies mixed-species flocks. Song a series of sharp metallic *shrik* notes, sometimes decelerating at the end.

Buff-throated Foliage-gleaner
Automolus ochrolaemus

7 in (18 cm). This is the most common and widespread foliage-gleaner in lowlands. **Conspicuous buff throat, eye-ring, and superciliary (behind eye)** are distinctive. Scaly-throated Foliage-gleaner has ochraceous eye-ring and superciliary; Russet Ant-shrike (p. 204) has heavier, hooked bill, lacks eye-ring, and shows brighter rufous on wings. Fairly common on entire Caribbean slope and on Pacific slope from eastern Panamá Province eastward; local on Pacific slope in Chiriquí and Veraguas; mostly below 3,000 ft (900 m), occasionally to 4,300 ft (1,300 m). Found in lower levels of forest. Forages actively in dense vegetation and dead-leaf clusters, but furtive and not often seen; often with mixed-species flocks. Song a rapid, descending series of sharp notes *ki-ki-kikikikikrrrr*; also a buzzy *krrrt!*

adult

Lineated
Foliage-gleaner

immature

Scaly-throated
Foliage-gleaner

Slaty-winged
Foliage-gleaner

Buff-fronted
Foliage-gleaner

Buff-throated
Foliage-gleaner

Ruddy Foliage-gleaner
Automolus rubiginosus

8 in (20 cm). Lacks any strong pattern. Best recognized by mostly **dark brown coloration**; note slightly contrasting **cinnamon-rufous throat and breast**. Race in western Panama has dark chestnut tail; race in eastern Panama is darker overall and has black tail. Streak-breasted Treehunter (p. 188) is streaked on chest; Ruddy Woodcreeper (p. 196) is brighter rufous and climbs on trunks; Tawny-throated Leaftosser (p. 194) has thinner bill and forages on ground. Rare and very local; mostly 2,000 to 4,500 ft (600 to 1,350 m). Found in lower levels of forest, particularly in dense vegetation in forest edge or in ravines. Calls include a harsh grating *kreee-YUP!* and a nasal, whining *keee-ahh*.

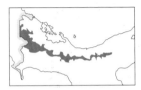

Buffy Tuftedcheek
Pseudocolaptes lawrencii

8 in (20 cm). Easily recognized by **conspicuous, flared, pale buffy tufts on cheeks**. Uncommon in western highlands eastward to Coclé; in Chiriquí, mostly above 6,000 ft (1,800 m); in eastern part of range, down to 4,000 ft (1,200 m). Found in middle and (more often) upper levels of forest. Forages actively in epiphytes, especially bromeliads; often with mixed-species flocks. Call a sharp *srit!*

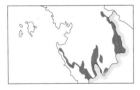

Sharp-tailed Streamcreeper
Lochmias nematura

6 in (15 cm). Resembles a leaftosser (p. 194), but conspicuous **white spotting on underparts** should prevent confusion. Very rare in foothills and highlands of eastern Darién; recorded from 2,200 to 5,000 ft (725 to 1,525 m). Found on ground and on rocks along small mountain streams in forest. Forages in dense undergrowth, flicking aside leaves with its bill in leaftosser fashion. Song a series of dry *chit* notes, accelerating and becoming louder, then dropping off abruptly.

Streaked Xenops
Xenops rutilans

4.5 in (12 cm). Shares **short wedge-shaped bill** and conspicuous **white malar stripe** with Plain Xenops, but **crown, nape, and back are streaked with buff** and **underparts are streaked with white** (race found in Darién has somewhat less streaking). Behavior similar to that of Plain Xenops. Very rare in highlands of western Panama and Darién (mostly 4,000 to 6,000 ft [1,200 to 1,800 m] in west, down to about 1,800 ft [550 m] in Darién); two recent records from lowlands of eastern Panamá Province. Found in middle and upper levels of forest. Song a series of six to eight thin, sibilant *swik* notes (less harsh than those of Plain Xenops).

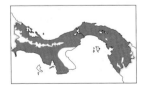

Plain Xenops
Xenops minutus

4.5 in (12 cm). Combination of **short wedge-shaped bill** with upturned lower mandible and conspicuous **white crescent-shaped malar stripe** distinguishes it from all other species except Streaked Xenops, from which it differs in **unstreaked back and underparts**. Wedge-billed Woodcreeper (p. 200) has similar bill but lacks facial stripe and has longer tail. Common on both slopes, usually below 3,000 ft (900 m), rarely to 6,200 ft (1,860 m). Found at middle and upper levels of forest. Gleans acrobatically on small branches and twigs, often hanging upside down. Usually found with mixed-species flocks. Song a rapid series of 8 to 12 high *chik* notes, accelerating slightly.

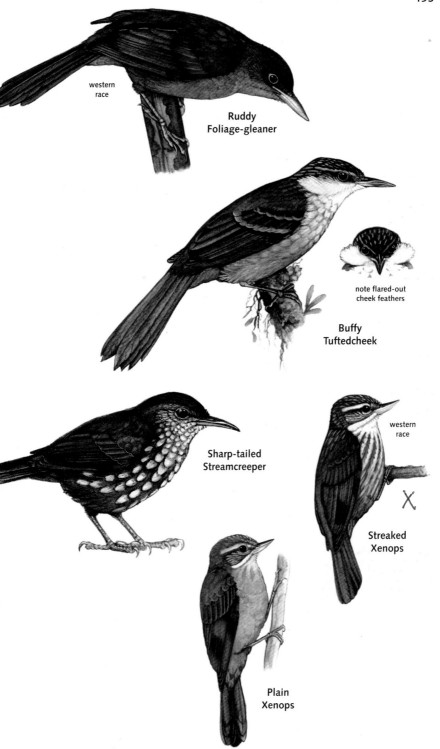

western race

Ruddy
Foliage-gleaner

note flared-out
cheek feathers

Buffy
Tuftedcheek

Sharp-tailed
Streamcreeper

western
race

Streaked
Xenops

Plain
Xenops

Tawny-throated Leaftosser — *Sclerurus mexicanus*

6.5 in (16 cm). **Tawny throat** distinguishes it from other leaftossers; further distinguished from Scaly-throated Leaftosser by rufous rump. Song Wren (p. 296) has conspicuous blue patch around eye and barred wings and tail. Rare and local in lowlands and foothills on Caribbean slope; also rare and local in foothills and lower highlands on Pacific slope; to 5,300 ft (1,600 m). Found on and near ground in forest. Furtive and inconspicuous, leaftossers forage by flicking up leaves from the forest floor with their long bills. Song a series of four to nine descending whistles, each becoming slightly shorter, sometimes beginning or ending with a trill or churr; call a sharp *fwhkk!*

Gray-throated Leaftosser — *Sclerurus albigularis*

6.5 in (16 cm). **Pale gray throat contrasting strongly with chestnut chest** distinguishes it from other leaftossers; further distinguished from Scaly-throated Leaftosser by rufous rump. Very rare in highlands of western Chiriquí; 4,000 to 6,000 ft (1,200 to 1,800 m). Found on and near ground in forest. Behavior similar to that of Tawny-throated Leaftosser. Song a long, variable series of high squeaky whistles (often in groups of three), interspersed with sharper notes.

Scaly-throated Leaftosser — *Sclerurus guatemalensis*

6.5 in (17 cm). **Scaly pattern on throat** (formed by white feathers with dark edges) and **lack of rufous rump** distinguish it from other leaftossers. Southern Nightingale-Wren (p. 296) has much shorter tail and lacks scaly throat. Behavior similar to that of Tawny-throated Leaftosser. Uncommon on both slopes, to 4,100 ft (1,250 m). Found on and near ground in forest. Song a long series (sometimes continuing for several minutes) of sharp whistles, each phrase first increasing in pitch and volume and then decreasing; call a sharp *shwek!*, sharper and harsher than that of Tawny-throated Leaftosser.

Olivaceous Woodcreeper — *Sittasomus griseicapillus*

6 in (15 cm). Only woodcreeper with **uniformly gray head and breast**; also note **short, straight bill**. Uncommon on Pacific slope, rare on Caribbean slope; to 5,000 ft (1,500 m). Found at middle levels in forest edge, adjacent clearings with trees, woodland, and mangroves. Song a high, fast musical trill.

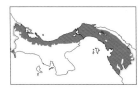

Long-tailed Woodcreeper — *Deconychura longicauda*

7 in (18 cm). Easily confused with several other woodcreepers; best distinguished by combination of medium-length, straight, dark bill, **unstreaked back**, and **buffy spots** (not streaks) **on chest**. Appears more slender with longer tail than other woodcreepers. Uncommon on Caribbean slope and on Pacific in western Chiriquí and from western Panamá Province eastward; to 3,500 ft (1,050 m). Found in lower and middle levels of forest. Song a series of sharp high chips, starting slowly, accelerating, and then trailing off gradually in an irregular rhythm.

Tawny-throated
Leaftosser

Gray-throated
Leaftosser

Scaly-throated
Leaftosser

Long-tailed
Woodcreeper

Olivaceous
Woodcreeper

Plain-brown Woodcreeper
Dendrocincla fuliginosa

8.5 in (21 cm). In its range, only woodcreeper with unstreaked dull brown crown, back, and underparts; also note **grayish cheeks and throat separated by dark malar stripe**. Ruddy Woodcreeper is bright rufous all over and lacks malar stripe; Tawny-winged Woodcreeper (no range overlap) has strong contrast between tawny flight feathers and rest of wing. Fairly common on entire Caribbean slope and on Pacific slope from western Panamá Province eastward; to 4,600 ft (1,400 m), sometimes higher. Found in lower and middle levels of forest. Regularly follows army-ant swarms. Call a sharp hoarse *spaik!*; song a loud churring, increasing in volume and then rapidly trailing off.

Tawny-winged Woodcreeper
Dendrocincla anabatina

7 in (18 cm). Best field mark is **tawny flight feathers** that contrast with olive-brown on rest of wing and on back; also note pale buff throat and narrow buffy superciliary. Plain-brown Woodcreeper (no range overlap) has uniform wings and dark malar stripe. Uncommon in lowlands, rare in foothills, of western Chiriquí; to 4,100 ft (1,250 m). Found in lower and middle levels of forest. Regularly follows army-ant swarms; puffs out throat, raises crown feathers, and flicks wings while foraging excitedly. Call a somewhat musical *dreeuh*; song a long series of rapid, evenly spaced *whicka* notes, all on the same pitch.

Ruddy Woodcreeper
Dendrocincla homochroa

7.5 in (19 cm). Only woodcreeper that is so **uniformly rufous** (brightest on crown); also note **gray lores**. Rare in lowlands and uncommon in foothills and lower highlands on Pacific slope; a few records from Caribbean slope in foothills of western Bocas del Toro and in lowlands in Canal Area; to 4,500 ft (1,350 m). Found in lower and middle levels of forest. Regularly follows army ants; often flicks wings. Song a series of *whik* notes, becoming slower toward end.

Strong-billed Woodcreeper
Xiphocolaptes promeropirhynchus

12 in (31 cm). Largest woodcreeper. Best recognized by **exceptionally long, heavy, slightly decurved bill**; also note indistinct dusky malar stripe. Cocoa Woodcreeper (p. 198), mostly at lower elevations, is smaller and has much thinner bill; Black-banded Woodcreeper (p. 198) is nearly as large but has less heavy bill and more distinct black barring on lower underparts (Strong-billed may have indistinct barring on belly). Very rare in western Panama eastward to Coclé; recorded from 3,000 to 3,600 ft (900 to 1,100 m). Found in lower and middle levels of forest. Song a descending series of loud, whistled, paired notes: *kur-WHEEP!, kur-WHEEP!, kur-WHEEP, kur-WHEEP, kur-wheep, kur-wheep, kur-wheep*; call a whining *kurrrrr-YAK!*

Northern Barred-Woodcreeper
Dendrocolaptes sanctithomae

10 in (26 cm). **Fine black barring above and below** is diagnostic (but may be difficult to see in poor light). On Black-banded Woodcreeper (p. 198), banding is confined to lower underparts. Uncommon in lowlands and rare in foothills. Occurs on entire Caribbean slope and on Pacific slope in Chiriquí and from eastern Panamá Province eastward; also found locally on Pacific slope in Veraguas and western Panamá Province, where it is restricted to foothills; to 3,600 ft (1,100 m). Inhabits lower levels of forest. Often found with army-ant swarms; occasionally found with mixed-species flocks. Song a series of three to six paired, whistled notes, each pair slurred upward *dooo-weeE, dooo-weeE, dooo-weeE*.

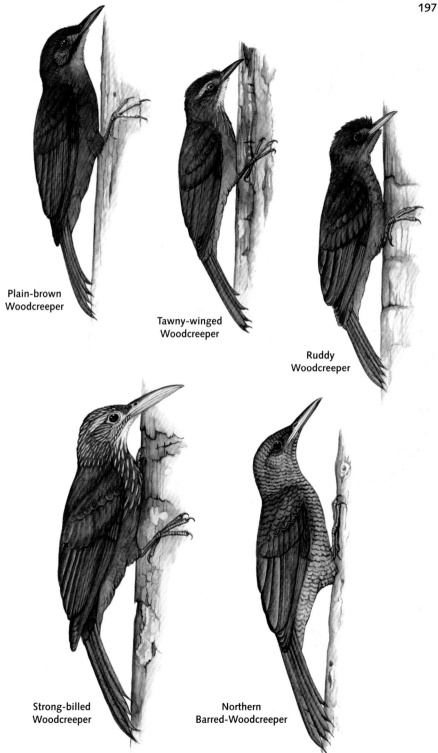

197

Plain-brown
Woodcreeper

Tawny-winged
Woodcreeper

Ruddy
Woodcreeper

Strong-billed
Woodcreeper

Northern
Barred-Woodcreeper

Black-banded Woodcreeper
Dendrocolaptes picumnus

10 in (25 cm). Only woodcreeper with **streaked breast** and **distinct fine black barring on belly** (though in poor lighting, the barring can be hard to see); also note large size and heavy black bill. Strong-billed Woodcreeper (p. 196) has even larger, heavier bill; has obscure, dusky malar stripe; and is, at most, only indistinctly barred on belly. Rare in western foothills and highlands eastward to Veraguas; recorded from 3,000 to 7,000 ft (900 to 2,100 m). Found in all levels of forest. Song a series of 8 to 20 (or more) *wherk* notes, becoming slower toward the end.

Straight-billed Woodcreeper
Xiphorhynchus picus

8 in (20 cm). **Straight whitish or pinkish bill** is diagnostic; also note **white throat and malar area** and **white spots on chest**. Streak-headed Woodcreeper (p. 200) has slightly decurved bill and less extensive white on throat (not extending to malar area); Cocoa Woodcreeper is larger and has dark bill and buff throat. Uncommon on and near the Pacific coast, from Los Santos to western Darién; also uncommon on and near the Caribbean coast in Canal Area. Found at all levels in mangroves (sometimes also in adjacent forest and woodland). Song a series of high nasal *whik* notes, slowing toward end.

Cocoa Woodcreeper
Xiphorhynchus susurrans

8.5 in (22 cm). This is the most common and widespread woodcreeper in lowlands. Best recognized by combination of **straight, fairly stout bill (note dark upper mandible), heavy buff streaking above and below**, and **buff throat**. Streak-headed (p. 200) and Straight-billed Woodcreepers have pale bills (slightly decurved in case of Streak-headed) and whitish throats; Long-tailed (p. 194) lacks streaking on back and has spots (not streaks) on chest. Occurs throughout much of the country, to 2,000 ft (600 m). Very common in forest edge and woodland; uncommon within forest. Found in lower levels of forest. Song a mournful series of loud whistled notes, which start slowly, then speed up and become louder before trailing off: *weep-weep-whe epWHEEPWHEEPWHEEPWHEEPWHEEPwheep-wheep-wheep—wheep— wheep———weep———weep.*

Black-striped Woodcreeper
Xiphorhynchus lachrymosus

9 in (23 cm). Easily recognized by conspicuous **black-and-white streaking above and below**. Fairly common on entire Caribbean slope and on Pacific in western Chiriquí and from eastern Panamá Province eastward; also found locally on Pacific slope in Veraguas, but only in foothills; to 4,000 ft (1,200 m). Occurs mainly in upper levels of forest. Call consists of three or four loud, sharp, descending whistles: *WHEU, hew, hew, hu* (similar to call of Cinnamon Woodpecker, p. 182, but faster).

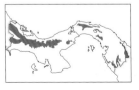

Spotted Woodcreeper
Xiphorhynchus erythropygius

8.5 in (22 cm). The only woodcreeper with such an **olive tone** to brownish plumage on head, back, and underparts; also note **distinct eye-ring** and **rounded buffy spots on breast and belly**. Long-tailed Woodcreeper (p. 194) also has buffy spots on breast but is smaller and has buffy superciliary, unstreaked back, streaks (not spots) on belly, and longer tail. Fairly common in foothills on both slopes, mostly 1,000 to 4,500 ft (300 to 1,350 m), sometimes to 5,300 ft (1,600 m); very rare in Caribbean lowlands. Found at all levels of forest; often with mixed-species flocks. Song a melancholy series of two or three descending whistles, each successively lower in pitch: *dreoo, dreooo, dreeeoou.*

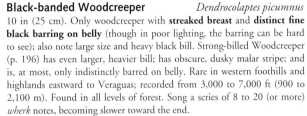

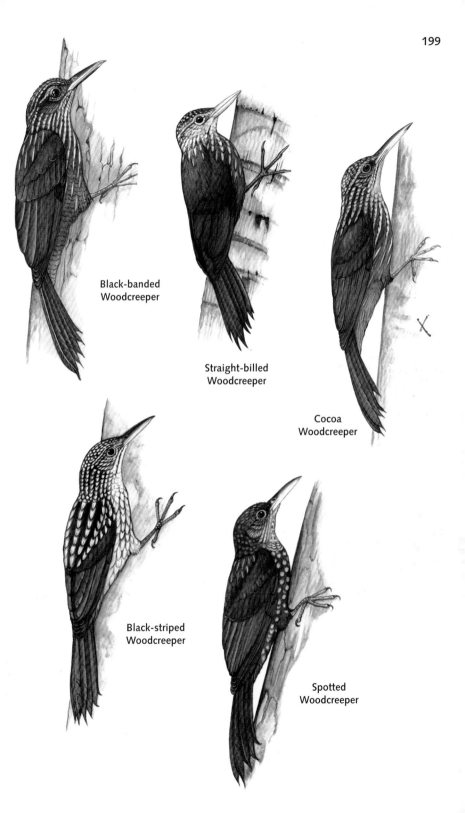

Black-banded
Woodcreeper

Straight-billed
Woodcreeper

Cocoa
Woodcreeper

Black-striped
Woodcreeper

Spotted
Woodcreeper

Wedge-billed Woodcreeper
Glyphorynchus spirurus

5.5 in (14 cm). Smallest woodcreeper. **Short bill with slightly upturned lower mandible** is diagnostic. Xenops (p. 192) have a similar bill but show a conspicuous white malar stripe. Fairly common on entire Caribbean slope; also fairly common on Pacific slope in western Chiriquí, Veraguas foothills, and from eastern Panamá Province eastward; to 5,000 ft (1,500 m). Found in lower levels of forest; occasionally with mixed-species flocks. Call a sharp sneezy *chif!*; also a short rapid trill that crescendos and then ends abruptly.

Streak-headed Woodcreeper
Lepidocolaptes souleyetii

7 in (18 cm). Combination of **slightly decurved bill (pale brownish or pinkish)** and **fine streaking on crown** distinguishes it from similar species. Spot-crowned Woodcreeper (mainly at higher elevations) has small spots instead of streaks on crown; Cocoa (p. 198) is larger and has larger, straight bill with dark upper mandible; Straight-billed (p. 198) is larger, with straight bill and white on throat extending to malar area. Fairly common on Pacific slope and on Caribbean in western Bocas del Toro and from Canal Area eastward; to 5,000 ft (1,500 m). Found in cleared areas with scattered trees and in open woodland and gallery forest. Song a short, rapid descending series of chittering notes.

Spot-crowned Woodcreeper
Lepidocolaptes affinis

8.5 in (21 cm). Shares **slightly decurved, pale bill** with Streak-headed Woodcreeper (mainly at lower elevations), from which it is distinguished by **small spots** (not streaks) **on crown**. Other similar woodcreepers are confined to lower elevations. Fairly common in western highlands eastward to Ngöbe-Buglé; mainly above 4,000 ft (1,200 m), rarely down to 3,600 ft (1,080 m). Found at all levels of forest. Often with mixed-species flocks. Song a very high-pitched thin *tsee-tsee* followed by a short accelerating twitter; call a sharp nasal *fweer*.

Red-billed Scythebill
Campylorhamphus trochilirostris

9 in (23 cm). Easily recognized by **extremely long decurved red bill**; Brown-billed Scythebill (mainly at higher elevations) has somewhat shorter dark brown bill. Rare on Caribbean slope from northern Coclé eastward, and on Pacific from eastern Panamá Province eastward; to 3,500 ft (1,050 m). Occurs in lower and middle levels of forest edge and woodland. Sometimes with mixed-species flocks. Song a series of six or seven whistled notes, slowing toward the end.

Brown-billed Scythebill
Campylorhamphus pusillus

9 in (23 cm). **Very long decurved dark brown bill** is diagnostic; Red-billed Scythebill (mainly at lower elevations) has even longer red bill. Uncommon in foothills and lower highlands; mainly 2,000 to 5,300 ft (600 to 1,600 m), but recorded down to 700 ft (200 m) in Bocas del Toro. Found at all levels of forest. Often with mixed-species flocks. Song variable; may include a series of four or five quavering, ascending, whistled notes followed by an accelerating trill (and sometimes concluded by a sharp *fweep!*).

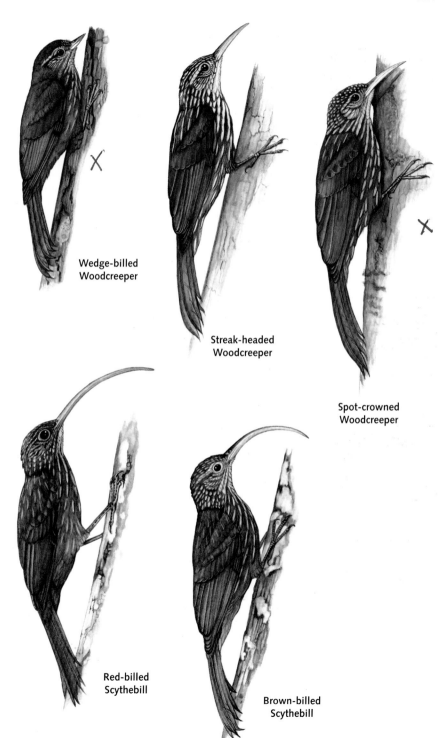

Wedge-billed
Woodcreeper

Streak-headed
Woodcreeper

Spot-crowned
Woodcreeper

Red-billed
Scythebill

Brown-billed
Scythebill

THAMNOPHILIDAE. The antbirds are a large and diverse family of mostly insectivorous birds found only in the neotropics. They reach their greatest diversity in lowland forests, though a few occur in foothills or highlands. The family name derives from the foraging behavior of a few species that follow swarms of army ants as they scour the leaf litter of the forest floor. The birds feed on insects and other arthropods fleeing from the ants, not on the ants themselves. In most species, the sexes differ in appearance; male plumage often features combinations of black, gray, or white, while females are more brownish or rufescent.

Fasciated Antshrike
Cymbilaimus lineatus

6.5 in (17 cm). Male similar to male Barred Antshrike, but has **finer black-and-white barring** and **red eye**. Female similar in pattern to larger Barred Puffbird (p. 170), but has **chestnut cap**, lacks buff collar on hindneck, and has a more horizontal stance. Fairly common on entire Caribbean slope and on Pacific slope from Canal Area eastward; also occurs on western Pacific slope in Veraguas foothills; usually below 2,000 ft (600 m), occasionally to 4,100 ft (1,250 m). Found in lower and middle levels of forest edge and woodland. Often difficult to see due to secretive behavior: searches slowly and deliberately through vine tangles and other dense vegetation. Song consists of a mournful series of 4 to 10 clear whistles slurring upward: *wheu . . . wheu . . . wheu . . . wheu.*

Great Antshrike
Taraba major

7.5 in (19 cm). In both sexes, two-tone color pattern is distinctive; **black above and white below** in male, **rufous above and white below** in female. Also note large size, **red eye**, and heavy hooked bill. Fairly common on both slopes; usually below 2,000 ft (600 m), occasionally to 4,300 ft (1,300 m). Found in lower levels of forest edge, young second growth, and in thickets in clearings. Usually remains hidden in dense vegetation. Detected mainly by song, a long, accelerating series of loud *hoot* notes, usually ending with a nasal, snarling *gwarr!* (call of White-tailed Trogon [p. 160] is similar but lacks final note).

Barred Antshrike
Thamnophilus doliatus

6 in (15 cm). Male distinguished from male Fasciated Antshrike by **coarser black-and-white barring** and **whitish eye**. Female is only Panama bird combining **rufous upperparts, cinnamon underparts**, and **streaking on sides of head**; also note **whitish eye**. Fairly common on Pacific slope eastward to eastern Panamá Province, and on Caribbean from northern Coclé to western Kuna Yala; to 2,000 ft (600 m). Found in dense vegetation of forest edge and in second growth, thickets in clearings, hedgerows, and gardens. Song a rapid, accelerating series of soft *heh* notes, ending in a longer nasal *hu-hek!*; call a growling *arrrh!*

Black Antshrike
Thamnophilus nigriceps

6 in (15 cm). Male, **entirely black** except for white underwing coverts, is distinguished from most other black birds by **heavy hooked black bill**. Smaller Jet Antbird (p. 210) has white on wing coverts and tail; male Immaculate Antbird (p. 212) has bare bluish skin around eye. On female, combination of **chestnut back** and **heavy whitish streaking on head and breast** is distinctive; no range overlap with Black-hooded Antshrike (p. 204). Uncommon in lowlands on Pacific slope, from eastern Panamá Province eastward. Found in dense vegetation in second growth, thickets in clearings, and forest edge. Song a series of resonant *koh* notes, starting slowly and accelerating near end.

Fasciated
Antshrike

female

male

Great
Antshrike

female

male

Barred
Antshrike

female

male

female

male

Black
Antshrike

Black-hooded Antshrike

Thamnophilus bridgesi

6.5 in (16 cm). Male distinguished from other mostly black birds by **heavy hooked black bill** and **small white spots on shoulders**; also note that underparts are paler than rest of body. Smaller Jet Antbird (p. 210) has conspicuous white spots on tail. On female, **heavy white streaking on head and breast** is distinctive; no range overlap with Black Antshrike (p. 202). Fairly common on Pacific slope eastward to Los Santos; mostly in lowlands, occasionally to 3,700 ft (1,100 m). Found in lower levels of forest, woodland, gallery forest, and mangroves. Song an accelerating series of harsh *ehnk* notes that ends in a sharp *har!*; also gives a descending *kow-kow-kow* or *kow-kow*. **PL**

Western Slaty-Antshrike

Thamnophilus atrinucha

5.5 in (14 cm). Male distinguished by combination of **mostly gray plumage** and **extensive white spotting on shoulders**; also note **white tips on tail feathers** and **black crown**. Male Dusky Antbird (p. 210) and male antvireos (p. 206) have much less extensive spotting on wings and lack solid black crown. Female distinguished from smaller female Spot-crowned Antvireo (p. 206) by more **extensive buffy feather edging and spotting on shoulders** and **lack of streaking on chest**. Very common on entire Caribbean slope and on Pacific slope from western Panamá Province eastward; to 3,000 ft (900 m). Found in lower levels of forest and woodland. Often with mixed-species flocks. Call a rapid, accelerating series of nasal *henh* notes, ending on a longer harsh *hu-henk!*; other calls include an abrupt *ak!* followed by a rolling *kur-r-r-r-r*, and a nasal *henk!* (usually doubled or tripled).

Speckled Antshrike

Xenornis setifrons

6.5 in (16 cm). Only antshrike with **streaked back**. On male, combination of **streaked brown upperparts** and **slate-gray underparts** and tail is unique among Panama birds. Female somewhat resembles in pattern both Striped Woodhaunter (p. 188) and Lineated Foliage-gleaner (p. 190); distinguished by heavy hooked bill, **pale wing-bars**, and lack of rufous in tail. Rare in lowlands and (especially) foothills of eastern Panama, mostly 500 to 3,000 ft (150 to 900 m). Found in lower levels of very wet forest; particularly favors steep wet ravines. Song a series of three to nine thin whistles, rising in pitch and volume and then falling off; also gives a harsh *chak-chak-chak*. Called Spiny-faced Antshrike by AOU. **EL**

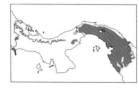

Russet Antshrike

Thamnistes anabatinus

5.5 in (14 cm). The **heavy hooked bill** and **bright rufous wings that contrast with duller brownish back** distinguish it from other birds with rufous upperparts and cinnamon underparts; also note **pale cinnamon superciliary extending behind eye**. Buff-throated Foliage-gleaner (p. 190) lacks rufous in wings; very rare Buff-fronted Foliage-gleaner (p. 190) has gray crown; Cinnamon Becard and females of other becards (pp. 260-263) lack contrast between wings and back and have superciliaries that do not extend behind eye. Fairly common in foothills throughout the country, mostly 1,000 to 3,000 ft (300 to 900 m), occasionally to 5,000 ft (1,500 m); rare in lowlands, in western Chiriquí and from Canal Area eastward. Found in middle levels of forest. In behavior, resembles a foliage-gleaner, foraging higher and more actively than typical antshrikes. Often with mixed-species flocks. Song a series of six or seven sharp whistles, becoming louder and then falling off; call a thin *wee-sip*.

male

Black-hooded
Antshrike

female

Western
Slaty-Antshrike

male

female

male

Speckled
Antshrike

female

Russet
Antshrike

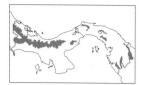

Plain Antvireo
Dysithamnus mentali.

4.5 in (11 cm). Stockier and has heavier head and bill than antwrens. Botl sexes distinguished from respective sexes of Spot-crowned Antvireo (littl elevational overlap) by **unmarked crown and chest** and **dark eye**. Mal similar to male Dusky Antbird (p. 210), but latter differs in larger size thinner bill, uniform gray underparts, and tail that is longer and shows whit tipping. Female distinguished from female antwrens by **distinct russe crown,** and from Tawny-crowned Greenlet (p. 276) by dark eye and whitisl eye-ring. Fairly common in lower highlands; mostly 2,000 to 5,000 ft (60(to 1,500 m), occasionally to 6,100 ft (1,850 m). Found in lower levels o forest. Sometimes with mixed-species flocks. Song a series of sharp *pu* notes at first evenly spaced and then accelerating.

Spot-crowned Antvireo
Dysithamnus puncticep:

4.5 in (12 cm). Only antbird with **spotted crown**; also note **pale eye** Stockier and with heavier head and bill than antwrens. Plain Antvireo (littl elevational overlap) lacks spots on crown and streaking on chest and has darl eye. Uncommon on entire Caribbean slope and on Pacific slope from easterr Panamá Province eastward; to 2,500 ft (750 m). Found in lower levels o forest, occasionally with mixed-species flocks. Song a soft, rolling trill tha fades off at end.

Checker-throated Antwren
Epinecrophylla fulviventri:

4 in (10 cm). On male, **throat speckled with black and white** is diagnostic Female is very similar to female White-flanked Antwren (p. 208), from which it is distinguished by **pale eye, black wing coverts**, and **lack of whit patch on flank**. Female Slaty Antwren (p. 208) has plain wings and darl eye. Common on entire Caribbean slope and on Pacific slope from westerr Panamá Province eastward; to 3,000 ft (900 m). Found in lower and middl levels of forest. Pairs or small family groups often accompany pairs or smal family groups of Dot-winged and White-flanked Antwrens (p. 208), thes species forming the core of mixed-species flocks. Mostly forages in hangin dead-leaf clusters. Song a series of evenly spaced, high, thin *seek* notes, all o the same pitch; call a single thin *tsik!*

Moustached Antwren
Myrmotherula ignota

3 in (7 cm). **Tiny size, almost tailless appearance**, and combination o **streaked upperparts** and **yellowish underparts** should prevent confusion Female is buffier than male. Black-capped Pygmy-Tyrant (p. 230) is also smal and almost tailless but lacks streaked upperparts. Uncommon on Caribbear slope from Canal Area to western Kuna Yala, and on Pacific from easterr Panamá Province eastward; to 2,000 ft (600 m). Found in middle levels o forest, often with mixed-species flocks; frequents dense vegetation and vine tangles. Song a series of high-pitched chirps, accelerating near the end.

Pacific Antwren
Myrmotherula pacifica

3.5 in (9 cm). On male, **bold black-and-white streaking above and below** is distinctive; on female, note combination of **bright tawny head and underparts** and **black-and-white streaked back**. Moustached Antwren ha unstreaked pale yellow underparts; Black-and-white Warbler (p. 320) resemble male in pattern but differs in shape and behavior. Fairly common in lowland on Caribbean slope from western Bocas del Toro eastward, and on Pacific from eastern Panamá Province eastward; to 2,000 ft (600 m). Found in thickets ir open areas, and in young second growth and forest edge; often near water. Song a series of sharp chips, rising and accelerating slightly; call a thin *nyeahh*.

Plain
Antvireo

male

female

Spot-crowned
Antvireo

male

female

Checker-throated
Antwren

male

female

Moustached
Antwren

male

female

Pacific
Antwren

male

female

White-flanked Antwren
Myrmotherula axillaris

4 in (10 cm). On male, **white flank patch** is diagnostic; male Dot-winged Antwren has longer tail and more white on wings and tail. Female very similar to female Checker-throated Antwren (p. 206), but distinguished by **dark eye, brown** (not black) **wing coverts**, and **whitish patch on flank**. Female Slaty Antwren has plain wings and lacks white flank patch. Common on entire Caribbean slope and on Pacific in western Chiriquí and from western Panamá Province eastward; to 3,000 ft (900 m). Found in lower and middle levels of forest. Small groups frequently travel with parties of Checker-throated and Dot-winged Antwrens, forming the core of mixed-species flocks. Song a descending series of thin whistles; call a squeaky *wheek-whup!* (usually two notes, sometimes three).

Slaty Antwren
Myrmotherula schisticolor

4 in (10 cm). Generally occurs at higher elevations than other antwrens. Male distinguished from male White-flanked and Dot-winged Antwrens by **mostly slaty** coloration (black only on throat and breast); from male White-flanked by lack of white flank patch; and from Dot-winged by shorter tail that lacks conspicuous white tipping. Female differs from female White-flanked and Dot-winged by **lack of spotting on wings**; female Plain Antvireo (p. 206) has russet crown. Dusky Antbird (p. 210) is larger with longer tail; male Dusky is also distinguished from male Slaty by lack of black on breast; female Dusky is distinguished from female Slaty by its richer tawny underparts. Fairly common in foothills and lower highlands; 2,000 to 5,800 ft (600 to 1,750 m); rare in lowlands in western Chiriquí and in western and southern Azuero Peninsula. Found in lower levels of forest, often with mixed-species flocks. Calls include a sharp high-pitched *tsip!* and a nasal descending *nyaarr*.

Rufous-winged Antwren
Herpsilochmus rufimarginatus

4 in (10 cm). Conspicuous **rufous patch on flight feathers** is diagnostic; also note prominent white superciliary, white wing-bars, and pale yellow breast and belly. Fairly common in eastern Panamá Province and in Darién; to 3,500 ft (1,050 m). Found in middle and upper levels of forest. Frequently forages in vine tangles and other dense vegetation, often with mixed-species flocks. Song a short, accelerating series of churring notes, with an accent on the final note: *chu-chu-chuchuchchchchueeer!*

Dot-winged Antwren
Microrhopias quixensis

4 in (10 cm). Male distinguished from male White-flanked and Slaty Antwrens by **longer tail with more extensive white tipping** and **wider white wing-bar**; male White-flanked has white flank patch; male Slaty is mostly slate gray; male Jet Antbird (p. 210) is larger and has only narrow white edging on wing. Female, with **dark gray upperparts** and **bright chestnut underparts**, is unmistakable. Common on entire Caribbean slope and on Pacific in westernmost Chiriquí and from Canal Area eastward; to 3,500 ft (1,050 m). Found in lower and middle levels of forest and woodland, often with mixed-species flocks. Favors vine tangles and other dense growth, especially along edge of forest and woodland. Song a series of sharp notes that first ascend in pitch and then descend more rapidly; call a descending *cheeu!*

White-flanked
Antwren

male

female

Slaty
Antwren

male

female

male

female

Rufous-winged
Antwren

Dot-winged
Antwren

male

female

White-fringed Antwren

Formicivora grisea

4.5 in (12 cm). Easily recognized in its restricted Panama range on the Pearl Islands, where it is the only antwren. The only other antbirds in the archipelago are the very different Barred Antshrike (p. 202) and Jet Antbird. Common on Isla del Rey, San José, Pedro González, and Viveros islands. Found in lower levels of forest, woodland, and second growth. Song a series of evenly spaced chirps, all on the same pitch; call a soft squealing *chu-ik!*

Rufous-rumped Antwren

Terenura callinota

4 in (10 cm). **Rufous rump patch** is diagnostic; also note two prominent pale yellow wing-bars and pale yellow breast and belly. Uncommon in western Panama (recorded mainly from Fortuna in Chiriquí and in adjacent Ngöbe-Buglé) and in eastern Darién; mostly from 2,500 to 4,000 ft (750 to 1,200 m). Found in upper levels of wet forest. Forages actively in outer leaves and branches, sometimes hanging upside down. Call a high, thin, hissing *tzizzzss.*

Dusky Antbird

Cercomacra tyrannina

5 in (13 cm). Male differs from male Western Slaty-Antshrike (p. 204) in having **much less white on wing** and in **lacking strong contrast between crown and rest of head**; male Black-hooded Antshrike (p. 204) has small white spots on shoulder; male Slaty Antwren (p. 208) is smaller with shorter tail and black throat and breast. Male of eastern Panama race is distinctly grayer than male of western race; female of eastern race is paler overall than female of western race. Female is **brighter tawny below** than female Slaty Antwren; female Bare-crowned Antbird has bare blue skin around eye and is larger. Common on both slopes, to 5,000 ft (1,500 m). Found in lower levels of forest edge, second growth, and thickets in forest clearings; somewhat secretive and often hard to see in dense vegetation. Usually in pairs. Song a series of about 10 piping notes, the first several notes ascending in pitch and the final notes descending; calls include a sharp *chee-do!* and a descending buzzy *whrrr.*

Jet Antbird

Cercomacra nigricans

6 in (15 cm). Conspicuous **white spots on tail** distinguish both sexes from male Dusky Antbird and male Black (p. 202) and Black-hooded Antshrike (p. 204); male Dot-winged Antwren (p. 208) is much smaller and has bolder white wing-bar. On female, also note **white streaking on throat and upper breast**. Uncommon and local on Pacific slope from Veraguas eastward, and on Caribbean slope from western Colón Province to western Kuna Yala; to 2,000 ft (600 m). Found in lower levels of forest edge, second growth, and thickets in forest clearings (frequently near streams); often remains concealed in thick vegetation. Usually in pairs. Song a series of nasal paired notes: *kick-KO! kick-KO! kick-KO!* (accented emphatically on second syllable); call a harsh *whark!*

Bare-crowned Antbird

Gymnocichla nudiceps

6 in (15 cm). Male's **bare blue forecrown** is unique; also note white edging on wing coverts. On female, combination of **blue orbital skin** and **rufous underparts and wing-bars** is distinctive; female Immaculate and Chestnut-backed Antbirds (p. 212) lack wing-bars. Uncommon on entire Caribbean slope and on Pacific slope in western Chiriquí and from eastern Panamá Province eastward; to 2,000 ft (600 m). Found in lower levels of forest edge, second growth, and thickets near forest. Mostly found at army-ant swarms, although sometimes seen away from them. Usually in pairs. Song a series of sharp, clear piping notes, all on the same pitch and accelerating slightly near end.

White-fringed
Antwren

male

female

Rufous-rumped
Antwren

male

female

Dusky Antbird

male
western race

male
eastern race

female
western race

Jet Antbird

male

female

Bare-crowned
Antbird

male

female

Chestnut-backed Antbird
Myrmeciza exsul

5.5 in (14 cm). Both sexes distinguished from much rarer Dull-mantled Antbird by **bare blue orbital skin** and **brown** (not red) **eye**. Female differs from female Immaculate and Bare-crowned (p. 210) Antbirds by **slaty crown and sides of head**. Male and female of eastern Darién race have small white spots on wing coverts (like Dull-mantled); female has bright rufous on breast (like female Bare-crowned) but lacks wing-bars. Common on entire Caribbean slope; also common on Pacific, from Chiriquí eastward to western side of Azuero Peninsula, and from Canal Area eastward; to 3,000 ft (900 m). Found in lower levels of forest, usually close to ground. Song consists of two or three emphatic whistles, with the last note lower in pitch: *whit, wheer!* or *whit, whit, wheer!* (often paraphrased as "Come HERE! Come right HERE!"); call a nasal *nyaah*. Call of Black-faced Antthrush (p. 216) is similar but accented on first note instead of last.

Dull-mantled Antbird
Myrmeciza laemosticta

5.5 in (14 cm). Distinguished from Chestnut-backed Antbird by **red eye** and **lack of bare blue orbital patch**; on female, **black-and-white checkered throat** is also distinctive. Both sexes have a concealed white patch on back (displayed when excited) that is lacking in Chestnut-backed. Chestnut-backed also lacks white spots on wing coverts, except in eastern Darién. Rare and local on both slopes, from Veraguas eastward; favors foothills, but also found in lowlands; to 2,800 ft (850 m). Inhabits forest, usually in undergrowth along streams and in wet ravines. Call a series of 8 to 10 clear high-pitched whistles, the first two or three given at a slower cadence than the remaining ones: *wheet-wheet-wheet-wit-wit-wit-wit-wit-wit*.

Immaculate Antbird
Myrmeciza immaculata

7 in (18 cm). Male distinguished from other mostly black birds by **bare bluish white orbital skin**. On male Bare-crowned Antbird (p. 210), entire front of crown is bare. Female Immaculate is larger than female Chestnut-backed Antbird and has brown (not slaty) crown; female Bare-crowned is bright rufous below and has rufous wing-bars. Uncommon; most numerous in foothills, from 1,000 to 6,300 ft (300 to 1,900 m). Found in lower levels of forest, often at army-ant swarms. Song a series of 6 to 10 loud clear whistles, evenly spaced and all on same pitch.

White-bellied Antbird
Myrmeciza longipes

5.5 in (14 cm). On male, combination of **bright rufous-chestnut upperparts, black throat and chest**, and **white lower breast and belly** is distinctive. On female, combination of **rufous-chestnut upperparts, buffy chest**, and **white lower breast and belly** is distinctive. Fairly common on Pacific slope, from Coclé eastward to central Darién; also fairly common on Caribbean slope, in Canal Area and adjacent parts of Panamá and Colón Provinces; to 2,000 ft (600 m). Found in lower levels of forest edge, young second growth, and thickets. Song a series of loud chirps, beginning very rapidly, then gradually slowing down and finally trailing off (often likened to sound made by mechanical wind-up bird).

male

male

eastern
Darién race

female

female

**Chestnut-backed
Antbird**

male

female

**Dull-mantled
Antbird**

male

male

female

female

**Immaculate
Antbird**

**White-bellied
Antbird**

Spotted Antbird

Hylophylax naevioides

4.5 in (11 cm). On male, **bold black spotting on white chest, chestnut back**, and **mostly gray head** render it unmistakable. Female, though duller, is easily recognized by combination of **spotting on chest** and prominent **buffy wing-bars**. Common on entire Caribbean slope and on Pacific slope from western Panamá Province eastward; also occurs on western Pacific slope but only in foothills; to 3,000 ft (900 m). Inhabits lower levels of forest. Frequently found at army-ant swarms but also forages independently. Song a series of 8 to 10 wheezy doubled notes that first rise in pitch and volume and then descend and fall off: *kiba keeba KHEEBA KHEEBA KHEEBA KHEEBA kheeba kheeba keeba kiba*; calls include a buzzy *zhirr* and a sharp *tsik!*

Wing-banded Antbird

Myrmornis torquata

6 in (15 cm). Combination of prominent **buffy wing-bars** and **nearly tailless appearance** makes this species virtually unmistakable. Antthrushes and antpittas (pp. 216-219) lack wing-bars; much smaller Spotted Antbird has spots on chest. Rare and local on Caribbean slope in Canal Area and eastern Kuna Yala; also rare and local on Pacific slope, from eastern Panamá Province eastward; to over 4,000 ft (1,200 m). Found in lower levels of forest. Typically forages on ground, flicking up leaves like a leaftosser. Song a long series of evenly spaced whistled notes that rise slightly in pitch and become louder; also gives a nasal *chirr*.

Bicolored Antbird

Gymnopithys leucaspis

5.5 in (14 cm). Combination of **bare blue orbital patch** and **mostly white underparts** is unique. Race found in western Panama lacks gray band along edge of crown. Fairly common on entire Caribbean slope and on Pacific slope in western Chiriquí and from Veraguas eastward; usually below 3,000 ft (900 m), but locally to over 5,000 ft (1,500 m). Inhabits lower levels of forest. One of the most common birds at army-ant swarms, and only rarely found away from them. Song a series of sharp whistled notes, the first three or four rising sharply in pitch and intensity, then rapidly decelerating and falling off, sometimes ending in a *churr*; calls include a harsh grating *gwarrrr!* and a thin descending *zhrooo*.

Ocellated Antbird

Phaenostictus mcleannani

8 in (20 cm). This spectacular species is easily recognized by **large bright blue bare facial patch** and conspicuous **scalloping above and below**. Uncommon on entire Caribbean slope and on Pacific slope from eastern Panamá Province eastward; also occurs on western Pacific slope but only in foothills; to 3,000 ft (900 m). Found in lower levels of forest, nearly always at army-ant swarms. Often pumps tail up and down. Song a series of piping notes, rising in pitch and intensity, sometimes falling off at end; similar in pattern to that of Bicolored Antbird, but initial rise is slower and notes are not as emphatic. Call a sharp *dzerrr*.

Spotted Antbird

male

female

Wing-banded Antbird

male

female

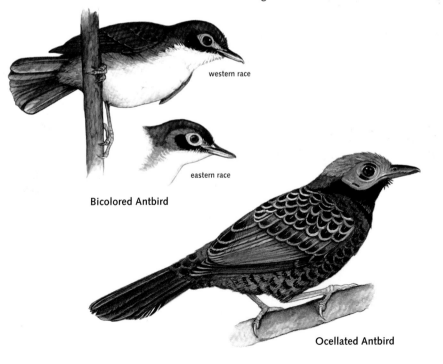

western race

eastern race

Bicolored Antbird

Ocellated Antbird

FORMICARIIDAE. Members of this exclusively neotropical family were formerly placed in the typical antbird family (Thamnophilidae) along with the antpittas. Antthrushes walk about slowly and deliberately on the forest floor searching for insects, often cocking their tail upward, the source of their local Spanish name *gallito* (little rooster). Highly secretive, they are far more often heard than seen. Panama's three species can easily be distinguished by the color and pattern of the head and breast, as well as by voice.

Black-faced Antthrush
Formicarius analis

7 in (18 cm). The most common and most widespread antthrush, and the only one in lowlands. Distinguished from other antthrushes by **gray breast** and **olive-brown crown and nape**. Common on entire Caribbean slope; also common on Pacific slope in western Chiriquí and from western Panamá Province eastward; occurs elsewhere on western Pacific slope only in foothills; recorded to 5,000 ft (1,500 m). Inhabits forest floor; often found at army-ant swarms. Song a slow, hesitant series of plaintive whistles (usually 3 or 4, sometimes as many as 15); the first whistle is longer and has a slightly higher pitch: *peeu, pew, pew* (similar to call of Chestnut-backed Antbird [p. 212] but accented on first note instead of last). Call a sharp chuckling *fweek!*

Black-headed Antthrush
Formicarius nigricapillus

6.5 in (17 cm). Distinguished from other antthrushes by **all-black head and breast**. Chestnut-backed Antbird (p. 212) is similar in pattern but differs markedly in shape and behavior; its bare blue orbital patch extends to lores. Rare and local in foothills and lower highlands; mainly on Caribbean slope, eastward to eastern Panamá Province and western Kuna Yala; recorded from 1,500 to 5,000 ft (450 to 1,500 m). Found on ground in wet forest. Song a series (10 to 20 or more) of mournful, short, hollow whistles, accelerating slowly and becoming louder, then ending abruptly.

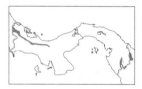

Rufous-breasted Antthrush
Formicarius rufipectus

7.5 in (19 cm). Distinguished from other antthrushes by **bright rufous crown, nape, and breast**. Rare in foothills and lower highlands of western Panama eastward to Veraguas; also rare in eastern Darién; mostly 2,500 to 5,000 ft (750 to 1,500 m). Found on ground in wet forest. Song consists of two short, clear whistles, the second usually slightly higher: *pew-piw*.

Gnateaters

CONOPOPHAGIDAE. The gnateaters are a small family of insectivorous birds of tropical forest understory, closely related to antbirds and confined mainly to South America. The Black-crowned Antpitta is the largest member of its family and the only to occur in Central America; until recently it was classified with the rest of the antpittas.

Black-crowned Antpitta
Pittasoma michleri

6.5 in (17 cm). **Bold black-and-white scalloping** below and **black crown** make this spectacular species unmistakable. In race on western Caribbean slope, male has almost entirely black head (cheeks brownish); female is similar but with white speckling on throat. In rest of Panama, both sexes have sides of head chestnut (female has more white speckling on throat than male). Rare on entire Caribbean slope, and on Pacific slope from eastern Panamá Province eastward; also found on western Pacific slope, but only in foothills; to 4,100 ft (1,250 m). Found on ground in forest, often at army-ant swarms. Song a series of whistled *piw* notes, starting rapidly and then very gradually slowing down (often lasting a minute or more); also gives a rapid series of harsh *wak* notes, slowing near the end. **CL, EL**

Black-faced
Antthrush

Black-headed
Antthrush

Rufous-breasted
Antthrush

male
western
race

male
eastern
race

Black-crowned
Antpitta

GRALLARIIDAE. The antpittas, along with the antthrushes, were formerly classified with the typical antbirds (Thamnophilidae) but have recently been separated into their own family. Like antthrushes, the antpittas frequent the forest floor, but they have a more upright stance than antthrushes and often hop rather than walk. Secretive and generally inconspicuous, antpittas are far more often heard than seen.

Scaled Antpitta
Grallaria guatimalensis

6.5 in (17 cm). The only antpitta with **scaling on back**; also note **rufous breast**. **Throat is mostly dark brown** (pale line down center); it is enclosed by **pale malar streaks** on each side and a **pale bar below**. Rare in foothills and highlands, above 1,900 ft (570 m). Found on ground in forest. Song a rapid series of quavering hollow notes lasting about 3 to 5 seconds; slowly becomes louder and then rapidly falls off (similar in quality to that of a screech-owl, p. 126).

Streak-chested Antpitta
Hylopezus perspicillatus

5.5 in (14 cm). The most common and most widespread antpitta in lowlands. Distinguished from Thicket Antpitta by **wider, more distinct buffy eye-ring, much heavier blackish streaking on breast**, dark malar stripe, and small pale spots on wing coverts. Fairly common on entire Caribbean slope and on Pacific slope in western Chiriquí and from eastern Panamá Province eastward; also found on Pacific slope in Veraguas foothills; to 4,100 ft (1,250 m). Found on ground in forest. Song a slow, mournful series of about 10 clear whistles, the first few notes rising, then leveling off for several notes, finally slowing down and descending slightly.

Thicket Antpitta
Hylopezus dives

5.5 in (14 cm). Distinguished from Streak-chested Antpitta by **ochraceous breast** (with only indistinct streaking) and **cinnamon-rufous flanks, lower belly, and vent**; also note indistinct eye-ring and lack of dark malar stripe or spotting on wings. Ochre-breasted Antpitta is much smaller, has yellow bill, and lacks rufous on lower belly and vent. Uncommon in Bocas del Toro, eastern Panamá Province, Kuna Yala, and Darién; to 2,500 ft (750 m). Found on ground in very dense undergrowth at forest edge and in thickets in nearby clearings. Song a series of 5 to 12 whistled notes, rising slowly and becoming louder and then ending abruptly (similar to call of Streak-chested Antpitta but faster and does not trail off at end).

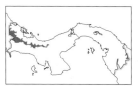

Ochre-breasted Antpitta
Grallaricula flavirostris

4 in (10 cm). Much smaller than other antpittas; **entirely yellowish bill** is diagnostic. Also note **prominent eye-ring, ochraceous breast**, and **mostly white lower underparts**. Rare in foothills and lower highlands of western Panama eastward to Veraguas, and in eastern Darién; recorded 2,100 to 5,200 ft (650 to 1,600 m). Found near ground in forest; usually perches low in vegetation rather than walking on ground like other antpittas. Song a high thin whistle: *fwee!* (sometimes two notes: *fwee-up!*).

Scaled
Antpitta

Streak-chested
Antpitta

Thicket
Antpitta

Ochre-breasted
Antpitta

RHINOCRYPTIDAE. Tapaculos are a small family of insectivorous birds, found mainly in temperate and mountainous areas of South America. Panama's three species inhabit dense undergrowth in forest in foothills and highlands, scurrying about on or near the ground, almost like mice. Secretive and difficult to see, their calls are often the best clue to their presence. Some species (including those found in Panama) frequently cock their tails, the origin of the Spanish name *tapa culo*, meaning "cover your rear."

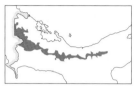

Silvery-fronted Tapaculo
Scytalopus argentifrons

4.5 in (12 cm). On male, **silvery forehead and superciliary** distinguish it from other small birds of forest undergrowth. In race that occurs from Ngöbe-Buglé to Coclé, male's brow line does not extend behind eye. Female (both races) lacks brow line; **barred flanks** distinguish female from larger Wrenthrush (p. 330), which has rufous crown, and from Southern Nightingale Wren (p. 296), which has longer bill and shorter tail. Fairly common in highlands and upper foothills eastward to Coclé, above 3,500 ft (1,050 m). Found near ground in dense undergrowth in forest. Favors steep hillsides and wet ravines. Song a series of sharp notes, initially accelerating rapidly and becoming louder, then continuing on same pitch as tempo very gradually slows down; usually lasts 5 to 7 seconds, sometimes 15 seconds or more. **WH**

Choco Tapaculo
Scytalopus chocoensis

4.5 in (11 cm). Male **lacks pale superciliary** of other male tapaculos (although some male Chocos may show a trace). Both sexes distinguished from other small understory birds by **rufous barring on flanks**. Female browner than male, and rufous areas somewhat brighter. Uncommon in highlands and upper foothills in southeastern Darién, from 3,500 to 5,000 ft (750 to 1,500 m). Found near ground in dense undergrowth in forest. Song a series of loud *kek* notes, accelerating quickly at beginning, then very gradually slowing down, often continuing for more than 30 seconds; slower than call of Silvery-fronted Tapaculo, and notes are not as sharp. **EH**

Tacarcuna Tapaculo
Scytalopus panamensis

4.5 in (12 cm). Both sexes are very similar to male Silvery-fronted Tapaculo; distinguished by **black forehead** and **paler throat**. Female browner above and paler gray on throat and breast than male. Reportedly common in highlands and upper foothills of Cerro Tacarcuna in eastern Darién; 3,600 to 4,800 ft (1,100 to 1,460 m). Found near ground in dense undergrowth in forest. Song described as a piping *tseety-seety seety seety*. **EH**

Broadbills

EURYLAIMIDAE. The classification of the enigmatic Sapayoa has long been controversial. Placed with the manakins until recently, it is now considered the sole New World representative of the broadbills, a family of mostly insectivorous birds otherwise confined to the tropics of Asia and Africa.

Sapayoa
Sapayoa aenigma

5.5 in (14 cm). Nearly **uniformly olive** (somewhat yellower on throat and lower underparts); male has yellow crown patch (usually concealed). Also note **broad bill**. Most similar to Olivaceous Flatbill (p. 234) but lacks yellow wing-bars and edging and streaking on chest. Female manakins (pp. 268-271) are smaller, with shorter tail; see also Thrush-like Schiffornis (p. 258) and Carmiol's Tanager (p. 368). Rare on Caribbean slope from Canal Area eastward and on Pacific from eastern Panamá Province eastward; to 4,600 ft (1,400 m). Found in lower levels of forest, usually near streams or in wet ravines. Sallies for insects from a perch; sometimes joins mixed-species flocks. Makes a short (about 1 second in duration), somewhat musical trill that rises abruptly and then falls more slowly.

female

Silvery-fronted
Tapaculo

male
western race

male

Choco Tapaculo

male

Tacarcuna Tapaculo

male

Sapayoa

TYRANNIDAE. This is the largest family of birds in the New World (where they exclusively occur), and also the family with by far the most species in Panama. Although very diverse in form, many species have a characteristic upright stance. Most tyrant flycatchers are insectivorous, but the larger species also take small vertebrates, and a few eat primarily eat fruit. Many species forage by sallying out repeatedly from the same perch to catch small insects in flight; others snatch or glean insects from leaves. Tyrant flycatchers are mostly dull in coloration, although a few are boldly patterned; many have a brightly colored crown patch that is normally concealed. Some genera, in particular the migrant *Contopus* and *Empidonax*, present some of the most difficult identification problems among Panama birds; voice is often a critical clue.

Brown-capped Tyrannulet
Ornithion brunneicapillus

3 in (8 cm). Combination of small size, **short tail, distinct white superciliary, yellow underparts**, and **lack of wing-bars** is distinctive. In westernmost Chiriquí, see Yellow-bellied Tyrannulet (no range overlap). Fairly common on Caribbean slope from western Bocas del Toro eastward, and on Pacific from western Panamá Province eastward; to 2,500 ft (750 m). Found in middle and upper levels of forest. Sometimes with mixed-species flocks. Often difficult to see due to small size and tendency to forage high. Usually detected by call, a series of four to seven high-pitched whistled notes; the first one or two notes slurring upward, followed by a distinct pause, with the final series of notes then descending rapidly: *fwee, feee-fee-fii-fi*.

Yellow-bellied Tyrannulet
Ornithion semiflavum

3 in (8 cm). **Gray** (not brown) **crown** distinguishes it from very similar Brown-capped Tyrannulet (no range overlap). Rare in westernmost Chiriquí. Found in middle and upper levels of forest and woodland. Sometimes with mixed-species flocks. Call a series of three to five whistled notes, descending only slightly, the last note slurring upward (slower and more deliberate than call of Brown-capped Tyrannulet).

Southern Beardless-Tyrannulet
Camptostoma obsoletum

3.5 in (9 cm). Combination of **distinct whitish wing-bars** and **slight crest** distinguishes it from other small flycatchers. Yellow-crowned Tyrannulet (p. 224) has more prominent superciliary and darker crown (yellow crown patch often visible); Paltry Tyrannulet (p. 230) has wing edging rather than wing-bars; Lesser Elaenia (p. 226) and Northern Scrub-Flycatcher (p. 232) are distinctly larger. Common on entire Pacific slope and on Caribbean slope from Canal Area eastward; to 2,000 ft (600 m). Found in scrub, young second growth, hedgerows, and forest edge (sometimes in forest canopy). Often cocks tail. Call a series of three to six high-pitched, plaintive *pwee* notes, descending slightly.

Mouse-colored Tyrannulet
Phaeomyias murina

4.5 in (11 cm). Very drab; best recognized by combination of **brownish upperparts, buffy wing-bars**, and dull whitish superciliary. Southern Beardless-Tyrannulet is smaller, has whitish wing-bars, and often cocks tail. Fairly common in lowlands on Pacific slope, from western Chiriquí to eastern Panamá Province. Found in scrub, open areas with scattered trees, and hedgerows. Call a series of sharp, high-pitched *djiw* notes, accelerating near end and then dropping off sharply on final one or two notes.

Brown-capped
Tyrannulet

Yellow-bellied
Tyrannulet

Southern
Beardless-Tyrannulet

Mouse-colored
Tyrannulet

Yellow Tyrannulet
Capsiempis flaveola

4.5 in (11 cm). Combination of **yellow superciliary, wing-bars, and underparts** is distinctive. Yellow-winged Vireo (p. 272) is similar in pattern but has thicker bill (little elevational overlap); Yellow-breasted Flycatcher (p. 234) has wider bill, and orange lores and eye-ring (no range overlap). Fairly common on Pacific slope eastward to eastern Panamá Province, and on Caribbean in western Bocas del Toro and from northern Coclé to western Kuna Yala; to 3,900 ft (1,300 m). Found in scrub, young second growth, and thickets in open areas. Call a variety of *whit* and *whee-dup* notes given in a jumbled series.

Yellow-crowned Tyrannulet
Tyrannulus elatus

4.5 in (11 cm). Distinguished from other small flycatchers by combination of **grayish superciliary, pale yellowish wing-bars**, and **yellow breast and belly**; yellow crown patch is often displayed, especially when calling. Also note very short bill. Paltry Tyrannulet (p. 230) has wing edging rather than wing-bars; Southern Beardless-Tyrannulet (p. 222) has less prominent superciliary and paler crown and usually appears slightly crested; in Rough-legged Tyrannulet (p. 228) superciliaries meet on forehead (no elevational overlap). Common on entire Pacific slope and on Caribbean from northern Coclé to western Kuna Yala. Occurs in lowlands, in forest edge, woodland, clearings, and gardens. Call a clear, whistled *fwee-DEER* (paraphrased as "three BEERS!").

Forest Elaenia
Myiopagis gaimardii

4.5 in (12 cm). Confusing; best distinguished from similar species by combination of **narrow bill** and **yellow wing-bars and wing edging**. Yellow crown patch is usually concealed. Greenish Elaenia is very similar but lacks wing-bars or edging; Yellow-olive Flycatcher (p. 236) has a much broader bill; Yellow-crowned Tyrannulet has smaller bill, lacks yellow edging on wing coverts (but has wing-bars), and has more distinct superciliary. See also Yellow-margined Flycatcher (p. 236) and female Gray Elaenia. Fairly common in lowlands on Caribbean Slope from northern Coclé eastward, and on Pacific slope from Canal Area eastward. Occurs in upper levels of forest; often with mixed-species flocks. Call an emphatic, sharp *fwee-iik!* (two distinct notes repeated at well-spaced intervals).

Greenish Elaenia
Myiopagis viridicata

5 in (13 cm). Nondescript and easily confused with other species; note **indistinct grayish superciliary** and **lack of distinct markings on wings**. Forest Elaenia has wing-bars and wing edging; Yellow-olive and Yellow-margined Flycatchers (p. 236) have distinct wing markings and broader bills. Uncommon in lowlands on Pacific slope eastward to western Darién, and on Caribbean slope in Canal Area. Occurs in forest edge, woodland, and gallery forest. Call a sharp *pseeer!* (not two distinct notes like call of Forest Elaenia).

Gray Elaenia
Myiopagis caniceps

4.5 in (12 cm). On male, **bluish gray upperparts** and **white wing-bars and wing edging** are distinctive. Female very similar to Forest Elaenia, but back is brighter olive (contrasting more with gray crown) and wings are blacker (contrasting more with yellow wing-bars and wing edging). Rare in lowlands; recorded from Caribbean slope in Canal Area and from eastern Darién. Occurs in canopy of forest. Often with mixed-species flocks. Call a very rapid trill of sharp high-pitched notes; also a sharp *wheek!*

Yellow
Tyrannulet

Yellow-crowned
Tyrannulet

Forest
Elaenia

Greenish Elaenia

female

male

Gray Elaenia

Yellow-bellied Elaenia

Elaenia flavogaster

6 in (15 cm). **Crest (slightly divided in center** and usually **showing white at base)** is distinctive when raised (which it frequently is). Very similar to Lesser Elaenia (see for distinctions). Northern Scrub-Flycatcher (p. 232) lacks crest; Panama Flycatcher (p. 248) is larger, has longer, heavier bill, and has only slight crest. Very common on entire Pacific slope and on Caribbean in Bocas del Toro and from northern Coclé eastward to western Kuna Yala; to over 6,300 ft (1,900 m). Found in scrub, young second growth, open areas with trees, gardens, and hedgerows. Very active and noisy; one common call is a descending series of hoarse notes: *FWEER-fweer-fwir*; also gives a harsh descending *fwirrr!*

Lesser Elaenia

Elaenia chiriquensis

5.5 in (14 cm). Very similar to Yellow-bellied Elaenia, but is somewhat smaller and has only **slight crest** (which may show white in center, like that of Yellow-bellied); also shows less contrast between gray breast and yellow belly. Mountain Elaenia (limited elevational overlap) lacks crest entirely and is nearly uniformly light yellowish olive below. Fairly common on Pacific slope eastward to eastern Panamá Province; uncommon on Caribbean slope in Canal Area and adjacent Colón Province; to 5,000 ft (1,500 m), rarely to 6,300 ft (1,900 m). Found in scrub, young second growth, and open areas with trees. Calls include a buzzy *chwik!* and a soft *fwir* (not nearly as loud or harsh as the calls of Yellow-bellied Elaenia).

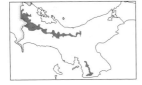

Mountain Elaenia

Elaenia frantzii

6 in (15 cm). Closely resembles Lesser Eleania (little elevational overlap) but has **rounded head** (lacks crest entirely), never shows white on crown, and is almost **uniformly light yellow-olive below** (lacks contrasting gray chest). Also note **wide, pale edging on tertials**. Very common in western highlands eastward to Veraguas; mostly 5,000 to 8,000 ft (1,500 to 2,400 m), but recorded 2,500 to 11,000 ft (750 to 3,300 m). Found in scrub, thickets in pastures, hedgerows, and forest edge. Call a short, descending, whistled *pwir*

Ochre-bellied Flycatcher

Mionectes oleagineus

5 in (13 cm). Best distinguished by distinctly **ochraceous belly** (contrasting with plain olive plumage) and by habit of frequently **flicking wings up over back**, one after the other. Race found in eastern Panama shows two indistinct ochraceous wing-bars. Common on both slopes, to 4,100 ft (1,250 m). Found in lower levels of forest. Feeds on fruit and insects. Males sing in leks, giving an interminable series of sharp *tsik!* notes in an irregular rhythm (occasionally interspersed with two-syllable *chwik* notes).

Olive-striped Flycatcher

Mionectes olivaceus

5 in (13 cm). Best identified by combination of **conspicuous whitish spot behind eye** and **streaking on breast**. Flatbills (p. 234) are larger, have very broad bills, and lack spot behind eye. Uncommon in lowlands, fairly common in foothills and lower highlands; occurs on entire Caribbean slope and on Pacific slope from Canal Area eastward; on western Pacific slope found only in foothills and lower highlands; usually below 4,000 ft (1,200 m), sometimes to above 6,000 ft (1,800 m). Found in lower levels of forest; favors moist ravines. Inconspicuous; feeds mainly on fruit. Like Ochre-bellied Flycatcher, occasionally flicks wings over back one at a time. Male gives long series of very high, thin *tsi* notes that rise and fall.

Yellow-bellied
Elaenia

Lesser Elaenia

Mountain Elaenia

Ochre-bellied Flycatcher

western race

Olive-striped
Flycatcher

Sepia-capped Flycatcher
Leptopogon amaurocephalus

4.5 in (12 cm). Combination of **distinct dark patch on ear coverts, brown cap**, and **buffy wing-bars** is distinctive. Flicks wings up over back, one at a time. Slaty-capped Flycatcher (little elevational overlap) is similar but has dark gray crown. Rare on Pacific slope, eastward to eastern Panamá Province, to 2,100 ft (650 m); a few records from Caribbean slope in Canal Area. Found in lower levels of gallery and dry forests. Sometimes with mixed-species flocks. Call a rough, high-pitched trill: *chchchrrrrrreeeew*.

Slaty-capped Flycatcher
Leptopogon superciliaris

5 in (13 cm). Has **dark patch on ear coverts** and **buffy wing-bars** like Sepia-capped Flycatcher (little elevational overlap) but is distinguished from that species by **dark gray cap**. Like Sepia-capped, flicks wings over back one at a time. Uncommon in western foothills and highlands eastward to Coclé, and in eastern Darién; mostly 1,500 to 4,500 ft (450 to 1,350 m). Found in lower levels of forest, often with mixed-species flocks. Call a squeaky *whikup!*

Yellow-green Tyrannulet
Phylloscartes flavovirens

4 in (10 cm). Small and slender. Best recognized by combination of **white eye-ring, two yellowish wing-bars**, and nearly uniform yellow underparts. Uncommon in lowlands on Pacific slope from Canal Area eastward, and on Caribbean slope in Canal Area. Occurs in forest canopy. Perches horizontally, often cocking tail; frequently droops both wings at same time, or lifts wings over back one at a time. Frequently with mixed-species flocks. Call a short, very rapid descending *chchchrritt*. **EL***

Rufous-browed Tyrannulet
Phylloscartes superciliaris

4 in (10 cm). Easily recognized by **thin black crescent surrounding whitish cheeks**; also note rufous brow (sometimes hard to see) and white forehead. Uncommon and local in foothills; 2,000 to 4,000 ft (600 to 1,200 m). Found in canopy of wet forest. Often with mixed-species flocks. Calls include a high-pitched *sheet!* and a rapid series of *chit* notes delivered in an irregular pattern.

Rough-legged Tyrannulet
Phyllomyias burmeisteri

4.5 in (11 cm). Best recognized by **broad white superciliaries that meet on forehead, gray crown, yellowish wing-bars**, and **yellowish breast and belly**; also note pale lower mandible. Yellow-crowned Tyrannulet (no elevational overlap, p. 224) has grayish superciliaries that do not meet or forehead and a stubbier, all-black bill. Rare in western highlands eastward to central Chiriquí; recorded mostly 4,000 to 7,000 ft (1,200 to 2,100 m), one record from 3,500 ft (1,050 m). Found in canopy of forest and in forest edge. Often with mixed-species flocks. Call a sharp whistled *shrreeek!*

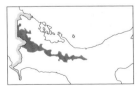

Torrent Tyrannulet
Serpophaga cinerea

4 in (10 cm). Of Panama birds that occur in mountain streamside habitat, the only species with combination of **black cap, wings, and tail** and **gray back**. Black Phoebe (p. 244) is mostly black; American Dipper (p. 296) is more uniformly gray and very different in shape. Common in foothills and highlands in western Panama eastward to Veraguas; mostly 4,000 to 6,600 ft (1,200 to 2,000 m), sometimes down to 2,500 ft (750 m), especially on Caribbean slope. Found along swiftly flowing rivers and streams. Often perches on rocks along edge or in middle of streams; frequently wags tail up and down. Call a repeated *tsip*.

Sepia-capped
Flycatcher

Slaty-capped
Flycatcher

Yellow-green
Tyrannulet

Rufous-browed
Tyrannulet

Rough-legged
Tyrannulet

Torrent
Tyrannulet

Sooty-headed Tyrannulet
Phyllomyias griseiceps

4 in (10 cm). Combination of **dusky cap** (slightly crested), **lack of wing-bars**, and **yellowish belly** distinguishes it from similar species. Paltry Tyrannulet has slaty cap, conspicuous yellow wing edging, and grayish underparts (no yellow). Uncommon on Pacific slope from eastern Panamá Province eastward; to 2,000 ft (600 m). Found in forest canopy and in adjacent clearings with trees. Call a chipper, musical *deet-diddlydeedit*.

Paltry Tyrannulet
Zimmerius vilissimus

4 in (10 cm). Wings with **bright yellow edging (but no wing-bars)** distinguish it from other small flycatchers. Also note **pale gray underparts**; most other tyrannulets have mainly yellow underparts. Yellow-margined Flycatcher (p. 236) is much larger and has yellow belly. Common on both slopes; mostly below 4,000 ft (1,200 m), but to 7,000 ft (1,200 m) in western Chiriquí. Inhabits forest canopy. Often feeds on mistletoe berries. Call a whistled *peee-yup!* (accented on the second syllable).

Bronze-olive Pygmy-Tyrant
Pseudotriccus pelzelni

4.5 in (11 cm). Darker and more uniformly colored than any other small flycatcher; also note **rufous wing edging, pale yellowish belly**, and red or reddish brown eye. Female manakins (pp. 268-271) are more olive green and have shorter tail. Uncommon in lower levels of forest in highlands of eastern Darién, mostly above 4,000 ft (1,200 m). Sometimes with mixed-species flocks. Call a short, high-pitched buzzy trill. Frequently snaps bill; in flight, makes whirring sound with its wings.

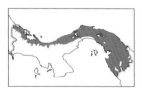

Black-capped Pygmy-Tyrant
Myiornis atricapillus

2.5 in (6 cm). **Tiny size, black cap,** and **almost tailless appearance** make this species easy to recognize; also note **white spectacles**. Black-headed Tody-Flycatcher (p. 232) lacks spectacles and has much more yellow on underparts. Fairly common in lowlands on Caribbean slope and on Pacific in westernmost Chiriquí and from eastern Panamá Province eastward. Found in middle and upper levels of forest; difficult to observe due to its small size and tendency to forage high. Call is a sharp, high-pitched *cheet!* given singly or repeated at intervals of 1 or 2 seconds (easily mistaken for call of an insect); call of Black-headed Tody-Flycatcher is similar, but notes are repeated more rapidly, with barely a pause between them.

Scale-crested Pygmy-Tyrant
Lophotriccus pileatus

4 in (10 cm). Easily recognized by **short black and rufous crest** (rarely raised, but color pattern and small projection behind crown are evident even when crest is laid flat). Common in foothills; mostly 2,000 to 4,000 ft (600 to 1,200 m), but recorded from 1,500 ft (450 m) to over 5,000 ft (1500 m). Found in lower levels of forest. Male's calls are surprisingly loud for a bird of its size, and include various sharp *krik!* or *kryik!* notes, given singly or strung together in a series.

Pale-eyed Pygmy-Tyrant
Lophotriccus pilaris

3.5 in (9 cm). Best distinguished by **buffy face** and **obscure brownish streaking on breast**; pale eye is often not conspicuous. Slate-headed Tody-Flycatcher (p. 232) has wider bill, grayer head, and white spectacles. Fairly common on Pacific slope from western Chiriquí to eastern Panamá Province; mostly in lowlands, rarely to 3,000 ft (900 m). Found in scrub, young second growth, hedgerows, and in lower levels of dry woodland. Calls include a harsh, grating *brrrrt* and a series of sharp, burry *whik* notes.

Sooty-headed
Tyrannulet

Paltry Tyrannulet

Bronze-olive
Pygmy-Tyrant

Black-capped
Pygmy-Tyrant

Scale-crested
Pygmy-Tyrant

Pale-eyed
Pygmy-Tyrant

Northern Scrub-Flycatcher *Sublegatus arenarum*

5.5 in (14 cm). Best recognized by combination of **short, mostly black bill** (base of lower mandible paler), **white supraloral stripe**, and **sharp contrast between pale yellow belly and pale gray throat and breast**. Lesser and Mountain Eleanias (p. 226) have less contrast on underparts, and lower mandible that is more extensively pale; Yellow-bellied Elaenia (p. 226) is strongly crested; Panama Flycatcher (p. 248) is larger, has longer bill, and lacks supraloral stripe. Uncommon in lowlands on Pacific slope (especially near coast), eastward to western Darién. Occurs in scrub, dry forest, and mangroves. Call a sibilant whistled *fweep!* (often extended to two notes: *fweee-yip!*).

Slate-headed Tody-Flycatcher *Poecilotriccus sylvia*

3.5 in (9 cm). Combination of **long, slightly flattened black bill** and **light gray throat and chest** distinguishes it from other small flycatchers; also note gray crown and sides of head that contrast with olive back, white supraloral stripe, and broken eye-ring. Pale-eyed Pygmy-Tyrant (p. 230) is somewhat similar but has fine streaking on breast and lacks supraloral stripe and eye-ring; other tody-flycatchers have similar bills but differ in bright yellow underparts. Uncommon on Pacific slope eastward to eastern Panamá Province, and on Caribbean slope in western Bocas del Toro and in western Colón Province and Canal Area; to 2,700 ft (800 m). Found in lower levels of forest edge and in thickets and scrub. Difficult to see, usually remaining in dense vegetation. Calls include a short, descending burry trill, *burrrrr*, and a sharp *chip* (sometimes doubled).

Common Tody-Flycatcher *Todirostrum cinereum*

4 in (10 cm). Bicolored appearance, with **slaty upperparts** (blackish on face) and **bright yellow underparts**, makes identification easy. Also note long, slightly flattened bill and yellow eye. Black-headed Tody-Flycatcher has olive back and white throat. Common on both slopes, to 5,000 ft (1,500 m). Found in forest edge, woodland, scrub, thickets, and gardens. An active and sprightly bird, frequently flipping up its tail or flicking it from side to side. Calls include a sharp *tchk!* and a rapid descending trill.

Black-headed Tody-Flycatcher *Todirostrum nigriceps*

3 in (8 cm). Combination of **black cap that contrasts with olive back, white throat**, and **bright yellow breast and belly** is distinctive. Common Tody-Flycatcher has slaty back, all-yellow underparts, and yellow eye; Black-capped Pygmy-Tyrant (p. 230) has white spectacles and is almost tailless. Uncommon on Caribbean slope eastward to western Kuna Yala, and on Pacific slope from Canal Area eastward; to 3,500 ft (1,050 m). Found in upper levels of forest edge and adjacent clearings with trees. Difficult to observe since it typically forages high up within dense vegetation. Call a series of high, sharp, emphatic notes (8 to 20 or more), evenly spaced and on the same pitch, given at a rate of about 2 per second: *chit!-chit!-chit!-chit!-chit!* (call of Black-capped Pygmy-Tyrant is similar but slower, with notes repeated at 1- or 2-second intervals).

Black-billed Flycatcher *Aphanotriccus audax*

4.5 in (12 cm). Somewhat resembles some of the migrant *Empidonax* species (pp. 242-245) but distinguished by **all-black bill, narrow white supraloral stripe, broken eye-ring**, and **broad pale olive green band** across breast separating white throat from yellowish belly (some migrant *Empidonax* flycatchers have an olive wash on chest but it does not form such a definite band); also note pale buff wing-bars. Forest Elaenia and female Gray Elaenia (p. 224) have gray crown that contrasts with olive back and lack olive band across chest. Uncommon in eastern Panamá Province and in Darién; to 2,000 ft (600 m). Found in lower levels of forest. Call an explosive, wheezy *FWEEdididew*. **EL**

Northern
Scrub-Flycatcher

Slate-headed
Tody-Flycatcher

Common
Tody-Flycatcher

Black-headed
Tody-Flycatcher

Black-billed
Flycatcher

Brownish Twistwing *Cnipodectes subbrunneus*

6.5 in (16 cm). A dull brown bird, lacking obvious field marks; best recognized by its **habit of lifting one wing and then the other over back** (shared by *Mionectes* [p. 226] and *Leptopogon* [p. 228] flycatchers). Thrush-like Schiffornis (p. 258) has shorter bill, shorter and less rufous tail, and lacks buffy brown wing-bars and wing edging; it does not lift its wings. Bran-colored Flycatcher (p. 238) is smaller and has streaking on breast and more obvious wing-bars; it inhabits more open areas (not forest interior). Royal Flycatcher appears crested and has small buffy spots on wing coverts. Fairly common in lowlands on Caribbean slope from northern Coclé eastward, and on Pacific slope from Canal Area eastward. Occurs in lower levels of forest, often near streams. Call usually consists of two (sometimes one or three) short emphatic whistles, each note descending: *fweer, fweer.*

Olivaceous Flatbill *Rhynchocyclus olivaceus*

5.5 in (14 cm). Distinguished from most other flycatchers by **broad, flat bill**, mostly dull olive plumage, and **yellowish olive wing-bars and wing edging**. Eye-ringed Flatbill is very similar but has more conspicuous eye-ring, less conspicuous wing-bars and wing edging, and is more uniformly olive on chest (less yellowish streaking). Smaller Olive-striped Flycatcher (p. 226) has narrower bill and whitish spot behind eye; Sapayoa (p. 220) has plain wings and lacks streaking on breast. Fairly common on Caribbean slope from western Colón Province eastward, and on Pacific slope from Canal Area eastward; to 2,000 ft (600 m). Found in lower and middle levels of forest. Not very active, usually perching quietly; sometimes accompanies mixed-species flocks. Call a short, harsh, descending *khrrrt!*

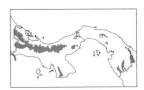

Eye-ringed Flatbill *Rhynchocyclus brevirostris*

6 in (15 cm). Resembles Olivaceous Flatbill, but has **more conspicuous eye-ring** (Olivaceous has slight eye-ring), less prominent wing-bars and wing edging, and a **more uniformly olive chest**. See Olivaceous Flatbill for comparisons with other species. Uncommon in foothills and lower highlands; 2,000 to 6,000 ft (600 to 1,800 m); rare in lowlands of western Chiriquí. Found in lower and middle levels of forest. Behavior similar to that of Olivaceous Flatbill. Call a high, sharp *shreep!*

Yellow-breasted Flycatcher *Tolmomyias flaviventris*

4.5 in (12 cm). **Orange-yellow lores** are distinctive. Much yellower overall than all other flycatchers except Yellow Tyrannulet (no range overlap, p. 224), which has narrower bill and lacks orange-yellow on face. Locally common in lowlands in Tuira River Valley in Darién; probably spreading westward. Found in forest edge and second growth. Call a shrill, high pitched whistle, *shureep*, given at intervals of 1 or 2 seconds.

Royal Flycatcher *Onychorhynchus coronatus*

6.5 in (16 cm). Spectacular red and blue crest is rarely displayed; even when closed, however, crest projects at rear of crown, producing a distinctive **hammerheaded look**. Also note **small buffy spots on wing coverts** and **tawny rump and tail**. Uncommon on both slopes (relatively more numerous on Pacific); to 3,700 ft (1,100 m). Found in lower levels of forest, usually near streams. Call a squealing, emphatic, two-note *kwheee-up!*

Brownish
Twistwing

Olivaceous
Flatbill

Eye-ringed
Flatbill

Yellow-breasted
Flycatcher

female

male
crest raised

Royal
Flycatcher

Yellow-olive Flycatcher
Tolmomyias sulphurescens

5.5 in (14 cm). **Pale eye** and **yellow wing-bars** (not just wing edging) distinguish it from very similar Yellow-margined Flycatcher. Forest Elaenia, Greenish Elaenia, and female Gray Elaenia (p. 224) have dark eyes and narrower bills; larger Olivaceous Flatbill has dark eyes and olive crown. Uncommon on entire Pacific slope and on Caribbean in western Bocas del Toro and from northern Coclé to western Kuna Yala; mostly below 3,000 ft (900 m), occasionally as high as 5,500 ft (1,650 m) in western Chiriquí. Inhabits middle levels of dry forest, gallery forest, and woodland; often found along streams. Call consists of one or two sharp, high-pitched, sibilant *tshrik!* notes.

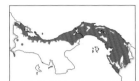

Yellow-margined Flycatcher
Tolmomyias assimilis

5 in (13 cm). **Broad, somewhat flattened bill** (shared with Yellow-olive and Yellow-breasted [p. 234] Flycatchers; not as broad as that of flatbills) distinguishes it from Forest Elaenia, Greenish Elaenia, and female Gray Elaenia (p. 224). Very similar to Yellow-olive Flycatcher; distinguished by **dark eye** (pale in Yellow-olive) and **distinct whitish patch at base of primaries**; note that it has broad yellow wing edging but **no wing-bars** (Yellow-olive has distinct wing-bars); also differs in habitat. Common on entire Caribbean slope; on Pacific slope, common from western Panamá Province eastward, but rare in western Chiriquí; to 2,500 ft (750 m). Found in middle and upper levels of forest, often with mixed-species flocks. Call a series of three to five sharp, high-pitched notes usually with a slight pause after the first note: *shrik, shrik-shrik-shrik.*

Stub-tailed Spadebill
Platyrinchus cancrominus

3.5 in (9 cm). Very similar to White-throated Spadebill (no range overlap) but slightly paler overall, with less yellow in crown. No similar species in limited Panama range; uncommon on larger islands of Bocas del Toro (one record from adjacent mainland). Inhabits lower levels of forest. Call a rapid staccato *whitididit.*

White-throated Spadebill
Platyrinchus mystaceus

3.5 in (9 cm). Combination of stubby shape, **broad flat bill**, and **complex facial pattern** distinguishes it from all Panama species except Stub-tailed Spadebill (no range overlap) and Golden-crowned Spadebill (limited elevational overlap), the latter of which has conspicuous golden rufous (no yellow) crown and olive (not brown) back. Uncommon in foothills and highlands, from 2,500 to 6,000 ft (750 to 1,800 m). Found in lower levels of forest. Call a sharp, squeaky *wheek!* (sometimes doubled).

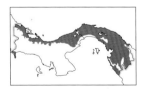

Golden-crowned Spadebill
Platyrinchus coronatus

3.5 in (9 cm). Easily recognized by stubby shape, **broad flat bill**, and **complex facial pattern**; black-bordered **golden rufous crown** and olive back distinguish it from other spadebills. Fairly common on entire Caribbean slope; also fairly common on Pacific slope, from eastern Panamá Province eastward and in western Chiriquí; elsewhere on western Pacific slope found only in foothills; to 3,500 ft (1,050 m). Found in lower levels of forest. Call a weak, buzzy, insect-like trill, lasting about 2 seconds.

Ruddy-tailed Flycatcher
Terenotriccus erythrurus

4 in (10 cm). Combination of tiny size, **gray head**, and **rufous underparts, wings, rump, and tail** makes this species easy to identify. Common on both slopes, to 2,600 ft (800 m). Found in lower and middle levels of forest. Occasionally with mixed-species flocks. Call a high, thin *pseee-sit!*

Yellow-olive
Flycatcher

Yellow-margined
Flycatcher

Stub-tailed
Spadebill

White-throated
Spadebill

Golden-crowned
Spadebill

Ruddy-tailed
Flycatcher

Sulphur-rumped Flycatcher
Myiobius sulphureipygius

4.5 in (12 cm). Conspicuous **pale yellow rump** distinguishes it from all other widespread small flycatchers except nearly identical Black-tailed, from which it differs by **tawny chest and flanks**; also differs in habitat. In Darién highlands, compare also with Tawny-breasted Flycatcher. Fairly common on entire Caribbean slope; also fairly common on Pacific slope, from eastern Panamá Province eastward and in western and central Chiriquí; elsewhere on western Pacific slope, occurs only in foothills; to 4,000 ft (1,200 m). Found in lower levels of forest, often near streams. Frequently with mixed-species flocks. Forages very actively, often fanning tail and drooping wings while displaying rump. Call a sharp thin *psit!*

Black-tailed Flycatcher
Myiobius atricaudus

4.5 in (12 cm). Shares conspicuous **pale yellow rump** with very similar Sulphur-rumped Flycatcher, from which it differs in **dull buffy olive** (not tawny) **chest**. Uncommon in lowlands on both slopes. Found in lower levels of dry forest, gallery forest, forest edge, and woodland; often near streams. Behavior similar to that of Sulphur-rumped Flycatcher. Call a thin *wi* (softer than that of Sulphur-rumped).

Tawny-breasted Flycatcher
Myiobius villosus

5.5 in (14 cm). Very similar to Sulphur-rumped Flycatcher, but slightly larger, darker olive above, and **more extensively tawny on underparts** (yellow limited to center of belly). Known in Panama from only two specimens collected in forest on Cerro Tacarcuna in Darién at 4,125 and 4,800 ft (1,250 and 1,460 m); may occur elsewhere in highlands of eastern Darién. Call similar to that of Sulphur-rumped Flycatcher.

Bran-colored Flycatcher
Myiophobus fasciatus

4.5 in (12 cm). Combination of distinctly **brown upperparts, streaked breast**, and conspicuous **buff wing-bars** distinguishes it from other small flycatchers. Brownish Twistwing (p. 234) is larger, has less conspicuous wing-bars, and lacks streaking on breast; also differs in habitat. Uncommon on Pacific slope eastward to eastern Panamá Province, and on Caribbean slope in Canal Area and eastern Colón Province; also occurs on Caribbean slope of western Panama in the foothills of Ngöbe-Buglé and Veraguas; to over 4,300 ft (1,300 m). Found in scrub, second growth, and thickets in open areas. Call a thin, whistled *whee-he-he-he-he*.

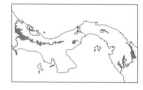

Tufted Flycatcher
Mitrephanes phaeocercus

4.5 in (12 cm). Only small flycatcher with such a **pointed crest**; also note **bright tawny breast** (brightest on race found in westernmost Panama, paler in central Panama, and palest in race found in Darién). Rare Ochraceous Pewee is much larger, with longer bill, and darker below. Common in foothills and highlands; mostly 2,000 to 5,000 ft (600 to 1,500 m), sometimes to 7,100 ft (2,150 m). Found in lower and middle levels of forest. Sallies for insects like a small pewee, often returning to same perch and shivering tail on alighting. Call a rapid series of high chirping *pip* notes.

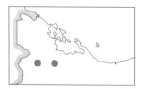

Ochraceous Pewee
Contopus ochraceus

6.5 in (16 cm). Combination of **crest, ochre breast**, and **ochre wing-bars** is distinctive. Tufted Flycatcher is much smaller with brighter tawny on breast. Very rare in western Chiriquí; recorded 4,000 to 8,000 ft (1,200 to 2,400 m). Found at forest edge. Call a sharp, repeated *pwit;* also gives a *pip-pip-pip.* **WH**

Sulphur-rumped
Flycatcher

Black-tailed
Flycatcher

Tawny-breasted
Flycatcher

Bran-colored
Flycatcher

western
race

Tufted Flycatcher

Ochraceous
Pewee

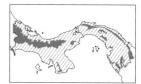

Olive-sided Flycatcher
Contopus cooperi

6.5 in (17 cm). **Dark flanks** (narrowly separated by pale underparts) **almost meet across breast**, creating a distinctive "vested" look. Compared to pewees, has large head and short tail; also distinguished by white tufts that often show behind wings on sides of rump. Uncommon transient, from late Aug to mid-Nov and from mid-March to late May; rare winter resident. Occurs mostly in foothills and highlands. Usually seen on high exposed perch, from which it makes long sallies for insects, often returning to original perch. Call a series of three loud whistles, the first note brief, followed by two longer ones (often paraphrased as "quick, three-beers"); also gives a rapid *pip-pip-pip*.

Dark Pewee
Contopus lugubris

6.5 in (16 cm). Recognized by combination of **distinct crest** and nearly uniformly **dark underparts** (slightly paler on throat and lower belly). Fairly common in western foothills and highlands eastward to central Chiriquí; mostly 3,000 to 7,500 ft (900 to 2,250 m). Found in canopy of forest and in adjacent open areas with large trees. Behavior similar to that of Olive-sided Flycatcher. Call a variable series of high thin *pip* notes. **WH**

Eastern Wood-Pewee
Contopus virens

5.5 in (14 cm). Nearly identical to Western Wood-Pewee, from which it is reliably distinguished only by voice. Tends to be somewhat paler and has more distinct wing-bars; lower mandible is mostly pale (on Western Wood-Pewee, lower mandible is pale only on basal half), but these characters are variable. Very similar Tropical Pewee is distinguished by pale lores. *Empidonax* flycatchers (pp. 242-245) are slightly smaller and have relatively shorter wings; most (with the exception of Willow and Alder Flycatchers) have distinct eye-rings and brighter wing-bars. Common transient, mostly in lowlands; mainly Sept to Nov and March to mid-May. Found in forest edge. Sallies out after insects from perch, to which it then returns; does not flick tail (unlike Tropical Pewee and *Empidonax* flycatchers). Call a sharp, whistled, rising *pee-wee* (sometimes gives full song: *pee-a-wee*).

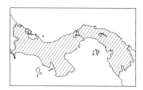

Western Wood-Pewee
Contopus sordidulus

5.5 in (14 cm). Very similar to Eastern Wood-Pewee and Tropical Pewee; see those species for comparisons. Common transient, mainly early Aug to late Nov and early March to May; possibly rare winter resident. Mainly occurs in western foothills and highlands. Found in forest edge. Behavior similar to that of Eastern Wood-Pewee. Call a burry *fwee-urrr* slurring downward (rougher sounding than that of Eastern).

Tropical Pewee
Contopus cinereus

5 in (13 cm). Best distinguished from Eastern and Western Wood-Pewees by **pale lores** and by voice; slightly smaller and has darker head, with proportionately shorter wings and longer tail; has mostly pale lower mandible like Eastern. Fairly common on Caribbean slope eastward to western Kuna Yala, and on Pacific eastward to western Darién. Occurs in lowlands, in scrub and in pastures with scattered shrubs and trees. Sallies for insects from low perch, often shaking tail on re-alighting. Call a rapid, musical trill: *dredidididee* (quite different in quality from calls of Eastern and Western Wood-Pewees).

Olive-sided
Flycatcher

Dark Pewee

Eastern
Wood-Pewee

Western
Wood-Pewee

Tropical Pewee

The *Empidonax* flycatchers are notoriously difficult to identify to the species level. Variation in plumage due to age and wear presents additional complications. Voice is often the most reliable clue, but most migrants call infrequently. Habitat preferences can also aid in identification. Species on this page can generally be distinguished from Eastern and Western Wood-Pewees (p. 240) by being slightly smaller, having proportionately shorter wings in comparison with tail (in wood-pewees, wings extend one-third to one-half distance to tail tip), and having a shorter primary projection. In addition, Yellow-bellied, Acadian, and Least Flycatchers have distinct eye-rings and brighter wing-bars than the wood-pewees or Tropical Pewee (p. 240). When perched, all *Empidonax* species flick wings and tail at least occasionally (like Tropical Pewee but unlike the two wood-pewees).

Yellow-bellied Flycatcher · *Empidonax flaviventris*

4.5 in (12 cm). **Distinctly yellow throat** distinguishes it from most other migrant *Empidonax* species. Acadian also sometimes has yellow throat but is slightly larger and has longer primary projection; it also differs in usual winter range. Yellowish Flycatcher (p. 244) is brighter yellow overall and eye-ring is wider behind eye. Fairly common winter resident, mostly in foothills and highlands (rare in lowlands), from early Sept to late April. Occurs eastward to Veraguas and to western side of Azuero Peninsula; mostly 2,000 to 5,000 ft (600 to 1,500 m). Found in lower levels of forest. Call (frequently given) is a musical whistled *pur-whee*, rising at the end (reminiscent of call of Eastern Wood-Pewee, p. 240, but more rapid).

Acadian Flycatcher · *Empidonax virescens*

5 in (13 cm). Generally the most common *Empidonax* species within lowland forest. Has **longer primary projection** than other *Empidonax*; tends to be more olive above (with exception of Yellow-bellied Flycatcher) and paler below. Sometimes has strong yellow cast below (including on throat), and then can easily be confused with Yellow-bellied. Fairly common transient and winter resident, mostly Sept to late April. Occurs mainly in lowlands, occasionally in foothills and highlands. Found in lower levels of forest. Call a loud, sharp, squeaky *fweet!*

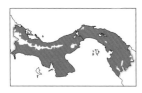

Willow Flycatcher · *Empidonax traillii*

5 in (13 cm). Essentially identical to Alder Flycatcher, distinguishable only by voice. In comparison to other *Empidonax* species, note less distinct eye-ring (sometimes even absent) and often relatively dull wing-bars; white throat usually contrasts noticeably with face. Fairly common transient mainly in lowlands, occasionally in foothills and highlands, from Sept to Nov and April to mid-May; rare winter resident. Found in shrubby areas and in forest edge; often near water. Calls include a burry *fitz-breer*, with the accent on the first syllable, and a rough *brrit!*

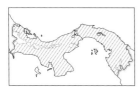

Alder Flycatcher · *Empidonax alnorum*

5 in (13 cm). Distinguishable from Willow Flycatcher only by voice. Migrant, apparently only as a transient. Habitat, behavior, and distribution are probably the same as those of Willow, but exact status is uncertain due to identification problem. Calls include a burry *free-breeo*, with accent on second syllable, and a flat *kep*. **Not illustrated**.

Least Flycatcher · *Empidonax minimus*

4.5 in (12 cm). Distinguished from other *Empidonax* species by slightly smaller size, smaller bill, grayer upperparts, and whiter underparts; also has a more conspicuous eye-ring than most others. Vagrant, with records from Chiriquí, Bocas del Toro, and Canal Area. Favors shrubby areas and forest edge. Call a thin, dry *whit*.

Yellow-bellied
Flycatcher

Acadian Flycatcher

Willow Flycatcher

Least Flycatcher

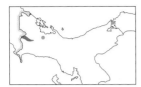

White-throated Flycatcher
Empidonax albigularis

4.5 in (12 cm). Browner than most migrant *Empidonax* species; also note **buffy wing-bars** and buff cast on lower underparts; **white throat contrasts with brownish chest**. Immatures of Willow Flycatcher and Alder Flycatcher (p. 242) can also be brownish above and have buffy wing-bars but are slightly larger. Rare in highlands of western Chiriquí, mostly 4,000 to 6,000 ft (1,200 to 1,800 m); a few records from lowlands. Found in shrubby areas, thickets in pastures, and on fencerows. Calls include a burry, upward-inflected *b-r-r-riik!* and a rough *whirk!*

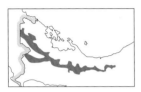

Yellowish Flycatcher
Empidonax flavescens

4.5 in (12 cm). **Asymmetrical yellowish eye-ring** (broader behind eye) and brighter yellow coloration (especially below) distinguish it from other *Empidonax* species, including Yellow-bellied Flycatcher (p. 242). Fairly common in western highlands, eastward to Veraguas; mostly 3,500 to 7,300 ft (1,050 to 2,200 m). Found in lower and middle levels of forest and coffee plantations. Call a short, thin, high *tsee.*

Black-capped Flycatcher
Empidonax atriceps

4.5 in (11 cm). Combination of **blackish cap** and **white eye-ring** (often incomplete) **that is broader behind eye** is distinctive. Fairly common in highlands of western Chiriquí and Bocas del Toro; mostly above 7,000 ft (2,100 m). Found in shrubby areas. Often shakes tail sideways. Call a short high *chit.*

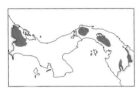

Black Phoebe
Sayornis nigricans

6.5 in (16 cm). Readily recognized by **mostly black plumage that contrasts with white belly**; also note white outer tail feathers. Race found in western Panama has gray wing-bars; eastern race has white wing-bars and less white on belly. Torrent Tyrannulet (p. 228) is much smaller and has mostly gray upperparts. Fairly common in foothills and highlands, mostly 3,000 to 6,000 ft (900 to 1,800 m); occurs locally down to near sea level, especially in Bocas del Toro. Often perches on rocks along or in streams, sallying out for insects; frequently wags tail. Call a high, shrill, whistled *pseeeer* or *ki-seeeeer.*

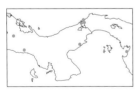

Vermilion Flycatcher
Pyrocephalus rubinus

5 in (13 cm). Male unmistakable, with **scarlet crown and underparts** and **blackish mask and upperparts**. Female grayish brown above; females of migratory races that breed north of Panama are **streaked dusky on breast** and **pinkish or pinkish red on flanks, lower belly, and vent** (immature has pale yellow flanks, lower belly, and vent); females of races that breed in South America **have dusky streaking extending to belly**, and little or no pink below. Vagrant; migrants of either northern or southern races are possible in Panama. Inhabits open country, perching on wires, fences, and trees. Call a thin sibilant *tseek!*

Pied Water-Tyrant
Fluvicola pica

4.5 in (12 cm). **Bold black-and-white pattern** together with waterside habitat should preclude confusion. Locally common in lowlands in eastern Panamá Province and western Darién, and in Canal Area along section of Chagres River that runs above Lake Gatún. Found in marshes and in vegetation along rivers and streams, irrigation ditches, lakes, and ponds. Gleans insects from streamside vegetation; sometimes forages on ground. Call a nasal, buzzy *zhreeeoo.*

245

White-throated
Flycatcher

Yellowish Flycatcher

Black-capped
Flycatcher

western
race

Black Phoebe

male

female
northern race

Vermilion
Flycatcher

Pied
Water-Tyrant

Long-tailed Tyrant　　　　　　　　　　*Colonia colonus*

4.5 in (12 cm); elongated central tail feathers may add 4 in (10 cm). Easily recognized by combination of **mostly black plumage**, **wide white band encircling head** below gray crown, and **thin, elongated central tail feathers** (longer in males than females; may be absent when molting); vertical white stripe down center of back is sometimes concealed. Fairly common on entire Caribbean slope and on Pacific slope from eastern Panamá Province eastward; also occurs on Pacific slope in Veraguas foothills; to 4,000 ft (1,200 m). Found in forest edge and in clearings within forest. Typically sallies for insects from an exposed perch, to which it returns after making a capture. Call a musical, rising, whistled *fweeEET!*

Cattle Tyrant　　　　　　　　　　*Machetornis rixosa*

7.5 in (19 cm). Combination of **brown upperparts, all-yellow underparts, red eyes**, and **long legs** is distinctive. Somewhat resembles a terrestrial kingbird. Tropical Kingbird (p. 254) is greener on back and has gray throat and olive on breast; not usually found on ground. Rare; recorded in Canal Area, eastern Panamá Province, Darién, and the Pearl Islands. Found in cattle pastures and on lawns, airstrips, and other areas with short grass. Forages mainly on the ground, where it runs rapidly; perches on low shrubs or lower branches of trees, sometimes on backs of cattle. Call consists of high-pitched metallic *chit* notes given in a variable series, sometimes strung together as a trill.

Bright-rumped Attila　　　　　　　　　　*Attila spadiceus*

7 in (18 cm). Combination of **heavy hooked bill with pink base, red eyes, bright yellow rump** (sometimes buff), and **streaked breast** is distinctive; bull-headed look and erect posture also aid in identification. Fairly common on both slopes, to 6,000 ft (1,800 m). Found in lower and middle levels of forest. Call a series of emphatic two-note whistles, which rise and become louder, then conclude with a single descending note: *whe-dup, whee-dup, Whee-dup, WHEE-dup, WHEE-DUP, WEeerrr.*

Sirystes　　　　　　　　　　*Sirystes sibilator*

7 in (18 cm). Black, white, and gray pattern is distinctive; **white rump contrasting with gray back** distinguishes it from any similar flycatcher or becard. Uncommon on Caribbean slope from Canal Area eastward, and on Pacific slope from eastern Panamá Province eastward; to 3,500 ft (1,050 m). Found in forest canopy. Call consists of loud, emphatic *chup* notes in a variable series, sometimes run together rapidly: *ch-ch-ch-ch-chup-chup, chup.*

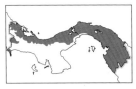

Rufous Mourner　　　　　　　　　　*Rhytipterna holerythra*

7 in (18 cm). Very similar to larger Rufous Piha (p. 258); best distinguished by voice. Mourner has **thinner bill, darker throat** (Piha's paler throat contrasts slightly with breast), **flatter crown** (Piha has rounded head), **wings duller than back** (on Piha, wings are same color or brighter than back), and tends to perch more horizontally. Color more uniform than on female becards (pp. 260-263) or Russet Antshrike (p. 204); Speckled Mourner (p. 258) has pale spots on wing coverts. Uncommon on entire Caribbean slope; also uncommon on Pacific slope in Chiriquí and from eastern Panamá Province eastward; elsewhere on Pacific slope, occurs only in foothills; to 4,600 ft (1,400 m). Found at all levels of forest. Call a mournful, two-note "wolf-whistle," the first note rising, the second falling: *wheeEET, WHEeerrr* also a whistled *wheer-wheer* (both notes on the same pitch).

Long-tailed
Tyrant

Cattle Tyrant

Sirystes

Bright-rumped
Attila

Rufous Mourner

Dusky-capped Flycatcher — *Myiarchus tuberculifer*

6.5 in (16 cm). Distinguished from Panama Flycatcher and Great Crested Flycatcher by **blackish cap** (dusky in immature). Adults of race in western Panama (eastward to Veraguas) and immatures of all races have some cinnamon edging on wings and tail; this is absent on adults of race in eastern Panama. Common on both slopes; to 6,000 ft (1,800 m), most numerous in foothills. Found in forest, in middle and upper levels and in canopy. Calls include a hoarse whistled *wheEEeer* that rises and then falls; also a thinner, flatter *feeeer*.

Panama Flycatcher — *Myiarchus panamensis*

7.5 in (19 cm). Very similar to Great Crested Flycatcher but not as strongly crested, and lower underparts are paler yellow. Adults **lack rufous on wings and tail**; immature has some rufous edging but underside of tail is grayish (not rufous as in Great Crested). Dusky-capped Flycatcher has dark cap; Northern Scrub-Flycatcher (p. 232) is smaller, and has shorter bill and supraloral stripe; Tropical Kingbird (p. 254) has gray crown and nape that contrasts with olive back and a slightly forked tail. Fairly common on both slopes; to 4,500 ft (1,350 m). Found in open areas with trees and in scrub, open woodland, and mangroves. Calls include a whistled *feeww-pik!* and a *wheerr*.

Great Crested Flycatcher — *Myiarchus crinitus*

7.5 in (19 cm). Distinguished from adult Panama Flycatcher by **rufous on wings and tail**; immature Panama has some rufous edging but underside of tail is grayish (rufous in Great Crested). On Great Crested, lower underparts are brighter yellow and contrast more strongly with gray chest. Common winter resident, mainly from Oct to April. Occurs throughout the country, to 3,500 ft (1,050 m). Found in middle and upper levels of forest. Call (frequently given) is a sharp, rising *fweeeUP!*

Lesser Kiskadee — *Pitangus lictor*

6.5 in (16 cm). Similar to Great Kiskadee, differing in smaller size and **more slender bill**. Distinguished from Rusty-margined Flycatcher (which is similar in size and habitat, p. 250) by longer bill and by **white superciliaries that completely encircle crown around back of head**. Fairly common on both slopes from Canal Area eastward. Occurs in lowlands, in shrubs and trees on the margins of lakes, ponds, marshes, and slow-moving rivers and streams. Call a hoarse, buzzy *wheeeerrr-bik!*

Great Kiskadee — *Pitangus sulphuratus*

8.5 in (22 cm). Distinguished from similar-sized Boat-billed Flycatcher (p. 252) by narrower (but still stout) bill with nearly straight culmen, and by **white superciliaries that completely encircle crown around back of head**. Adult further distinguished from adult Boat-billed by **brown** (not olive) **back** and **rufous in wings and tail** (young immature Boat-billed has rufous edging on upperparts, including on wings and tail). Lesser Kiskadee is much smaller with more slender bill. Very common on both slopes; to 4,600 ft (1,400 m). Found in trees in open and semi-open areas and in parks and gardens; often near water. Has a variety of loud raucous calls, including *khis, kha-DEE!* (from which it takes its name); *kik-Khoo* (descending on the second note); and *kik-kik-KA-doo*.

adult

Panama
Flycatcher

adult
western
race

Dusky-capped
Flycatcher

Great Crested
Flycatcher

Lesser
Kiskadee

Great
Kiskadee

Rusty-margined Flycatcher
Myiozetetes cayanensis

6 in (15 cm). Closely resembles Social Flycatcher; distinguished by **black** (not dark brownish gray) **crown and sides of head that strongly contrast with brown back** (back olive in Social) and by **lack of wing-bars** (Social has pale edging on wing coverts producing indistinct wing-bars); also distinguished by orange to yellow crown patch (vermilion in Social), which is usually concealed. Lesser Kiskadee (p. 248) is similar in size and habitat but has a longer, more slender bill and white superciliaries that completely encircle crown around back of head (narrowly divided in Rusty-margined). Fairly common on Caribbean slope from western Colón Province eastward and on Pacific slope from western Panamá Province eastward (more common in Darién, where it extends to open areas away from water); uncommon in Chiriquí and southern Veraguas; to 2,000 ft (600 m). Found in shrubs and other low vegetation; usually near water. Call a sharp, plaintive, prolonged *feeeeeeeerrrr* (lasting a second or more).

Social Flycatcher
Myiozetetes similis

6.5 in (16 cm). Very similar to Rusty-margined Flycatcher; distinguished by **dark brownish gray** (not black) **crown and sides of head, showing little contrast with olive back**, and **indistinct wing-bars**; crown patch is vermilion rather than orange to yellow but is usually concealed. Immature has some rusty edging on wings and tail, lacking in adult. White-ringed Flycatcher has longer bill and white superciliaries that completely encircle crown around back of head (narrowly divided in Social); Boat-billed Flycatcher (p. 252) is much larger with larger bill. Very common on Caribbean slope eastward to eastern Colón Province (isolated record from eastern Kuna Yala), and on Pacific slope eastward to eastern Panamá Province; mostly below 4,300 ft (1,300 m), rarely to 6,300 ft (1,900 m). Found in open areas with trees, forest edge, second growth, shrubby areas, and gardens. Sometimes forages on ground, on lawns and other areas with short grass. Noisy, with a variety of calls; one call consists of one or two sharp notes followed by a buzzy trill, *tseep, brit-buweeerr*; also gives a piercing *chi-wiww!*

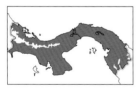

Gray-capped Flycatcher
Myiozetetes granadensis

6.5 in (16 cm). Resembles Social Flycatcher; distinguished by **gray crown and nape** and **white superciliaries extending only to just behind eye**. Tropical Kingbird (p. 254) lacks superciliaries. Fairly common on both slopes; most common in Darién; to 4,300 ft (1,300 m). Found in shrubby areas and clearings with trees; often near water. Call a short sharp *chik!*; also gives a *weer-weer-weer*.

White-ringed Flycatcher
Conopias albovittatus

6 in (15 cm). Similar to Social Flycatcher, but has **white superciliaries that completely encircle crown around back of head; longer bill**; and **no wing-bars**. Great and Lesser Kiskadees (p. 248) also have superciliaries that encircle crown but have more rufous upperparts and mostly occur in different habitat. Uncommon on Caribbean slope in Canal Area and western Colón Province, and on Pacific from eastern Panamá Province eastward; relatively more common in Darién; to 4,500 m (1,350 m). Found in upper levels and canopy of forest. Call a high rattling trill: *whiriririririririkkkkk*.

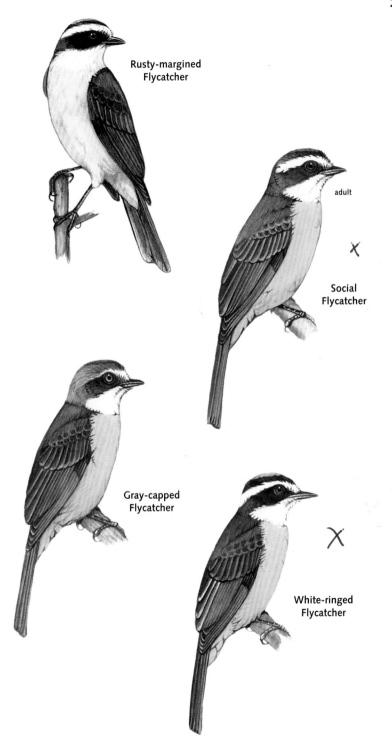

Rusty-margined
Flycatcher

adult

Social
Flycatcher

Gray-capped
Flycatcher

White-ringed
Flycatcher

Boat-billed Flycatcher

Megarynchus pitangua

8.5 in (22 cm). Resembles Great Kiskadee (p. 248) but has even **broader and heavier bill** (with a more arched culmen) and **white superciliaries that are narrowly separated on back of head**. Adult lacks rufous in wings and tail and has **olive** (not brown) **back**; young immatures have some rufous edging on upperparts (including wings and tail). Social Flycatcher (p. 250) is much smaller, with smaller bill. Common on both slopes, to 6,300 ft (1,900 m). Found in middle and upper levels of forest edge, woodland, and nearby clearings. Calls include a grating, rattling *ki-ki-ki-ki-ku-RAW!* (reminiscent of that of Red-crowned Woodpecker, p. 178), and a sharp whistled *fwirk!* that is sometimes followed by a burry trill: *fwik!, burrrrrik!*

Golden-bellied Flycatcher

Myiodynastes hemichrysus

8 in (20 cm). **White malar stripe with dusky submalar below it** distinguishes it from other large flycatchers with **yellow underparts** that occur within its range. Differs from Golden-crowned Flycatcher (no range overlap) in **lack of olive streaking across breast** (may show some vague olive streaking on sides). Fairly common in western foothills and highlands eastward to Coclé; recorded 2,500 to 6,300 ft (750 to 1,900 m). Found in middle and upper levels of forest edge and adjacent clearings with trees. Call a high, squeaky *fwee-ik!* **WH**

Golden-crowned Flycatcher

Myiodynastes chrysocephalus

8 in (20 cm). Shares **white malar stripe with dusky submalar below it** and **yellow underparts** with Golden-bellied Flycatcher (no range overlap); differs from that species in having **extensive indistinct olive streaking on breast**. Other large flycatchers with yellow underparts that occur within its range lack malar stripe. Uncommon in highlands of eastern Darién; mostly above 4,000 ft (1,200 m). Found in middle and upper levels of forest edge and in clearings in forest. Call is a sharp *kee-ip!* (similar to that of Golden-bellied).

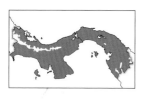

Streaked Flycatcher

Myiodynastes maculatus

8 in (20 cm). Similar to Sulphur-bellied Flycatcher, which is much rarer (see that species for comparisons). Distinguished from other large flycatchers by **streaked underparts** and **rufous tail**. Piratic Flycatcher (p. 254) is much smaller, with shorter bill, unstreaked back, and no rufous on rump and tail. Common on both slopes, to 5,600 ft (1,700 m). Migrants from farther north in Central America supplement resident population during winter. Calls include a strident whining *kee-YOOO* and a sharp *chik!*; at dawn sings a musical *wheet!-fididi-wheet!*

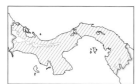

Sulphur-bellied Flycatcher

Myiodynastes luteiventris

7.5 in (19 cm). **Black chin** is diagnostic in comparison to much more common Streaked Flycatcher, which has white chin; also note **heavier submalar stripe, lower mandible with pink restricted to base** (on Streaked, basal half of lower mandible is pink), and whitish edging on wing coverts (on Streaked, edging is more buffy or rufous). Lower underparts are usually more yellowish than on Streaked (though some immature Sulphur-bellied have whitish underparts). Uncommon transient, mostly Sept to Oct and March to April. Occurs throughout the country, mainly in lowlands and foothills. Found in upper levels of forest and woodland. Call a high, squealing *squee-yup!*

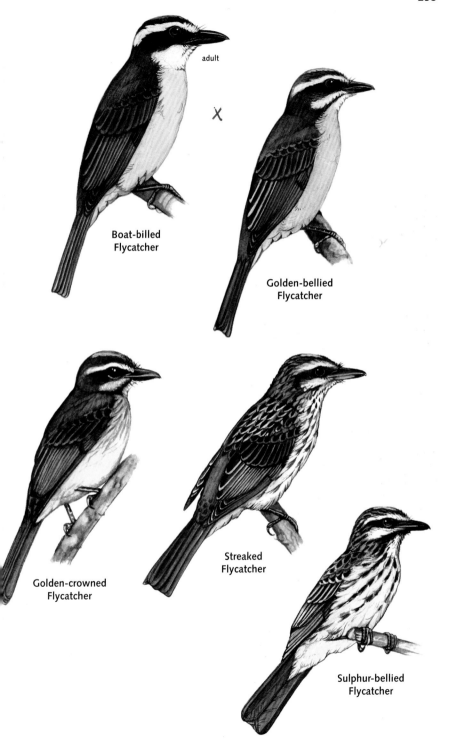

adult

Boat-billed
Flycatcher

X

Golden-bellied
Flycatcher

Golden-crowned
Flycatcher

Streaked
Flycatcher

Sulphur-bellied
Flycatcher

Piratic Flycatcher
Legatus leucophaius

5.5 in (14 cm). Similar in pattern to much larger Streaked and Sulphur-bellied Flycatchers (p. 252), but note **shorter all-dark bill, unstreaked olive-brown upperparts**, and **lack of rufous on rump and tail**. Fairly common on both slopes, to 5,300 ft (1,600 m). Breeds in Panama, but migrates to South America in nonbreeding season (Oct to Dec). Found in forest edge, clearings, and parks and gardens. Feeds mainly on fruit. Name derives from habit of harassing oropendolas, caciques, and other species to appropriate their nests for its own use. Males sing interminably during the breeding season (often from a high perch), giving a sibilant whistled *fee-eee*, usually followed after a pause by a staccato *didididi*.

Tropical Kingbird
Tyrannus melancholicus

8 in (20 cm). One of the most conspicuous and widespread birds in Panama; combination of **gray head that contrasts with olive back, yellow breast with olive wash, yellow belly**, and **slightly notched dusky brown tail** is distinctive. Compare vagrant Western Kingbird. Eastern and Gray Kingbirds have white underparts; on Panama Flycatcher (p. 248), crown and nape are same color as back (not contrasting); Gray-capped Flycatcher (p. 250) has white forehead and short white superciliary. Abundant throughout the country, to 6,300 ft (1,900 m). Found in open areas, forest edge and clearings, and urban habitats. Frequently seen perched on roadside wires. Call a high-pitched metallic chittering; dawn song consists of a few short notes followed by an undulating trill: *pip-pip-pip-deetdididideet*.

Western Kingbird
Tyrannus verticalis

8.5 in (22 cm). Very similar to much more common Tropical Kingbird; distinguished by shorter bill, by pale gray on underparts extending to breast (not just on throat), and by **unnotched black tail that contrasts strongly with back (outer tail feathers narrowly edged white)**. Tropical has dusky brown, notched tail that lacks white edging and contrasts little with back. Vagrant, recorded in westernmost Chiriquí and Canal Area. Call a high-pitched chittering (similar to that of Tropical Kingbird).

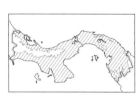

Eastern Kingbird
Tyrannus tyrannus

8 in (20 cm). Combination of **blackish upperparts, white underparts**, and conspicuously **white-tipped tail** is distinctive. Common transient (uncommon on western Pacific slope), mostly early Sept to late Nov and late March to mid-May; to 2,500 ft (750 m). Found in open areas and in forest edge and woodland edge. Often occurs in large flocks. Feeds mostly on fruit in migration. Usually silent in Panama.

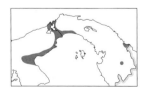

Gray Kingbird
Tyrannus dominicensis

8.5 in (21 cm). Distinguished from Tropical Kingbird by **white underparts** and **entirely pale gray upperparts** (no olive on back); Eastern Kingbird is much darker above and tail is tipped white. Uncommon winter resident, late Aug to late April. Occurs in lowlands on both slopes, mainly near coast. Found in open areas with scattered trees and in urban parks and residential areas. Call a high-pitched *chit-chirri*.

Piratic Flycatcher

Tropical Kingbird

Western Kingbird

Eastern Kingbird

Gray Kingbird

Southern Bentbill
Oncostoma olivaceum

4 in (10 cm). **Thick, downward-curving bill** should prevent confusion with any species but Northern Bentbill (little range overlap), from which it differs by **olive-yellow throat and chest** (not gray). Common in lowlands on Caribbean slope from northern Coclé eastward, and on Pacific slope from Canal Area eastward. Occurs in lower levels of forest. Inconspicuous, often perching quietly in dense vegetation and moving infrequently; usually detected by its frequently given call, a rolling, burry, froglike *bwwrrrrrr*.

Northern Bentbill
Oncostoma cinereigulare

4 in (10 cm). Shares odd **downward-curving bill** only with Southern Bentbill, from which it differs in **grayish throat and chest**. Uncommon in lowlands on Caribbean slope eastward to western Colón Province, and on Pacific slope in westernmost Chiriquí. Occurs in lower levels of forest and in thickets in nearby clearings. Calls and behavior similar to those of Southern Bentbill.

Fork-tailed Flycatcher
Tyrannus savana

M 14 in (36 cm); F 11.5 in (28 cm). Easily recognized by combination of **extremely long forked tail** and **dark cap**. Much rarer Scissor-tailed Flycatcher lacks dark cap. Common on Pacific slope eastward to eastern Panamá Province; less common on Caribbean slope, in Canal Area; to 5,000 ft (1,500 m). Found in open grassy and scrubby areas and in parks and residential areas. Calls include a sharp click and a dry buzzy chittering.

Scissor-tailed Flycatcher
Tyrannus forficatus

M 13 in (33 cm); F 10.5 in (27 cm). Shares **extremely long forked tail** with much more common Fork-tailed Flycatcher; distinguished by **lack of dark cap** and by **paler gray upperparts**. Adult has pink or salmon flanks, belly, and wing-linings; these areas are buff in immature, which has shorter tail. Uncommon and irregular winter resident, from Nov to March. Occurs in lowlands; found on Pacific slope, eastward to eastern Panamá Province (rare east of Coclé); on Caribbean slope, a few records from Bocas del Toro and one from Canal Area. Found in open areas. Call a flat *kip*.

Crowned Slaty-Flycatcher
Empidonomus aurantioatrocristatus

7 in (18 cm). Similar to a kingbird (p. 254) in shape. Has slaty gray upperparts and pale gray underparts; note **blackish crown** (with usually partially concealed yellow crown patch) and **broad black eye-line extending onto ear coverts**. Wings and tail are blackish; bill black. Inhabits forest edge, woodland, scrub, and open areas with trees. Vagrant; one record from Cerro Azul, eastern Panamá Province (2007). **Not illustrated.**

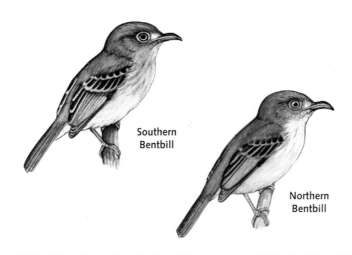

Southern
Bentbill

Northern
Bentbill

Fork-tailed
Flycatcher

Scissor-tailed
Flycatcher

adult

Incertae sedis. This group includes an assortment of species, formerly classified among the manakins, cotingas, or tyrant flycatchers, whose taxonomic position is presently uncertain.

Thrush-like Schiffornis *Schiffornis turdina*

6.5 in (16 cm). A nondescript brown bird that is best recognized by its round-headed and "wide-eyed" look. Birds in lowlands of central and eastern Panama, and in foothills and highlands of Cerro Pirre in Darién, are bright rufous brown, with contrasting grayish belly; those in the foothills and highlands of eastern Panama (except Cerro Pirre), and in the lowlands and foothills of western Panama, are olive-brown and show no contrast between belly and upperparts. Vocal differences between these forms suggest they may represent separate species. Brownish Twistwing (p. 234) has longer bill; longer, more rufous tail; and buffy brown wing-bars and wing edging; Sapayoa (p. 220) is more olive green and has broader bill. Common on Pacific slope and on Caribbean slope from Ngöbe-Buglé eastward; to 4,600 ft (1,400 m). Found in lower levels of forest. Call of rufous form is a series of four whistles, the first longer and slurred upward, the last three shorter and rhythmic: *wheeeeeuuu, whi-whit, wheet!* Call of olive-brown form is similar in quality but consists of three notes, the first one longer, rising and then falling, the last two sharper and more emphatic: *whEEEEuuuuuuuuu, wheet-wit!*

Gray-headed Piprites *Piprites griseiceps*

4.5 in (12 cm). Combination of **gray head, white eye-ring, mostly yellowish underparts** (including throat), and **plain wings** is distinctive. Yellow-olive and Yellow-margined Flycatchers (p. 236) have grayish throats and yellow wing markings. Very rare in lowlands of Bocas del Toro. Found in forest. Calls include a short mellow whistled *wheet!* and a series of staccato whistled notes: *whit-whit-whididi-di-deer.* **CL**

Rufous Piha *Lipaugus unirufus*

9 in (23 cm). Very similar to Rufous Mourner (p. 246), from which it is most reliably distinguished by voice. Piha has **heavier bill, paler throat, more rounded head** (crown somewhat flattened in Rufous Mourner), **wings of same color or brighter than back** (Mourner has wings duller than back), and perches more erectly. Larger and more uniformly colored than female becards (pp. 260-263) or Russet Antshrike (p. 204); Speckled Mourner has pale spots on wing coverts. Uncommon on entire Caribbean slope and on Pacific slope in western Chiriquí and from eastern Panamá Province eastward; to 4,000 ft (1,200 m). Found in middle and upper levels of forest. Call a loud, emphatic whistle, *wheOOOaa!*; also gives a softer *wheeee-oo.*

Speckled Mourner *Laniocera rufescens*

8 in (20 cm). Distinguished from similar Rufous Mourner (p. 246) and Rufous Piha by **rufous spots on dark wing coverts**; breast often shows dusky scaling. Males have pale yellow pectoral tufts on side of breast (often concealed by wings). Uncommon on Caribbean slope in western Bocas del Toro; also uncommon on both slopes from Canal Area eastward; to 6,500 ft (1,400 m). Found in middle levels of forest. Male's song is a prolonged series of loud, sharp, ringing two-note whistles (with an interval of 1 or 2 seconds between doublets): *kli-YI! . . . kli-YI! . . . kli-YI!*

rufous-brown race

olive-brown race

Thrush-like Schiffornis

Gray-headed Piprites

Rufous Piha

male

Speckled Mourner

Barred Becard

Pachyramphus versicolor

5 in (13 cm). Both sexes easily recognized by combination of **yellowish face and throat** and **indistinct dusky barring on underparts**; on female, also note rufous wing patch contrasting with green back. Uncommon in western highlands, mostly above 5,000 ft (1,500 m). Found in middle and upper levels of forest. Often with mixed-species flocks. Call a series of high-pitched notes, the first three or four evenly spaced, the last five or six accelerating slightly: *pii . . . pii . . . pii . . . pi-pi-pipipi.*

Cinereous Becard

Pachyramphus rufus

5.5 in (14 cm). Male distinguished from male White-winged Becard by **white forehead and supraloral stripe, gray back and tail, little white in wing**, and **paler underparts**; male Black-and-white Becard has more white in wing, and tail is blacker and has conspicuous white tipping. Female differs from both Cinnamon Becard and larger female One-colored Becard (p. 262) by **whitish lores and supraloral stripe** and **whiter underparts**. Rare in lowlands. Occurs on Pacific slope from eastern Panamá Province eastward. Found in woodland, forest edge, and clearings with trees. Call a fast trill that rapidly becomes louder at start and then, more slowly, decreases in volume.

Cinnamon Becard

Pachyramphus cinnamomeus

5.5 in (14 cm). Distinguished from female Cinereous Becard and female One-colored Becard (p. 262) by **distinct pale buff supraloral**; also note that Cinereous has whitish (not slaty) lores and is whiter below. Rufous Mourner (p. 246), Rufous Piha (p. 258), and female White-lined Tanager (p. 338) lack supraloral and are more uniformly colored; Russet Antshrike (p. 204) has larger bill, and rufous wings and tail that contrast with duller back. Fairly common on Caribbean slope; also fairly common on Pacific from eastern Panamá Province eastward; uncommon and local on western Pacific slope; to 4,300 ft (1,300 m). Found in woodland, forest edge, and clearings with trees. Call a series of mellow whistles, the first note longer, the remaining notes descending: *deeeew, dew-dew-diw-diw.*

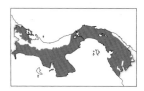

White-winged Becard

Pachyramphus polychopterus

5.5 in (14 cm). The most widespread becard. Male distinguished from male Cinereous and Black-and-white Becards by **black lores, black back, more extensive white in wing and on scapulars**, and **darker underparts**. Female best recognized by **white supraloral, broken white eye-ring**, and **broad buffy edging on scapulars and wing coverts**; female Black-and-white has chestnut cap and distinct blackish line through eye. Fairly common on both slopes, to 4,300 ft (1,300 m). Found in lower and middle levels of woodland, forest edge, and clearings with trees. Call a series of musical notes, the first note followed by a pause, the subsequent series beginning rapidly and then slowing down: *chew, chichichichichuchuchewchew.* Also gives a series of mellow, evenly spaced *dew* notes.

Black-and-white Becard

Pachyramphus albogriseus

5.5 in (14 cm). Male distinguished from male White-winged Becard by **white supraloral stripe, gray** (not black) **back, lack of white scapular bar**, and **paler underparts**; from male Cinereous Becard by more extensive white in wing and **black** (not gray) **tail with conspicuous white tipping**. On female, striking head pattern, including **chestnut cap** and **dark eye-line**, is distinctive; also note buffy wing-bars. Rare in western highlands, from 3,000 to 6,900 ft (900 to 2,100 m); two records from lowlands of Darién. Found in lower and middle levels of forest. Call a series of high, thin whistles: *sweeuh-sweeuh-sweeuh-sweeuh.*

female

male

Barred Becard

female

male

Cinereous Becard

Cinnamon Becard

X

female

male

White-winged Becard

female

male

Black-and-white Becard

Rose-throated Becard
Pachyramphus aglaiae

6.5 in (17 cm). Male is mostly **dark slaty gray** (paler below) **with blacker crown**. (Note that in races likely to occur in Panama, male either lacks rose on throat or has only small rose throat patch.) Unlikely to occur in range of male One-colored Becard. On female, combination of **slaty crown, rufous-brown back,** and **buffy face and underparts** is distinctive. Rare migrant (status uncertain, but probably winter resident) on western Pacific slope; to at least 4,300 ft (1,300 m). Found in forest canopy, forest edge, and woodland. Call a thin, rising *fweeee*.

One-colored Becard
Pachyramphus homochrous

6.5 in (17 cm). Male is **dark slaty gray above**, with **paler gray on breast and belly** (rarely, shows faint pink wash on throat); also note upright stance and bull-headed appearance. Male Rose-throated Becard unlikely to occur in range. Female distinguished from Cinnamon Becard and female Cinereous Becard (p. 260) by larger size and bushier crown; lacks distinct whitish supraloral of Cinnamon; female Cinereous has whiter underparts. Immature male initially like adult female, acquiring adult male plumage only gradually; may have slaty head and back, gray underparts, and rufous wings and tail. Uncommon in lowlands on Pacific slope, from eastern Panamá Province eastward; a few records from Caribbean slope in Canal Area and eastern Panamá Province; to 2,000 ft (600 m). Inhabits forest canopy, forest edge, and nearby clearings with trees. Call a thin, high *sweeooo* that rises and then falls (sometimes preceded by a brief twitter).

Masked Tityra
Tityra semifasciata

7.5 in (19 cm). Both sexes distinguished from Black-crowned Tityra by **bare red orbital patch** and **red base of bill**. Common on both slopes, to 6,100 ft (1,850 m). Found in middle and upper levels of forest and woodland, and in nearby clearings with trees. Call a dry, raspy, croaking *kwirrk* (often doubled, or repeated in a longer series).

Black-crowned Tityra
Tityra inquisitor

6.5 in (17 cm). Distinguished from Masked Tityra by **black crown, all-black bill**, and lack of red orbital patch; on female, also note buff forehead and **rufous sides of head**. Uncommon on both slopes, to 4,300 ft (1,300 m). Found in middle and upper levels of forest and woodland, and in nearby clearings with trees. Call similar to that of Masked Tityra, but thinner and not as rasping: *khhrrrt*.

Rose-throated
Becard

male

female

One-colored
Becard

adult
male

female

Masked
Tityra

male

female

Black-crowned
Tityra

male

female

COTINGIDAE. The cotingas are a highly varied family of mostly fruit-eating birds. They are restricted to the neotropics and reach their greatest diversity in South America. Males often differ markedly from females in plumage and sometimes in size; several species have courtship displays that are among the most spectacular known among birds. Members of the "blue" and "white" groups of cotingas, with three species each in Panama, are similar within each group but overlap little if at all in range. The other three Panama cotingas are very distinctive, and not readily confused.

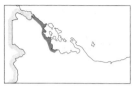

Lovely Cotinga   *Cotinga amabilis*

7 in (18 cm). Both sexes very similar to respective sexes of more widespread Blue Cotinga (known to overlap only in eastern Bocas del Toro); no range overlap with Turquoise Cotinga. Male distinguished from male Blue by **lack of black patch around eye**, more purplish (not as black) throat patch, larger purple patch on breast, and **longer blue uppertail coverts extending almost to tip of tail**; female is paler gray than female Blue and has less heavy speckling on breast. Rare in lowlands of Bocas del Toro eastward to Chiriquí Grande. Found in canopy of forest and in adjacent areas with tall trees. Generally silent.

Turquoise Cotinga   *Cotinga ridgwayi*

7 in (18 cm). Similar to Blue and Lovely Cotingas but no range overlap; male has more purplish (not as black) throat patch and larger purple belly patch than Blue; male Lovely lacks black patch around eye. Female is darker and more heavily speckled than female Lovely; very similar to female Blue. Uncommon in western Chiriquí (to 4,500 ft (1,350 m). Found in canopy of forest, woodland, and adjacent areas with tall trees. Generally silent. **PL**

Blue Cotinga   *Cotinga nattererii*

7.5 in (19 cm). See Lovely Cotinga (limited range overlap) for comparisons with that species; no range overlap with Turquoise Cotinga. Male could be confused with smaller male Blue Dacnis (p. 346) but lacks black back patch and has purple patch on breast; see also male Swallow Tanager (p. 348). Female somewhat resembles a dove or thrush but appears scaled both above and below; also note buffy eye-ring that gives a wide-eyed look. Uncommon on Caribbean slope from eastern Bocas del Toro (Chiriquí Grande area) eastward, and on Pacific slope from western Panamá Province eastward; to 3,000 ft (900 m). Found in canopy of forest, woodland, and adjacent areas with tall trees. Generally silent.

Purple-throated Fruitcrow   *Querula purpurata*

M 11.5 in (29 cm); F 10 in (26 cm). On male, **purple throat** (often flared in display) is diagnostic (though it can be difficult to see in poor light). Female and immature male lack purple throat but are distinguished by **broad silvery bill** (tip dark) and chunky appearance, with broad wings and short tail. Common on entire Caribbean slope and on Pacific slope from Canal Area eastward; to 2,000 ft (600 m). Found in upper and middle levels of forest. Troops about in noisy flocks, plucking fruit from trees in swooping flight; shakes tail on alighting. Call consists of loud, far-carrying, melodious whoops, sometimes rising at the end: *hoop, hoop, hoooOOP!* (interspersed with a variety of harsh grating and quacking notes).

Lovely
Cotinga

male

female

Turquoise
Cotinga

male

female

Blue Cotinga

male

female

Purple-throated
Fruitcrow

female

adult
male

Black-tipped Cotinga
Carpodectes hopkei

9.5 in (24 cm). **Black bill** distinguishes both sexes from Yellow-billed and Snowy Cotingas (no range overlap with either species); male has red eyes and inconspicuous black tipping on outer primaries. Tityras (p. 262) have red and/or black on head. Uncommon in lowlands of southeastern Darién, to about 2,000 ft (600 m). Found in forest canopy. No known calls.

Yellow-billed Cotinga
Carpodectes antoniae

8 in (20 cm). **Yellow bill** distinguishes both sexes from Snowy and Black-tipped Cotingas (no range overlap with either species). Tityras (p. 262) have red and/or black on head. Rare in Chiriquí and in southern Veraguas eastward to Gulf of Montijo; to 1,700 ft (500 m). Found in canopy of mangroves and in adjacent cleared areas with tall trees; occasionally occurs in canopy of non-mangrove forests. Call a trogon-like or dovelike *cuh* or *cow*. **PL**

Snowy Cotinga
Carpodectes nitidus

8 in (20 cm). **Blue-gray bill** distinguishes both sexes from Black-tipped and Yellow-billed Cotingas (no range overlap with either species). Tityras (p. 262) have red and/or black on head. Uncommon in Bocas del Toro and western Ngöbe-Buglé, to 1,500 ft (450 m). Found in canopy of forest and adjacent clearings with tall trees. Call a dry, scratchy *chih* or *chi*. **CL**

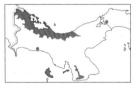

Three-wattled Bellbird
Procnias tricarunculatus

M 12 in (30 cm); F 10 in (25 cm). Male, with **white head, chestnut body,** and **three long pendulous wattles** dangling from bill, is unmistakable. Female can be recognized by large size, olive upperparts, and **olive streaking on yellow underparts**. During breeding season (March to Sept), fairly common in upper levels of forest in western foothills and highlands, mostly from 2,300 to 7,000 ft (700 to 2,100 m); in nonbreeding season, descends to lowlands, mostly on Caribbean slope (rarely on Pacific). Occurs also on Coiba Island and Cébaco Island. Found in upper levels of forest. Males call from high perches, often concealed by leaves and difficult to see. Calls vary locally; they include a harsh, grating *ihrk* and a loud, resonant *CLONG!*

Bare-necked Umbrellabird
Cephalopterus glabricollis

M 16 in (41 cm); F 14 in (36 cm). Male's bizarre **umbrella-like crest** and **bare red throat and chest** make it unmistakable. Female and immature male can be recognized by large size and smaller but still distinctive **crest**. In flight, note broad wings and short tail. Rare in western foothills and highlands; during breeding season (April to Sept), occurs mostly from 3,000 to 7,000 ft (900 to 2,100 m); in nonbreeding season, probably descends to foothills and lowlands on western Caribbean slope. Found in upper levels of wet forest. Displaying male spreads crest and inflates red chest sac while giving a deep, resonant, liquid *HOOM*. **WH**

male

Black-tipped
Cotinga

female

male

female

Yellow-billed
Cotinga

male

female

Snowy Cotinga

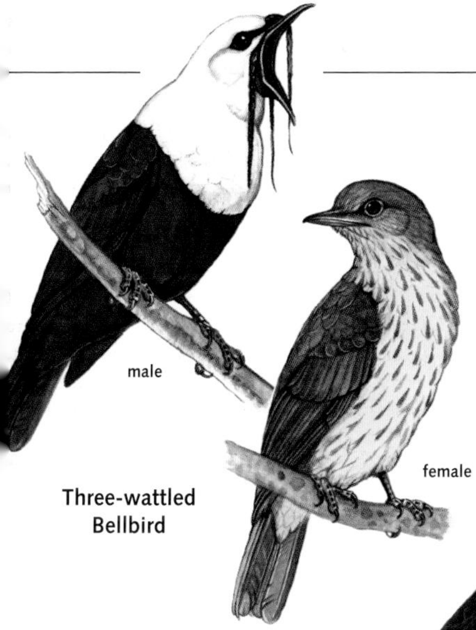

male

female

Three-wattled
Bellbird

female

breeding
male

Bare-necked
Umbrellabird

PIPRIDAE. This family of small fruit-eating birds occurs exclusively in the neotropics. Manakins primarily inhabit the understory of lowland forest and woodland, although a few species occur at higher elevations. Males of most species have bright or contrastingly patterned plumage and are distinctive, while females are mostly green and confusingly similar. In many species, males gather in leks where they engage in elaborate courtship displays—either singly or with a male partner—to attract females. These displays often include a variety of loud noises, some produced vocally and others mechanically by modified wing feathers.

Green Manakin
Chloropipo holochlora

4.5 in (12 cm). Resembles females of other manakin species but is larger, has proportionately **longer tail** than most, and has contrasting **yellowish belly**; female Lance-tailed (p. 270) is similar in size but has pointed tail; Sapayoa (p. 220) is larger and has broader bill and yellower throat. Rare in lowlands and foothills (relatively more numerous in foothills). Occurs in eastern Panamá Province, Kuna Yala, and Darién; to 4,100 ft (1,250 m). Found in lower levels of forest. Usually silent; call a high, rising *sweee!*

White-collared Manakin
Manacus candei

4.5 in (12 cm). Male distinguished from male Golden-collared Manakin by **white collar** and **yellow** (not green) **belly**. Female very similar to female Golden-collared but yellower on belly; distinguished from other female manakins in range by **orange legs**. Males in region between Changuinola and Almirante ("Almirante Manakin") have yellow collar and throat, distinguished from Golden-collared by collar that is broader across back and by yellow that extends lower on underparts. Fairly common in lowlands of western Bocas del Toro. Found in lower levels of forest edge and woodland. Calls and wing-snaps similar to those of Golden-collared.

Orange-collared Manakin
Manacus aurantiacus

4 in (10 cm). Male distinguished from male Golden-collared Manakin (no known range overlap) by **orange** (not golden yellow) **collar, yellow** (not olive) **lower underparts**, and olive (not black) tail. Female (almost identical to female White-collared, but no range overlap) is somewhat more yellow-olive above and yellower below than female Golden-collared; distinguished from other female manakins in range (except Lance-tailed, p. 270) by **orange legs**; female Lance-tailed is larger and has pointed tail. Uncommon on Pacific slope eastward to Azuero Peninsula; to 2,500 ft (750 m). Found in lower levels of forest edge, gallery forest, and woodland. Calls and wing-snaps similar to those of Golden-collared. **PL**

Golden-collared Manakin
Manacus vitellinus

4.5 in (11 cm). Male told from male Orange-collared (no known range overlap) and White-collared Manakins by **golden yellow collar** and **green lower underparts**. Female is more uniformly olive (less yellow) below than female Orange-collared and female White-collared; distinguished from other female manakins in range (except Lance-tailed, p. 270) by **orange legs**; female Lance-tailed is larger and has pointed tail. Common on Caribbean slope from Bocas del Toro (Almirante area) eastward, and on Pacific slope from western Panamá Province eastward; also occurs on western Pacific slope in Veraguas foothills; to 2,500 m (450 ft). Found in lower levels of forest edge and woodland. Displaying males make rapid, loud snapping noise with their wings, like a string of small firecrackers going off; calls include shrill *whee-yoo!* and a churring trill.

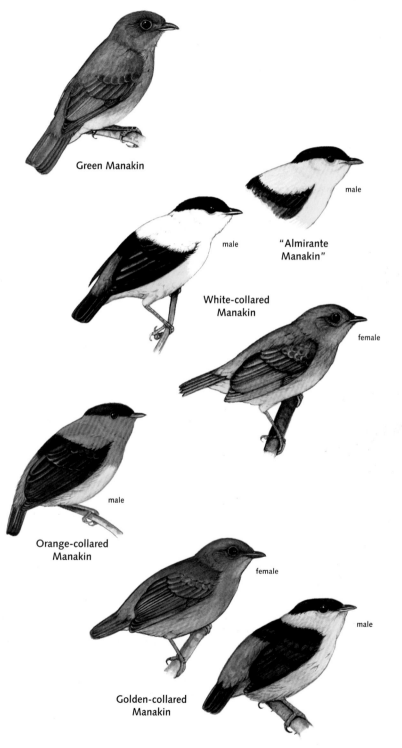

269

Green Manakin

"Almirante
Manakin"

male

White-collared
Manakin

male

male

female

Orange-collared
Manakin

male

female

Golden-collared
Manakin

male

White-ruffed Manakin
Corapipo alter

4 in (10 cm). On male, **white throat contrasting with blue-black head an** **body** is distinctive. Female differs from other female manakins by **distinc** **gray throat and cheeks** contrasting with olive head and body. Common i foothills and lower highlands on both slopes, from 1,500 to 5,000 ft (450 t 1,500 m); rarely down to near sea level on Caribbean slope. Found in lowe levels of forest. Call a high, rolling *prrreeeuw*.

Lance-tailed Manakin
Chiroxiphia lanceolat

4.5 in (12 cm). Male easily recognized by combination of **red cap** and **blu** **back** that contrast with **black body**. Female is larger than other manakin and has **pointed tail**; shares **orange legs** with female White-collarec Orange-collared, and Golden-collared Manakins (p. 268). Immatu male resembles female but has red cap, gradually acquiring full adult ma plumage over a period of several years. Common on Pacific slope westwar to western Darién; on Caribbean slope found only in central Canal Area; t over 5,300 ft (1,600 m). Common in lower levels of dry forest, woodlanc and scrub. Highly varied vocalizations include a mellow *doh!*, a musical *d* *ah*, a nasal *kwaah*, a sharp *kip*, and a hollow, churring *chochochochocho*.

White-crowned Manakin
Pipra pipr

3.5 in (9 cm). On male, **white cap** contrasting with **velvety black head an** **body** should preclude confusion. Female differs from other female manaki by **gray crown** and **red eye**. Rare. Occurs in western foothills and highland mostly on Caribbean slope; from about 1,500 to 4,000 ft (450 to 1,200 m Found in lower levels of forest. Call a harsh buzzy *shhreerr*.

Blue-crowned Manakin
Pipra coronat

3 in (8 cm). Male's **bright blue cap** contrasting with **velvety black hea** **and body** is distinctive. Female is a **brighter grass green** (not olive gree above than other female manakins. Common on entire Caribbean slope; als common on Pacific slope in western Chiriquí and from Canal Area eastwar also occurs on western Pacific slope in Veraguas foothills; to 2,000 (600 m). Found in lower levels of forest. Both sexes give a short musical tri displaying males follow this with a doubled, croaking, froglike *ku-wheek!*

Golden-headed Manakin
Pipra erythrocepha

3 in (8 cm). Male distinguished from male Red-capped Manakin by **brig** **yellow head** and red and white thighs. Female very similar to female Re capped; distinguished by **whitish bill**. Fairly common on Pacific slope fro eastern Panamá Province eastward, and on Caribbean slope in eastern Ku Yala; to 4,000 ft (1,200 m). Found in lower levels of forest. Calls inclu various high-pitched chips and trills; unlike Red-capped, does not snap wing

Red-capped Manakin
Pipra menta

4 in (10 cm). Male distinguished from male Golden-crowned Manakin **red head** and yellow thighs. Female differs from female Golden-crown by **darker bill**. Common on Caribbean slope eastward to western Ku Yala; also common on Pacific slope, in western Chiriquí, southern Veragua and from the Canal Area to eastern Panamá Province; to 2,000 ft (600 n Found in lower levels of forest. Call consists of several short *chit* notes, ther long undulating whistle, followed by a final *chit*: *chit-chit, suuuwhheeeeee, ch* Also makes loud explosive wing-snaps.

White-ruffed
Manakin

male

female

immature
male

male

female

Lance-tailed
Manakin

White-crowned
Manakin

male

female

Blue-crowned
Manakin

male

female

Golden-headed
Manakin

male

Red-capped
Manakin

male

female

VIREONIDAE. These mainly insectivorous birds occur only in the Americas. They resemble wood-warblers (p. 310), but most have heavier, slightly hooked bills and forage less actively (the greenlets are exceptions); the majority are rather drab in coloration. Panama's species include both typical vireos (genus *Vireo*), most of which are migrants, and the resident greenlets, shrike-vireos, and peppershrike. Migrant species are mostly silent but sometimes sing in late spring just before departing to the north.

White-eyed Vireo
Vireo griseus

4.5 in (12 cm). No other Panama bird combines **yellow spectacles, white wing-bars**, and **white throat**. Also note whitish eye on adult (dark in immature). Yellow-throated Vireo has yellow throat; Yellow-winged Vireo has yellow wing-bars and is yellower overall. Rare migrant, recorded from Dec to Feb. Occurs mainly near Caribbean coast; a few records from elsewhere. Found in shrubby areas and overgrown clearings. Song a rapid, variable series of sharp or buzzy notes, often beginning and ending with a short *chik* and including a longer slurred note: *chik, ka-di-deeeer-ka-chik!*

Yellow-throated Vireo
Vireo flavifrons

4.5 in (12 cm). Combination of **yellow spectacles, white wing-bars**, and **yellow throat** is unique. Yellow-winged Vireo has yellow wing-bars and is more extensively yellow below; rare White-eyed Vireo has white throat. Common transient and winter resident, mainly from late Oct to early April. Occurs almost throughout the country, to at least 5,000 ft (1,500 m). Found in forest canopy, in forest edge, and in woodland. Often with mixed-species flocks. Song a series of burry, two- or three-syllable whistles, given at intervals of 2 or 3 seconds; also gives a descending, rasping scold.

Blue-headed Vireo
Vireo solitarius

5.5 in (14 cm). No other Panama bird combines **gray head, greenish back, white spectacles and throat**, and **white wing-bars**. Vagrant; recorded from Nov to March. Reported from highlands of western Chiriquí and near Caribbean coast in Canal Area. Inhabits forest.

Yellow-winged Vireo
Vireo carmioli

4.5 in (11 cm). No other vireo or wood-warbler combines distinct **yellow wing-bars** with **unmarked, mainly yellow underparts**. Yellow Tyrannulet (little elevational overlap, p. 224) has thinner bill; Yellow Warbler (no elevational overlap, p. 312) has indistinct yellow wing-bars but lacks dark lores. Fairly common in western highlands; mainly above 6,000 ft (1,800 m), rarely down to 3,000 ft (900 m). Found in forest canopy, in forest edge, and in adjacent clearings with tall trees. Song a series of two- or three-syllable buzzy notes, given at intervals of 2 to 4 seconds. **WH**

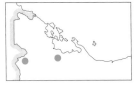

Warbling Vireo
Vireo gilvus

4.5 in (12 cm). Very similar to Philadelphia Vireo (p. 274), but has **much less distinct eye-line, paler lores**, and **lacks yellow on throat** (sometimes flanks and undertail coverts are washed with pale yellow). Brown-capped Vireo (p. 274) has brown crown. Vagrant; one record from foothills of Caribbean slope of Ngöbe-Buglé (1990) and one record from highlands of westernmost Chiriquí (2006). Found in woodland and second growth.

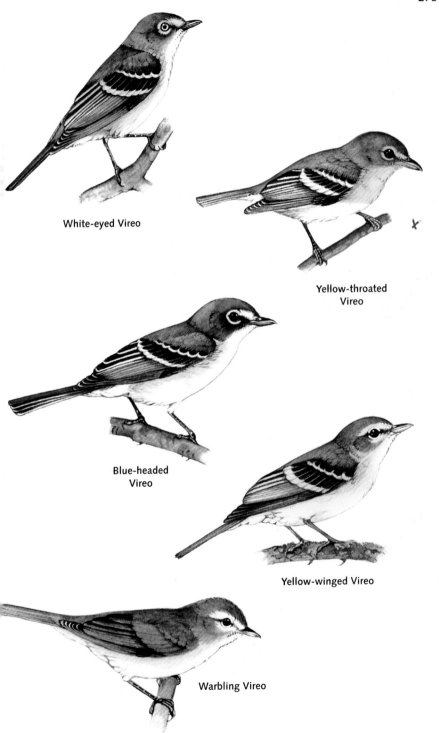

White-eyed Vireo

Yellow-throated
Vireo

Blue-headed
Vireo

Yellow-winged Vireo

Warbling Vireo

Brown-capped Vireo
Vireo leucophrys

4.5 in (11 cm). Very similar to Philadelphia Vireo; differs in **brown crown** and **white throat** (throat pale to bright yellow in Philadelphia). Red-eyed and Yellow-green Vireos have gray crowns. Common in western highlands in Chiriquí and Bocas del Toro; also one record from Cerro Tacarcuna in Darién; mostly 4,000 to 7,000 ft (1,200 to 2,100 m). Found in upper levels of forest edge, second growth, woodland, and overgrown clearings. Song, about 2 to 5 seconds in duration, consists of a rather musical series of short notes in which low notes alternate with high ones.

Philadelphia Vireo
Vireo philadelphicus

4.5 in (11 cm). Distinguished from very similar Brown-capped Vireo by **gray crown**; Philadelphia's underparts, including **throat**, vary from **pale to bright yellow** (white throat in Brown-capped). Red-eyed and Yellow-green Vireos are larger, with longer bill; Red-eyed has dark border to crown; Yellow-green has yellow on underparts restricted to sides, flanks, and undertail coverts. Nonbreeding Tennessee Warbler (p. 310) is similar but has slender bill and is brighter green on back. Winter resident, mainly Oct to early April. Common in foothills and highlands eastward to Veraguas; mostly 3,000 to 7,000 ft (900 to 2,100 ft); uncommon in lowlands eastward to eastern Panamá Province. Found in lower levels of forest edge, woodland, and shrubby areas. Usually silent.

Red-eyed Vireo
Vireo olivaceus

5 in (13 cm). Very similar to Yellow-green Vireo; distinguished by **dark lower border to crown** and more distinct line through eye, and by less yellow on underparts. Philadelphia Vireo lacks dark border to crown; it has mostly yellowish underparts. See also rare Black-whiskered Vireo. Very common transient, from Sept to mid-Nov and March to early May; a few may overwinter. Occurs nearly throughout the country; to 5,300 ft (1,600 m). Found in upper levels of forest and woodland. Usually silent; song like that of Yellow-green Vireo but slower and with longer phrases.

Yellow-green Vireo
Vireo flavoviridis

5 in (13 cm). Distinguished from very similar Red-eyed Vireo by less distinct facial pattern, **lack of dark lower border to crown**, and by more extensive, brighter yellow on side, flanks, and undertail coverts. Philadelphia Vireo is smaller, with shorter bill; the yellow on its underparts extends to breast and throat. See also Black-whiskered Vireo. Common nearly throughout the country; to 5,500 ft (1,650 m). Local breeding population migrates to South America between Oct and early Dec; migrants breeding in North America occur as transients in Sept, Oct, and March. Found in second growth, shrubby areas, scrub, and mangroves. Song an interminably repeated series of flat, two- to three-syllable whistles, with an interval of 1 or 2 seconds between phrases.

Black-whiskered Vireo
Vireo altiloquus

5.5 in (14 cm). Similar to Red-eyed and Yellow-green Vireos; distinguished by **thin dark lateral throat stripe** ("whisker") and heavier bill. Whisker can be difficult to see, and molting or wet individuals of Red-eyed and Yellow-green sometimes appear to have such a mark. Black-whiskered is also duller yellow on sides and flanks than Yellow-green. Very rare migrant (status uncertain, may be transient or winter resident); recorded Aug to April. Reported mostly near Caribbean coast. Usually silent.

Brown-capped
Vireo

Philadelphia
Vireo

Red-eyed
Vireo

Yellow-green
Vireo

Black-whiskered
Vireo

Scrub Greenlet

Hylophilus flavipes

4.5 in (11 cm). Adult is distinguished from any similar bird by combination of **entirely pinkish bill** and **pale eye**. Immature has dark bill and eye but can be recognized by combination of olive upperparts, plain wings, gray face, and yellow breast and belly. Occurs on Pacific slope eastward to eastern Panamá Province, and on Caribbean slope from northern Coclé to eastern Colón Province; usually below 1,500 ft (450 m), rarely to 3,300 ft (1,000 m). Common in scrub, second growth, woodland edge, and gardens. Song a mournful series of 10 to 20 mellow two-note whistles: *du-wee, du-wee, du-wee, du-wee, du-wee.*

Tawny-crowned Greenlet

Hylophilus ochraceiceps

4 in (10 cm). Distinguished from any similar bird by combination of **pale eye** and **tawny crown that contrasts with back** (color of back ranges from brown in western Chiriquí to olive green in Darién). Resembles a small antbird more than a vireo. Female Plain Antvireo (p. 206) has dark eye; Golden-fronted Greenlet has dark eye and occurs in different habitat. Rare locally on entire Caribbean slope and on Pacific slope in Chiriquí, southern Veraguas, and from eastern Panamá Province eastward; to 5,000 ft (1,500 m). Found in lower levels of forest. Often with mixed-species flocks. Call a rapid series of nasal, scolding *dwe* notes; song a leisurely series of evenly spaced, short, clear, rising whistles.

Golden-fronted Greenlet

Hylophilus aurantiifrons

4 in (10 cm). This drab species is best recognized by **light brown crown that contrasts with olive back**. Scrub Greenlet is yellower below; adult has pink bill and pale eye. Tawny-crowned Greenlet has pale eye and is found in different habitat. Fairly common in lowlands on Pacific slope from Herrera and southern Coclé eastward to western Darién; rare in lowlands on Caribbean slope in Canal Area. Found in second growth and scrub. Song a rapid, musical series of four (sometimes three or five) whistled notes: *chit-er-che-ew* or *che-eet-er-chew*.

Lesser Greenlet

Hylophilus decurtatus

3.5 in (9 cm). Best distinguished from other small birds of similar pattern by stubby shape, **relatively large, rounded head,** and **short tail**; also note **whitish eye-ring** and mostly white underparts (yellow confined to flanks). From the Canal Area westward, gray head contrasts with green back; in eastern Panama, head is greenish like back. Breeding male Tennessee Warbler (p. 310) is similar to gray-headed form but has distinct superciliary and lacks eye-ring. Very common on both slopes; to 6,000 ft (1,800 m). Found in middle and upper levels of forest. A frequent member of mixed-species flocks. Call a musical *chee-wit!* or *shr-ee-it!* (repeated almost incessantly).

Scrub Greenlet

Tawny-crowned
Greenlet

western
race

Golden-fronted
Greenlet

Lesser Greenlet

western
race

eastern
race

Green Shrike-Vireo
Vireolanius pulchellus

5.5 in (14 cm). Combination of mostly **bright emerald green upperparts** and **yellow throat** is unique; Yellow-browed Shrike-Vireo (no known range overlap) has broad yellow superciliary and blue crown. Chlorophonias (p. 388) have green throats. Common on Caribbean slope eastward to western Kuna Yala, and on Pacific slope in Panamá Province and Canal Area; rare in western Chiriquí and in Veraguas foothills; to 3,600 ft (1,100 m). Found in forest canopy. Occasionally with mixed-species flocks. Forages deliberately, moving relatively infrequently; this trait, along with canopy habitat and mostly green coloration, makes it very difficult to see. Song, constantly repeated, consists of three short, clear whistles, all on one pitch: *peer-peer-peer* (humorously paraphrased as "can't-see-me!").

Yellow-browed Shrike-Vireo
Vireolanius eximius

5.5 in (14 cm). Distinguished from very similar Green Shrike-Vireo (no known range overlap) by **broad yellow superciliary** and **blue crown**. Rare in eastern Darién; recorded between about 1,600 and 3,300 ft (480 and 1,000 m). Found in forest canopy. Habits similar to those of Green Shrike-Vireo. Song also similar, but consists of four notes instead of three.

Rufous-browed Peppershrike
Cyclarhis gujanensis

5.5 in (14 cm). Broad **orange-rufous superciliary on mostly grayish head** is unique. Fairly common throughout its Panama range; occurs in foothills and highlands in Chiriquí, mostly 2,600 to 8,300 ft (800 to 2,500 m); in lowlands on Pacific slope from southern Veraguas eastward to western Darién; and on Coiba Island. Found in forest edge and second growth; in lowlands on Pacific slope also occurs in gallery forest, coastal scrub, and mangroves; inhabits forest on Coiba. Song is grosbeak-like (pp. 368-371), consisting of variable, short musical whistled phrases; each phrase may be repeated for several minutes before being replaced by a new phrase that is also repeated.

Sharpbill

OXYRUNCIDAE. This odd species has been grouped with the cotingas or tyrant flycatchers, but presently is classified as the sole member of its own family. It feeds on insects, other small invertebrates, and fruit. The Sharpbill has a highly disjunct distribution, from Costa Rica to southeastern Brazil, mostly in foothills.

Sharpbill
Oxyruncus cristatus

6.5 in (16 cm). Combination of **sharply pointed bill, scaling on face,** and **heavy spotting on pale yellow underparts** is distinctive; also note red crown stripe with black edging (red often concealed). Speckled Tanager (p. 344) has stouter bill and spotting on both back and underparts. Uncommon in foothills and lower highlands. Occurs from western Chiriquí to Veraguas, and in eastern Darién; mostly 2,500 to 5,000 ft (750 to 1,500 m). Found in forest canopy. Often accompanies mixed-species flocks, searching for insects on branches and in foliage. Call a high buzzy trill that rises quickly and then slurs downward: *tseUUUuuurrrrrrrrrr!*

Green Shrike-Vireo

Yellow-browed
Shrike-Vireo

Rufous-browed
Peppershrike

Sharpbill

CORVIDAE. Crows and jays are a familiar family of mostly omnivorous birds. They occur nearly worldwide; however, in the Americas only jays occur south of Nicaragua. Panama's four species typically move about in active, noisy flocks.

Black-chested Jay
Cyanocorax affinis

13.5 in (34 cm). The most widespread jay. Easily recognized by distinctive **black, white, and blue pattern**; also note **yellow eye**. Fairly common on both slopes; to over 5,300 ft (1,600 m). Found in all levels of forest and woodland. Calls include a loud, ringing *cheowp, cheowp* and a staccato *chh-chh-chh-chowp!*

Brown Jay
Cyanocorax morio

15.5 in (40 cm). Combination of large size, mostly **dark brown upperparts**, whitish lower breast and belly, and white-tipped tail (conspicuous in flight) is distinctive. Immature has yellow bill and orbital skin. Uncommon in lowlands of western and central Bocas del Toro. Found in forest edge, second growth, and shrubby areas. Call a raucous, nasal, high-pitched *keeyowk!*

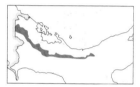

Azure-hooded Jay
Cyanolyca cucullata

11 in (28 cm). **Pale blue crown and nape** contrasting with mostly dark blue body is unique. Uncommon in foothills and highlands, mostly on Caribbean slope. Occurs in western Panama eastward to Veraguas; recorded 3,000 to 7,000 ft (900 to 2,100 m). Found in middle and upper levels of wet forest. Calls include a harsh, grating *cuh-renk, cuh-renk* and a piping *pink!*

Silvery-throated Jay
Cyanolyca argentigula

10 in (26 cm). **Silvery white throat** and **thin white brow stripe and superciliary** contrasting with dark head and body are diagnostic. Uncommon in highlands of western Chiriquí; recorded 5,000 to 9,900 ft (1,500 to 3,000 m). Found in upper levels of forest. Call a harsh, nasal *khir, khir, khir, khirr.* **WH**

Black-chested Jay

adult

immature

Brown Jay

Azure-hooded Jay

Silvery-throated Jay

HIRUNDINIDAE. The swallows and martins occur nearly worldwide. These are among the most aerial of birds, and they feed mostly on insects caught on the wing. Superficially similar to swifts (p. 134), they are distinguished by their more acrobatic flight and habit of perching in the open, often on wires or exposed branches; most Panama swallows are more strongly patterned than swifts. Only five species breed in Panama, the rest being migrants; both migrants and some residents can occur in large flocks during the nonbreeding season. Most swallows do not have distinctive calls, generally producing simple high-pitched chirps and chitters.

Tree Swallow *Tachycineta bicolor*

5.5 in (14 cm). Similar in pattern to Blue-and-white Swallow but has **white** (not black) **undertail coverts**. Mangrove and Violet-green Swallows have white on rump. Female duller than male. Usually rare (may not occur some years), occasionally common. Irregular winter resident, mainly Jan to March. Generally recorded from open areas near water, mostly on Caribbean slope of Canal Area and in eastern Panamá Province.

Mangrove Swallow *Tachycineta albilinea*

4.5 in (11 cm). Only common swallow with **completely white rump**; also note **thin white supraloral stripe**. Very rare White-winged Swallow also has white rump; it is distinguished by large white wing patches. Inhabits lowlands; common on Caribbean slope; uncommon on Pacific slope. Found near water.

White-winged Swallow *Tachycineta albiventer*

5.5 in (14 cm). Shares **white rump** with very similar Mangrove Swallow; distinguished by **large white wing patches** (formed by wide white edging on tertials, secondaries, and wing coverts), visible at rest and especially in flight; also lacks thin white supraloral. Note that Mangrove may have thin white edging on tertials and inner secondaries. Very rare vagrant in eastern Darién; recorded in July and Aug. Occurs on rivers. **Not illustrated**.

Violet-green Swallow *Tachycineta thalassina*

4.5 in (12 cm). Distinguished from Tree and Blue-and-white Swallows by **white patch on either side of rump**, and **white on face extending above eye**. Blue-and-white has black undertail coverts; Mangrove Swallow has all-white rump. Female duller than male. Rare and irregular migrant; recorded only in 1960, 1976, 1977, and 1983, from Dec to March. Flocks of up to 100 have occurred. Found in western highlands, eastward to western Panamá Province.

Blue-and-white Swallow *Pygochelidon cyanoleuca*

4.5 in (12 cm). **Black undertail coverts** distinguish it from other swallows with mostly white underparts. In migrant race, black on undertail coverts is less extensive and underwing coverts are paler. Resident race is common in western highlands eastward to western Panamá Province, mostly above 3,000 ft (900 m). Migrants from South America (present during southern winter, recorded April to Aug) are usually rare but occasionally common; occurs in lowlands of eastern Panama, westward to Canal Area. Found in open areas.

Bank Swallow *Riparia riparia*

4.5 in (12 cm). Distinguished from most other swallows by **brown chest band** separating white throat from white breast and belly. Brown-chested Martin (p. 286) shares breast band but is much larger and band is smudgier. Fairly common transient, mostly in Sept and Oct, and March and April (sometimes as early as Aug and as late as the start of June); rare winter resident. Found in open areas on both slopes.

Tree Swallow

male

male

Mangrove Swallow

Violet-green Swallow

male

male

resident race

resident race

resident race

Blue-and-white Swallow

Bank Swallow

White-thighed Swallow
Neochelidon tibialis

4.5 in (11 cm). Only **small all-dark** swallow (white thighs are inconspicuous in the field). Male Purple Martin (p. 286) and both sexes of Southern Martin (p. 286) are also entirely dark but much larger; both species of rough-winged swallows are pale on lower breast and belly. Uncommon; found on both slopes from Coclé eastward (on Pacific slope occurs mainly in foothills, except in Darién, where it is also found in lowlands); to 4,100 ft (1,250 m). Occurs over roads, streams, and small clearings within forest. Flight more twisting and erratic than that of most other swallows.

Northern Rough-winged Swallow
Stelgidopteryx serripennis

5 in (13 cm). Distinguished from Southern Rough-winged Swallow by **dark rump** and **lack of cinnamon on throat** (throat sometimes somewhat buffy) and upper chest. White-thighed Swallow is dark on lower breast and belly; Bank Swallow (p. 282) has white throat and distinct brown chest band. See also Gray-breasted Martin (p. 286). Fairly common winter resident, from Sept to April. Occurs mostly on Caribbean slope, eastward to Panamá and Colón Provinces. Found in open areas, especially near water.

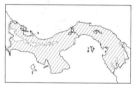

Southern Rough-winged Swallow
Stelgidopteryx ruficollis

5 in (13 cm). Differs from Northern Rough-winged Swallow in **cinnamon throat and upper chest** and **distinct pale band on rump** (see that species for other comparisons). Common on both slopes; to 6,000 ft (1,800 m). Found in open areas, especially near water.

Cliff Swallow
Petrochelidon pyrrhonota

5.5 in (14 cm). Prominent **buffy rump** and **narrow buff collar** contrasting with dark cap, back, and tail distinguish it from other swallows except very rare Cave Swallow (see for distinctions). Most races that occur in Panama have whitish or buffy foreheads; one race with rufous forehead and more rufous rump resembles Cave Swallow. Immature (all races) is duller; may have rufous forehead and pale throat but can be distinguished from Cave Swallow by **dark cheeks**. Common transient, mostly late Aug to late Oct and early March to early May; rare winter resident. Occurs mainly in lowlands near coast but can be found throughout the country. Inhabits open areas.

Cave Swallow
Petrochelidon fulva

5.5 in (14 cm). Similar in overall pattern to Cliff Swallow but usually has **pale cinnamon to light rufous** (not deep chestnut) **throat** and **lacks black mark on upper chest** (a few individuals of Cave have chestnut throat and black chest mark like Cliff). Most races of Cliff that occur in Panama have whitish or buffy forehead, but one race has rufous forehead (like Cave). Immature (all races) duller and can appear very similar to immature Cliff, but note **pale cheeks** (immature Cliff always has dark cheeks). In all plumages, Cave has **throat that is either paler than or about same color as rump**; Cliff has throat that is darker than rump. Vagrant, with only five records (Oct to Feb); recorded in Panamá Province and on Caribbean slope of Canal Area.

White-thighed
Swallow

Northern
Rough-winged
Swallow

Southern
Rough-winged
Swallow

x

adult

Cliff
Swallow
race with buff forehead

adult

adult

Cave Swallow

Barn Swallow
Hirundo rustica

6.5 in (17 cm). Only swallow with such a **deeply forked tail**. Immature and molting adults lack long tail streamers but can still be recognized by **uniformly dark upperparts** in combination with **chestnut throat and forehead** (duller in immature). Also note white spots on tail that form an incomplete band. Lower underparts vary from pale buff to rich cinnamon. Very common transient, late Aug to late Nov and early March to May; common winter resident; very rare in summer. Found throughout the country, especially near coast. Inhabits open areas.

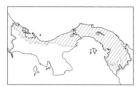

Purple Martin
Progne subis

7 in (18 cm). Male, entirely **glossy blue-black**, is only swallow with dark underparts aside from much smaller White-thighed Swallow (p. 284) and very rare Southern Martin; no swift shows such a distinct blue gloss. Female and immature similar to Gray-breasted Martin but have **grayish forehead** (sometimes absent) and **pale collar** (sometimes only sides of neck are pale). Fairly common fall transient, from early Aug to late Sept; uncommon in spring, from mid-Feb to mid-March. Most numerous along Caribbean coast; rare in lowlands on Pacific slope, from southern Coclé eastward. Inhabits open areas.

Gray-breasted Martin
Progne chalybea

6.5 in (17 cm). Larger than other swallows except for other martins. Adult male is **glossy blue-black** above; female and immature are duller. In all plumages, distinguished from female and immature Purple Martin by **dark forehead** and **lack of pale collar**. Both rough-winged swallows (p. 284) are also dingy below and can appear similar in poor light, but are smaller and have less deeply forked tails. Very common nearly throughout the country; to 5,000 ft (1,500 m). Found in open areas, including cities and towns; often near water.

Southern Martin
Progne elegans

7 in (18 cm). Male virtually identical to male Purple Martin, but slightly smaller and with a longer and more deeply forked tail; not safely distinguishable in the field. Female and immature blackish above, **entirely sooty brown below, including belly**; other female and immature martins are paler below. Vagrant (recorded late April to mid-July), with reports from eastern Kuna Yala, Caribbean slope of Canal Area, and eastern Panamá Province; breeds in South America. **Not illustrated**.

Brown-chested Martin
Progne tapera

6.5 in (16 cm). Similar in pattern to Bank Swallow (p. 282) but much larger; **brown chest band** is smudgier and **less distinctly demarcated from white breast** along lower margin; from above, long silky white undertail coverts often show along sides of rump and tail. Common some years and rare in others; irregular migrant from southern South America, present during southern winter (mostly mid-April to late Sept). Occurs in lowlands on both slopes. Found in open areas.

adult

adult

Barn Swallow

adult
male

**Purple
Martin**

female

adult
male

adult
male

**Gray-breasted
Martin**

**Brown-chested
Martin**

Incertae sedis. Formerly classified with either the mockingbirds or the wrens, the current taxonomic status of the Black-capped Donacobius is uncertain, although it is apparently linked to certain Old World Warblers or related groups. The species occurs from eastern Panama to northern Argentina.

Black-capped Donacobius
Donacobius atricapilla

9 in (22 cm). A slender, long-tailed bird. Easily recognized by combination of **dark upperparts** and **rich buff underparts**. Also note conspicuous **yellowish eye**, white tail tipping, and white patch on wings (visible in flight). A patch of bare orange skin on side of neck, usually concealed, is exposed when calling. Uncommon in lowlands of eastern Darién, to about 2,000 ft (600 m). Found in marshes and in dense vegetation along large rivers. Highly varied calls include a series of loud, vibrant, liquid *whoop* notes (reminiscent of a car alarm) and a harsh, descending *khyerrrr*.

Wrens

TROGLODYTIDAE. This family of small insectivorous birds is found almost exclusively in the Americas; only one species occurs in the Old World. Most species are mainly brown, often with rufous or chestnut tones. The majority have barring on their wings and tail, which distinguishes them from antbirds and other small brownish birds; also note the relatively long slender bill, often slightly curved. Wrens tend to be secretive, keeping out of sight in undergrowth or vine tangles. Accomplished vocalists, they most often reveal their presence with their melodious songs. In the genus *Thryothorus*, members of a pair sing antiphonally, the male giving one part of the call and the female the other.

White-headed Wren
Campylorhynchus albobrunneus

7.5 in (19 cm). Largest wren. Combination of **white head and underparts** and **dark brown back, wings, and tail** is unique. Uncommon on Caribbean slope from northern Coclé eastward, and on Pacific slope from eastern Panamá Province eastward; to 4,000 ft (1,200 m). Found in forest canopy. Forages in small flocks in vines and epiphytes, often giving its call, a harsh grating *khhrrr*.

Band-backed Wren
Campylorhynchus zonatus

6.5 in (16 cm). Only Panama bird that combines **barred back** with **heavy spotting on breast**. Uncommon on Caribbean slope from Bocas del Toro to Veraguas; occurs on Pacific slope in Veraguas foothills; to 3,300 ft (1,000 m). Found in forest canopy. Call a rhythmic series of squeaky, rasping notes.

Sooty-headed Wren
Thryothorus spadix

6 in (15 cm). **Dark head** (mostly black with slaty gray crown) contrasting with **rufous body** is distinctive. Uncommon in foothills in eastern Darién; recorded 1,500 to 4,000 ft (450 to 1,200 m). Found in lower levels of forest; occasionally with mixed-species flocks. Song consists of rich, musical whistled phrases, each phrase repeated several times before switching to a new phrase; typical phrases include *who-eer, wheedle, wheedle, whe-di* and *wheee, whidle, wheedle, whidle, wheeer*.

Black-throated Wren
Thryothorus atrogularis

6 in (15 cm). **Black throat and chest** distinguish it from any other wren within its range. Fairly common in western and central Bocas del Toro; to 2,400 ft (700 m). Found in lower levels of woodland, second growth, and shrubby and marshy areas. Song a melodious series of four or five whistled notes, followed by either a churr or a series of three evenly pitched notes: *whee-heer, wo-hi chuhchuhchuhchuhchuhchuh* or *weee-ur, whee-di, wheet, wheet, wheet*. **CL**

Black-capped
Donacobius

White-headed
Wren

Band-backed
Wren

Sooty-headed
Wren

Black-throated
Wren

Black-bellied Wren
Thryothorus fasciatoventris

5.5 in (14 cm). **White throat and breast,** contrasting sharply with mostly dark plumage, are distinctive; also note fine white barring on lower underparts. Immature duller, with gray throat and chest. Common in lowlands; occurs on Caribbean slope from northern Coclé eastward, and on Pacific slope in western Chiriquí and from Canal Area eastward. Found at lower levels of forest and woodland, in dense undergrowth and vine tangles, often near water. Song a series of short phrases composed of loud, resonant, whistled notes, often inflected upward at end: *hooo-eer, hoo-it!* Each variant is repeated many times before being switched to another.

Bay Wren
Thryothorus nigricapillus

5.5 in (14 cm). Several races occur in Panama; all can be distinguished from other wrens with long tails by **black crown and nape contrasting with chestnut back**. Race on western Caribbean slope has white throat that contrasts with bright chestnut underparts; race in eastern Panama has mostly white underparts, heavily barred with black on breast and belly; intermediate forms in eastern Colón and eastern Panamá Provinces have mostly rufous underparts that are barred with black. White-breasted and Gray-breasted Wood-Wrens (p. 294) are much smaller and have much shorter tails. Common on entire Caribbean slope; also common on Pacific slope from Canal Area eastward; found on western Pacific slope in foothills of Veraguas and Coclé; to 2,500 ft (750 m). Inhabits forest edge and second growth, in dense vegetation (especially *Heliconia* thickets); often near streams. Song consists of a rapid series of loud, ringing, high-pitched whistled phrases, each variant repeated several times before changing to another.

Riverside Wren
Thryothorus semibadius

5 in (13 cm). Combination of **bright chestnut upperparts** and **white underparts with fine black barring** is distinctive. Fairly common in western Chiriquí; to 4,000 ft (1,200 m). Found at lower levels of forest and woodland, in dense undergrowth; also inhabits edges of mangroves; often near streams. Song similar to that of Bay Wren but less ringing in tone. **PL**

Stripe-throated Wren
Thryothorus leucopogon

4.5 in (12 cm). Combination of **streaked throat, tawny underparts,** and **barred wings** is distinctive. Rufous-breasted Wren (p. 292) has speckled rather than streaked throat, has brighter rufous on chest, and lacks barring on wings. Stripe-breasted Wren (no known range overlap) has black streaking extending to breast, not just on throat. Fairly common on both slopes, from eastern Panamá Province eastward; to 2,500 ft (750 m). Found at middle levels of forest edge, in vine tangles and other dense growth. Often with mixed-species flocks. Song consists of short whistled phrases repeated several times: *wheet-er-deet, wheet-er-deet, wheet-er-deet.* Also gives a more chirping *chu, chuh-chew.*

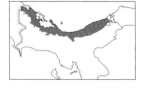

Stripe-breasted Wren
Thryothorus thoracicus

4.5 in (11 cm). No other wren has such **extensive streaking on underparts**. In Stripe-throated Wren (no known range overlap) streaking is confined to throat. Uncommon on Caribbean slope, eastward to Canal Area; occurs on Pacific slope in Veraguas foothills; to 2,500 ft (750 m). Found at lower and middle levels of forest and second growth, in vine tangles and other dense vegetation. Songs include variable short whistled phrases, repeated several times before changing; also gives a series of flat whistles, all on the same pitch.

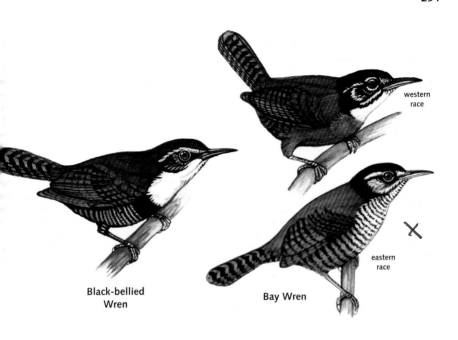

Black-bellied
Wren

western
race

eastern
race

Bay Wren

Riverside
Wren

Stripe-throated
Wren

Stripe-breasted
Wren

Rufous-breasted Wren
Thryothorus rutilus

4.5 in (12 cm). **Black throat** (speckled with white) **that contrasts with bright rufous chest** is distinctive. Rufous-breasted and Black-throated Wrens (p. 288) are only *Thryothorus* species that lack barring on wings. Stripe-throated Wren (p. 290) has streaked rather than speckled throat and is duller tawny on breast. Fairly common on Pacific slope eastward to eastern Panamá Province; uncommon on Caribbean slope in Canal Area and eastern Colón Province; to 5,200 ft (1,600 m). Found in lower levels of drier forest, woodland, and second growth. Song consists of rapid phrases of five to seven musical, whistled notes, often slurred downward at the end: *wheet, er, wheder wheder whee-oo*. Each phrase is repeated several times before switching to another. Song is somewhat less rich than those of other *Thryothorus* wrens.

Rufous-and-white Wren
Thryothorus rufalbus

5.5 in (14 cm). Easily recognized by **bright chestnut upperparts** contrasting with **white underparts**. Buff-breasted and Plain Wrens are much duller above and have less black streaking on sides of head. Fairly common on Pacific slope eastward to eastern Panamá Province; uncommon on Caribbean slope from northern Coclé to Canal Area; to about 5,000 ft (1,500 m). Found in lower levels of relatively dry forest and woodland and in second growth. Distinctive song is a series of deep mellow hooting whistles, with first few notes on the same pitch before changing to a different pitch, then ending with a note at a higher pitch: *whoo, whoo, wu-hu-hu-hu-hu-hu, whit!* (sometimes interspersed with trills, sharp whistles, and churrs).

Buff-breasted Wren
Thryothorus leucotis

5 in (13 cm). Very similar to Plain Wren; distinguished by **buffy** (not white) **breast** and **more distinct barring on wings and tail**; voice also differs. In area of overlap, tends to prefer wetter habitat. Rufous-and-white Wren is much brighter rufous above and whiter below; House Wren (p. 294) is smaller and has shorter tail, buffy (not white) superciliary, and less distinct barring on wings and tail. Fairly common in lowlands on both slopes, from Canal Area eastward. Found at forest edge and second growth, in dense undergrowth; usually near water. Song a rapid, rollicking series of musical whistled notes, each phrase repeated several times before changing to another; typical phrases include *chiri-chi, chiri-chi, chiri-chi, chiri-chi* and *chi-dit, chi-dit, churwee, chit-dit, chi-dit, churwee*.

Plain Wren
Thryothorus modestus

5 in (13 cm). Differs from very similar Buff-breasted Wren in **white breast** (has some buff on belly and flanks) and in **less distinct barring on wings and tail**. Canebrake Wren (no known range overlap, p. 294) is larger and darker. Rufous-and-white Wren is brighter above and has more distinct barring on wings and tail; House Wren (p. 294) is smaller, has shorter tail, buffy (not white) superciliary, and is duller white below. Fairly common on Pacific slope eastward to eastern Panamá Province, and on Caribbean slope from northern Coclé to eastern Colón Province; to over 6,000 ft (1,800 m). Found in cleared areas in thickets, scrub, and tall grass. Song similar to that of Buff-breasted but sharper and less musical.

Rufous-breasted
Wren

Rufous-and-white
Wren

Buff-breasted
Wren

Plain Wren

Canebrake Wren
Thryothorus zeledoni

5.5 in (14 cm). Very similar to Plain Wren (no known range overlap, p. 292) but larger, with heavier bill, darker olive-gray above, and lacking rufous on rump and tail and buff on flanks. Fairly common in lowlands in western Bocas del Toro. Found in cleared areas in thickets, scrub, and tall grass. Song similar to that of Plain Wren but somewhat higher pitched. Considered a subspecies of Plain Wren by AOU. **Not Illustrated**. **CL**

House Wren
Troglodytes aedon

4.5 in (11 cm). Nondescript; fine black barring on wings and tail distinguishes it from other small brown birds (except other wrens). Most similar to Plain Wren (p. 292) but differs by smaller size, **indistinct buffy superciliary** (Plain has distinct white superciliary), and duller white underparts. Ochraceous Wren is brighter, more distinctly patterned, and occurs in different habitat. Common on both slopes, to 7,000 ft (2,100 ft). Found in clearings and other open areas, especially around houses and other structures. Song a variable series of rapid musical notes, about 2 or 3 seconds in duration, often interspersed with short trills.

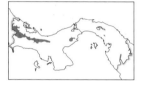

Ochraceous Wren
Troglodytes ochraceus

4 in (10 cm). **Bright brown upperparts** and **rich buff superciliary and underparts** are distinctive. House Wren is much duller overall and found in different habitat. Fairly common in foothills and highlands; mostly 2,500 to 8,300 ft (750 to 2,500 m). Found in middle and upper levels of forest. Forages especially in epiphytes; often with mixed-species flocks. Song a rapid series of thin, high-pitched notes. **WH, EH**

Sedge Wren
Cistothorus platensis

4 in (10 cm). Only wren with streaked back. Possibly extirpated from Panama; last reported in 1905. Recorded in western Chiriquí, from lowlands up to 9,000 ft (2,700 m) on Volcán Barú. Most likely to be found in wet grassy areas. Song a variable series of buzzy or high thin notes; also gives a dry *chrrr*. **No map**.

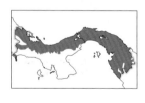

White-breasted Wood-Wren
Henicorhina leucosticta

4 in (10 cm). Distinguished from Gray-breasted Wood-Wren (little elevational overlap) by **white breast**. Differs from other wrens by combination of **small size, very short tail**, and **black crown and nape that contrast with chestnut back**. Common on entire Caribbean slope; also common on Pacific slope in western Chiriquí and from Canal Area eastward; occurs locally in foothills on western Pacific slope; mostly below 4,300 ft (1,300 m), occasionally to 6,300 ft (1,900 m). Found on and near ground in forest. Song a series of loud musical whistled phrases of three to five notes, each phrase repeated several times before changing to another; typical phrases include *dee-di-deet; cheee, churry churry*; and *chee-chee-cheery*; also gives a burry *bwerrr*.

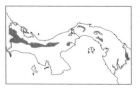

Gray-breasted Wood-Wren
Henicorhina leucophrys

4.5 in (11 cm). Distinguished from White-breasted Wood-Wren (little elevational overlap) by **gray breast**. Distinguished from other wrens by combination of **small size, very short tail**, and **black crown and nape that contrast with chestnut back**. Common in foothills and highlands throughout the country; mostly above 3,000 ft (900 m). Found on and near ground in forest and in coffee plantations with shade trees. Song a long series of loud musical notes, often jumbled and with virtually no clear pattern; sometimes includes repeated phrases, longer than those of White-breasted Wood-Wren.

House Wren

Ochraceous
Wren

Sedge Wren

White-breasted
Wood-Wren

Gray-breasted
Wood-Wren

Timberline Wren
Thryorchilus browni

4 in (10 cm). **White edging on primaries** is diagnostic; also note conspicuous white superciliary and white throat and breast. Ochraceous Wren (p. 294) has buff superciliary and underparts. Known in Panama mainly from Volcán Barú in Chiriquí, where it is fairly common above 9,000 ft (2,700 m); also reported from Cerro Fábrega in Bocas del Toro. Inhabits bamboo thickets in the understory of low forest near timberline; above timberline, found in shrubs. Song a high, thin, squeaky warbling. **WH**

Southern Nightingale-Wren
Microcerculus marginatus

4 in (10 cm). A tiny, nearly unpatterned brown bird; best identified by its **long thin bill, very short tail**, and habit of **constantly bobbing** rear end up and down as it walks about on the forest floor. Fairly common on entire Caribbean slope and on Pacific slope in western Chiriquí and from eastern Panamá Province eastward; occurs elsewhere on western Pacific slope only in foothills and highlands; mostly below 6,900 ft (2,100 m), recorded up to 9,900 ft (3,000 m). Found on and near ground in forest. Very furtive and difficult to see; recorded mainly by song, which consists of a short rapid introductory phrase, followed by a series of high sharp whistles, each about 1 second in duration, the intervals between notes very gradually becoming longer (up to 10 seconds near end). Called Scaly-breasted Wren by AOU.

Song Wren
Cyphorhinus phaeocephalus

4.5 in (12 cm). Combination of **bare blue orbital patch, bright chestnut throat**, and **barring on wings and tail** is unique. Could possibly be mistaken for certain antbirds (female Bare-crowned, p. 210, for example), but these lack barring on wings and tail; Tawny-throated Leaftosser (p. 194) lacks blue orbital patch and has much longer tail. Fairly common on entire Caribbean slope and on Pacific slope from western Panamá Province eastward; to 3,000 ft (900 ft). Found on and near ground in forest. Typically in small family groups; sometimes follows army-ant swarms. Song a series of sweet clear whistles of varying pitches, interspersed with guttural clucks and churrs; sounds like a haywire cuckoo clock. Group members often chime together in a complex medley.

Dippers

CINCLIDAE. The five species of this family are distributed in Europe, Asia, and the Americas. Dippers are the only truly aquatic songbirds. Chunky and with short tails, they swim underwater using their wings and are able to walk on the bottom of even swift-flowing streams in search of aquatic invertebrates. Their name is derived from their habit of "dipping," constantly bobbing the entire body up and down while standing or walking about.

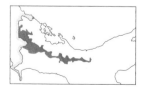

American Dipper
Cinclus mexicanus

6.5 in (17 cm). In its streamside habitat, easily recognized by **nearly uniform gray coloration** and distinctive **stocky shape, with short tail and long legs**. Immature is paler gray below and has narrow whitish edging on underparts and wings. Torrent Tyrannulet (p. 228) is smaller, shaped differently, and has dark cap, wings, and tail. Uncommon in highlands of western Panama, eastward to Veraguas; mostly 4,000 to 7,300 ft (1,200 to 2,200 m); locally down to 2,500 ft (750 m). Found along swift-flowing mountain streams; usually seen perched or walking on boulders in or alongside water, continually **bobbing up and down** and occasionally diving underwater. Song a complex series of high warbles and trills; call a sharp metallic *dzert!*

Timberline
Wren

Southern
Nightingale-Wren

Song Wren

adult

American
Dipper

SYLVIIDAE. The gnatwrens and gnatcatchers are tiny insectivorous birds found only in the Americas. Though presently assigned to the same family as the Old World Warblers, they are more likely allied to the wrens and merit their own family. Gnatcatchers are slender birds mostly found in forest canopy, while gnatwrens have long, thin bills and generally forage in forest undergrowth and vine tangles; both groups frequently cock their tails. Gnatwrens differ from most true wrens by not having barring on their wings and tail.

Tawny-faced Gnatwren   *Microbates cinereiventris*
4 in (10 cm). Combination of **long thin bill, tawny sides of head,** and **white throat** is distinctive; also note black submalar stripe and mainly gray underparts. Long-billed Gnatwren has longer bill and tail and is buffy below. Uncommon on entire Caribbean slope; on Pacific slope found in eastern Darién; elsewhere on Pacific slope occurs locally in foothills; to 3,000 ft (900 m). Found at lower levels of forest, in dense undergrowth and vine tangles. Song a flat clear descending whistle, repeated at intervals of 4 or 5 seconds; similar to that of Southern Nightingale-Wren (p. 296) but intervals between notes do not increase. Also gives a nasal *kheeerr* and a scolding chatter.

Long-billed Gnatwren   *Ramphocaenus melanurus*
4.5 in (11 cm). Easily recognized by **exceptionally long thin bill** and **long thin white-tipped tail** (see Tawny-faced Gnatwren for distinctions). Fairly common on both slopes, to 4,000 ft (1,200 m). Found at lower and middle levels of forest, woodland edge, and second growth; in undergrowth and vine tangles. Sometimes with mixed-species flocks. Song a chittering musical trill about 2 seconds long, often rising slightly near the end.

Tropical Gnatcatcher   *Polioptila plumbea*
4 in (10 cm). Both sexes distinguished from all other small birds by combination of **pale gray back** and **white face, superciliary, and underparts**. Common on both slopes, to 4,000 ft (1,200 m). Found in forest canopy and edge of forest and woodland; sometimes also found in shrubby areas and scrub. Very active, frequently cocking or flicking its long narrow tail. Often with mixed-species flocks. Song is a rapid trill of sharp high-pitched notes that lasts 1 or 2 seconds.

Slate-throated Gnatcatcher   *Polioptila schistaceigula*
4 in (10 cm). Combination of **slaty upperparts and breast** that contrast with **white lower underparts** is unique; also note **thin white eye-ring**. Rare and local; recorded from eastern Colón Province, western Kuna Yala, and eastern Darién; to 2,600 ft (800 m). Found in forest canopy and edge. Behavior similar to that of Tropical Gnatcatcher; often with mixed-species flocks. Song like that of Tropical Gnatcatcher, but faster, shorter (about a half second long), and slightly ascending.

Tawny-faced
Gnatwren

Long-billed
Gnatwren

Tropical
Gnatcatcher

male

female

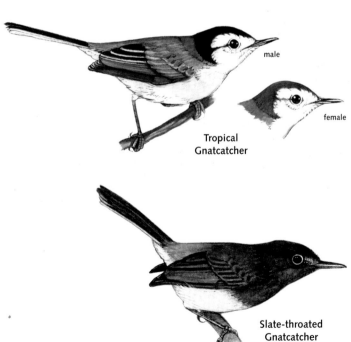

Slate-throated
Gnatcatcher

TURDIDAE. The thrushes are a large, cosmopolitan family whose members feed on insects, fruit, or a combination of both. Most Panama species are plump birds of subdued coloration, although some have brightly colored bare parts. Immatures of many species are spotted. Most of Panama's resident thrushes are birds of foothills and highlands; the resident Clay-colored Thrush and the four migrant species also occur widely in lowlands. Thrushes are among the most notable songsters among birds, and the haunting, ethereal calls of solitaires and nightingale-thrushes are some of the most evocative sounds of Panama's montane and cloud forests.

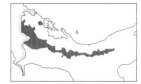

Black-faced Solitaire
Myadestes melanops

6.5 in (17 cm). Combination of mainly **gray plumage, black mask,** and **bright orange bill and legs** is unique. In flight, shows a flash of white in wings. Varied Solitaire (no range overlap) has brown back. Slaty-backed Nightingale-Thrush (p. 302) is darker slaty in color and has whitish belly and pale eye with orange orbital ring. Common in highlands of western Panama, eastward to Coclé; mostly above 5,000 ft (1,500 m), sometimes down to 2,500 ft (750 m). Found in middle levels of forest. Perches rather upright; moves infrequently and usually hard to see. Song consists of ethereal fluting notes (sometimes interspersed with more metallic notes) given in variable, one- to five-note phrases, with the notes in a single phrase rising and falling: *dee . . . . dee-deedle-lee . . . . dee-urr . . . . dee-lee-ur-dee.* Also gives a harsh *khrrrr.*

Varied Solitaire
Myadestes coloratus

6.5 in (17 cm). Differs from Black-faced Solitaire (no range overlap) in **brown back.** Fairly common in eastern Panama highlands; mostly above 4,000 ft (1,200 ft), sometimes down to 3,000 ft (900 m). Found in middle levels of forest. Habits similar to those of Black-faced Solitaire. Song also similar: gives a series of single fluting notes and short phrases, at leisurely intervals; also gives a whining *nyaahh.*

Black-billed Nightingale-Thrush
Catharus gracilirostris

6 in (15 cm). Only nightingale-thrush with **all-dark bill;** also note **brown band across chest** separating gray throat from gray lower breast and belly. Ruddy-capped Nightingale-Thrush has orange on lower mandible, rufous-brown crown, and lacks brown chest band. Fairly common in western highlands; mostly above 7,000 ft (2,100 m), sometimes down to 5,000 ft (1,500 m). Found on and near ground in forest and nearby clearings. Song consists of variable phrases of four to six thin, high-pitched reedy notes.

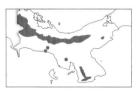

Orange-billed Nightingale-Thrush
Catharus aurantiirostris

5.5 in (14 cm). **Orange bill and legs** and **orange orbital ring** distinguish it from Black-billed and Ruddy-capped Nightingale-Thrushes. Differs from Black-headed Nightingale-Thrush (p. 302) in having gray rather than blackish head. Fairly common in western foothills and lower highlands eastward to Coclé; mostly 3,000 to 5,500 ft (900 to 1,650 m), but has been recorded down to near sea level on western Pacific slope. Found on and near ground in forest edge, woodland, shrubby clearings, and gardens. Song consists of variable phrases of four to six notes with a squeaky or metallic quality.

Ruddy-capped Nightingale-Thrush
Catharus frantzii

6.5 in (16 cm). Distinguished from other nightingale-thrushes by **entirely rufous-brown crown;** also note mostly dark bill with orange on lower mandible. Veery has indistinct spotting on chest. Common in western highlands; mostly above 5,000 ft (1,500 m), sometimes down to 4,000 ft (1,200 m). Found on and near ground in forest. Song consists of variable phrases of one to five fluting notes; resembles that of Black-faced Solitaire, but notes are somewhat burrier and less ethereal.

adult

immature

**Black-faced
Solitaire**

adult

Varied Solitaire

adult

**Black-billed
Nightingale-Thrush**

adult

**Orange-billed
Nightingale-Thrush**

adult

**Ruddy-capped
Nightingale-Thrush**

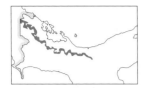

Black-headed Nightingale-Thrush   *Catharus mexicanus*

6.5 in (16 cm). Most similar to Slaty-backed Nightingale-Thrush; distinguished by **brownish olive back** and **dark eye**. Fairly common in foothills on Caribbean slope from Bocas del Toro to Veraguas; on Pacific slope, occurs only in Veraguas foothills; mostly 2,500 to 3,500 ft (750 to 1,050 m). Found on and near ground in wet forest. Song includes variable, rhythmic phrases of five or six sharp, somewhat shrill notes.

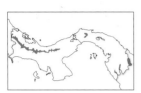

Slaty-backed Nightingale-Thrush   *Catharus fuscater*

6.5 in (17 cm). No other nightingale-thrush has either **gray back** or **pale eye**. Sooty Thrush (p. 304) is larger and blacker and lacks white on belly; also see Black-faced Solitaire (p. 300). Fairly common in foothills and highlands; recorded from 2,000 to 9,900 ft (600 to 3,000 m). Found on and near ground in wet forest and cloud forest. Shy and usually very difficult to see. Song consists of variable phrases of two to five liquid fluting notes; similar to song of solitaires, but notes are clearer and less reedy.

Veery   *Catharus fuscescens*

6.5 in (16 cm). **Less distinctly spotted on chest** than Gray-cheeked, Swainson's, and Wood Thrushes. More rufous above than Gray-cheeked and most Swainson's Thrushes; flanks are pale gray rather than olive. Some Swainson's are almost as rufous above but differ in having distinct buffy spectacles and olive flanks. Uncommon fall transient, late Sept to mid-Nov; very rare spring transient, early March to early April. Occurs mainly in lowlands of Caribbean slope (especially near coast); rare elsewhere. Found at lower levels of forest and on ground. Call a sharp reedy *hrr-ik!*

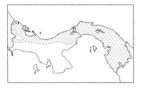

Gray-cheeked Thrush   *Catharus minimus*

6.5 in (17 cm). Very similar to Swainson's Thrush, but **lacks buffy spectacles** (may have indistinct gray area around eye) and has **grayish** (not buffy) **cheeks**. Also compare with Veery. Uncommon fall transient, late Sept to early Dec; rare winter resident and spring transient, to mid-April. Occurs mainly in lowlands of Caribbean slope; also occurs in lowlands on Pacific slope, from western Panamá Province eastward. Found in lower levels of forest and on ground. Call a sharp *fweet!*

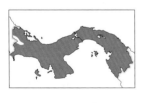

Swainson's Thrush   *Catharus ustulatus*

6.5 in (17 cm). Distinct **buffy spectacles** distinguish it from Gray-cheeked Thrush and Veery. Very common transient, mostly in Oct and Nov, and in March and April; uncommon winter resident. Occurs throughout the country, to about 6,000 ft (1,800 m). Found in lower levels of forest and on ground. Often sings in late spring before migration; song is a rising series of musical trilling notes. Call a sharp rising *wheeik!*

Wood Thrush   *Hylocichla mustelina*

7 in (18 cm). Much more **heavily spotted** below than any other thrush. Also note **rufous crown** and contrasting brown back; other thrushes with spotted underparts lack contrast between head and back. Uncommon winter resident, mostly mid-Oct to mid-April. Occurs mainly on Caribbean slope in western and central Panama; becomes rare from Canal Area eastward; to at least 6,000 ft (1,800 m). Found in lower levels of forest and on ground. Song (sometimes given in spring) consists of several fluting notes ending in a rapid trill. Call is a rapid *whik-whik-whik*.

adult

**Black-headed
Nightingale-Thrush**

adult

**Slaty-backed
Nightingale-Thrush**

Veery

**Gray-cheeked
Thrush**

**Swainson's
Thrush**

Wood Thrush

Sooty Thrush
Turdus nigrescens

10 in (25 cm). Combination of entirely **blackish** plumage and **orange bill, legs, and orbital ring** is unique; also note **pale eye**. Slaty-backed Nightingale-Thrush (p. 302) is smaller and has white on belly. Fairly common in western highlands; best known from Volcán Barú and vicinity; mostly above 7,500 ft (2,250 m), occasionally down to 6,000 ft (1,800 m). Found in forest edge, clearings in forest, and in other open areas. Song consists of short buzzy or squeaky phrases; call a low grating *grrek*.

Mountain Thrush
Turdus plebejus

9.5 in (24 cm). Duller and more **evenly colored** than any other thrush; also note **all-black bill** (shared only with Pale-vented Thrush and Black-billed Nightingale-Thrush, p. 300). Pale-vented Thrush is richer reddish brown and has white belly and vent; Black-billed Nightingale-Thrush is much smaller and has brown band across chest. Clay-colored Thrush is lighter sandy brown and has yellow bill. Fairly common in western highlands eastward to Ngöbe-Buglé; mostly 4,000 to 8,000 ft (1,200 to 2,400 m), sometimes down to 3,000 ft (900 m). Mainly arboreal; found in middle and upper levels of forest and in adjacent clearings. Song a monotonous series of chirping notes, varying only slightly in pitch, given at a rate of about two notes per second.

Pale-vented Thrush
Turdus obsoletus

8.5 in (22 cm). Combination of **dark bill, white belly and vent**, and mainly dark, reddish brown plumage distinguishes it from all other thrushes. Uncommon in foothills and lower highlands; occurs mostly on Caribbean slope, except in eastern Panama, where it also occurs on Pacific slope; from 1,500 to 5,000 ft (450 to 1,500 m), with a few records from lowlands in Canal Area. Mainly arboreal; found in middle and upper levels of wet forest. Song similar to that of Clay-colored Thrush, but somewhat faster and with less varied notes; call a series of two to four rising whistles: *whiurk, whirk, wheek!*

Clay-colored Thrush
Turdus grayi

8.5 in (22 cm). Only resident thrush that is widespread and common in lowlands. Nondescript, but recognized by combination of **nearly uniform light sandy brown** coloration and **yellow-green bill**. Very common on both slopes, but not found in Darién; to 6,500 ft (1,950 m). Inhabits gardens, forest edge, second growth, and open areas with shrubs. Often seen hopping about on lawns in urban and suburban areas. Frequently flicks tail when alighting. During dry season, males sing tirelessly (often beginning in middle of night), giving melodious series of varied notes, including slurred whistles, trills, and clucks. Calls include a nasal *nnyaowk!* and a rising *wheur-wheur-whiirk!*

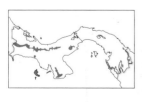

White-throated Thrush
Turdus assimilis

8.5 in (21 cm). **White crescent on upper chest** between **black-and-white streaked throat** and brown breast is distinctive. Also note yellow bill (in most of Panama), orbital ring, and legs; birds in eastern Darién and on Coiba Island have partly or entirely dark bills and are ruddier above. Common on Coiba Island; elsewhere, fairly common in foothills and lower highlands, 1,500 to 5,000 ft (450 to 1,500 m). Rare in lowlands on Caribbean slope, where it may disperse seasonally from foothills and highlands; reported mainly Nov to Jan, sometimes as early as Oct or as late as April (however, there are no recent records). Mainly arboreal; found in middle and upper levels of forest. Song a musical series of varied notes (often doubled), including rich whistles, trills, and warbles.

Sooty Thrush

adult

Mountain Thrush

adult

Pale-vented Thrush

adult

Clay-colored
Thrush

adult

X

White-throated
Thrush

adult
yellow-billed
race

MIMIDAE. The mockingbirds and their relatives—catbirds, thrashers, and others—comprise a small family found only in the Americas. Generally plain in coloration, they are mainly insectivorous but eat some fruit. Several species are renowned for their talent at mimicking the calls of other birds or other sounds in their environment, a habit from which the name "mockingbird" is derived.

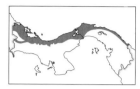

Gray Catbird
Dumetella carolinensis

8 in (20 cm). Combination of **mostly gray plumage**, **black cap**, and **chestnut vent** is unique. Transient and winter resident, mostly Oct to April but sometimes in Sept or May. Mostly in lowlands, occasionally into lower highlands. Fairly common on western Caribbean slope, but becomes uncommon eastward to Kuna Yala; uncommon to rare on Pacific slope, where it occurs eastward to eastern Panamá Province. Found in thickets, forest edge, and second growth. Skulking and often difficult to see. Call a mewling, nasal, catlike *myarr*, from which it takes its name.

Tropical Mockingbird
Mimus gilvus

10 in (26 cm). Only mostly **pale gray** bird with such a **long, conspicuously white-tipped tail**; also note **narrow white wing-bars** and relatively long slender bill. Introduced from Colombia; first recorded in 1932. Common in Canal Area and adjacent Colón Province; also common on Pacific slope from Panamá Province to Darién, and near Chitré, Herrera; isolated records from elsewhere. Found in urban and suburban areas and other open habitats; often seen on lawns and grassy fields, running for a short distance and then raising wings above back. Song a long, melodious series of varied, whistling trills and warbles, some repeated several times. Apparently does not mimic other birds.

Pipits & Wagtails

MOTACILLIDAE. These small, insectivorous, mainly ground-dwelling birds occur principally in the Old World. Only the drab pipits range into the Americas south of Alaska.

Yellowish Pipit
Anthus lutescens

4.5 in (11 cm). **Thin bill** and habit of **walking** (rather than hopping) distinguish it from all other small, brown-streaked birds of grasslands; also note **blackish tail with white outer tail feathers** (conspicuous in flight). Uncommon and local in lowlands on Pacific slope, from Chiriquí eastward to eastern Panamá Province; a few records from Caribbean slope in Canal Area. Found in pastures, on airstrips, and in other areas with short grass. Displaying male flies up in a loop, giving a series of rising *dzee* notes, then glides down with a slurred *je-je-jeeeeerrrrrrr* (from the ground, also gives a shorter *tssirrt*).

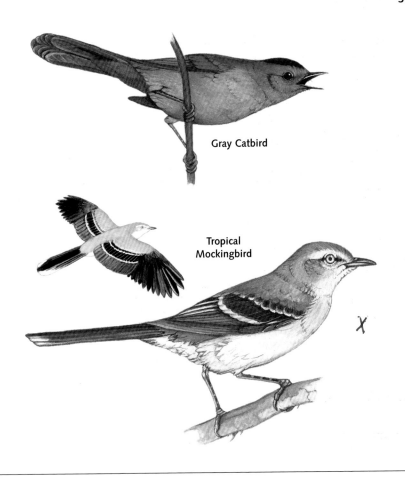

Gray Catbird

Tropical
Mockingbird

𝑋

Yellowish Pipit

BOMBYCILLIDAE. The three species of waxwings are mainly frugivorous birds that breed in the northern regions of North America, Europe, and Asia. They take their name from the waxy red tips on their secondary feathers. One species reaches Panama as an occasional migrant.

Cedar Waxwing
Bombycilla cedrorum

6.5 in (16 cm). Easily recognized by combination of conspicuous **pointed crest, black mask,** and **short, square, yellow-tipped tail**. Immature mostly brownish gray and somewhat streaked below. Long-tailed Silky-Flycatcher also has crest but lacks mask and has much longer tail. Rare and irregular migrant, from Jan to March (not recorded every year). Scattered records from lowlands to lower highlands; occurs eastward to Canal Area, and on Pearl Islands. Usually seen in trees in open areas or at forest edge; may occur alone or in small flocks. Call, often given in flight, is a very high, thin trilling *tseeeep!*

Silky-flycatchers

PTILOGONATIDAE. The four members of this family occur from the southwestern United States to western Panama. Silky-flycatchers feed on both fruit and insects. They are generally thought to be nearest to the waxwings and, despite their name, are not closely related to the tyrant flycatchers. Panama's two species are quite dissimilar, but both are distinctive.

Black-and-yellow Silky-flycatcher
Phainoptila melanoxantha

8 in (20 cm). Both sexes distinctively patterned; note especially **yellow flanks** (male also has yellow rump) and glossy black head (male) or crown (female). Plump shape could suggest a thrush, but no thrush has bright yellow plumage. Uncommon in western highlands eastward to Coclé; above 3,500 ft (1,050 m), relatively more common above 7,500 ft (1,650 m). Found in lower and middle levels of forest. Regularly accompanies mixed-species flocks. Call a short, high, metallic *chrrit.*

Long-tailed Silky-flycatcher
Ptilogonys caudatus

8.5 in (22 cm). **Conspicuous crest, long graduated tail,** and gray and yellow plumage make this species unmistakable. Cedar Waxwing has black mask; its tail is much shorter and square (not graduated). Common in western highlands; mostly above 5,000 ft (1,500 m), sometimes down to 3,500 ft (1,050 m). Found in canopy of forest and in adjacent clearings with tall trees. Usually in small flocks. Call a high thin *drrrt.*

adult

Cedar Waxwing

male

**Black-and-yellow
Silky-flycatcher**

female

**Long-tailed
Silky-flycatcher**

PARULIDAE. This large family of mainly insectivorous birds occurs exclusively in the Americas. A majority of Panama's species are migrants that breed in temperate zones, particularly eastern North America. Although many migrant species have colorful and distinctive breeding plumages, when they arrive in the fall, a good number are in duller nonbreeding or immature plumages. Differences between males and females and individual variation create additional challenges for identification. Just before departure from Panama in the spring, migrants may put on breeding dress and occasionally sing (while wintering, they rarely give more than brief *chip* notes). Most of Panama's resident warblers are found primarily in foothills and highlands. Dull-plumaged warblers are most likely to be confused with vireos (pp. 272-279), but they generally have sharper bills and forage more actively.

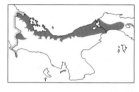

Blue-winged Warbler
Vermivora pinus

4.5 in (11 cm). Distinguished from other **mostly yellow** warblers by **narrow black eye-line** and **two distinct white wing-bars** (sometimes yellowish in female). Hybridizes with Golden-winged Warbler. The most common hybrid form, "Brewster's Warbler," has been reported from western Panama. It resembles Blue-winged but has yellow wing-bars and whitish underparts with a variable amount of yellow; males have yellow crown. Rare winter resident, from mid-Oct to late March. Inhabits lowlands and foothills eastward to eastern Panamá Province. Found in second growth, woodland, and forest edge.

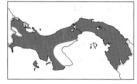

Golden-winged Warbler
Vermivora chrysoptera

4.5 in (11 cm). In all plumages, identified by **large yellow wing patch** and **distinctive facial pattern** (less obvious in female but still recognizable). Hybridizes with Blue-winged Warbler. "Lawrence's Warbler," a rare hybrid form with that species, could occur in Panama but has not yet been reported. It resembles Golden-winged but has yellow facial stripes and underparts, and two white or yellow wing-bars. Frequently with mixed-species flocks. Fairly common transient and winter resident; mostly Oct to April, occasionally in Sept and May. Most common in foothills and highlands of western Panama.

Nashville Warbler
Vermivora ruficapilla

4.5 in (12 cm). Note **gray head, white eye-ring**, and **mostly yellow underparts**. Male's chestnut crown patch is usually concealed; female and immature are duller overall; on immature, head may have strong olive wash. Similar in pattern to gray-headed race of Lesser Greenlet (p. 276) but has longer tail, thinner, more pointed bill, and is yellower below. Immature Yellow (p. 312) and Tennessee Warblers lack eye-ring; Mourning, MacGillivray's, and Connecticut Warblers (p. 324) show a hooded pattern, have pink (not dark) legs, and are found near ground (unlike arboreal Nashville). Vagrant; two records, one in western Chiriquí highlands, the other near Caribbean coast of Canal Area.

Tennessee Warbler
Vermivora peregrina

4.5 in (11 cm). In all plumages, note **narrow dark eye-line, pale superciliary**, and **white undertail coverts** (may be yellowish in immature). Breeding male resembles gray-headed race of Lesser Greenlet (p. 276) but has superciliary and lacks white eye-ring of that species. Nonbreeding male similar to adult female. Immature usually shows narrow, pale wing-bars. Philadelphia Vireo (p. 274) has thicker bill and is less active; it always has some yellow on breast and undertail coverts and lacks wing-bars. Immature Yellow Warbler (p. 312) lacks dark eye-line and has yellow in tail. Common transient and winter resident; mostly Oct to April, sometimes in Sept and May. Occurs throughout the country; to 7,000 ft (2,100 m). Found in forest canopy, forest edge, woodland, and clearings with trees. Frequently in small flocks of its own species; also joins mixed-species flocks. Often visits flowering trees for nectar.

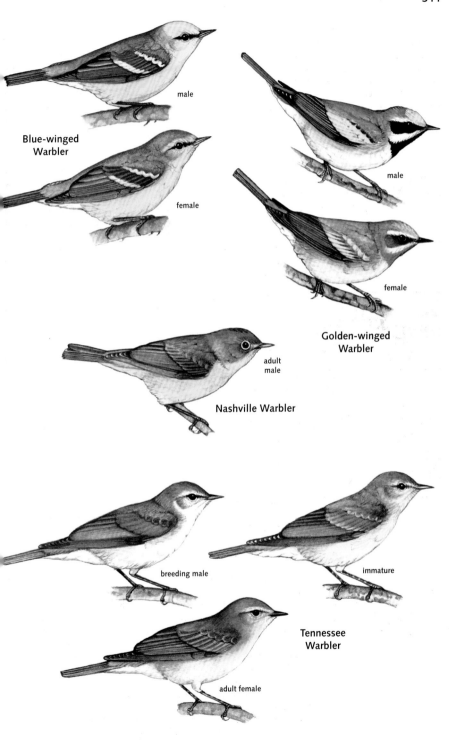

Blue-winged
Warbler

male

female

Golden-winged
Warbler

male

female

Nashville Warbler

adult
male

breeding male

immature

Tennessee
Warbler

adult female

Flame-throated Warbler
Parula gutturalis

4.5 in (11 cm). Combination of slate-gray upperparts, **black patch on back, bright orange throat and upper breast**, and **plain wings** is distinctive; also note whitish lower breast and belly. Tropical and Northern Parulas have white wing-bars and are bluer above with a greenish back patch. Fairly common in western highlands, mostly above 5,000 ft (1,500 m). Found in middle and upper levels of forest. Often with mixed-species flocks. Song a thin, high-pitched, rising buzzy trill: *zhreeeh*. **WH**

Tropical Parula
Parula pitiayumi

4 in (10 cm). Distinguished from much rarer Northern Parula by **black face mask**, lack of white eye-ring, **single** (not double) **white wing-bar**, and yellow on underparts that extends to belly. Flame-throated Warbler lacks wing-bars, is grayer above, and has brighter orange on throat and upper breast and whitish lower breast and belly. Fairly common. Occurs mostly in foothills and highlands, from 1,000 to 5,000 ft (300 to 1,500 m); occurs in lowlands in eastern Panamá Province and on Coiba Island. Found in middle and upper levels of forest and woodland. Sometimes with mixed-species flocks. Song a high-pitched buzzy trill, variably accelerating and/or decelerating.

Northern Parula
Parula americana

4.5 in (11 cm). In all plumages, differs from Tropical Parula in **broken white eye-ring** (faint in immature), **two white wing-bars** (single in Tropical), whitish lower breast and belly, and lack of black mask. Breeding male has distinctive black and rufous breast band, which is less distinct in nonbreeding male, immature male, and adult female; absent in immature female. See also Flame-throated Warbler. Rare winter resident; recorded mid-Oct to late April. Reported most often from Caribbean coast of Canal Area; also recorded from elsewhere in Canal Area, Bocas del Toro, and in Chiriquí highlands; to 4,300 ft (1,300 m). Found in middle and upper levels of forest edge and woodland.

Yellow Warbler
Dendroica petechia

4.5 in (11 cm). In all plumages, can be distinguished from similar species by **yellow inner webs of tail feathers**, creating a yellow flash when tail is spread. Two rather different forms, one resident (known as "Mangrove Warbler") and one migrant, occur in Panama. Males of both forms have distinctive **chestnut streaking on bright yellow breast**. Resident male also has all-chestnut head (except in Darién, where only the crown is chestnut, with the cheeks and throat yellowish). Females of both forms are drabber, with chestnut breast streaking reduced or absent; immatures are even duller. Mangrove female and immature male may show some rufous on head; females and immatures are often grayer above and whiter below than migrant females and immatures. Mangrove Warbler is fairly common in mangroves along both coasts, ranging into non-mangrove forest on some offshore islands. Migrants are very common transients and winter residents; mostly Sept to April, sometimes mid-Aug to mid-May. They occur in lowlands on both slopes, in open and scrubby areas, second growth, woodland, and mangroves. Song of resident form is a variable series of musical notes, often with last note emphasized: *chew-chew-chew-chu-wee-dit-chew!* Both migrants and residents frequently give a sharp *tsip!* note.

Flame-throated
Warbler

Tropical
Parula

breeding
male

Northern Parula

immature
female

migrant
adult male

immature female

Yellow Warbler

resident adult male
"Mangrove Warbler"

Chestnut-sided Warbler — *Dendroica pensylvanica*

4.5 in (11 cm). Adults in breeding plumage have **chestnut flanks** and **distinctive facial pattern**; compared to male, female has less chestnut on flanks and reduced facial pattern. Nonbreeding adults and immatures can be identified by **bright yellow-green upperparts** (spotted with black in adults, nearly plain in immatures), **distinct white eye-ring, gray face**, and **whitish underparts**; nonbreeding adults usually have some chestnut on flanks. Nonbreeding and immature Bay-breasted Warblers (p. 318) lack eye-ring, are duller olive above with at least obscure streaking, and are buffier below. Winter resident; mostly late Sept to early April, sometimes early Sept to early May. Found in lowlands and foothills on both slopes; common eastward to Canal Area; uncommon in eastern Panama. Inhabits middle and upper levels of forest and woodland. Frequently a member of mixed-species flocks. Often **cocks tail** like a gnatcatcher; also droops wings.

Magnolia Warbler — *Dendroica magnolia*

4.5 in (11 cm). In all plumages, can be recognized by **incomplete white band across tail** (from below, basal half of tail appears white); also note **yellow rump**. Breeding female similar to breeding male but grayer on back and face; nonbreeding female very similar to nonbreeding male. Immature has thin gray band across upper chest. Uncommon in lowlands on Caribbean slope, eastward to eastern Colón Province; rare in lowlands on Pacific slope, eastward to Darién. Found in lower and middle levels at forest edge and in adjacent clearings. Often with mixed-species flocks.

Cape May Warbler — *Dendroica tigrina*

5 in (13 cm). On breeding male, **rufous cheeks** are distinctive; also note **yellow rump**. Adult female can be recognized by combination of **yellow patch on side of neck, streaked underparts**, and **unstreaked back**. Immature female can be confused with several other species but usually shows pale yellowish patch on neck and has blurry streaking on breast and dull yellow or greenish rump. Yellow-rumped Warbler has more conspicuous yellow rump and streaked back; Palm Warbler (p. 318) has yellow undertail coverts and wags tail almost constantly. Very rare winter resident; recorded Dec to March. Occurs eastward to eastern Panamá Province; to 4,300 ft (1,300 m). Found in upper levels of forest edge, woodland, and nearby clearings. Favors flowering trees.

Black-throated Blue Warbler — *Dendroica caerulescens*

5 in (13 cm). **Blue, black, and white pattern** of male is unique. Immature male similar, but has brown wash on back. Male Cerulean Warbler (p. 320) has white throat and wing-bars. Female can be distinguished by **small white patch at base of primaries** (absent in some immatures), **white superciliary**, and **white arc below eye**. Very rare winter resident; recorded Oct to April; reported to 5,300 ft (1,600 m). Found in lower levels of forest and woodland.

Yellow-rumped Warbler — *Dendroica coronata*

4.5 in (12 cm). In all plumages, recognized by **bright yellow rump** and **yellow patch on sides of breast** (latter sometimes faint in immature female); also note streaking on whitish underparts and streaked back. Magnolia and Cape May Warblers also have yellow rump patches but are yellower below. Most individuals in Panama are of white-throated "Myrtle" form; only two records of yellow-throated "Audubon's" form. Irregular winter resident, common in some years and nearly absent in others; recorded early Nov to late March. Most common in western Panama, rare in eastern Panama; to 4,300 ft (1,300 m). Typically feeds on ground in open areas; when not foraging, perches in low trees and shrubs. Often in small flocks of its own species.

Chestnut-sided
Warbler

breeding
male

immature
female

Magnolia
Warbler

breeding
male

nonbreeding
male

immature

Cape May
Warbler

breeding
male

immature
female

breeding
female

male

Black-throated
Blue Warbler

female

breeding male
"Audubon's"

breeding
male "Myrtle"

immature female
"Myrtle"

Yellow-rumped
Warbler

Golden-cheeked Warbler
Dendroica chrysoparia

4.5 in (12 cm). In all plumages, can be distinguished by combination of **narrow dark eye-line** and **yellow cheeks**. On male, note black back and crown. Adult female similar to male but has reduced black on throat and olive back and crown. Black-throated Green and Townsend's Warblers have olive or black cheeks and at least some yellow on underparts; Hermit Warbler lacks eye-line. Vagrant in western Chiriquí; two records, both above Cerro Punta (2005, 2006). Inhabits forest.

Black-throated Green Warbler
Dendroica virens

4.5 in (11 cm). In all plumages, can be recognized by combination of **unstreaked green upperparts, bright yellow sides of head**, **indistinct olive patch on cheek**, and **yellow wash across vent**. Nonbreeding male, immature male, and adult female similar to breeding male but with reduced black on throat and chest. Townsend's Warbler is similar but has darker and more distinct cheek patch, more extensive yellow on breast and flanks, and lacks yellow wash on vent; Blackburnian Warbler has pale stripes on back. Very common in western Panama, becoming progressively less common eastward; rare in Darién; to at least 8,900 ft (2,700 m). Occurs in foothills and highlands as a winter resident. Birds that occur in lowlands are usually transient; mostly Oct to late March, sometimes in early Sept and mid-April. Found in upper levels of forest and woodland. Generally with mixed-species flocks.

Townsend's Warbler
Dendroica townsendi

5 in (13 cm). In all plumages, distinguished from much more common Black-throated Green Warbler by **distinct dark cheek patch on yellow sides of head**, more extensive yellow on breast and flanks, and lack of yellow wash across vent. Adult female and immature male similar to breeding male but with reduced black on throat and chest and less distinct cheek patch. Blackburnian Warbler has pale stripes on back. Vagrant; recorded from mid-Nov to early April. Occurs in western Chiriquí, above 4,000 ft (1,200 m). Found in middle and upper levels of forest and woodland.

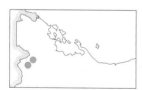

Hermit Warbler
Dendroica occidentalis

5.5 in (14 cm). Breeding male easily recognized by combination of almost entirely **bright yellow head** (including crown) and **small black throat patch**. Other plumages have reduced black on throat (absent in immature female), olive on crown, and indistinct olive patch on cheek. In all plumages, can be distinguished from much more common Black-throated Green Warbler by **grayish back** and **lack of streaking on underparts**; in immature female, note yellow eye-ring. Vagrant; recorded late Dec to early March. Occurs in highlands of western Chiriquí. Inhabits forest.

Blackburnian Warbler
Dendroica fusca

4.5 in (11 cm). On breeding male, striking **bright orange and black head** is unmistakable. In other plumages, head pattern is similar but less distinct, and orange is replaced by yellow-orange (in nonbreeding male and adult female) or dull yellow (in immature female). In all plumages, distinguished from Black-throated Green and Townsend's Warblers by **whitish stripes on back**. Fairly common transient and winter resident, mostly Sept to April. Occurs in foothills and highlands (transients uncommon in lowlands throughout the country). Found in middle and upper levels in forest and woodland. Often with mixed-species flocks.

male

Golden-cheeked
Warbler

female

Black-throated
Green Warbler

breeding
male

immature
female

breeding
male

Townsend's
Warbler

immature
female

breeding
male

Hermit Warbler

immature
female

breeding
male

Blackburnian
Warbler

immature
female

Yellow-throated Warbler · *Dendroica dominica*

5.5 in (14 cm). Facial pattern distinctive, with black mask bordered by white superciliary; **white cheek patch**; and yellow throat. Also note **unstreaked back**. All plumages are similar; female and immature somewhat duller than adult male. Nonbreeding and immature Blackburnian Warbler (p. 316) has yellow superciliary, yellow patch on side of neck, and whitish stripes on back. Rare winter resident; recorded mid-Aug to late March. Occurs eastward to eastern Panamá Province, to at least 5,300 ft (1,600 m). Found in forest edge, second growth, and gardens; most often seen in palms or introduced pines.

Palm Warbler · *Dendroica palmarum*

4.5 in (12 cm). Breeding adults have distinctive **chestnut cap** (absent in other plumages). In all plumages, can be recognized by combination of **yellow undertail coverts** and habit of almost **constantly pumping tail up and down**. Prairie Warbler also bobs tail but has different face pattern and is more extensively yellow below. Rare winter resident; recorded mid-Nov to mid-March. Occurs mostly in lowlands. Found in open and grassy areas; feeds on or near ground.

Prairie Warbler · *Dendroica discolor*

4.5 in (12 cm). On breeding male, combination of black eye-line and stripe above malar, black streaking on flanks, and **chestnut stripes on back** is distinctive. These features are reduced or absent in other plumages, but Prairie can always be recognized by **pale crescent below eye** (ranging from yellow to whitish) **bordered below by a dark semicircle** (ranging from black to gray) and habit of **constantly bobbing tail**. Palm Warbler also bobs tail but has different face pattern and is less yellow on underparts. Immature most similar to immature Magnolia Warbler (p. 314) but has yellowish rump and lacks white tail band and gray band across chest. Very rare winter resident; recorded mid-Nov to early Feb. Occurs eastward to Canal Area, to 4,600 ft (1,400 m).

Bay-breasted Warbler · *Dendroica castanea*

4.5 in (12 cm). On breeding male, combination of **chestnut head, throat, and flanks, black mask**, and **buff patch on neck** is distinctive. Breeding female has chestnut flanks and **pale neck patch**. Most nonbreeding adults, especially males, show some chestnut on flanks. Immature female can be recognized by combination of streaked back (streaking sometimes obscure), nearly unstreaked underparts (may have faint streaks on sides of breast), and buffy wash on flanks and vent. Similar in some plumages to Chestnut-sided Warbler (p. 314), but latter has gray face, white eye-ring, whiter underparts, and upperparts that are brighter green and unstreaked. See also very rare Blackpoll Warbler. Common transient and winter resident; mostly late Sept to mid-April, sometimes in early Sept or early May. Occurs in lowlands and foothills. Found in middle and upper levels of forest and woodland. Frequently with mixed-species flocks.

Blackpoll Warbler · *Dendroica striata*

4.5 in (12 cm). Breeding male recognized by combination of **black cap** and **white cheeks**. Black-and-white Warbler (p. 320) differs in having white stripes on crown. Nonbreeding adults (both sexes) similar to breeding female but have olive wash on back and sides; in all adult plumages, note dark lateral throat stripe (sometimes reduced to just streaking in nonbreeding female). Dull immatures (both sexes) can easily be confused with Bay-breasted Warbler individuals that lack chestnut on flanks. Blackpolls have at least faint streaking on breast and flanks and have whiter underparts including **white undertail coverts** (these usually washed buff in Bay-breasted). Legs are typically pale but can be dark as in Bay-breasted. Very rare transient and winter resident; recorded late Oct to late March. Occurs in lowlands, in middle and upper levels of forest and woodland.

Yellow-throated
Warbler

adult male

breeding
male

breeding
adult

immature
female

Palm Warbler

nonbreeding
adult

Prairie Warbler

breeding
male

breeding
female

Bay-breasted
Warbler

immature
female

breeding
male

breeding
female

Blackpoll Warbler

immature

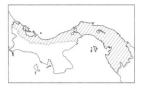

Cerulean Warbler
Dendroica cerulea

4.5 in (11 cm). On adult male, combination of **azure blue upperparts** and **narrow black chest band** is diagnostic; also note white wing-bars and black streaking on flanks. Male Black-throated Blue Warbler (p. 314) has black throat and lacks wing-bars. Female and immature (both sexes) can be recognized by unique **blue-green upperparts**; also note prominent **pale superciliary** and whitish wing-bars. Uncommon transient; late Aug to early Oct and mid-March to mid-April. Very rare winter resident. Occurs in lowlands and foothills, in canopy of forest and woodland. Often with mixed-species flocks.

Worm-eating Warbler
Helmitheros vermivorum

4.5 in (12 cm). Combination of **bold black stripes on buff head** and **buff underparts** is distinctive. All plumages similar. Three-striped Warbler (p. 330) has black patch on cheek and yellowish underparts. Uncommon winter resident; mostly Oct to April, sometimes arriving as early as late Sept. Occurs eastward to western Kuna Yala and eastern Panamá Province; more numerous in west, increasingly rare in central and eastern Panama; to at least 4,000 ft (1,200 m). Found in lower levels of forest and woodland; usually near ground, in undergrowth.

Black-and-white Warbler
Mniotilta varia

4.5 in (12 cm). **Heavy black-and-white streaking both above and below** is unique. Very rare Blackpoll Warbler (breeding male, p. 318) has solid black cap, and streaking is not as bold; male Pacific Antwren (p. 206) is also streaked but differs in shape, habitat, and behavior. Common transient and winter resident; mostly late Aug to early April. Occurs throughout the country; to 5,300 ft (1,600 m). Found in middle and upper levels of forest and woodland. Creeps on trunks and larger branches, often accompanying mixed-species flocks.

American Redstart
Setophaga ruticilla

4.5 in (12 cm). Conspicuous **red or yellow patches in wings, tail, and on sides** render this species unmistakable (patches are red on male, yellow on female and immatures). Immatures of both sexes resemble adult female (immature female sometimes lacks yellow in wings). Young males gradually acquire adult plumage over two years and may show black blotches on face and neck and have orange wing, tail, and side patches. Fairly common transient and uncommon winter resident; late Aug to late April, sometimes as late as May. Occurs throughout the country; to at least 5,500 ft (1,650 m); winters mainly in foothills. Found at all levels in forest, woodland, and mangroves. Usually with mixed-species flocks. Behavior is distinctive: **constantly fans tail** and droops wings as it sallies out for small flying insects (resident redstarts, p. 322, display same behavior).

Prothonotary Warbler
Protonotaria citrea

4.5 in (12 cm). In both sexes, combination of **yellow head and breast, plain blue-gray wings**, and **pure white undertail coverts** is distinctive. In flight, shows conspicuous white patches in tail. Immature similar to female. Blue-winged Warbler (p. 310) has black eye-line and white wing-bars. Fairly common transient and winter resident; mostly Sept to March, sometimes as early as Aug. Occurs in lowlands throughout the country; occasionally in foothills and highlands during migration. Found in lower levels of mangroves and other vegetation near water. Often in small groups of its own species; occasionally with mixed-species flocks.

Cerulean
Warbler

breeding
male

immature
female

Worm-eating
Warbler

Black-and-white
Warbler

male

female

American
Redstart

adult
male

adult
female

Prothonotary
Warbler

male

female

Ovenbird
Seiurus aurocapilla

5 in (13 cm). **Orange crown bordered with black** distinguishes it from any similar species; also note **white eye-ring**. Waterthrushes lack crown patch, have pale superciliary instead of an eye-ring, and teeter almost constantly. Could recall some migrant thrushes, but those are larger, lack crown patch, and hop on ground rather than walk (as Ovenbird does). Fairly common winter resident in western Panama, becoming rare in central and eastern Panama; two records from Darién (not mapped); late Sept to late April. Occurs throughout the country, ; to 9,600 ft (2,900 m). Found on and near ground in forest.

Northern Waterthrush
Seiurus noveboracensis

5 in (13 cm). Combination of **pale superciliary, streaked underparts,** and habit of **constantly teetering** as it walks on ground distinguishes it from all other species except very similar Louisiana Waterthrush (see for distinctions). Ovenbird has orange crown patch and white eye-ring (instead of superciliary). Very common transient and common winter resident; late Sept to late April, sometimes mid-Sept to May. Occurs in lowlands, on ground along streams; in mangroves; and around edges of bodies of water; to about 5,300 ft (1,600 m). In migration, may be found in highlands and in other habitats. Call a sharp metallic *tchink!*

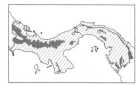

Louisiana Waterthrush
Seiurus motacilla

5.5 in (14 cm). Very similar to much more common Northern Waterthrush, including behavior of **constantly teetering**. In Louisiana, **superciliary is both broader and pure white behind eye** (narrower and buffy in front of eye); in Northern, superciliary narrows behind eye, where color varies from buff to white. Louisiana shows a **buffy patch on rear flanks** that contrasts with white underparts; Northern's underparts vary from white to pale yellow but are uniform on individual bird, with no contrast on flanks. Louisiana also has longer, thicker bill; little or no speckling on **pure white throat** (throat usually with small speckles in Northern); and is less heavily streaked below. Uncommon transient and winter resident; mostly Aug to March, sometimes to early April. Winters mostly in foothills and highlands; to at least 5,500 ft (1,650 m). Found in forest and woodland, on ground along streams (usually fast flowing). Call similar to that of Northern Waterthrush.

Slate-throated Redstart
Myioborus miniatus

4.5 in (12 cm). Combination of **slate-gray head and upperparts, yellow breast and belly,** and **tail-fanning behavior** should prevent confusion. Collared Redstart has yellow face. Common in foothills and highlands; mostly 2,000 to 6,900 ft (600 to 2,100 m). Found in lower and middle levels of forest, woodland, and adjacent clearings with trees. Very active, frequently spreading tail and making short sallies after insects; often with mixed-species flocks. Song a series of 6 to 10 high-pitched *chee* notes, often rising slightly and becoming louder before falling off near end.

Collared Redstart
Myioborus torquatus

5 in (13 cm). Narrow **dark chest band separating all-yellow face from yellow breast and belly** is unique; also note **tail-fanning behavior**. Slate-throated Redstart lacks yellow on face and throat. Common in western highlands eastward to Coclé; mostly above 6,000 ft (1,800 m), sometimes down to 3,500 ft (1,050 m). Found in lower and middle levels of forest and woodland. Like other redstarts, forages actively with short sallies, and fans tail frequently; often with mixed-species flocks. Song a thin, high-pitched warbling; variable in phrasing. **WH**

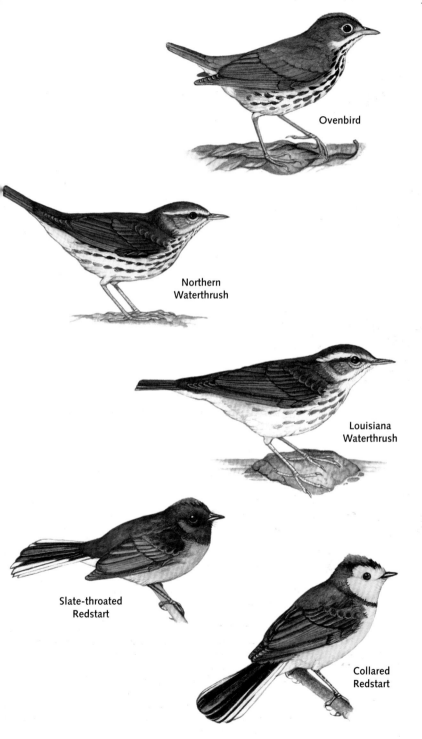

Ovenbird

Northern
Waterthrush

Louisiana
Waterthrush

Slate-throated
Redstart

Collared
Redstart

Mourning Warbler
Oporornis philadelphia

4.5 in (12 cm). **Gray hood** (dark gray in male, pale gray in female) distinguishes adults from other warblers except for much rarer MacGillivray's and Connecticut (see for comparisons); on immature, hood is incomplete, with broken breast band and usually yellowish throat. Adult male lacks eye-ring; immature and some adult females have a narrow eye-ring that is usually broken above and behind. Fairly common transient and uncommon winter resident; mid-Sept to mid-May. Winters mainly in western highlands; recorded to about 4,800 ft (1,600 m). Found in dense undergrowth in forest edge and woodland edge; also found in thickets in clearings and other open areas. Skulking and often difficult to see.

MacGillivray's Warbler
Oporornis tolmiei

4.5 in (12 cm). In all plumages, distinguished from Mourning and Connecticut Warblers by **white arcs above and below eye** (in adult female and immature, eye-arcs are somewhat less distinct than in male). Male further distinguished from male Mourning by black lores that connect across forehead. Adult female similar to female Mourning except for eye-arcs; immature distinguished from immature Mourning by eye-arcs and complete, grayish hood. Rare winter resident; mid-Oct to mid-May. Occurs principally in western Chiriquí highlands; recorded between 4,000 and 5,900 ft (1,200 and 1,800 m). A few records from lowlands in Chiriquí and Canal Area. Found in dense undergrowth in forest edge and woodland edge, and in thickets in clearings.

Kentucky Warbler
Oporornis formosus

4.5 in (12 cm). In all plumages, **incomplete yellow spectacles with dark streak below** are distinctive. Female and immature resemble male but black mask is less extensive. Nonbreeding and immature Canada Warblers (p. 328) can show similar facial pattern but have white eye-ring and gray rather than olive upperparts. Fairly common winter resident; early Sept to late April. Occurs in lowlands and foothills of western and central Panama, uncommon in eastern Panama; in migration, also occurs in highlands; to 8,000 ft (2,300 m). Found on and near ground in forest.

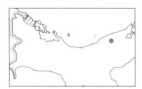

Connecticut Warbler
Oporornis agilis

4.5 in (12 cm). Similar to much more common Mourning Warbler; adult male lacks black on chest. In all plumages, distinguished by more conspicuous, **complete white eye-ring** (immature and some female Mournings have narrow eye-ring that is usually broken); **long undertail coverts** reaching more than halfway to tip of tail; paler yellow underparts; and habit of walking rather than hopping when on ground. Adult female resembles male but is paler and brown (not gray) on head. See also MacGillivray's Warbler. Very rare transient; late Sept to late Oct and late March to early April. Recorded from Caribbean lowlands eastward to northern Coclé. Found in forest edge and thickets, on and near ground in dense undergrowth.

Swainson's Warbler
Limnothlypis swainsonii

5 in (13 cm). Rather nondescript; note **large, straight bill** and short tail. Upperparts are dull brown, with **rufous tinge on crown**; also note **whitish superciliary, straight dark eye-line**, and whitish throat. Underparts are pale buff. Found in dense understory within forest. One record, from central Canal Area (2004). **Not illustrated**.

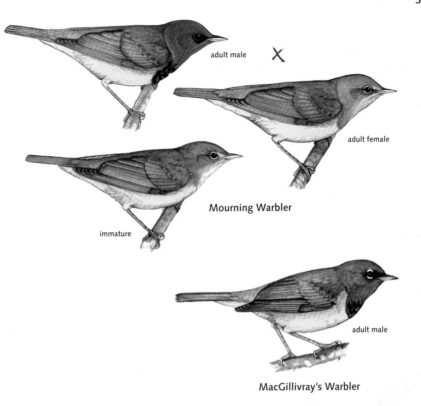

adult male

X

adult female

immature

Mourning Warbler

adult male

MacGillivray's Warbler

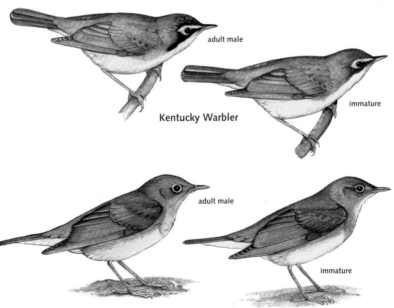

adult male

immature

Kentucky Warbler

adult male

immature

Connecticut Warbler

Common Yellowthroat
Geothlypis trichas

4.5 in (12 cm). Male recognized by **extensive black mask with whitish band above**; also note **buffy belly**. Other male yellowthroats lack white border to mask and are entirely yellow below. Adult female distinguished from similar warblers that have mainly yellow underparts by buffy lower breast and belly. Immature similar to adult female but paler yellow on throat and undertail coverts. Gray-crowned Yellowthroat has black lores and thicker bill. Rare winter resident; mostly mid-Oct to late April. Mostly in lowlands, but also recorded in Chiriquí highlands; to about 4,300 ft (1,300 m). Found near water, close to ground in shrubs or thick grass.

Olive-crowned Yellowthroat
Geothlypis semiflava

4.5 in (12 cm). On male, **black mask, lacking any gray or whitish border above**, is distinctive; also note **uniformly yellow underparts**. Male Common Yellowthroat has white border above black mask and whitish belly. Female and similar immature differ from other warblers in nearly **uniform olive green upperparts** and **completely yellow underparts** (immature somewhat buffier below). Female and immature Common have whitish belly. No range overlap with Masked and Gray-crowned Yellowthroats. Common in lowlands of Bocas del Toro. Found near water, in shrubs, thickets, and dense grass. Male sings from an exposed perch, giving a series of variably rising and falling musical notes, including *chuweechuwedit-chuweechuwedit-chuweechuwedit*.

Masked Yellowthroat
Geothlypis aequinoctialis

5 in (13 cm). Male distinguished by **large black mask bordered above by gray**. Male Common Yellowthroat has white border above mask and buffy belly. Female can be recognized by **grayish forecrown and cheeks** and **yellow supraloral and eye-ring**. Female and immature Common Yellowthroat lack these facial markings and have buffy belly. Both sexes of Gray-crowned Yellowthroat have black restricted to lores and thicker bill; no range overlap with Olive-crowned Yellowthroat. Uncommon in western Chiriquí; 1,600 to 4,500 ft (500 to 1,350 m). Found near water in shrubs and dense growth, and in wet grassy areas. Male sings from an exposed perch, giving a rapid musical warbling.

Gray-crowned Yellowthroat
Geothlypis poliocephala

4.5 in (12 cm). In both sexes, combination of **black lores** and **gray on head** is distinctive; has **thicker bill** than other yellowthroats. On male Masked Yellowthroat, mask extends behind eye; other female yellowthroats lack black on lores. Uncommon in western Chiriquí; 1,650 to 7,400 ft (500 to 2,250 m). Found in grassy areas with scattered trees or shrubs. Male sings from an elevated perch, giving a series of somewhat jumbled musical phrases.

Common
Yellowthroat

male

adult
female

Olive-crowned
Yellowthroat

male

female

Masked
Yellowthroat

male

female

Gray-crowned
Yellowthroat

male

female

Hooded Warbler
Wilsonia citrina

4.5 in (12 cm). In all plumages, distinguished from other warblers by combination of **extensive white in tail, plain wings**, and **uniformly olive back and rump**. Male's **black hood surrounding yellow face** renders it unmistakable. Female shows black hood to variable degree: on some, hood is similar to that of male; others have reduced black around face and across breast; some individuals (including all immature females) lack black entirely. Female Wilson's Warbler resembles females that lack black markings, but is smaller, lacks white in tail, and has yellow lores (lores dark in Hooded); female and immature Yellow Warbler (p. 312) have yellow instead of white in tail; female Prothonotary Warbler (p. 320) has gray rump. Rare winter resident; late Sept to early May. Occurs in lowlands; recorded eastward to eastern Panamá Province. Found in lower levels of forest edge and in second growth and thickets. Sometimes with mixed-species flocks.

Wilson's Warbler
Wilsonia pusilla

4.5 in (11 cm). On male, **small black cap** is distinctive. Black on crown is reduced in immature male and in female; often absent in immature female (crown then olive). In all plumages, note **yellow face, including forehead and lores**, and **uniformly olive tail**. Female Hooded Warbler is larger and has white in tail and dark lores; female and immature Yellow Warblers (p. 312) have yellow in tail; female yellowthroats (p. 326) lack yellow on forehead. Very common winter resident; Sept to mid-May. Occurs in foothills and highlands, from Chiriquí to eastern Panamá Province; mostly above 3,300 ft (1,000 m); becomes progressively rarer eastward. Found in lower and middle levels of forest, forest edge, and nearby clearings with shrubs. Frequently with mixed-species flocks.

Canada Warbler
Wilsonia canadensis

4.5 in (12 cm). On adult male, **yellow breast with necklace of dark streaks** is diagnostic; necklace is fainter on adult female and immatures of both sexes (some immatures almost lack streaking). In all plumages, combination of **uniformly grayish upperparts** (tinged olive in some immatures), **yellow supraloral**, and **white eye-ring** is distinctive. Fairly common transient; mostly late Sept to early Oct and late April to early May; rare winter resident. Occurs mainly in foothills, to over 5,300 ft (1,600 m). Found in lower levels of forest edge and nearby shrubby areas. Regularly accompanies mixed-species flocks.

Golden-crowned Warbler
Basileuterus culicivorus

4.5 in (12 cm). Only warbler that has combination of **yellow-orange crown stripe** (with black border) and **all-yellow underparts**. Three-striped Warbler (p. 330) has buff crown stripe, a black patch on cheeks, paler yellow underparts, and whitish throat. Uncommon in western highlands, eastward to Veraguas, mostly 3,300 to 5,500 ft (1,000 to 1,650 m); also uncommon on western side of Azuero Peninsula, above 1,000 ft (300 m). Found in lower levels of forest and woodland. Often accompanies mixed-species flocks. Song a series of 5 to 10 musical notes; the next-to-last note is lower pitched, the final note is inflected upward.

Rufous-capped Warbler
Basileuterus rufifrons

4.5 in (12 cm). Combination of **rufous crown and cheeks** and **white superciliary** is unique. Fairly common on Pacific slope eastward to eastern Panamá Province, and on Caribbean slope in Canal Area and Colón Province; to 5,300 ft (1,600 m). Found in undergrowth in woodland, forest edge, and second growth. Often cocks tail. Song a jumbled series of thin, dry notes that vary in pitch.

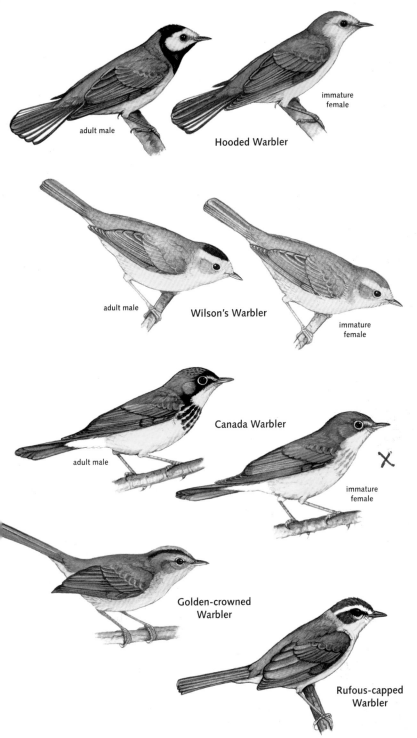

adult male

immature female

Hooded Warbler

adult male

Wilson's Warbler

immature female

Canada Warbler

adult male

immature female

Golden-crowned Warbler

Rufous-capped Warbler

Black-cheeked Warbler — *Basileuterus melanogenys*

5 in (13 cm). Combination of **chestnut crown, white superciliary**, and **blackish sides of head** is distinctive; also note buffy whitish underparts. In eastern Darién, see Pirre Warbler (no range overlap). Common in western highlands eastward to Veraguas; mostly above 5,000 ft (1,500 m), sometimes down to 4,000 ft (1,200 m). Found in lower levels of forest and woodland. Often in small groups of its own species, occasionally with mixed-species flocks. Song a sputtering series of sharp metallic notes. **WH**

Pirre Warbler — *Basileuterus ignotus*

5 in (13 cm). Similar to Black-cheeked Warbler (no range overlap) but yellower overall, with **greenish yellow superciliary, pale yellow underparts**, and more olive (not as grayish) back; sides of head not as black. Fairly common in highlands of eastern Darién, mostly above 4,500 ft (1,350 m). Found in lower levels of forest. Behavior similar to that of Black-cheeked. Song undescribed. **EH**

Three-striped Warbler — *Basileuterus tristriatus*

4.5 in (12 cm). Combination of **black cheek patch** and **bold buff and black stripes on head** is distinctive. Worm-eating (p. 320) and Golden-crowned (p. 328) Warblers lack black cheek patch; latter has orange-yellow crown stripe and yellower underparts. Fairly common in foothills and highlands; mostly 2,000 to 7,500 ft (600 to 2,250 m). Found in lower levels of forest and woodland. Usually in small groups of its own species, sometimes with mixed-species flocks. Song consists of a series of rapid, sharp, twittering notes.

Buff-rumped Warbler — *Phaeothlypis fulvicauda*

4.5 in (12 cm). Easily recognized by conspicuous **buff rump and base of tail**; also note habit of **fanning and flicking tail** from side to side. Waterthrushes (p. 322) have rump and tail same color as back, show streaking below, and teeter rather than flick tail. Uncommon; to 4,300 ft (1,300 m). Usually found in forest or woodland, along streams (often swiftly flowing, rocky ones); sometimes found in mangroves or other wet areas. Typically hops rather than walks. Song a series of ringing, chirping notes (often 20 or more) that build to a crescendo (loud enough to be heard over the noise of a rushing stream).

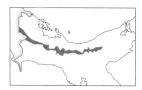

Wrenthrush — *Zeledonia coronata*

4 in (10 cm). Combination of **plump body, short tail, golden tawny crown**, and **slaty gray underparts** is distinctive. Uncommon in western highlands, eastward to Coclé; in Chiriquí occurs mostly above 5,900 ft (1,800 m), elsewhere down to 3,500 ft (1,050 m). Found on and near ground in forest, in dense undergrowth. Often flicks wings. Very secretive and difficult to see, usually remaining in dense cover; detected mainly by voice. Frequently given call is a high piercing *shreeii* that rises slightly near the end; song a variable series of three to six sibilant whistles that change in pitch: *tisee, tsup, tisee*. **WH**

Yellow-breasted Chat — *Icteria virens*

6.5 in (16 cm). Combination of **white spectacles, plain wings**, and **yellow throat and breast** is unique. Larger, with heavier bill than other warblers. Uncommon winter resident; early Oct to late April. Occurs in lowlands of western Bocas del Toro; one record from western Panamá Province. Found in thickets and second growth, and in dense vegetation in forest edge and woodland edge.

Black-cheeked
Warbler

Pirre Warbler

Three-striped
Warbler

Buff-rumped
Warbler

Wrenthrush

Yellow-breasted Chat

THRAUPIDAE. The members of this large and diverse family occur only in the Americas, where they are most diverse in the tropics. Many species have rather stout bills, sometimes with a sharp toothlike projection near the tip, but the conebills, honeycreepers, and dacnises have long thin bills suited for probing flowers for nectar. Most tanagers eat mainly fruit, supplemented by small arthropods, but some species are more insectivorous. This family is known for its many brightly colored species, especially the honeycreepers and those in the genus *Tangara*.

White-eared Conebill — *Conirostrum leucogenys*

3 in (8 cm). On male, combination of **black crown**, prominent **white cheek stripe**, and **unstreaked gray back** is unique; also note rufous undertail coverts. Female can be distinguished by combination of **gray upperparts, whitish rump**, and **buffy yellowish underparts and face**. Female Scarlet-thighed Dacnis (p. 346) also has buffy underparts but buff does not extend up to eye; also note pale bluish green upperparts (including rump). Fairly common in lowlands in eastern Panamá Province and Darién. Found in forest canopy and forest edge (especially in drier forest); also inhabits woodland. Forages in flowering trees for nectar and gleans leaves and branches for insects. Call undescribed.

Common Bush-Tanager — *Chlorospingus ophthalmicus*

5 in (13 cm). A conspicuous **white spot behind eye** distinguishes this species from other birds with olive backs and yellow underparts. Birds in Veraguas and Coclé have blacker head, orange throat flecked with black, and deeper orange breast. Sooty-capped Bush-Tanager has long white superciliary (rather than white spot behind eye). Very common in western foothills and highlands, eastward to Coclé; mostly 2,000 to 7,500 ft (600 to 2,250 m). Found at all levels (most often low) in forest and woodland, and in adjacent clearings with trees. Forages in active, noisy flocks; often joined by other species. Flocks give a rapid, sharp, high-pitched twittering.

Tacarcuna Bush-Tanager — *Chlorospingus tacarcunae*

5.5 in (14 cm). Best recognized by combination of **pale eye, uniformly olive upperparts**, and **yellow throat and chest**. Yellow-throated Bush-Tanager (p. 334) has dark eye, and yellow on underparts is restricted to throat. Pirre Bush-Tanager (no range overlap) has blackish crown and sides of head. Fairly common in foothills and highlands of eastern Panama (absent from southeastern Darién); above 2,300 ft (700 m). Found in lower and middle levels of forest. Usually in small flocks, sometimes with other species. Calls include a buzzy trill and a sharp *chit!* **EH**

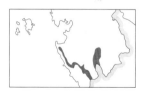

Pirre Bush-Tanager — *Chlorospingus inornatus*

6 in (15 cm). Only bush-tanager in its limited range. Larger, with heavier bill than other bush-tanagers; note **pale eye, blackish crown and sides of head that contrast with olive back**, and **all-yellow underparts**. Common in foothills and highlands of southeastern Darién; mostly above 4,000 ft (1,200 m), sometimes down to about 2,600 ft (800 m). Found in lower and middle levels of forest. Usually in small flocks, sometimes accompanied by other species. Call a sharp *chit!* **EH***

Sooty-capped Bush-Tanager — *Chlorospingus pileatus*

5.5 in (14 cm). **Broad, jagged, white superciliary** (beginning over eye) on **mostly black head** is distinctive. Common Bush-Tanager has only a small white spot behind eye, not a stripe. In poor light, Black-cheeked Warbler (p. 330) can appear similar, but its superciliary extends to bill, and it has chestnut crown and gray underparts. Common in western highlands eastward to Ngöbe-Buglé; mostly above 7,000 ft (2,100 m), sometimes down to 5,300 ft (1,600 m). Found at all levels (most often low) in forest and woodland. Typically in small flocks, sometimes with other species. Flocks give high twittering calls. **WH**

White-eared
Conebill

male

female

western
Chiriquí race

Common
Bush-Tanager

Veraguas and
Coclé race

Tacarcuna
Bush-Tanager

Pirre
Bush-Tanager

Sooty-capped
Bush-Tanager

Yellow-throated Bush-Tanager 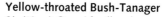 *Chlorospingus flavigularis*

5 in (13 cm). **Orangish yellow throat** contrasting with **brownish buff breast** is distinctive; also note dark eye. All other bush-tanagers have yellow on breast. Common Bush-Tanager (p. 332) further distinguished by white spot behind eye; Tacarcuna Bush-Tanager (p. 332) by pale eye. Fairly common but local in foothills; from Bocas del Toro to western Kuna Yala (mostly on Caribbean slope); generally 450 to 900 ft (1,500 to 3,000 m). Found in middle and upper levels of forest. Usually in small flocks, sometimes joined by other species. Call consists of sharp metallic *shrt* notes, given singly or run together in a rapid series.

Yellow-backed Tanager *Hemithraupis flavicollis*

4.5 in (12 cm). Male recognized by combination of **mostly black upperparts** and **bright yellow rump and throat**. Female similar to female Black-and-yellow Tanager, differing in **pale yellowish eye-ring, partly yellow** (not entirely black) **bill**, and, in area of range overlap, whitish belly (not uniformly yellow underparts). Uncommon in eastern Darién; to 3,300 ft (1,000 m). Found in upper levels of forest. Often with mixed-species flocks. Calls include a high *tssit* and a sharp *chrrt!*

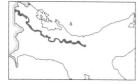

Ashy-throated Bush-Tanager *Chlorospingus canigularis*

5.5 in (14 cm). **Greenish yellow band across chest** separates pale gray throat and upper breast; also note **grayish sides of head**. Common Bush-Tanager (p. 332) has white spot behind eye; Yellow-throated Bush-Tanager has orangish yellow throat and lacks yellow on chest. Rare in western foothills eastward to Veraguas; mostly 2,600 to 4,000 ft (800 to 1,200 m). Found in upper levels of wet forest. Usually in small groups, sometimes with other species. Calls include a sharp high *chit!*, a rapid *chi-di-di-dit*, and a jumbled twittering.

Black-and-yellow Tanager *Chrysothlypis chrysomelas*

4.5 in (11 cm). Striking male, **bright yellow with black back, wings, and tail**, is unmistakable. Nondescript female has uniformly yellow underparts in most of Panama, but whitish lower breast and belly in Chiriquí and Bocas del Toro; both forms can be distinguished from any similar warbler by **longer, thicker all-black bill** (although bill is thin for a tanager); also note whitish tufts that often project on sides of breast from under wings. Female White-shouldered Tanager (p. 338) has bicolored bill, whitish throat, and, in most of Panama, contrasting gray head. In eastern Darién, compare female Yellow-backed Tanager. Fairly common in foothills; mostly 1,300 to 4,000 ft (400 to 1,200 m). Found in upper levels of forest and forest edge. Frequently in small groups accompanying mixed-species flocks. Call a sharp descending *shrreet*.

Rosy Thrush-Tanager *Rhodinocichla rosea*

7 in (18 cm). On male, **bright rose-red breast and supraloral area** are unique. Female, similar in pattern but with rose-red replaced by **orange-tawny**, is also distinctive. Fairly common on Pacific slope eastward to eastern Panamá Province, and on Caribbean slope from northern Coclé to eastern Colón Province; to about 4,000 ft (1,200 m). Found on and near ground in both young second growth and in dense undergrowth at edge of woodland and forest. Skulking and difficult to see in the thick tangled vegetation it prefers; forages by flicking dead leaves aside with bill. One of Panama's best songsters; the rich, resonant, wrenlike song is very atypical for a tanager (including the fact that it is sung antiphonally, with each member of a pair giving part of the song): gives a rhythmic *che-ow-whedup, chuwee-dup* and variants. Has a variety of other calls, including a sharp *wheet, chu-wu* and a descending *whiwhiwiwiwi* that alternates with single or double melodious whistles.

Yellow-throated
Bush-Tanager

Yellow-backed
Tanager

male

female

Ashy-throated
Bush-Tanager

Black-and-yellow
Tanager

male

female
eastern race

female
western race

Rosy
Thrush-Tanager

male

female

White-throated Shrike-Tanager

Lanio leucothorax

7.5 in (19 cm). Male is only mainly **black and yellow** bird with **white throat;** also note distinctive pattern. Pacific-slope males have black lower back, rump, and vent; Caribbean-slope males have mostly yellow lower back, rump, and vent. Female distinguished by combination of **brown upperparts, yellowish lower underparts**, and **heavy hooked black bill**. Rare and local on Pacific slope in western Chiriquí and in the foothills of Veraguas; also rare and local in foothills on Caribbean slope eastward to Coclé; mostly 1,500 to 3,000 ft (450 to 900 m); rarely to near sea level in Chiriquí. Found in middle levels of moist forest. Often a core species in mixed-species flocks. Has a variety of calls, including a sweet *chi-dew* (with the second note lower).

Dusky-faced Tanager

Mitrospingus cassinii

6.5 in (17 cm). Combination of **pale eye on blackish face** and **olive crown** that contrasts with mostly dark gray upperparts is distinctive. Fairly common on entire Caribbean slope; fairly common on Pacific slope from eastern Panamá Province eastward; also occurs on western Pacific slope but only in foothills; to at least 3,500 ft (1,050 m). Found in lower levels of forest, especially in dense vegetation along streams or edges. Usually in active flocks of up to a dozen individuals. Flocks constantly give harsh *khhtt!* notes.

Gray-headed Tanager

Eucometis penicillata

6.5 in (17 cm). **Slightly crested gray head**, contrasting strongly with **olive green upperparts** and **bright yellow underparts**, is distinctive; also note heavy, all-black bill. Female White-shouldered Tanager (p. 338) is similar in pattern but has bicolored bill, lacks crest (appears round-headed), and is smaller and more arboreal. Fairly common on Pacific slope and on Caribbean slope from northern Coclé eastward; to 5,300 ft (1,600 m). Inhabits lower levels of forest. Frequently found at army-ant swarms. Song a jumbled series of spluttering whistles and sharp notes; calls include a clucking *chut!* and a sharp thin *tseet.*

Sulphur-rumped Tanager

Heterospingus rubrifrons

6 in (15 cm). Combination of mostly gray plumage and **yellow rump** is distinctive (rump usually concealed, except in flight); also note conspicuous **white tufts at sides of breast** (often more readily seen than rump). Similar female Scarlet-browed Tanager (no known range overlap) occurs only in Darién. Uncommon on entire Caribbean slope; also uncommon on Pacific slope in eastern Panama Province and in Veraguas foothills; to 3,000 ft (900 m). Found in middle and upper levels of forest. Usually in small groups that accompany mixed-species flocks. Calls include a thin *tsit* (given alone or strung together in a twitter) and various squeaky notes. **CL, EL**

Scarlet-browed Tanager

Heterospingus xanthopygius

6.5 in (16 cm). On male, **scarlet tufts behind eye** are unique; also note yellow rump and wing patch and white tufts on side of breast. Female very similar to Sulphur-rumped Tanager (no known range overlap); slightly larger and with little if any yellow on undertail coverts. Uncommon in eastern Darién; to 3,000 ft (900 m). Found in middle and upper levels of forest. Often with mixed-species flocks. Calls similar to those of Sulphur-rumped.

male
Pacific slope
race

male
Caribbean slope
race

White-throated
Shrike-Tanager

female

Dusky-faced
Tanager

Gray-headed
Tanager

Sulphur-rumped
Tanager

Scarlet-browed
Tanager

male

female

White-shouldered Tanager
Tachyphonus luctuosus

5 in (13 cm). Male is only mostly black bird with conspicuous **white shoulder patch**. Males of races that occur in western Panama have smaller white patch than males in east; within western Panama, males in Chiriquí also have yellow crown and pale eye. Larger male White-lined Tanager usually looks all black but may show narrow white line at top of shoulder, and flashes white wing-linings in flight; male Dot-winged Antwren (p. 208) and both sexes of Jet Antbird (p. 210) have white wing-bars instead of distinct patch, and also have white tail tipping. Male Tawny-crested Tanager resembles Chiriquí male but lacks white in wing. In most of Panama, female has gray head, contrasting with olive back and yellow underparts; in western Panama, female has a more olive head showing less contrast with back. Gray-headed females resemble larger Gray-headed Tanager (p. 336) but have **bicolored** (not all-black) **bill**, lack crest, are duller, and forage higher above the ground; olive-headed female distinguished from female Black-and-yellow Tanager (p. 334) by bicolored bill and whitish throat. Common on entire Caribbean slope and on Pacific slope from Canal Area eastward; rare and local in western Chiriquí; to 2,500 ft (750 m). Found at all levels of forest and woodland. Usually with mixed-species flocks. Calls include squeaky *chew* and *chut* notes (sometimes given in series) and a thin *tsit*.

Tawny-crested Tanager
Tachyphonus delatrii

5.5 in (14 cm). Male's **bright tawny crest** is distinctive. Female is overall duller and more uniform brown in color than other similar female tanagers. Male of Chiriquí race of White-shouldered Tanager (which has yellow crown) looks somewhat similar to male Tawny-crested but shows white patch in wing (Tawny-crested does not occur in Chiriquí). Fairly common in lowlands on entire Caribbean slope; uncommon in lowlands on Pacific slope in eastern Panamá Province and in Darién; occurs on western Pacific slope in Veraguas foothills. Found in lower levels of forest. Goes about in active flocks of up to a dozen individuals, occasionally with other species. Flocks give a constant chatter of *zhrit* notes (often doubled or tripled) and other *tsk* notes.

White-lined Tanager
Tachyphonus rufus

6.5 in (17 cm). Male has **white wing-linings** that are concealed when perched but conspicuous in flight; a narrow white line at top of shoulder sometimes shows on closed wing. Male White-shouldered Tanager's wing patch is visible when perched. Bright rufous female (somewhat paler below) can be distinguished from other similarly colored birds by **bluish gray base to lower mandible**. Fairly common in lowlands on entire Caribbean slope; uncommon in lowlands on Pacific slope from western Panamá Province eastward; rare in western Chiriquí, where it extends into lower highlands. Found in open areas with shrubs, and in second growth and gardens. Usually in pairs, which facilitates identification. Calls include a chirping *chiddit!* (the second note higher) and a squeaky *fee-deet*.

Crimson-collared Tanager
Ramphocelus sanguinolentus

7 in (18 cm). Combination of **broad red collar and crown** and **black face** is unmistakable. Immature somewhat duller but still recognizable. Uncommon in lowlands and foothills of Caribbean slope, eastward to Coclé; occurs on Pacific slope in Veraguas foothills; to 3,000 ft (900 m). Found in lower levels of forest edge, woodland edge, shrubby areas, and second growth. Call a thin descending *zhreee*. Song a leisurely series of phrases of sibilant notes that rise and fall, interspersed with high-pitched hissing notes.

White-shouldered Tanager

male
eastern race

female
eastern race

female
western race

male
Chiriqui race

male western
Caribbean slope
race

Tawny-crested Tanager

male

female

White-lined Tanager

male

female

Crimson-collared Tanager

adult

Crimson-backed Tanager
Ramphocelus dimidiatus

6.5 in (16 cm). In both sexes, **bright crimson lower back, rump, and lower underparts** are distinctive; male has dull red head, upper back, and breast; on female, these areas are reddish brown. On male, also note **silvery base to lower mandible**. Ant-tanagers (p. 366) are much duller on lower back and underparts; male Passerini's and Cherrie's Tanagers are black (not reddish or brown) on head, back, and breast. Common on Caribbean slope from northern Veraguas eastward, and on Pacific slope from Chiriquí eastward; to over 5,300 ft (1,600 m). Found in shrubby areas, second growth, clearings, and gardens. Often in small groups. Locally known as *sangre de toro* ("bull's blood," from its dark red coloration). Call a nasal *whenkh*. Song, given at dawn, a musical whistled *chid-dee-chew* or *chit, dew, dew.*

Passerini's Tanager
Ramphocelus passerinii

6.5 in (16 cm). In both sexes, note **thick bluish bill** with dark tip. Male is **black with bright red lower back and rump**; virtually identical to male Cherrie's Tanager (no range overlap) but slightly redder on lower back and rump. See Scarlet-rumped Cacique (p. 380). Female, duller than female Cherrie's, has yellowish ochre on rump and greenish orange on chest. Female Flame-rumped Tanager is pale yellow on lower back and underparts. Common in lowlands of Bocas del Toro and western Ngöbe-Buglé. Found in second growth, shrubby areas, and gardens. Males often perch in open, puffing out their brilliant rump. Usually in small groups. Call a thin, high-pitched *whik!* Song consists of variable phrases of three or four whistled notes: *wheet, wheedip, wheet.* Passerini's and Cherrie's were formerly considered a single species, the Scarlet-rumped Tanager.

Cherrie's Tanager
Ramphocelus costaricensis

6.5 in (16 cm). Both sexes have **thick bluish bill** with dark tip. Male (not illustrated) essentially identical to male Passerini's Tanager (no range overlap) but slightly more orange on lower back and rump. Crimson-backed Tanager is dull red or brownish on head, upper back, and upper breast and has red lower underparts. See also Scarlet-rumped Cacique (p. 380). Female is brighter than female Passerini's, with more **orange on chest and rump**. Very common on Pacific slope, eastward to southern Veraguas; to 5,300 ft (1,600 m). Found in second growth, shrubby areas, and gardens. Behavior and calls similar to Passerini's; song is more musical and given more frequently. Cherrie's and Passerini's were formerly considered a single species, the Scarlet-rumped Tanager. **WL**

Flame-rumped Tanager
Ramphocelus flammigerus

6.5 in (16 cm). Male, **black with yellow lower back and rump**, is distinctive. Yellow-rumped Cacique (p. 380) has much larger bill and yellow on wing and undertail coverts. On female, **lemon yellow rump and underparts** are distinctive. Female Passerini's Tanager is orangish rather than yellow on rump and breast; Sulphur-rumped Tanager (p. 336) lacks yellow on breast. Occurs in lowlands and lower foothills. Common on Caribbean slope from eastern Bocas del Toro eastward; also common on Pacific slope from eastern Panamá Province eastward; rare on Pacific in Canal Area; occurs on western Pacific slope in foothills of Veraguas and Coclé; to about 2,500 ft (750 m). Found in second growth, shrubby areas, and gardens. Often in small groups. Calls include a thin *zhreet* and a nasal *whank*. Song consists of two-note phrases repeated in a regular cadence.

Crimson-backed Tanager
male
female

Passerini's Tanager
male
female

Cherrie's Tanager
female

Flame-rumped Tanager
male
female

Blue-gray Tanager

Thraupis episcopus

5.5 in (14 cm). **Pale blue-gray on head and underparts, bright blue on wings and tail;** no other Panama bird is as bluish overall. In poor light could be mistaken for Palm Tanager, which is similar in size and shape, but that species has contrasting dark flight feathers; smaller Plain-colored Tanager has entirely dark wings. One of the most familiar and ubiquitous birds in Panama; very common almost throughout the country; to 5,300 ft (1,600 m). Found at all levels in open areas with trees, second growth, shrubby areas, gardens, and urban areas; also in forest canopy, forest edge, and woodland. Often with Palm Tanager in small flocks. Locally called *azulejo* (in reference to its blue color). Call a thin *seee*. Song consists of squeaky notes rising and falling in pitch, with no set pattern.

Palm Tanager

Thraupis palmarum

6.5 in (16 cm). Combination of **grayish olive plumage** and contrasting **dark flight feathers with pale band across base** is distinctive. Smaller Plain-colored Tanager is gray without olive tone and has entirely dark, unmarked wings and black lores. Common almost throughout the country; to 4,500 ft (1,350 m). Found at all levels in open areas with trees, second growth, shrubby areas, and gardens; also in forest canopy, forest edge, and woodland. Often with Blue-gray Tanager in small flocks. Call a thin *seee*. Song like that of Blue-gray Tanager, but faster and with sharper and less squeaky notes.

Blue-and-gold Tanager

Bangsia arcaei

5 in (13 cm). Combination of uniformly **dark blue head and upperparts** and **yellow breast and belly** is unique; also note **dark red eye**. Some male euphonias (pp. 384-389) are similar in pattern, but these are much smaller and have yellow or tawny on head and dark eyes. Uncommon in foothills, mostly on Caribbean slope eastward to western Kuna Yala; very locally on Pacific slope in Chiriquí, Veraguas, and eastern Panamá Province; recorded 1,000 to 4,000 ft (300 to 1,200 m). Found in upper levels of wet forest. Sometimes with mixed-species flocks. Call a sharp, high-pitched *zhree*. Song consists of a medley of sharp high-pitched notes. **CL, EL**

Plain-colored Tanager

Tangara inornata

4.5 in (12 cm). Best identified by combination of uniformly lead gray head and body, **dark unpatterned wings**, and **black lores**. Bright blue patch on shoulder is usually concealed when perched. Larger Palm Tanager has olive tone; wings are dark only on flight feathers, which have pale band across base. Sulphur-rumped Tanager and female Scarlet-browed Tanager (p. 336) can appear similar when their yellow rumps are concealed, but they have longer bills and usually show white tufts on side of breast. Common on entire Caribbean slope; also common on Pacific slope, from western Panamá Province eastward; to about 2,500 ft (750 m). Found in forest canopy, forest edge, woodland edge, and in clearings with trees. Usually in small flocks of its own species. Call a high-pitched metallic *dziit*.

Gray-and-gold Tanager

Tangara palmeri

6 in (15 cm). **Black spotting around back of neck and across whitish chest** (forming a necklace) is distinctive; also note black mask. Gold tinge on chest can be hard to see. Rare in foothills, from eastern Panamá Province eastward; mostly 1,500 to 3,300 ft (450 to 1,000 m). Found in upper levels of moist forest. Usually in small groups, often associating with mixed-species flocks. Calls include a sweet *chweet* and a high-pitched *chit chup swee* (with the last note rising).

Blue-gray
Tanager

Palm Tanager

Blue-and-gold
Tanager

Plain-colored
Tanager

Gray-and-gold
Tanager

Emerald Tanager
Tangara florida

4.5 in (11 cm). Combination of mostly **bright green plumage** and conspicuous **squarish black ear patch** is distinctive. Female lacks yellow on crown. Occurs in foothills; fairly common on entire Caribbean slope and on Pacific slope from eastern Panamá Province eastward; mostly 1,000 to 3,000 ft (300 to 900 m). Found in upper levels of moist forest. Usually in mixed-species flocks. Calls include a sharp *psik!* and a whining *fweeer*.

Silver-throated Tanager
Tangara icterocephala

5 in (13 cm). On male, **bright yellow plumage**, **black streaking on back**, and **white throat bordered by black moustachial stripe** should prevent confusion. Female and immature are duller but retain basic pattern, including whitish throat and streaked back. Common in foothills and highlands on both slopes; mostly 2,000 to 7,400 ft (600 to 2,250 m), a few records from near sea level on Caribbean slope. Found in upper levels of forest. Usually in groups, sometimes numbering more than 20 individuals, and frequently associating with mixed-species flocks. Call a sharp buzzy *bzeet*.

Speckled Tanager
Tangara guttata

4.5 in (12 cm). **Heavy black spotting both above and below** is unique. Immature less heavily spotted and lacks yellow superciliary. If seen from below, Sharpbill (p. 278) could be confused, but that species has a pointed bill and lacks spotting on back. Fairly common in foothills and highlands on both slopes (more local on western Pacific slope); recorded 1,000 to 5,000 ft (300 to 1,500 m). Found in upper levels of forest. Often in mixed-species flocks. Calls consist of weak, thin chipping notes, sometimes accelerated into a twitter.

Bay-headed Tanager
Tangara gyrola

5 in (13 cm). Combination of **chestnut head** and mostly **bright turquoise underparts** is distinctive. Female duller, but retains basic pattern; immature even duller, and sometimes mostly green, but usually retains some chestnut on head and blue on underparts. Rufous-winged Tanager (much less common) has rufous in wings and mostly green underparts. Fairly common in foothills and lower highlands, mostly 2,000 to 5,300 ft (600 to 1,600 m); rare in lowlands of western Chiriquí and of Caribbean slope of Canal Area. Found in upper levels of forest and in adjacent clearings with tall trees. Often in mixed-species flocks. Calls include a sibilant *tsit* and a descending *dzeee*.

Rufous-winged Tanager
Tangara lavinia

4.5 in (12 cm). Distinguished from Bay-headed Tanager by mainly **rufous wings** and mostly **bright green underparts** (has variable amount of blue on throat and along center of underparts); on male, also note broad yellow patch on upper back (Bay-headed has thin yellow line across nape). Female and immature duller, often mostly green; they usually have some rufous in the wing by which they can be distinguished from immature Bay-headed. Rare in foothills; occurs on Caribbean slope eastward to western Kuna Yala, and on Pacific slope in eastern Panamá Province and Darién; 1,000 to 3,000 ft (900 to 3,000 m); one record from lowlands on Caribbean slope of Canal Area. Found in upper levels of forest. Often in mixed-species flocks, sometimes associating with Bay-headed. Call a thin *tsit*, sometimes accelerated into a rapid chittering.

Emerald Tanager

male

Silver-throated
Tanager

adult male

Speckled Tanager

adult

Bay-headed
Tanager

adult
male

adult
male

adult
female

Rufous-winged
Tanager

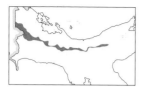

Spangle-cheeked Tanager
Tangara dowii

4.5 in (12 cm). Within its range, combination of **cinnamon lower underparts** and **pale green spangling on sides of head** is unique; compare Green-naped Tanager (no range overlap). Elegant Euphonia (p. 384) shares cinnamon underparts but has entirely pale blue crown and dark rump. Uncommon in western highlands eastward to Coclé; recorded 4,000 to 7,400 ft (1,200 to 2,250 m). Found in upper levels of forest. Often in small groups that associate with mixed-species flocks. Call a high-pitched metallic *tsit* (sometimes run into a twitter). **WH**

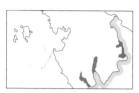

Green-naped Tanager
Tangara fucosa

4.5 in (12 cm). Distinguished from Spangle-cheeked Tanager (no range overlap) by **crown with pale green spots** (not reddish brown), **blue spangling on chest** (not bluish green and buff), and **buffier lower underparts**. Uncommon in highlands of eastern Darién; mainly above 4,500 ft (1,350 m), rarely down to 2,000 ft (600 m). Found in upper levels of forest. Often in small groups that associate with mixed-species flocks. Call a high-pitched *tsit* (sometimes strung together rapidly). **EH***

Golden-hooded Tanager
Tangara larvata

4.5 in (12 cm). Recognized by elaborate pattern: mostly **golden head, black back and chest**, and **blue on face, wings, and rump**. Immature similar but duller; green replaces gold on head. Common on both slopes; to 5,000 ft (1,500 m). Found in upper levels of forest edge, woodland, and clearings with trees. Usually in small groups, sometimes associating with mixed-species flocks. Call a thin metallic *chit* (sometimes accelerated into a rapid chatter).

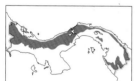

Scarlet-thighed Dacnis
Dacnis venusta

4.5 in (11 cm). On male, combination of **bright blue upperparts** and **black underparts** is distinctive. Scarlet thighs are usually inconspicuous. On female, combination of **bluish green upperparts** and **buffy underparts** is unique; female Blue Dacnis is mainly green below; female Viridian Dacnis is duller, with pale eye and two-tone wings; female White-eared Conebill (p. 332) has grayish upperparts, and buff underparts extend higher on face (up to eye); female Cerulean Warbler (p. 320) has wing-bars and prominent pale superciliary. Fairly common in foothills and highlands, mostly 1,000 to 6,300 ft (300 to 1,900 m); uncommon in lowlands on Caribbean slope and in Darién. Found in upper levels of forest. Usually in small groups of its own species. Calls include a thin buzzy *whik*, a metallic *zhrik*, and a rapid twittering.

Blue Dacnis
Dacnis cayana

4.5 in (11 cm). On male, combination of **mostly blue plumage, black throat**, and **black patch on back** is unique. On female, combination of **blue head** and **mostly green body** is distinctive; also note pinkish legs. In eastern Darién, compare Viridian Dacnis. Common on both slopes; to 3,000 ft (900 m). Found in upper levels of forest, woodland, and clearings with trees. Often in small groups that associate with mixed-species flocks. Calls include a very high-pitched sharp *tsit* and a harsher *chut*.

Viridian Dacnis
Dacnis viguieri

4 in (10 cm). Male similar in pattern to male Blue Dacnis, but is bluish green rather than blue; further distinguished by **bicolored wings, pale eye**, and lack of black throat patch. Female is distinguished from female Blue Dacnis by **bicolored wings** and **pale eye**; it is also much duller (paler green below and lacks blue on head). Rare in southeastern Darién; to 2,000 ft (600 m). Found in upper levels of forest, woodland, and clearings with trees. Call undescribed. **EL**

Spangle-cheeked
Tanager

Green-naped
Tanager

Golden-hooded
Tanager

adult

male

female

Scarlet-thighed
Dacnis

Blue Dacnis

male

female

Viridian
Dacnis

male

female

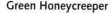

Green Honeycreeper
Chlorophanes spiza

4.5 in (12 cm). Male recognized by combination of mostly **emerald green plumage** and **partial black hood**. Female can be distinguished from other green birds by **long, slightly decurved, mostly yellow bill** (dark along culmen). Female Blue Dacnis (p. 346) has shorter, darker bill, bluish head, and pinkish legs. Fairly common on both slopes; to 4,100 ft (1,200 m). Found in upper levels of forest and woodland. Often with mixed-species flocks. Call a chirping *cheet!*

Shining Honeycreeper
Cyanerpes lucidus

4 in (10 cm). Male's **bright yellow legs** distinguish it from male Red-legged Honeycreeper; further distinguished by black throat patch, lack of pale blue crown, and lack of black back patch. Female differs from other female honeycreepers by **blue streaking on breast**. In eastern Darién, compare very similar Purple Honeycreeper. Fairly common in foothills and lower highlands on entire Caribbean slope, and on Pacific from eastern Panamá Province eastward (uncommon in lowlands); uncommon and local on western Pacific slope; recorded to 5,300 ft (1,600 m). Found in upper levels of forest and woodland. Often in small groups that associate with mixed-species flocks. Calls include high-pitched chittering notes.

Purple Honeycreeper
Cyanerpes caeruleus

4 in (10 cm). Male is nearly identical to male Shining Honeycreeper but has **paler blue forecrown**; on Purple, forecrown contrasts slightly with rest of crown; on Shining, crown is uniformly colored. (Contrary to many references, black throat patch of Shining is not more extensive than that of Purple; the species overlap in this character.) Female is more distinctive; distinguished from female Shining by **green** (not blue) **streaking on chest**, **buffy** (rather than dusky) **lores and sides of head**, and deeper buff on throat. Rare and apparently local in eastern Darién; to 2,600 ft (800 m). Found in upper levels of forest. Often in small groups that associate with mixed-species flocks. Call a sharp *chit!*

Red-legged Honeycreeper
Cyanerpes cyaneus

4.5 in (11 cm). Male differs from male Shining and Purple Honeycreepers in **bright red legs, sky blue crown**, black back patch, and lack of black on throat. Female differs from other female honeycreepers in **reddish legs** and **indistinct olive streaking on breast**; female Shining Honeycreeper has distinct blue streaking on breast; female Purple Honeycreeper has distinct green streaking on breast; female Green Honeycreeper lacks streaking on breast and has mostly yellow bill. Unusual for a breeding resident, male has a distinct nonbreeding plumage (July to Sept), similar to that of female except that male retains black wings and tail. In all plumages, bright yellow underwings are visible in flight. Common throughout most of the country; to 5,300 ft (1,600 m). Found in forest edge, woodland, shrubby areas, and gardens. Often in groups of a dozen or more, frequently with mixed-species flocks. Calls include a thin *dzt* and a piercing *chuweet!*

Swallow Tanager
Tersina viridis

5.5 in (14 cm). Both sexes can be distinguished from any similarly colored species by **distinct barring on flanks** (black in male, green in female). Also note **broad bill** and erect posture. Uncommon in eastern Darién, with a few records westward to the Canal Area. Found in upper levels of forest edge and woodland. Usually in small flocks of its own species. Often perches on exposed branches, sallying out to catch small insects; also eats fruit. Call a high-pitched *tsee*.

male

female

Green
Honeycreeper

Shining
Honeycreeper

male

female

Purple
Honeycreeper

male

female

nonbreeding
male

breeding
male

Swallow
Tanager

underwing

female

Red-legged
Honeycreeper

male

female

Incertae sedis. The dapper little Bananaquit occurs in much of the neotropics, including on Caribbean islands. It feeds on flower nectar, fruit, and small insects. This species was formerly either placed in its own family or linked with the wood-warblers, but at present its taxonomic position is uncertain.

Bananaquit
Coereba flaveola

3.5 in (9 cm). Recognized by combination of **thin, slightly decurved bill** and **long white superciliary**; also note **white spot on wing** and yellow rump. Immature similar in pattern but duller, with olive upperparts and more greenish yellow underparts. Common on both slopes (less common in dry areas), to 5,300 ft (1,600 m). Inhabits shrubby areas, gardens, forest canopy, and forest edge. Can be found almost anywhere there are flowers; it obtains nectar by either probing directly with its beak or making a hole in the base of longer flowers. Also eats berries and picks at larger fruits. Very tame, regularly visiting hummingbird feeders and fruit tables. Song, given throughout the year, consists of thin, sharp, high-pitched trills, whistles, and warbles.

Saltators

Incertae sedis. These heavy-billed, mostly dull-colored birds were formerly included with the grosbeaks and buntings (family Cardinalidae), but their taxonomic position is currently uncertain. They are probably closest to the tanagers. Several species have musical songs.

Streaked Saltator
Saltator striatipectus

7 in (18 cm). Only finchlike bird with combination of **plain olive upperparts** and **olive streaking on underparts**. Common on Pacific slope eastward to Darién, and on Caribbean slope from northern Coclé eastward to western Kuna Yala; to 5,700 ft (1,700 m). Found in shrubby areas, second growth, woodland, and gardens. Song consists of three to five sweet whistled notes, the last one (sometimes two) slurred and longer: *tew-tew-tew-teeeuuw*.

Black-headed Saltator
Saltator atriceps

9 in (23 cm). Distinguished from smaller Buff-throated Saltator by **black crown and nape** and **all-white throat** (no buff). Uncommon in lowlands on Caribbean slope eastward to western Kuna Yala; rare and local (mainly in foothills) on Pacific slope; to 4,000 ft (1,200 m). Often in small noisy flocks. Found in lower levels of forest edge, woodland edge, and adjacent shrubby areas. Call a loud explosive *chak*, sometimes run together into a chatter. Song consists of harsh scratchy notes.

Buff-throated Saltator
Saltator maximus

8 in (20 cm). Resembles larger Black-headed Saltator but **lacks black on crown** and has **buff on lower throat** (although this is sometimes faint). In race in eastern Panama, black around throat is restricted to submalar stripe and does not extend across chest. Common on both slopes throughout most of the country; to 5,900 ft (1,800 m). Found in lower and middle levels of forest edge, woodland, and adjacent shrubby areas. Song consists of variable warbled phrases of mellow whistles, such as *chuweet, cheet, choo-a-wheet*.

adult

Bananaquit

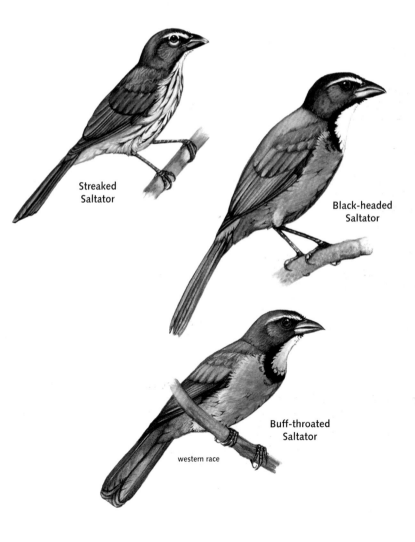

Streaked
Saltator

Black-headed
Saltator

Buff-throated
Saltator

western race

Grayish Saltator

Saltator coerulescens

8.5 in (22 cm). Combination of **mostly gray plumage** with **white superciliary and throat** is distinctive. A recent colonist from Costa Rica, first recorded in 2003. Fairly common in lowlands of western Bocas del Toro; a few records from Chiriquí highlands. Found in shrubby areas, second growth, and hedgerows. Song a variable series of sweet whistled or sputtering notes, ending on a whistle that slurs upward.

Slate-colored Grosbeak

Saltator grossus

7 in (18 cm). Easily recognized by combination of **heavy, bright red bill** (more orange in female) and **mostly slate-gray plumage**. Female is somewhat paler below and has less black on face and around throat. Fairly common on entire Caribbean slope; also fairly common on Pacific slope from Canal Area eastward; occurs on western Pacific slope in foothills; to 3,000 ft (900 m). Found in middle and upper levels of forest. Song consists of variable, deliberate phrases made up of loud rich whistles (rather wrenlike in quality). Calls include a sharp metallic *spiik!* and a whining, descending *caaaah*.

Seedeaters, Finches & Sparrows

EMBERIZIDAE. Most species in this cosmopolitan family have stout bills designed for cracking seeds; although seeds are a major part of their diet, they also feed on insects and, sometimes, on fruit. A few species have thinner bills; the Slaty Flowerpiercer's bill is oddly modified to procure nectar from flowers. Note that the names "finch" and "sparrow" are applied to members of several different families of seed-eating birds and have no taxonomic significance.

Blue-black Grassquit

Volatinia jacarina

4 in (10 cm). In both sexes, **bill is thinner and more pointed** than in any similar species. Male is glossier than male Thick-billed Seed-Finch (p. 356) and black forms of Variable Seedeater (p. 354), and **lacks the white wing spot** of those species. Much rarer male Blue Seedeater (p. 370) is larger with heavier bill, lacks gloss, and is found in different habitat. Female is distinguished from female seedeaters by **streaked breast**; female Indigo Bunting (p. 372) is less strongly streaked below, has more contrastingly whitish throat, and shows faint buffy wing-bars. Compare with rare Slaty Finch (no range overlap, p. 356). Very common on both slopes; to 5,300 ft (1,600 m). Often in small flocks that associate with other grassquits and seedeaters. Found near ground in grassy and shrubby areas. From an exposed perch, males give a buzzy *zzzhhhREEET*, often jumping up a few feet during the song before returning to the same perch or one nearby.

Slate-colored Seedeater

Sporophila schistacea

4.5 in (11 cm). Male's **yellow bill** distinguishes it from any similar species; also note **white wing spot**. Female has **whiter lower underparts** than other female seedeaters and female Thick-billed Seed-Finch (p. 356). Generally rare, but sometimes locally common in areas where bamboo is seeding. Occurs on entire Caribbean slope and on Pacific slope from western Panamá Province eastward (a few records from Chiriquí); to 3,000 ft (900 m). Found in lower and middle levels of forest and woodland. Song consists of fast, high-pitched, metallic notes, often beginning with a trill that is followed by a series of notes on the same pitch: *zhhhreeee zit zit zit zit zit zit zit*.

Grayish
Saltator

Slate-colored
Grosbeak

male

Blue-black
Grassquit

female

male

female

Slate-colored
Seedeater

Variable Seedeater
Sporophila americana

4 in (10 cm). Males vary regionally. All-black form (with white wing spot) occurs on Caribbean slope eastward to Canal Area; distinguished from male of larger Thick-billed Seed-Finch (p. 356) by **smaller bill with arched culmen**. Pied forms occur on entire Pacific slope and on Caribbean slope of Canal Area. These show varying amounts of white below and on rump; throat mostly black in Chiriquí and on Coiba Island; throat usually mostly white eastward; intermediates between black and pied forms occur on central Caribbean slope and on Pacific in and near Canal Area. Pied forms distinguished from male White-collared Seedeater by **lack of white wing-bars**; see also vagrant Lesson's Seedeater. Female distinguished from female Ruddy-breasted, Yellow-bellied, and Slate-colored (p. 352) Seedeaters by **blackish bill**; female Yellow-bellied Seedeater is also more yellowish below (some female Variable Seedeaters are yellowish buff on belly); female Thick-billed Seed-Finch is warmer brown and has larger bill. Very common on both slopes; to at least 4,600 ft (1,400 m). Found in grassy areas, clearings, and gardens. Usually in small groups that frequently associate with other seedeaters and grassquits. Sometimes feeds on flowers or buds in trees. Song consists of sweet twittering and warbling notes that rise and fall in no particular sequence.

White-collared Seedeater
Sporophila torqueola

4 in (10 cm). Only seedeater with **wing-bars**; in area of range overlap, pied form of male Variable Seedeater has black throat. Common in lowlands of Bocas del Toro and Chiriquí. Found in grassy fields and other open areas. Usually in small groups that often associate with other seedeaters and grassquits. Song, a series of musical whistled notes, is slower and more melodious than that of Variable.

Lesson's Seedeater
Sporophila bouvronides

4.5 in (11 cm). Male distinguished from male of pied forms of Variable Seedeater by **broad white malar stripe**, lack of wide black band across upper breast, and lack of partial white collar. Female distinguished from other female seedeaters by **pale yellow bill**. Vagrant in eastern Darién. Found in grassy areas. Song a short, rapid, musical twitter, accelerating near end. **Not illustrated**.

Yellow-bellied Seedeater
Sporophila nigricollis

4 in (10 cm). On male, combination of **black face and upper breast, olive back**, and **yellowish** (whitish in some individuals) **lower breast and belly** is distinctive. Female very similar to female Variable Seedeater, but is usually **more yellowish below** and usually has slaty gray rather than blackish bill. Common on entire Pacific slope and on Caribbean slope in western Colón Province and Canal Area; to 5,900 ft (1,800 m). Found in grassy fields and shrubby areas. During dry season, leaves drier areas to congregate in wetter regions; flocks associate with other seedeaters and grassquits. Song a rapid musical warbling, often ending with a buzzy note.

Ruddy-breasted Seedeater
Sporophila minuta

3.5 in (9 cm). Male easily recognized by **chestnut underparts**. Female distinguished from other female seedeaters by smaller size, **buffy underparts and rump**, and buffy edging on wing feathers. Common in lowlands on entire Pacific slope; rare in lowlands on Caribbean slope in Colón Province, Canal Area, and western Kuna Yala. Vacates drier areas during dry season. Found in open grassy areas. Often in small groups that associate with other seedeaters and grassquits. Song consists of deliberate series of sweet whistles, often with some notes doubled.

male
western Pacific
slope form

Variable
Seedeater

male
western Caribbean
slope form

female

male

female

Yellow-bellied
Seedeater

male

female

White-collared
Seedeater

female

male

Ruddy-breasted
Seedeater

Nicaraguan Seed-Finch
Oryzoborus nuttingi

5.5 in (14 cm). On male, **enormous pinkish bill** makes it unmistakable in range. Female is larger and has **heavier bill** than female Thick-billed Seed-Finch; female Blue-black Grosbeak (p. 370) is larger, darker, and lives in different habitat. No range overlap with Large-billed Seed-Finch. Rare and apparently irregular in lowlands of western Bocas del Toro. Found in open grassy fields and shrubby areas, often near water. Song a series of slurred whistled notes, often doubled or tripled. **CL**

Large-billed Seed-Finch
Oryzoborus crassirostris

5.5 in (14 cm). Male has **enormous whitish bill**; distinguished from male Nicaraguan Seed-Finch (no range overlap) by conspicuous **white wing spot** and white wing-linings (usually concealed), and whitish rather than pinkish bill; female is less rufous brown than female Nicaraguan. A recent colonist from Colombia, first recorded in 2007. Now occurs in lowlands of Darién and easternmost Panamá Province; may be spreading westward. Found in wet grassy areas. Song consists of mellow whistles, including some doubled notes, such as *tu-deer*.

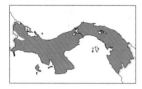

Thick-billed Seed-Finch
Oryzoborus funereus

4.5 in (11 cm). Male similar to black form of Variable Seedeater (p. 354), but has **larger, heavier bill with nearly straight culmen**. Female likewise differs from female seedeaters in size and shape of bill and also is **richer brown** in color. Nicaraguan and Large-billed Seed-Finches are larger and have even heavier bills (pinkish or whitish in male). Fairly common on both slopes; to 3,300 ft (1,100 m). Found in lower levels of forest edge, and in shrubby areas and clearings. Song a prolonged, jumbled series of sweet chirps, whistles, and twitters.

Yellow-faced Grassquit
Tiaris olivaceus

3.5 in (9 cm). Male easily recognized by **bright yellow superciliary and throat**. Female distinguished from all female seedeaters (pp. 352-355) by fainter version of male's facial pattern (including yellow superciliary and throat); also has more **olive coloration** overall. Found on both slopes; common in foothills and highlands, uncommon in lowlands; to over 5,600 ft (1,700 m). Found in grassy areas. Often in small flocks that associate with other grassquits and seedeaters. Song a thin, high, rapid trill.

Slaty Finch
Haplospiza rustica

4.5 in (12 cm). On male, combination of uniform gray coloration and **slender conical bill** distinguishes it from other finches. Male Peg-billed Finch and Slaty Flowerpiercer (p. 358) have distinctly different bill shapes. Female resembles female Blue-black Grassquit (p. 352), but **streaking on underparts extends onto throat** (unstreaked in grassquit). Female Peg-billed Finch has wing-bars. Rare in Chiriquí; one record from western Panamá Province; mostly 5,000 to 5,900 ft (1,500 to 1,800 ft), rarely down to 3,000 ft (900 m). Found on and near ground in forest and adjacent clearings. Usually in pairs, sometimes in small groups. Song a jumbled series of very high thin buzzy and squeaky notes.

Peg-billed Finch
Acanthidops bairdii

5.5 in (14 cm). Both sexes can be recognized by **long, pointed, bicolored bill** (lower mandible yellow); also note female's **cinnamon wing-bars**. Evidently an occasional invader from Costa Rica; usually very rare, but sometimes temporarily common when bamboo is seeding. Occurs in highlands of western Chiriquí; from 6,900 to 7,900 ft (2,100 to 2,400 m). Found in middle levels of forest. Song consists of several harsh notes followed by a descending buzz. **WH**

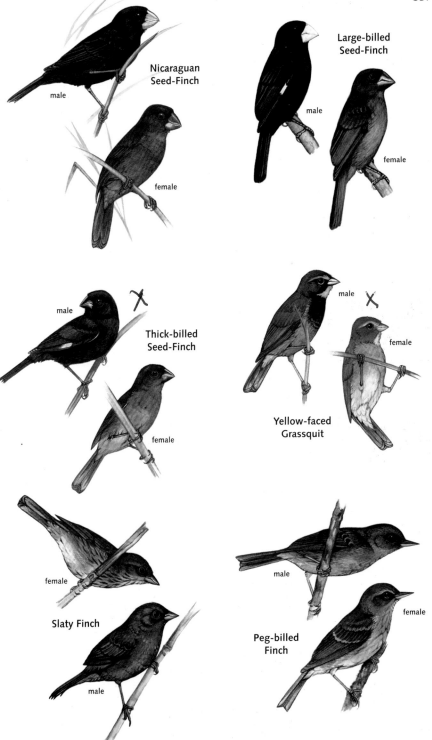

Nicaraguan
Seed-Finch

male

female

Large-billed
Seed-Finch

male

female

Thick-billed
Seed-Finch

male

female

male

female

Yellow-faced
Grassquit

Slaty Finch

female

male

Peg-billed
Finch

male

female

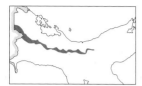

Slaty Flowerpiercer
Diglossa plumbea

4.5 in (11 cm). Odd bill, with **hooked upper mandible and paler, slightly upturned lower mandible**, is unique. Uses bill to pierce the base of flowers and steal nectar while not pollinating the plant. Common in western highlands eastward to Veraguas; above 4,300 ft (1,300 m). Found in lower levels of forest edge, shrubby clearings, and gardens. Song a weak, rapid, high-pitched twittering. **WH**

Saffron Finch
Sicalis flaveola

5 in (13 cm). Adult is **yellower overall** than any other finch. On female orange on head is reduced or lacking. Immature is streaked above and has mostly whitish underparts, with yellow collar across breast and hindneck and yellow vent. Grassland Yellow-Finch (not recorded in range) distinguished from adult by streaked crown and back, and from immature by yellow throat and belly. Probably introduced from South America; first recorded in 1951. Now locally common near both coasts of Canal Area; rare in central Canal Area. Found on lawns and other areas with short grass. Often feeds in small groups. Song a long-repeated series of sharp chipping notes.

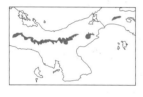

Wedge-tailed Grass-Finch
Emberizoides herbicola

6.5 in (17 cm). **Long pointed tail** is distinctive. Nonbreeding Bobolink (p. 374) has shorter tail and striped crown. Uncommon and local in foothills on Pacific slope eastward to western Panamá Province; 2,000 to 3,300 ft (600 to 1,100 m); also recorded in lowlands in eastern Panamá Province. Found in grassy areas. Males sing from a rock, shrub, or grass clump; song is a short series of musical chirps: *dee-dee-dee.*

Grassland Yellow-Finch
Sicalis luteola

4 in (10 cm). No other small finchlike bird combines **streaked back** and **mostly yellow underparts** (female is buffy on breast). On immature Saffron Finch (not known to occur together), yellow on underparts is restricted to band across breast and to vent; female Lesser Goldfinch (p. 388) lacks streaking on back and has white markings in wing and tail. Rare and local in lowlands of southern Coclé, with isolated records from Chiriquí and eastern Panamá Province. Found in pastures and other areas with short grass. Breeds in loose colonies. Song a thin, buzzy trill.

Yellow-thighed Finch
Pselliophorus tibialis

6.5 in (17 cm). Within its range, adult distinguished by **conspicuous yellow thighs**. Immature lacks yellow thighs; it is more uniformly dark slaty than any other finch. Compare Yellow-green Finch (no range overlap). Very common in western Chiriquí; mostly above 5,000 ft (1,500 m). Found in lower and middle levels of forest. Forages in active noisy groups. Flocks give metallic *tink* notes; song a jumbled series of squeaky notes. **WH**

Yellow-green Finch
Pselliophorus luteoviridis

7 in (18 cm). Very similar to Yellow-thighed Finch (no range overlap), but has **olive green** (not slaty) **back and underparts**. Fairly common in highlands of eastern Chiriquí, Ngöbe-Buglé, and Veraguas; above 4,000 ft (1,200 m). Found in lower and middle levels of forest. Habits similar to those of Yellow-thighed Finch. **WH***

Slaty
Flowerpiercer

male

female

Saffron Finch

adult
male

immature

Wedge-tailed
Grass-Finch

Grassland
Yellow-Finch

male

Yellow-thighed
Finch

adult

Yellow-green
Finch

Large-footed Finch
Pezopetes capitalis

7.5 in (19 cm). This large species is best recognized by combination of **dark head** (slaty gray with black face and crown stripes) and dull **olive body**. Yellow-green Finch (no range overlap, p. 358) is smaller and lacks striping on head. Fairly common in highlands of western Chiriquí and Bocas del Toro; mostly above 6,900 ft (2,100 m), sometimes down to 5,000 ft (1,500 m). Found on and near ground in forest and shrubby clearings. Scratches in leaf litter using both feet simultaneously. Song consists of phrases of musical but rather metallic notes; reminiscent of song of Orange-billed Nightingale-Thrush (p. 300).

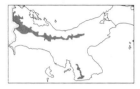

White-naped Brush-Finch
Atlapetes albinucha

6.5 in (17 cm). Combination of **yellow throat** and **white crown stripe** on black head is distinctive. Common in foothills and highlands of western Panama; mostly above 3,000 ft (900 m). Found in forest edge and shrubby clearings. Song a leisurely series of variable phrases of high, thin, sibilant notes.

Orange-billed Sparrow
Arremon aurantiirostris

5.5 in (14 cm). On adult, **bright orange bill** is diagnostic; also note **striking head pattern** and **black band on white breast**. Immature has black bill but shares the distinctive head and breast markings. Stripe-headed Brush-Finch and Black-striped Sparrow (p. 362) lack black breast band. Fairly common on both slopes; to at least 4,600 ft (1,400 m). Found on and near ground in forest and woodland. Song a fast series of very high thin notes.

Sooty-faced Finch
Arremon crassirostris

6.5 in (16 cm). Combination of **chestnut cap, mostly black face and throat** (except for whitish malar stripe), and **yellow center of breast and belly** is distinctive. Chestnut-capped Brush-Finch has white throat and belly. Uncommon in foothills and highlands in western Panama; mainly on Caribbean slope, eastward to Coclé; recorded 2,000 to 7,900 ft (600 to 2,400 m); also occurs on Cerro Tacarcuna in Darién. Found on and near ground in forest undergrowth. Call a high, thin *psee-PSEET*.

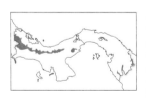

Chestnut-capped Brush-Finch
Arremon brunneinucha

7 in (18 cm). Recognized by combination of **chestnut crown, white throat**, and **black chest band**. Sooty-faced Finch has black throat and yellow belly. Common in foothills and highlands; mostly above 3,000 ft (900 m). Found on and near ground in forest undergrowth. Flicks leaves aside with bill rather than scratching with feet. Song consists of short rhythmic phrases of very high, thin, sibilant notes.

Stripe-headed Brush-Finch
Arremon torquatus

7 in (18 cm). Distinguished from smaller Black-striped Sparrow (p. 362) by **broad black mask** (not thin black eye-stripe) and **whiter underparts**. On race found in most of eastern Panama, gray crown stripes are narrower and sometimes obscure; on race that occurs on Cerro Pirre, crown is almost entirely black, without gray striping. Rare in foothills and highlands; mostly 2,000 to 5,000 ft (600 to 1,500 m); formerly occurred in lowlands of Chiriquí but no recent records. Found on and near ground in forest undergrowth and in thickets in adjacent clearings. Song composed of repeated phrases of very high thin notes.

Large-footed
Finch

White-naped
Brush-Finch

Orange-billed
Sparrow

adult

Sooty-faced
Finch

Chestnut-capped
Brush-Finch

western
race

Stripe-headed
Brush-Finch

Black-striped Sparrow
Arremonops conirostris

6.5 in (16 cm). Combination of **gray head with black striping** and contrasting **green back** is distinctive. Stripe-headed Brush-Finch (p. 360) is larger, has more black on head (including a broad black mask), and is whiter below. Common on both slopes; to 5,500 ft (1,650 m). Found on and near ground in shrubby areas, young second growth, undergrowth in woodland edge, and thickets in open areas. Distinctive song is a series of mellow *cho* notes that last 15 to 20 seconds; initially slow and then gradually accelerating (like sound of a ball bouncing to a halt). Also gives various *cho!* and *wheet!* calls, singly or in short series.

Lark Sparrow
Chondestes grammacus

6.5 in (17 cm). **Complex chestnut and black head pattern, black spot on breast**, and **extensive white in tail** make this species unmistakable. On immature, chestnut on head is replaced by brown. Vagrant, with two records from Tocumen Marsh in eastern Panamá Province (1985, 2008). Inhabits grassland.

Grasshopper Sparrow
Ammodramus savannarum

4.5 in (11 cm). Combination of **unstreaked buffy breast, pale median crown stripe**, and **short tail** is distinctive. Wedge-tailed Grass-Finch (p. 358) is larger with much longer tail and lacks crown stripe; nonbreeding Bobolink (p. 374) is larger and has pale nape; Lincoln's Sparrow is streaked below. Possibly extirpated. Formerly bred in scattered localities in grasslands on the Pacific slope, from Chiriquí to eastern Panamá Province, but no records since the late 1960s. Migrants from the north have been recorded twice as vagrants in Bocas del Toro (1963, 1967). Usually difficult to see, hiding in tall grass and flying only a short distance when flushed. Males sing from exposed perches; song consists of two or three short chips followed by an insect-like trill.

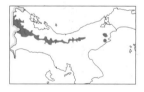

Rufous-collared Sparrow
Zonotrichia capensis

5 in (13 cm). Adult recognized by **gray and black striped head, slight crest**, and **rufous collar** across hindneck. Duller immature, which also appears to have crest, can be distinguished from other sparrow-like birds by combination of buffy superciliary and streaking below. See vagrant Lincoln's Sparrow. Very common in highlands of western Chiriquí; mostly above 4,000 ft (1,200 m); becomes less common moving eastward to western Panamá Province, where recorded down to about 1,650 ft (500 m). Found in fields, gardens, towns, and other open areas. Song a sweet, whistled *cheeeow, cheeeuuww.*

Lincoln's Sparrow
Melospiza lincolnii

5 in (13 cm). Combination of **broad gray superciliary** and **fine crisp black streaking below** is distinctive; also note **buffy malar stripe** and narrow whitish eye-ring. Immature Rufous-collared Sparrow is most similar but has buffy rather than gray superciliary and lacks buffy malar stripe and eye-ring. Vagrant, with three records, from Bocas del Toro (1967), Chiriquí (1988), and Canal Area (before 1866). Favors grassy and brushy areas.

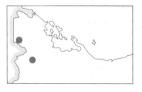

Volcano Junco
Junco vulcani

6.5 in (16 cm). **Yellow eye** and **pink bill** make recognition easy in its very restricted Panama range. Fairly common above timberline on Volcán Barú in Chiriquí; mostly above 10,000 ft (3,000 m), rarely down to 9,000 ft (2,700 m); recently found on Cerro Fábrega in Bocas del Toro. Occurs in open and shrubby areas. Often in small flocks. Song consists of phrases of squeaky or buzzy notes.

Black-striped
Sparrow

Lark Sparrow

adult

Grasshopper
Sparrow

Rufous-collared
Sparrow

immature

adult

Lincoln's
Sparrow

Volcano Junco

CARDINALIDAE. This family, found only in the Americas, is closely related to the Emberizidae. The Blue Seedeater has recently been moved here from that family, as have tanagers of the genera *Piranga*, *Habia*, and *Chlorothraupis* from the Thraupidae. Most Panama species have rather stout bills (especially heavy in the grosbeaks); they feed mainly on seeds and fruits. Several of the resident species have melodious songs.

Hepatic Tanager
Piranga flava

6.5 in (16 cm). Male similar to male Summer Tanager, but has more distinctly **dark lores, darker bill**, and is a duller **brick red** (tinged red-orange on underparts) rather than the rosy red of Summer. Female and similar immature male distinguished from female Summer Tanager and from nonbreeding Scarlet Tanager by **dark lores** and **darker bill**; bill is heavier than that of Scarlet. Female also resembles Carmiol's Tanager (p. 368) but is brighter yellow below and more arboreal. Fairly common in foothills on both slopes; mainly 2,000 to 4,500 ft (600 to 1,350 m), a few records from near sea level. Found in upper levels of forest and adjacent clearings with trees. Usually alone or in pairs. Call a rapid *chit-chi-dit* or *chu-chit*. Song is a series of phrases composed of burry notes that go up and down in pitch.

Summer Tanager
Piranga rubra

6.5 in (16 cm). Both sexes resemble corresponding sexes of Hepatic Tanager but have **paler bill** and lores that are not as dark; male is a brighter **rosy red** than male Hepatic. Immature male resembles female but is tinged with red, as are some adult females. Female and nonbreeding male Scarlet Tanager differ from female Summer by having smaller, darker bill and darker wings and tail. Common transient and winter resident, early Sept to late April. Occurs mostly below 5,900 ft (1,800 m), but recorded to 7,400 ft (2,250 m). Found in forest edge, second growth, shrubby areas, clearings with trees, and gardens. Call a staccato *chiddidup*.

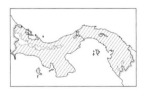

Scarlet Tanager
Piranga olivacea

6.5 in (16 cm). On breeding male (seen only during spring migration), combination of **black wings and tail** and **scarlet body** is distinctive. (First-year breeding males are somewhat duller than older ones; molting male may show splotches of red on green body.) Nonbreeding male is mostly olive and has **black wings**; female similar but wings are dusky rather than black. Female Summer Tanager has larger, paler bill and wings that are not as dark; also compare female Hepatic Tanager. Some females and immatures show faint wing-bars. Uncommon transient, mostly from Oct to Nov and in April; rare winter resident. Occurs in lowlands throughout the country. Found in upper levels of forest and woodland. Call consists of a short *chip* followed by a hoarse *whirr*.

Western Tanager
Piranga ludoviciana

6.5 in (17 cm). In all plumages, note **pale bill** and **two wing-bars**. On breeding male, combination of **bright red head** and **yellow body** is distinctive. Nonbreeding male has little or no red on head and has olive mottling on black back; immature male Flame-colored Tanager (p. 366) is similar but is larger and has distinct dark streaking on back and white tail tipping. On female, combination of pale bill and **dusky or gray unstreaked back that contrasts with yellower nape and rump** distinguishes it from other female tanagers with wing-bars. Female Flame-colored has streaked back and white tail tipping; female White-winged (p. 366) is smaller, brighter yellow below, and has bicolored bill; female Scarlet is uniformly olive green on upperparts. Some female Westerns are whitish below. Rare winter resident; recorded late Nov to late March. Occurs in western Chiriquí, to at least 5,000 ft (1,500 m). Found in upper levels of forest and woodland. Call a rapid *whiddidick*.

Hepatic Tanager — male, female

Summer Tanager — male, female

Scarlet Tanager — breeding male, nonbreeding male

Western Tanager — breeding male, female

Flame-colored Tanager
Piranga bidentata

6.5 in (17 cm). **Distinct dark streaking on back** and **white tipping on tail** distinguish both sexes from all similar tanagers. On White-winged Tanager, also note smaller size and bicolored bill; male is deep red (not orangish) and has black mask. Immature male resembles female but is brighter; some immature males show orange on head and resemble nonbreeding male Western Tanager (p. 364), but can be set apart by streaking on back and white tail tipping. Common in western highlands; mostly 4,000 to 7,600 ft (1,200 to 2,300 m). Found in forest canopy, forest edge, and clearings with trees. Occasionally with mixed-species flocks. Call a loud, hoarse *fiDEEK*. Song consists of phrases of three to six burry notes.

White-winged Tanager
Piranga leucoptera

5 in (13 cm). Male is only mainly **red** tanager with **black mask**. Both sexes differ from corresponding sexes of larger Flame-colored Tanager in **bicolored bill, unstreaked back**, and lack of white tail tipping; male is brighter red than male of that species. Female differs from rare female Western Tanager (p. 364) in bicolored bill and brighter yellow underparts. Fairly common in foothills and highlands of Chiriquí, Ngöbe-Buglé, and Veraguas; recorded 3,000 to 7,400 ft (900 to 2,250 m); also found locally in foothills on Azuero Peninsula. Occurs in upper levels of forest. Often with mixed-species flocks. Calls include a sharp *pit!* and a sweet whistled *wheet*, each given singly or combined as a *pit-whee-wheet*.

Red-crowned Ant-Tanager
Habia rubica

6.5 in (17 cm). Male distinguished from male Red-throated Ant-Tanager by **bright red crown patch with narrow dark border** (on male Red-throated, crown patch lacks border) and by lack of bright red throat. Female similar to female Red-throated but is more olive above, usually has **large yellow crown patch** (Red-throated rarely shows yellow in crown), and lacks female Red-throated's distinctly yellow throat. Uncommon on entire Pacific slope; rare on Caribbean slope in central Canal Area; to 7,400 ft (2,250 m). Found in lower and middle levels of forest. Usually in small groups. Groups frequently give rapid chittering calls, much less harsh and grating than those of Red-throated. Song a series of loud musical notes; examples include *chee-dup, chee-dup, chee-dup* and *he-dup, he*.

Red-throated Ant-Tanager
Habia fuscicauda

7.5 in (19 cm). Male distinguished from male Red-crowned Ant-Tanager by **bright red throat** and by lack of dark border on red crown patch. Female's best field mark is **yellow throat**; overall, female is browner (less olive) than female Red-crowned Ant-tanager and Carmiol's Tanager (p. 368). Common in lowlands and lower foothills on entire Caribbean slope; uncommon and local on Pacific slope from Veraguas eastward. Found in lower levels of forest edge and woodland. Usually in small groups of up to about eight individuals; furtive, often remaining in cover. Scolds with rasping notes that sound like tearing paper. Song consists of musical but somewhat squeaky notes that rise and fall in pitch.

White-winged
Tanager

male

female

Flame-colored
Tanager

male

female

Red-crowned
Ant-Tanager

male

female

Red-throated
Ant-Tanager

male

female

Carmiol's Tanager
Chlorothraupis carmioli

6.5 in (16 cm). This mostly olive green species (yellower below, especially on throat) resembles females of several other tanagers. Female Hepatic Tanager (p. 364) is brighter yellow below; female Red-throated Ant-Tanager (p. 366) is browner overall, with more clearly defined yellow throat patch; female Red-crowned Ant-Tanager (p. 366) has yellow crown bordered with black. Sapayoa (p. 220) has broader bill, is less yellow on throat, and is different in behavior. In eastern Darién, see Lemon-spectacled Tanager (no range overlap). Fairly common in foothills and lower highlands; found on entire Caribbean slope and locally on Pacific slope; mostly 1,000 to 4,800 ft (300 to 1,450 m); on Caribbean slope occurs locally to near sea level. Found in lower levels of forest. Travels in active, noisy flocks of twenty or more. Flocks give a nearly continuous chatter of squeaky *wheek* notes, interspersed with a rasping *khrrrrhhh* and other snarling calls.

Lemon-spectacled Tanager
Chlorothraupis olivacea

6.5 in (16 cm). **Bright yellow spectacles** contrasting with mainly olive green plumage (yellower on throat) are diagnostic. Carmiol's Tanager (no range overlap) lacks spectacles. Fairly common in southeastern Darién; to 4,000 ft (1,200 m). Found in lower levels of forest. Forages in small flocks (typically smaller than those of Carmiol's). Calls similar to Carmiol's, but the harsher notes are higher pitched and thinner, not as rasping.

Black-faced Grosbeak
Caryothraustes poliogaster

6.5 in (16 cm). Within its range, combination of heavy bill, **black mask**, and **yellow head and breast** is distinctive. Compare with Yellow-green Grosbeak (no range overlap). Prong-billed Barbet (p. 174) has differently shaped bill and is more ochraceous on head and breast. Fairly common on Caribbean slope eastward to northern Coclé; to 3,500 ft (1,050 m). Found in middle and upper levels of forest and in adjacent clearings with trees. Usually in groups, sometimes of 20 or more individuals; regularly with mixed-species flocks. Song a series of short phrases of sharp squeaky whistles. Call consists of a buzzy note followed by three or four sharp whistles: *brrrt, chew-chew-chew.*

Yellow-green Grosbeak
Caryothraustes canadensis

6 in (15 cm). Very similar to Black-faced Grosbeak (no range overlap); shares **black mask** and **yellow head and breast** but distinguished by **yellow lower underparts** (not gray) and **lack of gray on rump**. Fairly common in foothills of southeastern Darién; mostly between 2,500 and 4,000 ft (750 and 1,200 m). Found in middle and upper levels of forest. Usually in groups that often associate with mixed-species flocks. Call a sharp, metallic, descending *chrrrrt!*

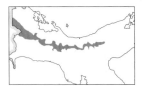

Black-thighed Grosbeak
Pheucticus tibialis

7.5 in (19 cm). Combination of **heavy bill** and **black and yellow pattern** is diagnostic; also note white wing spot. Uncommon in western highlands and upper foothills, eastward to Coclé; mostly above 2,500 ft (750 m). Found in upper levels of forest and in adjacent clearings with trees. Song consists of variable phrases of high sweet notes that rise and fall; phrases sometimes end in rapid trill. Call a sharp *pik.*

Carmiol's Tanager

Lemon-spectacled
Tanager

Black-faced
Grosbeak

Yellow-green
Grosbeak

Black-thighed
Grosbeak

Rose-breasted Grosbeak *Pheucticus ludovicianus*

7 in (18 cm). On breeding male, combination of **rosy breast patch** and mainly black-and-white plumage make it unmistakable. Nonbreeding male has brownish mottling on head and back but retains at least some rose on breast. Female and immature male are distinguished from other streaked finchlike birds by heavy, pale bill and **two conspicuous whitish wing-bars**; also note prominent striping on head. Fairly common transient and uncommon winter resident; mostly from Oct to early April, sometimes arriving in late Sept and leaving in late April. Occurs throughout the country; to 5,900 ft (1,800 m). Found in upper levels of forest, woodland, and clearings with trees. Often in small groups. Call a sharp metallic *chink!*

Blue-black Grosbeak *Cyanocompsa cyanoides*

6.5 in (16 cm). On male, combination of large size, **heavy dark bill, unmarked wings**, and **bluish gloss** distinguishes it from any other dark finchlike bird. Male Blue Seedeater, Blue-black Grassquit (p. 352), and Indigo Bunting (p. 372) are smaller and have smaller bills; male Blue Grosbeak has chestnut wing-bars; male Nicaraguan Seed-Finch and male Large-billed Seed-Finch (p. 356) have pale bills. Female is larger and has **stouter bill** than most other brown finchlike birds; female Nicaraguan Seed-Finch and female Large-billed Seed-Finch have even heavier bills and are found in more open habitat. Common on both slopes; to 4,000 ft (1,200 m). Found in lower levels of forest and woodland. Tends to remain in cover; often difficult to see. Song a leisurely series of sweet notes, hesitant and jerky at the beginning, speeding up and more jumbled toward the end. Call a sharp metallic *chirrt!*

Blue Grosbeak *Passerina caerulea*

6 in (15 cm). Both sexes distinguished from similar species by **chestnut or cinnamon wing-bars**. In immature male, body plumage may be partially brown. Female Indigo Bunting (p. 372) is smaller, with smaller bill, and has less conspicuous buffy wing-bars. Rare winter resident; early Oct to late March. Occurs in lowlands on both slopes, eastward to Canal Area. Found in shrubby areas and second growth. Sometimes in groups. Call a sharp metallic *tchink*.

Blue Seedeater *Amaurospiza concolor*

4.5 in (12 cm). Male's **dull blue coloration** is apparent only in good light, otherwise appearing blackish. Male Blue-black Grassquit (p. 352) is smaller and has smaller bill; appears glossy in good light. Male Thick-billed Seed-Finch (p. 356) and male of black forms of Variable Seedeater (p. 354) have white wing patches. Female is **richer, more uniform brown** than other female seedeaters; female Thick-billed Seed-Finch has heavier bill. Both sexes of Blue-black Grosbeak are much larger, with heavier bill. Rare and local in foothills and highlands, eastward to western Panamá Province; mostly 2,000 to 8,900 ft (600 to 2,700 m), with a few records from lowlands in Canal Area. Found in lower levels of forest and woodland. Song a short series of sweet notes, *su-su-suwheet*.

breeding
male

female

Rose-breasted
Grosbeak

immature
male

Blue-black
Grosbeak

Blue
Grosbeak

adult male

male

female

female

Blue
Seedeater

male

female

Indigo Bunting
Passerina cyanea

4.5 in (12 cm). Male is **brighter blue** overall than other similar finchlike birds; male Blue Grosbeak (p. 370) has chestnut wing-bars and is larger. Female resembles female Blue-black Grassquit (p. 352) but has paler throat, **only indistinct streaking below**, and often shows **indistinct buffy wing-bars**. Nonbreeding male is brown like female but with a variable amount of blue splotching. Winter resident; mostly Oct to April, sometimes to late May. Fairly common in western Panama, becoming less common eastward to Canal Area and eastern Panamá Province; to 5,900 ft (1,800 m). Found in shrubby and overgrown areas. Often in small flocks. Call a dry *tsik*.

Painted Bunting
Passerina ciris

5 in (13 cm). **Multicolored** adult male is unmistakable. Female and similar (but drabber) immature can be distinguished from other small finchlike birds by **greener upperparts** and **lack of markings on head or wings**. Female Yellow-faced Grassquit (p. 356) has yellowish superciliary and throat; female Lesser Goldfinch (p. 388) has small white patch on blackish wings. Uncommon winter resident; recorded late Oct to late April. Uncommon in western Bocas del Toro; rare on Pacific slope, eastward to western Panamá Province. Found in shrubby and overgrown areas. Call a sharp *chip*.

Dickcissel
Spiza americana

5.5 in (14 cm). On breeding male, combination of **yellow markings on face and chest, black bib**, and **chestnut shoulders** is distinctive. Nonbreeding male has less distinct black bib; duller female and immature lack black bib entirely. In all plumages, usually shows some **yellow on superciliary, a yellow wash on chest**, and some **chestnut on shoulders**. Female House Sparrow resembles immature but lacks yellow on superciliary and chest and lacks streaking below. Common transient and rare winter resident (late Aug to May) on entire Pacific slope; rare transient on Caribbean slope; to 4,000 ft (1,200 m). Found in grassy and open areas. Often occurs in large flocks, sometimes numbering in the thousands. Flocks constantly give twittering and sharp buzzy calls.

Old World Sparrows

PASSERIDAE. This Old World family of seed-eating birds is represented in Panama by a single species. A native of Eurasia, the House Sparrow was introduced to North America in the mid-nineteenth century, and has since spread through much of the hemisphere. In 1976 it was first recorded in Panama, where it is mainly confined to cities and towns; unlike in the United States and elsewhere, it does not occur in agricultural areas to any great extent.

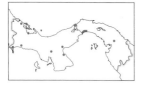

House Sparrow
Passer domesticus

6 in (15 cm). **Head pattern of chestnut, gray, and black** makes male easily recognizable. Female and similar immature differ from other streaked finchlike birds by combination of **single white wing-bar** and **unmarked underparts**. Immature Rufous-collared Sparrow (p. 362) is streaked below; female and immature Dickcissels lack wing-bar and usually show rufous on shoulder and yellow wash on breast. Uncommon and local in lowlands on the Pacific slope eastward to Panama City area, and in lowlands on Caribbean slope in Bocas del Toro and the Colón area. Found in urban areas; often in small flocks. Call a chirping *chirrup* or *cheep*.

breeding
male

nonbreeding
male

Indigo Bunting

female

male

Painted Bunting

female

breeding
male

Dickcissel

immature
female

male

**House
Sparrow**

female

ICTERIDAE. This family occurs only in the Americas. Species characteristically have long, conical, pointed bills but are otherwise quite diverse in appearance, ecology, and nesting habits. Most eat a combination of fruits and insects, but the diet may also include seeds and, sometimes, small vertebrates. Males of some species are distinctly larger than females. Orioles, oropendolas, and most caciques make elaborate woven pouchlike nests that they hang from branches; the oropendolas and Yellow-rumped Cacique nest in large noisy colonies. The cowbirds, by contrast, are brood parasites that deposit their eggs in the nests of other birds to be raised by unwitting foster parents; cowbirds themselves construct no nests.

Bobolink
Dolichonyx oryzivorus

6 in (15 cm). In nonbreeding plumage, combination of conical pointed bill, **buffy and blackish crown striping**, and **pointed tail feathers** is distinctive; also note **pale unstreaked nape** and distinct streaking below. Breeding male is unique: **mostly black**, with a **large pale yellow patch on nape** and **white patches on scapulars and rump**. Immature has obscure streaking below. Female and immature Red-breasted Blackbirds have streaked napes and unpointed tail feathers; female has rosy wash on breast (absent in female Bobolink); immature is more distinctly streaked below than immature Bobolink. Uncommon fall transient and rare spring transient; mid-Sept to late Oct and mid-April to early May. Occurs mainly on Caribbean slope, near coast; occasionally found on Pacific slope in central and eastern Panama. Found in grassy areas. Often in small groups. In flight, gives a sharp *chit*.

Red-breasted Blackbird
Sturnella militaris

6.5 in (16 cm). Breeding male, with **bright red throat and breast,** is unmistakable. On nonbreeding male, feathers are tipped brown, partially obscuring the red on underparts; upperparts appear streaked. Adult female usually shows a **rosy wash on underparts** (brighter in breeding plumage). Young immature is similar to female but more heavily streaked below and lacks rosy wash. Nonbreeding Bobolink lacks rosy tones, is less streaked below, and has pale unstreaked nape and pointed tail feathers. Common on entire Pacific slope; local on Caribbean slope in Canal Area and in adjacent Colón Province; to 4,000 ft (1,200 m). Found in pastures and other grassy areas. Gathers in flocks in nonbreeding season. Males sing from elevated perches, giving a few sharp dry *chip* notes followed by a harsh buzzy trill.

Yellow-hooded Blackbird
Chrysomus icterocephalus

M 7 in (18 cm); F 6.5 in (16 cm). Both sexes resemble very rare Yellow-headed Blackbird (unlikely to occur within range; see for distinctions, p. 380). Male distinguished from other species by **bright yellow head and chest**. Female can be recognized by **yellowish superciliary and throat** and **indistinct dark streaking on back and underparts**. A recent colonist from Colombia, first recorded in 2007. So far reported only from freshwater marshes near El Real in Darién (evidently breeding, though possibly present only seasonally), but likely to spread. Song consists of an introductory *chip* followed by a nasal whining trill that becomes louder and then falls off, sometimes followed by a rapid twitter.

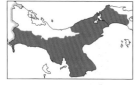

Eastern Meadowlark
Sturnella magna

8 in (20 cm). **Bold black V on yellow breast** makes recognition easy. In flight, shows **white outer tail feathers**. Common on Pacific slope eastward to eastern Panamá Province; local on Caribbean slope from northern Coclé to eastern Colón Province; to 5,900 ft (1,800 m). Found in pastures and other grassy areas. Walks on ground when feeding; when alarmed, flies up (showing white outer tail feathers), then drops down into grass again. Males sing from fence posts or other exposed perches, the song consisting of two or more liquid whistled phrases, with the last note descending: *cheedlyee, cheedlyoo*. Call a buzzy *dzerp*.

Bobolink

breeding
male

nonbreeding
adult

**Red-breasted
Blackbird**

breeding
male

female

**Yellow-hooded
Blackbird**

male

female

**Eastern
Meadowlark**

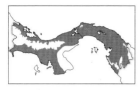

Giant Cowbird
Molothrus oryzivorus

M 13 in (33 cm); F 11.5 in (29 cm). Much larger than Shiny and Bronzed Cowbirds and has longer, heavier bill. Distinguished from Great-tailed Grackle by **tail that is shorter** and **appears flat in flight** (not folded in a V). Male has **large ruff on nape** (expanded in courtship display) that gives it an odd, small-headed look. On adult, also note **reddish or orangish eyes** (eyes dark in immature); Shiny Cowbird and Great-tailed Grackle lack red eyes. Fairly common in lowlands on both slopes; to 2,000 ft (600 m). Found in grassy fields and other open areas, and along river banks. The Giant Cowbird is a brood parasite on oropendolas and caciques; during the breeding season it is most readily seen around colonies of these species. In nonbreeding season, occurs in flocks. In courtship male gives a shrill ascending whistle.

Bronzed Cowbird
Molothrus aeneus

M 8 in (20 cm); F 7 in (18 cm). Adults of both sexes have **red eyes**; eye is dark in immature. Male has **distinct ruff on nape** that is sometimes raised; distinguished from male Shiny Cowbird and from male Giant Cowbird by greenish bronze (not purplish) **sheen on head and body** (although wings and tail are glossed purple); male Shiny has dark eye and lacks ruff; male Giant shares red eye but is much larger. Female is duller and lacks sheen; female Shiny is paler, with dark eye; female Giant is much larger. Fairly common on Pacific slope eastward to eastern Panamá Province, and on Caribbean slope in Bocas del Toro, Canal Area, and eastern Colón Province; to 6,600 ft (2,000 m). Found in grassy fields and other open areas; sometimes occurs in cities and towns. Like Shiny, in nonbreeding season usually seen in flocks; often associates with cattle. Song a sharp shrill whistle that becomes louder and then falls off.

Shiny Cowbird
Molothrus bonariensis

M 9 in (23 cm); F 8.5 in (21 cm). Male distinguished from Bronzed Cowbird by **purplish gloss on head and body** and **dark eye**, but these features can be hard to see in poor light; also note absence of neck ruff. Female is paler than female Bronzed and has **dark eye**. Respective sexes of Giant Cowbird are much larger and have red or orangish eyes (except in immature). Uncommon and local in lowlands of eastern Panama, westward to Canal Area. Found in pastures and other grassy, open areas. In nonbreeding seasons, occurs in flocks; often associates with cattle. Song a musical warbling consisting of sharp high notes occasionally interspersed with harsher ones.

Great-tailed Grackle
Quiscalus mexicanus

M 15.5 in (40 cm); F 12 in (31 cm). Male distinguished from other blackish birds by **exceptionally long tail (folded downward in center to form a V)** and **pale eye**. Female has **longer tail** and is more slender than other similar birds; also note **pale eye**. Immatures similar to respective sexes of adults, but younger individuals have dark eyes. Very common in urban areas and along coast; uncommon in open areas inland. Occurs on Pacific slope and on Caribbean slope in Bocas del Toro and Ngöbe-Buglé (where rare) and from Canal Area eastward; to about 6,600 ft (2,000 m). A bold and aggressive bird that forages for food on city streets and scavenges along beaches; communal roosts may number in the hundreds or even thousands. Has wide variety of calls, including a strident *wheeek-wheeek-wheeek*, a rising *whuREEEK*, and various other whining and chattering vocalizations. In Panama, commonly known as *talingo*.

immature

male

Giant
Cowbird

immature

male

Bronzed
Cowbird

male

female

Shiny
Cowbird

adult
male

female

Great-tailed
Grackle

Black-cowled Oriole

Icterus prosthemelas

7 in (18 cm). Adult is only oriole that has combination of **all-black head** and **yellow lower underparts, lower back, and rump**. Immature distinguished from Yellow-backed and Yellow-tailed Orioles by **olive upperparts**; further distinguished from Yellow-tailed by lack of yellow in tail; immature Orchard Oriole and immature Baltimore Oriole (p. 380) have wing-bars. Uncommon in lowlands of Caribbean slope eastward to northern Coclé. Found in middle and upper levels of forest edge, woodland edge, clearings with trees, and trees along rivers. Usually near water. Song a series of soft, mellow whistles.

Orchard Oriole

Icterus spurius

6.5 in (16 cm). **Black and chestnut pattern** of adult male is distinctive. Female distinguished from female and immature Baltimore Oriole (p. 380) by **olive upperparts** and **greenish yellow underparts**. Immature male distinguished from immature Black-cowled Oriole by **wing-bars**. Common winter resident; mostly early Aug to mid-March, sometimes arriving in late July and leaving in early April. Found in upper levels of forest edge, woodland, and open areas with trees; also inhabits residential areas and parks of cities and towns. Often visits flowering trees to feed on nectar. Call a sharp *chack!*

Yellow-backed Oriole

Icterus chrysater

7.5 in (19 cm). Distinguished from Yellow-tailed Oriole by **yellow back** and by lack of yellow in tail and on wing coverts. Immature Black-cowled Oriole has olive upperparts. See also Orange-crowned Oriole. Fairly common on both slopes from Veraguas eastward; to 3,000 ft (900 m). Found in upper levels of forest and woodland, and in shrubby areas with trees. Song a lackadaisical series of clear mellow whistles that vary disjointedly both in pitch and in the intervals between notes.

Orange-crowned Oriole

Icterus auricapillus

7 in (18 cm). **Bright orange crown, nape, and sides of head** are distinctive. Further distinguished from Yellow-backed Oriole by black back and from Yellow-tailed Oriole by lack of yellow in tail. Uncommon in lowlands in eastern Panamá Province, Darién, and western Kuna Yala; a small introduced population occurs along Chagres River in central Canal Area. Found in upper levels of forest and woodland, and in shrubby areas with trees. Often seen in flowering trees. Song consists of a series of single whistled notes or short phrases repeated for long periods.

Yellow-tailed Oriole

Icterus mesomelas

8.5 in (22 cm). Only oriole with **yellow in tail**. Tail has yellow sides when seen from above; appears mostly yellow when seen from below. Fairly common in lowlands on entire Caribbean slope and on Pacific slope from western Panamá Province eastward. Found in lower and middle levels of woodland (often in dense undergrowth and thickets), and in shrubby areas and clearings with trees; usually near water. Song a series of short, mellow phrases, each one repeated several times before changing to another. Calls include an emphatic *chup-cheer*.

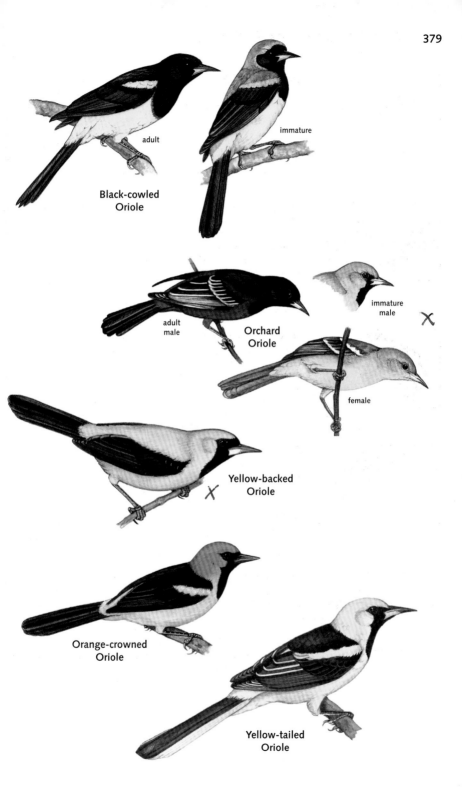

Black-cowled
Oriole

adult

immature

Orchard
Oriole

adult
male

immature
male

female

Yellow-backed
Oriole

Orange-crowned
Oriole

Yellow-tailed
Oriole

Baltimore Oriole   *Icterus galbula*

6.5 in (17 cm). Male is only oriole that is mostly **orange and black**. Female and immature distinguished from female Orchard Oriole (p. 378) by browner upperparts and **orangish underparts** (orange restricted to upper breast on drabber immature females; in this case the belly is whitish rather than yellow as in Orchard). Fairly common winter resident; mostly early Oct to late April, sometimes arriving in late Sept and leaving in early May. Found throughout the country; to 5,900 ft (1,800 m). Occurs in upper levels of forest edge, woodland, and open areas with trees. Call a harsh chattering.

Yellow-billed Cacique   *Amblycercus holosericeus*

8.5 in (21 cm). Only **all-black** bird with combination of **pale yellow eye** and **pale yellowish bill**. Scarlet-rumped Cacique appears similar when perched (with rump concealed) but has pale blue eye and usually forages in flocks in upper levels of the forest. Fairly common on both slopes; to 10,200 ft (3,100 m). Found in forest thickets, woodland edge, second growth, and nearby clearings. Often difficult to see, usually skulking in dense vegetation near ground, but sometimes ranges higher to forage in fruiting or flowering trees; most often found singly or in pairs. Song includes variable phrases composed of mellow, slurred whistles, including *wheeee-heuuu*; also sings one or two slurred whistles followed by a churr. Gives a variety of other musical whistling and trilling notes.

Scarlet-rumped Cacique   *Cacicus uropygialis*

8.5 in (22 cm). Distinctive **scarlet rump** is conspicuous in flight but often concealed when perched; also note **light blue eye** and **pointed whitish bill**. Yellow-billed Cacique has pale yellow eye; male Cherrie's and Passerini's Tanagers (p. 340) have differently shaped, bluish bills. Fairly common on entire Caribbean slope; also fairly common on Pacific slope in Darién; uncommon and more local on Pacific slope in western Chiriquí, eastern Panamá Province, and in Veraguas (foothills only); to 3,000 ft (900 m). Found in middle and upper levels of moist forest and woodland. Breeds in pairs or small groups; when not breeding, usually forages in active noisy groups. Flocks give loud, sharp whistles slurring downward, sometimes strung together in a rapid series.

Yellow-rumped Cacique   *Cacicus cela*

M 11 in (28 cm); F 9 in (23 cm). Combination of **large pale bill** and **bright yellow lower back, rump, and vent** is unique; also note yellow patch on wing and pale blue eye. Oropendolas (p. 382) have yellow only on tail, not on body or wings. Fairly common on Caribbean slope from western Colón Province eastward, and on Pacific slope in southern Veraguas and Los Santos, and from Canal Area eastward; to 2,300 ft (700 m). Found in upper and middle levels of forest, woodland, and cleared areas with large trees. Breeds in colonies, often in association with oropendolas; frequently forages in groups. Gives a variety of liquid whistling and burbling calls, as well as grating churrs, squeaks, and sharp notes.

Yellow-headed Blackbird   *Xanthocephalus xanthocephalus*

M 10 in (25 cm); F 8 in (20 cm). Male similar to Yellow-hooded Blackbird (p. 374), but is much larger and has **white patch near bend of wing** (especially conspicuous in flight, but also visible when perched). Female resembles female Yellow-hooded but is larger, browner, **lacks streaking on back**, and has **whitish streaking on lower underparts**. Immature male similar to female but darker on body. Vagrant, recorded from Caribbean side of Canal Area and eastern Panamá Province. Call a harsh clacking *krruk*. **Not illustrated**.

male

immature

**Baltimore
Oriole**

female

**Yellow-billed
Cacique**

**Scarlet-rumped
Cacique**

**Yellow-rumped
Cacique**

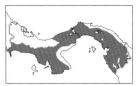

Crested Oropendola
Psarocolius decumanus

M 17 in (43 cm); F 13 in (33 cm). Only oropendola with **all-black head**; also note **whitish bill**. Chestnut-headed Oropendola has chestnut head and chunkier shape; Montezuma and Black Oropendolas have colorful facial patches and bicolored bills. Uncommon on Caribbean slope from northern Coclé to eastern Colón Province; fairly common on Pacific slope, in eastern Panamá Province and Darién; rare and local from Chiriquí to Canal Area; to 3,000 ft (900 m). Found in upper and middle levels of forest, woodland, and clearings with large trees. Not as gregarious as other oropendolas but sometimes forages in small groups. In display males give a rising bubbling rattle, often followed by a few low hooting notes and noisy wing flapping; also gives a harsh *chak* note.

Chestnut-headed Oropendola
Psarocolius wagleri

M 14 in (35 cm); F 11 in (28 cm). Only oropendola with **chestnut head and neck**; smaller and chunkier than other oropendolas. Note also that base of upper mandible is more bulbous than in Crested Oropendula (creating a more distinct notch between mandible and crown), so that the two species can often be distinguished even in poor light. Common on both slopes; to 4,500 ft (1,350 m). Found in middle and upper levels of forest, woodland, and clearings with large trees. Breeds in large colonies of 25 to 50 nests (occasionally up to 100) placed in an isolated tree (often one that overhangs a stream or road); away from colonies, often forages in groups. Gives a variety of calls, including a gurgling rattle followed by a churr, an explosive resonant *whhhuurk!*, and other chortling and bubbling notes.

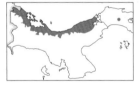

Montezuma Oropendola
Psarocolius montezuma

M 20 in (51 cm); F 16 in (41 cm). Within its range, combination of very large size, **bare blue and pink facial patches**, and **black bill with orange tip** is unique; also note **chestnut back**. Black Oropendola (no range overlap) has mostly black body. Fairly common in lowlands of Caribbean slope eastward to Canal Area; one record from eastern Panamá Province. Found in middle and upper levels of forest, woodland, and clearings with large trees. Often forages in groups. In display, male gives an ascending series of musical bubbling notes followed by a gurgle.

Black Oropendola
Psarocolius guatimozinus

M 18 in (46 cm); F 15.5 in (39 cm). Resembles Montezuma Oropendola (no range overlap), sharing **bare blue and pink facial patches** and **black bill with orange tip**, but is distinguished by **black** (not chestnut) **upper back, flight feathers, and underparts** (except for vent). Crested Oropendola lacks facial patches and has whitish bill. Fairly common in Darién. Found in middle and upper levels of moist forest, woodland, and clearings with large trees. Often forages in groups. Display call of male similar to that of Montezuma Oropendola.

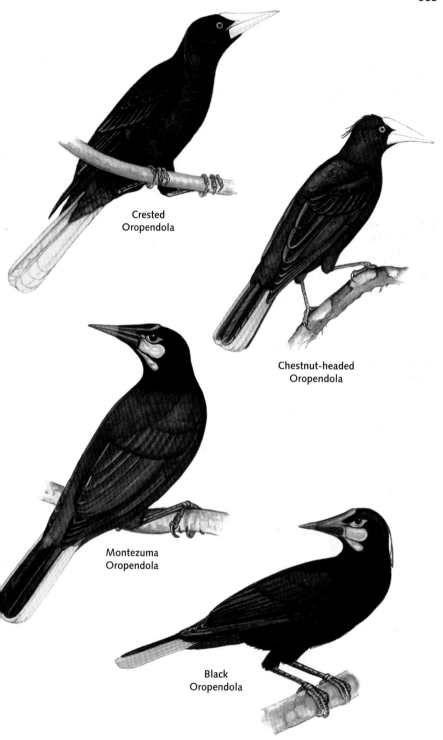

Crested
Oropendola

Chestnut-headed
Oropendola

Montezuma
Oropendola

Black
Oropendola

FRINGILLIDAE. The members of this large family are found nearly worldwide. Among the species that occur in Panama, the goldfinches and siskins have stout conical bills and feed principally on seeds, while the euphonias and chlorophonias (formerly classified with the tanagers in the family Thraupidae) eat mostly fruit, especially mistletoe berries. In most Panama species, males are boldly patterned, while females are relatively nondescript. Male euphonias that are mainly blue and yellow are best distinguished by the color and pattern of the crown, throat, and vent; on female euphonias, note the color of the head and underparts. Immature males of some species resemble females and acquire adult male plumage gradually; they sometimes show a blue-black head or blackish spots on otherwise female-type plumage.

Yellow-crowned Euphonia
Euphonia luteicapilla

3.5 in (9 cm). Male is only euphonia with both **dark throat** and **all-yellow crown** (extends back to top of nape). Male Orange-bellied Euphonia (p. 388) is very similar, but yellow does not extend as far back on crown as it does on Yellow-crowned; the species also differ in habitat. On other dark-throated male euphonias, yellow on crown does not extend much behind eye. Female is more uniformly olive above and yellow below than all other female euphonias except Thick-billed; latter has slightly heavier bill, though this is difficult to discern in field. Common on Pacific slope; uncommon on Caribbean slope, in Bocas del Toro and from northern Coclé to Canal Area; to 3,000 ft (900 m). Found in shrubby areas, cleared areas with trees, forest edge, and gardens. Typically occurs in small groups. Constantly gives a sharp, high-pitched *beem-beem* or *beem-beem-beem*, the source of its local name, *bim-bim*. Song consists of phrases of high-pitched, sputtering notes.

Thick-billed Euphonia
Euphonia laniirostris

4 in (10 cm). In most of Panama, only male euphonia with **all-yellow underparts** (including throat and vent); distinguished from rare male Yellow-throated Euphonia (which also has all-yellow underparts) by **yellow crown that extends behind eye**. Female very similar to female Yellow-crowned Euphonia. Common on entire Pacific slope and on Caribbean slope from northern Coclé eastward; to 4,000 ft (1,200 m). Found in shrubby areas, cleared areas with trees, forest edge, and gardens. Usually in small groups. Calls include a sweet clear *fweet*, a burry *brreet*, and a clear *dee-dit*, the latter softer and faster than common call of Yellow-crowned Euphonia.

Yellow-throated Euphonia
Euphonia hirundinacea

4 in (10 cm). Male very similar to male Thick-billed Euphonia (both have **all-yellow underparts**), but **yellow crown extends back only to eye**. Female distinguished from female Thick-billed and Yellow-crowned Euphonias by **white on belly**; note that female White-vented Euphonia (p. 386) has whitish throat. Very rare in foothills and highlands of western Chiriquí; 3,000 to 4,000 ft (900 to 1,200 m). Found in forest edge and cleared areas with trees. Calls include include a sharp *fwi-dirrr* and a rapid *chee-dee-dee*.

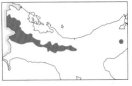

Elegant Euphonia
Euphonia elegantissima

4.5 in (11 cm). **Sky blue cap** makes both male and female unmistakable. Fairly common in western foothills and highlands, eastward to western Panamá Province; mostly 3,500 to 5,000 ft (1,050 to 1,500 m), occasionally to 7,500 ft (2,300 m). Found in middle and upper levels of forest edge, woodland, and cleared areas with trees. Usually in small groups. Calls include a clear musical *cheuu* and a sharp high *fwit*.

Yellow-crowned
Euphonia

adult male

female

Thick-billed
Euphonia

adult male

female

Yellow-throated
Euphonia

adult male

female

Elegant Euphonia

adult male

female

Fulvous-vented Euphonia
Euphonia fulvicrissa

3.5 in (9 cm). Within range, both sexes are distinguished from all other euphonias by **rufous lower belly and vent**. Common in lowlands on Caribbean slope, from northern Coclé eastward; also common in lowlands on Pacific slope, from western Panamá Province eastward; to 3,000 ft (900 m). Found in lower and middle levels of forest. Usually in small groups; sometimes with mixed-species flocks. Call a short rolling *churrrit* that is often doubled or tripled.

Spot-crowned Euphonia
Euphonia imitans

3.5 in (9 cm). On male, **yellow crown that extends to just behind eye** distinguishes it from male Yellow-crowned Euphonia (on which yellow crown extends back to top of nape, p. 384). Male is distinguished from male White-vented Euphonia by **yellow vent**. Small black spots on crown are inconspicuous. In range, female is only euphonia with **rufous belly and vent**. Uncommon in western Chiriquí; to 5,000 ft (1,500 m). Found in lower and middle levels of forest. Regularly occurs in small groups. Call similar to that of Fulvous-vented Euphonia.

Olive-backed Euphonia
Euphonia gouldi

3 in (8 cm). Male is only adult euphonia that combines **yellow forecrown** and **green back**; both sexes distinguished from all other euphonias in range by **rufous belly and vent**. Common on Caribbean slope eastward to northern Veraguas; to 2,000 ft (600 m). Found in lower and middle levels of forest, woodland, and cleared areas with trees. Usually in small groups. Call a rolling *churr-churr* or *churridiit*.

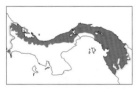

White-vented Euphonia
Euphonia minuta

3.5 in (9 cm). **White lower belly and vent** distinguish both sexes from respective sexes of other euphonias, except for female of very rare Yellow-throated (p. 384), which has yellow throat (female White-vented has whitish throat). Male Tawny-capped shares white vent but is otherwise distinctive. Fairly common in lowlands and foothills on entire Caribbean slope; uncommon and local on Pacific slope in western Chiriquí, eastern Panamá Province, and Darién; also occurs on Pacific slope in Veraguas and western Panamá Province but only in foothills. Found in upper levels of forest. Usually in small groups that often accompany mixed-species flocks. Calls include a thin high *tsip* and a short *chrrt*.

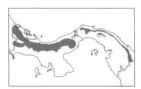

Tawny-capped Euphonia
Euphonia anneae

4.5 in (11 cm). Male is only euphonia with **tawny crown**. Female is only euphonia that combines **tawny forecrown** and **gray throat and breast**; also note **gray tinge on hindcrown**. Female Fulvous-vented, Spot-crowned, and Olive-backed Euphonias also have rufous forecrown, but they have rufous lower belly and vent. Fairly common on both slopes in foothills and highlands (with a few records from lowlands on Caribbean slope); mostly 1,500 to 4,000 ft (450 to 1,200 m), occasionally to above 5,600 ft (1,700 m). Found in all levels of forest and in adjacent clearings with trees. Usually in small groups that often accompany mixed-species flocks. Calls include a high *piim-piim* and various harsh and whining notes.

Fulvous-vented
Euphonia

adult male

female

Spot-crowned
Euphonia

adult male

female

Olive-backed
Euphonia

adult male

female

Tawny-capped
Euphonia

adult male

female

White-vented
Euphonia

adult male

female

Orange-bellied Euphonia
Euphonia xanthogaster

4 in (10 cm). Male distinguished from very similar male Yellow-crowned Euphonia (p. 384) by **less extensive yellow crown patch** (does not extend to top of nape) with a **rounded rear margin** (in Yellow-crowned, crown patch is squared off behind); habitat also differs. Female is only euphonia with combination of **yellow forecrown** and **gray throat and breast**; also note **gray hindcrown and nape**; female Tawny-capped Euphonia (no range overlap, p. 386) has tawny forecrown. Fairly common in foothills and highlands of southeastern Darién; mostly 1,500 to 5,000 ft (450 to 1,500 m). Found in lower levels of forest. Often in small groups that accompany mixed-species flocks. Calls include *dee-deet* and *dee-dee-deet* (both calls with the last note higher), and a sharp *fwit*.

Yellow-collared Chlorophonia
Chlorophonia flavirostris

4 in (10 cm). Male, **bright green with yellow collar, breast, and belly**, should not be confused in range. Female and similar immature can be recognized by combination of mostly **bright green plumage** and **orange bill and legs**. Rare on Cerro Pirre in eastern Darién, mostly above 4,000 ft (1,200 m). Found in upper levels of forest. Calls include a high-pitched melancholy *peerr* slurring downward and a soft *pik*.

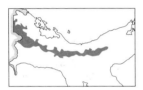

Golden-browed Chlorophonia
Chlorophonia callophrys

5 in (13 cm). In range, combination of mostly **bright green head and upperparts** and **bright yellow breast and belly** is unique. Green Shrike-Vireo (p. 278) has yellow throat and occurs mostly at lower elevations. Uncommon in western foothills and highlands, eastward to Coclé; above 2,500 ft (750 m). Found in upper levels of forest and in clearings with trees. Often in small groups. Call a soft, plaintive, whistled *wheeeuuu* on a single pitch.

Yellow-bellied Siskin
Spinus xanthogastrus

4 in (10 cm). Male distinguished from male Lesser Goldfinch by **black throat;** female distinguished from female Lesser Goldfinch by **whitish** (not yellow) **lower belly**. Both sexes have **yellow** (not white) **patches in wings and tail**. (Euphonias lack wing and tail patches.) Common in Chiriquí; from 4,000 to 8,000 ft (1,200 to 2,400 m). Found in upper levels of forest edge and in clearings and gardens. Usually in small flocks; sometimes feeds on seeding plants near ground. Call a high-pitched *pseee* slurring downward. Song consists of rapid high-pitched twittering.

Lesser Goldfinch
Spinus psaltria

3.5 in (9 cm). Both sexes distinguished from respective sexes of Yellow-bellied Siskin by **uniformly yellow underparts** and **white** (not yellow) **patches in wings and tail**. Euphonias lack wing and tail patches. Common in lowlands and foothills on Pacific slope eastward to Darién; rare in lowlands and foothills on Caribbean slope in Canal Area. Found in open areas with some shrubs or trees, woodland, and gardens. Usually in small flocks. Call consists of two notes, a high-pitched descending *tsee-ee*. Song consists of high-pitched warbles and twitters.

Orange-bellied
Euphonia

adult male

female

Yellow-collared
Chlorophonia

male

female

Golden-browed
Chlorophonia

male

female

Yellow-bellied Siskin

male

female

Lesser Goldfinch

male

female

Acknowledgments

I would first and foremost like to thank all the birders who have visited Panama and provided records and reports of their observations. This information has been invaluable in enhancing our understanding of the distribution and status of many species in Panama. I would particularly like to thank my fellow members of the Panama Records Committee of the Panama Audubon Society, Robert Ridgely, Dodge and Lorna Engleman, and Darién Montañez, for providing review and comments on reports of rare species. Dodge Engleman also reviewed the species accounts (any errors, however, remain my own). It is impossible to mention everyone who has contributed to the information contained in this book, but among them are Bill Adsett, Angel Aguirre, Ken Allaire, Maria Allen, Carlos Bethancourt, Guido Berguido, Michael Braun, Bob Brown, Robb Brumfield, Euclides Campos, Alberto Castillo, Dan Christian, Paul Coopmans, Jan Axel Cubilla, Francisco Delgado, Dale Dyer, José Carlos García, Danny George, John Guarnaccia, Karl Kaufmann, Andrew Kratter, Jim Kushlan, Howard Laidlaw, George Ledec, Mark Letzer, Horace Loftin, Rosabel Miró, Randy Moore, the Montañez family (Darién, Camilo, Delicia, and Pedro), Jacobo Ortega, Clemente Quiroz, Doug Robinson, Ghislain Rompré, Loyda Sánchez, Gilles Seutin, José Tejada, Gary Vaucher, Dan and Kay Wade, Brian Watts, and Venicio Wilson. Others who have provided assistance or information include Carlos Alfaro, Raul Arias de Para, Marco Gandasegui, Jackie Howard, and Iñaki Ruíz. I would also like to thank my many local guides and others who have assisted with my field work in many parts of Panama.

This book would have been impossible without the work of generations of ornithologists who have studied the birds of Panama. I would especially like to recognize Robert Ridgely, whose *Field Guide to the Birds of Panama* (in collaboration with artist John Gwynne), one of the first modern field guides to any tropical country, was indispensible to me in learning about Panama's birds when I first arrived here. Alexander Wetmore's monumental work, the four-volume *Birds of the Republic of Panama* (the fourth volume co-authored with Roger Pasquier and Storrs Olson), is also an invaluable source of information. At an early stage of my career, Eugene Eisenmann, Panama's pre-eminent native ornithologist, provided encouragement on my visits to the Ornithology Department of the American Museum of Natural History. More recently, the collections staff of the museum, Paul Sweet and Paul Capainolo in particular, have assisted me on visits to examine specimens.

I would like to thank my collaborator, artist Robert Dean, for his keen attention to detail and commitment to the highest levels of accuracy in the illustrations, as well as for companionship in the field in our two expeditions to Darién in pursuit of the birds of eastern Panama. I also thank our publishers, John McCuen and Marc Roegiers of Zona Tropical, and Heidi Lovette of Cornell University Press, for having taken on this project and for overseeing the whole production process from start to finish. John's editing, as well as that of Mary

Babcock from Cornell University Press, helped to improve the text. Gabriela Wattson at Zona Creativa created an attractive design for the book, and I would especially like to thank her for converting my hundreds of hand-drawn range maps to clear digital versions. I would also like to thank Rob Clay, of BirdLife International's Quito office, for proposing me to John and Marc as a possible author for this book when they were first considering the project.

From my first arrival in Panama as a graduate student more than 30 years ago, my work in this country has been made possible by the Smithsonian Tropical Research Institute (STRI). I would like to thank current Director Eldredge "Biff" Bermingham and former Director Ira Rubinoff for their support. I also thank the staff of STRI's Tropical Sciences Library for assisting me in obtaining many hard-to-locate references in ornithology.

George R. Angehr

First I would like to thank the creators of the field guides to neotropical birds that preceded ours. Without those, this book would be a lesser work.

I wish to thank the following people for their friendship and for their suggestions for seeking out and illustrating the majority of the birds found in this guide. Not all of these are birdwatchers but in their own way they aided me in the execution of the artwork: Larry Landstrom, Ruth Rodriguez, Bob Proniewych, Michael Duffy, Colonel Steve Guy, Richard Garrigues, Pat O'Donnell, Nick Athenas, Olger Licuy, Luis Eduardo Uruena, Barry Walker, Juan Carlos Calvechi, Jim Zook, Kevin Easley, Eduardo Amengual, Dev and Harriet Joslin, Ron and Dollyann Hoff, Daryl Loth, my sister Janice and her family, Annie Wenz, Larry French, Tricia Wagner and all my pals in Monteverde, the Chanchos—Walter Marin, Arturo Cruz Obando, and Federico Moises Chinchilla Salvatierra—and, last but not least, Alan and Karen Masters.

For their guiding skills and general assistance while in the field in Panama I would like to thank Bill Adsett, José Tejada, Euclides Campos, Marco Gandesegui at Ancon Expeditions, Inaki Ruiz and the staff of Burbayar Lodge, Rosabel Miro and Karl Kaufmann at Birder's View on Cerro Jefe, and the Panama Audubon Society.

I should also like to thank Heidi Lovette at Cornell University Press, our designer Gabriela Wattson at Zona Creativa, and Marc Roegiers at Zona Tropical for making this book a reality.

My deep appreciation goes out to my co-author, George Angehr, for his abundant knowledge of Panamanian birds, his assistance in and out of the field, and for his helpful suggestions throughout the creative process.

Finally a special thank you to John McCuen at Zona Tropical for his persistence, belief in the project, passion, criticism, editing skills, and, above all, determination to create the best book possible. We'll make a birder out of you yet, John.

Robert Dean

Appendix: Additional Species

The first part of this appendix contains a list of vagrant species not included within the main body of the text. This is followed by a list of species whose arrival in Panama is most likely due to human intervention.

Vagrants. The following species have been recorded only one or two times in Panama.

Gray-headed Albatross
Thalassarche chrysostoma

32 in (81 cm); WS 87 in (220 cm). Very large. Head and neck are pale gray; back, wings, and tail are gray; underparts and rump white; bill black with yellow lines along culmen and bottom of lower mandible. Immature has black bill. One doubtful nineteenth-century record from Pacific coast.

Wandering Albatross
Diomedea exulans

47.5 in (121 cm); WS 119 in (302 cm). Enormous; one of the largest flying birds. Adult mostly white with black wing tips and secondaries; bill pink. Immature mostly brown with white face; individuals become gradually whiter with age. One record, Bay of Panama (1937).

Cory's Shearwater
Calonectris diomedea

19.5 in (50 cm); WS 44 in (111 cm). Pale grayish brown above, white below; underwings mostly white; bill yellowish. One record, off Caribbean coast north of Colón (1985).

Christmas Shearwater
Puffinus nativitatis

14.5 in (37 cm); WS 30 in (76 cm). Resembles Sooty Shearwater (p. 16), but underwings are entirely dark brown. One record, far offshore western Pacific coast (1990).

Manx Shearwater
Puffinus puffinus

13.5 in (34 cm); WS 32.5 in (83 cm). Very similar to Audubon's and Galapagos Shearwaters (p. 16), but has white undertail coverts. One record from Isla Margarita, off Caribbean coast near Colón City (2003).

Townsend's Shearwater
Puffinus auricularis

13 in (33 cm); WS 30 in (76 cm). Very similar to Audubon's and Galapagos Shearwaters (p. 16), but browner above, and white on underparts extends up onto sides of rump; also note that legs are blackish (not pinkish). One record, Gulf of Panama (1977).

Wilson's Storm-Petrel
Oceanites oceanicus

7 in (18 cm); WS 16 in (40 cm). Mostly black, with pale band on upper wing above secondaries; white rump patch, with rounded lower margin, extends down sides onto flanks. Southern race may have some white on vent. Tail square; webs of feet are yellow. One record, on Pearl Islands in Pacific (1969).

White-vented Storm-Petrel
Oceanites gracilis

6 in (16 cm); WS not recorded. Similar to Wilson's Storm-Petrel, including white rump patch (with rounded lower margin) and yellow webs of feet, but is smaller and has white belly (separated from white rump by dark line on side). Underwing is paler than on Wilson's. One record, Gulf of Panama (1937).

Markham's Storm-Petrel
Oceanodroma markhami

9 in (23 cm); WS not recorded. Nearly identical to Black Storm-Petrel (p. 18) but browner (not as black) and has more deeply forked tail; pale bar on upper wing is longer, extending almost to bend of wing. One record off western Pacific coast (1937).

Galapagos Penguin
Spheniscus mendiculus

21 in (53 cm). A small penguin with slaty gray upperparts and white underparts. Face black, separated from dark crown and neck by narrow white line; two gray bands across chest. Immature lacks white line around face. One record from Puerto Armuelles, Chiriquí (1955).

American Bittern
Botaurus lentiginosus

23 in (58 cm). Similar in general appearance to a juvenile tiger-heron (p. 26), but upperparts lack barring. Upperparts dull brown; underparts whitish, with bold chestnut stripes running down neck; blackish malar stripe extends down along side of upper neck. Flight feathers slaty. One record, Canal Area (1862).

Black-legged Kittiwake
Rissa tridactyla

17 in (43 cm); WS 36 in (91 cm). Breeding adult resembles Ring-billed Gull (p. 88), but has more slender, entirely yellow bill; black legs; and wing tips that are entirely black (without white spots). Nonbreeding adult has gray smudge on ear coverts. Immature has black bill, black spot on ear coverts, and partial black collar across hind neck. In flight, immature shows bold black "M" across back and wings, formed by black outer primaries and black stripe across wing coverts; secondaries and inner primaries are white. One record of an immature at Costa del Este in eastern Panamá City (2009).

Swallow-tailed Gull
Creagrus furcatus

22.5 in (57 cm); WS 52 in (132 cm). A large gull with white underparts and a deeply forked white tail. Pattern in flight like Sabine's Gull (p. 86), with gray back and wing coverts, black outer primaries, and large white triangle on secondaries and inner primaries. Breeding adult has slaty hood; nonbreeding adult has white head and black patches around eye and on ear coverts. Immature like nonbreeding adult, but back and wing coverts are brown with white scaling; tail has black terminal band. One record off coast of Darién (1957).

Great Horned Owl
Bubo virginianus

19 in (49 cm). Very large, with conspicuous ear tufts. Brown above, mottled with gray or tawny. Face tawny, outlined in black; lower throat white; underparts whitish, heavily barred with black. Two records, from Chitra, Veraguas (1868), and Rancheria Island, near Coiba Island (1956).

Burrowing Owl
Athene cunicularia

10 in (25 cm). Has long legs and short tail; lacks ear tufts. Upperparts brown, spotted with whitish; forehead and superciliaries white; face gray; throat white. Underparts whitish with irregular brown barring on breast and sides. One record from Divalá, Chiriquí (1900).

Hammond's Flycatcher
Empidonax hammondii

5 in (13 cm). Very similar to Least Flycatcher (p. 242), but slightly larger, with very short, thin, mostly dark bill; also slightly darker below. One record, near Boquete, Chiriquí (1982).

Northern Wheatear
Oenanthe oenanthe

5.5 in (14 cm). A long-legged, short-tailed, mostly terrestrial thrush. In all plumages, shows conspicuous white rump and base of tail; has broad black terminal tail band. Breeding male pale gray above, with white superciliary and throat, black mask, and black wings; breast and belly buffy, vent and undertail coverts white. Breeding female similar to male, but has only a trace of gray mask. Nonbreeding female similar to breeding female, but browner above and more cinnamon below, with buffy edging on wings. One record, Chiriquí (2008).

Virginia's Warbler
Vermivora virginiae

4.5 in (12 cm). Similar to Nashville Warbler (p. 310), but grayer overall. Mostly gray above and below, with white eye-ring; has yellow on breast (lacking in some immatures), rump, and upper and under tail coverts. Adult male has chestnut crown patch. One record from Pacific side of Canal Area (2001).

Lined Seedeater
Sporophila lineola

4.5 in (11 cm) Very similar to Lesson's Seedeater (p. 354); male differs in having narrow white stripe down center of crown. Sides, flanks, and breast lack black mottling (sometimes present in Lesson's). Female indistinguishable in the field from female Lesson's. One record from Sherman, on Caribbean side of Canal Area (2000).

Human Assisted Birds. The occurrence in Panama of the following birds is almost certainly due to human assistance. Included are probable ship-assisted vagrants and escaped cage birds. The Panama Canal is a major artery of world commerce, and some birds have undoubtedly arrived by hitchhiking onboard transiting ships. Probable ship-assisted birds are those species that do not regularly migrate south of Mexico (or that are non-migratory); are omnivorous or granivorous (and hence likely to be able to find suitable food on shipboard); and that have only been recorded in the immediate area of the Panama Canal. Note that some species thought to be escaped caged birds could actually be natural vagrants.

Common Raven
Corvus corax

24 in (61 cm). A very large, entirely black, crowlike bird with a shaggy throat and wedge-shaped tail. One record near Gatún, Canal Area (1971). Almost certainly ship-assisted.

European Starling
Sturnus vulgaris

8 in (20 cm). Has straight, pointed bill and short tail. Breeding adult mostly glossy black with green and purple highlights; bill yellow. Nonbreeding adult similar but with profuse whitish speckling all over; bill black. Immature is uniformly gray-brown. Three records from Canal Area (1979, 2001, 2008). Probably ship-assisted.

Great Tit
Parus major

5 in (13 cm). Bill is short and black. Head glossy black, with large white cheek patch. Back olive green; wings grayish, with single white wing-bar; tail gray. Throat black; rest of underparts yellow, with broad black stripe extending down center from throat to vent. One record at a feeder in Gamboa, central Canal Area (2006). A European species. Probably ship-assisted; possibly an escaped cage bird.

White-crowned Sparrow
Zonotrichia leucophrys

7 in (18 cm). Adult has crown striped black and white. Back brown with black streaks; two white wing-bars. Throat, lower face, and breast gray; flanks brownish. On immature, crown striped with brown and buff. One record from Colón City (1982). Probably ship-assisted.

Savannah Sparrow
Passerculus sandwichensis

5.5 in (14 cm). Grayish to rufous brown above, with dark streaks on back. Pale median stripe on crown; superciliary is grayish, with yellowish tinge above lores; dark eye-line, moustachial stripe, and submalar streak. Underparts whitish, with crisp dark streaking on breast and sides. Two records, Caribbean side of Canal Area (1976, 1982). Probably ship-assisted.

Dark-eyed Junco
Junco hyemalis

6 in (15 cm). Has several distinctive races; only the "Slate-colored" form has occurred in Panama. Bill pink. Adult male has slate gray upperparts, throat, breast, and sides; lower underparts white. Outer tail feathers white. Adult female and immature similar to adult male, but paler gray, with a brownish tinge above. Two records, Caribbean side of Canal Area (1992, 2006). Probably ship-assisted.

American Goldfinch
Spinus tristis

5 in (13 cm). Breeding male mostly bright golden yellow, with black forehead, crown, wings, and tail; white wing-bars; and white rump and undertail coverts. Breeding female similar, but lacks black cap, and is yellowish olive above and dull yellow below. Nonbreeding adults are mostly grayish brown, with prominent buffy wing-bars; nonbreeding male has yellow on face and yellow shoulders. Bill pink in breeding birds, dusky when not breeding. One record from western Panamá Province (2003). Probably an escaped cage bird, possibly a natural vagrant.

Nutmeg Munia
Lonchura punctulata

4 in (10 cm). A small finchlike bird with a stout silvery gray bill and a short tail. Adult has chestnut face, grayish brown nape and back, and buffy brown rump and tail. Underparts white, with bold black scalloping on breast and sides. Immature buffy brown above, paler buffy brown on throat and breast, and whitish on belly. One record from Gamboa, central Canal Area (2003). Probably an escaped cage bird, possibly a natural vagrant. Called Nutmeg Mannikin by AOU.

Tricolored Munia
Lonchura malacca

5 in (12 cm). Similar in shape to Nutmeg Munia; bill stout and silvery gray. Male has black head; chestnut back, rump, and tail; white breast and sides; and black belly, vent, and undertail coverts. Female duller; immature is grayish brown above and buffy below. Two records, southern Canal Area (2006). Probably an escaped cage bird, possibly a natural vagrant. Called Tricolored Mannikin by AOU.

Glossary

See Anatomical Features, page xxiv, for additional definitions.

abundant. Abundance category that describes a species recorded in the field every day, often in large numbers.

AOU. The American Ornithologists' Union is the organization that publishes the official *Checklist of North American Birds*. Common and scientific names in this book mostly follow this reference; those that differ are noted.

army-ant swarms. Army ants (genera *Eciton* and *Labidus*) forage for insects and other small animals in large swarms that search through the leaf litter on the forest floor. Many species of birds, including the Rufous-vented Ground-Cuckoo, woodcreepers, antbirds, and tanagers follow these swarms in order to capture insects fleeing from the ants.

axillars. An area of feathers at the base of the underwing; corresponds to the armpit of a mammal.

back. Area of the upperparts located between the nape and the rump, and between the base of each wing.

bare parts. A term describing unfeathered parts of a bird, including the beak, cere, orbital area, legs, and feet.

barred. Marked with alternating bands of different colors, with the bands running perpendicular to the long axis of the bird's body.

belly. The area of the underparts between the breast and the vent.

breast. The area of the underparts between the throat and the belly; the front part of a bird's body.

breeding migrant. A species that breeds in Panama, but migrates out of the country during the nonbreeding season.

breeding plumage. A distinctive plumage assumed by many bird species during the breeding season; breeding plumage is usually more colorful or more boldly marked than that worn during the nonbreeding season. Some birds also show more brightly colored **bare parts** when breeding. Distinctive breeding plumages are common among migrant species that arrive in Panama from the north; some birds may still retain these plumages when they arrive in the fall (Sept-Oct), or molt into them before they depart in the spring (March-May).

breeding resident. A species that breeds in Panama, and that remains in the country during the nonbreeding season.

brood parasite. A species that deposits its eggs in the nests of other species, thus delegating the task of raising its nestlings to the host parents. Examples of such species in Panama include the Striped and Pheasant Cuckoos and the cowbirds.

canopy. The uppermost level of the forest; when describing foraging height, refers to the area within about 10 feet of the upper level of leaves.

cap. When the top of a bird's head (crown) has a color that is distinct from the rest of the head, it is called a cap.

cere. A fleshy covering, at the base of the upper mandible, through which the nostrils open. It is found in several groups of birds, including hawks, falcons, owls, pigeons, and parrots.

cheek. A patch of feathers below and behind the eye that covers the ear opening; also known as **ear coverts**. When this patch (or sometimes the feathers bordering its outer edge) is distinctly colored from the surrounding area, it is known as a **cheek patch** or **ear patch**.

chest. The upper part of the breast.

chin. The upper part of the throat, immediately below the base of the lower mandible.

cloud forest. A type of forest that occurs in mountainous areas and that is characterized by the formation, and persistence, of clouds. Much of the moisture available to plants is obtained by condensation directly from these clouds rather than from rainfall. The canopy is typically relatively low, and trunks and branches are often covered with a thick mat of mosses, ferns, bromeliads, and other epiphytes.

common. Abundance category that describes a species recorded on substantially more than half of all days in the field.

cosmopolitan. Refers to a group or species with a range that includes much of the world.

crest. Feathers (usually elongated) on the top of the crown that are capable of being raised.

crown. The entire top portion of the head, from just above the upper mandible to the neck.

crown patch. A colorful patch of feathers in the center of the crown that is usually concealed but sometimes raised in display. Crown patches are found in many tyrant flycatchers.

cryptic. Describes birds that are difficult to see, either due to color pattern (often a mottled combination of brown and gray that blends in with leaf litter or branches) or secretive behavior.

culmen. The top edge of the upper mandible, as seen in profile.

decurved. Describes a bill that is curved downward.

dry forest. A forest type that has low annual rainfall and a prolonged dry season, during which many of the trees lose their leaves.

dry season. The part of the year with relatively low rainfall; in most of Panama this occurs from mid-December to mid-April.

ear coverts. A patch of feathers below and behind the eye that covers the ear opening; see also **cheek**.

ear patch. When the ear coverts (or the feathers bordering it) are distinct in color from the surrounding feathers, they are referred to as an ear patch (also called a **cheek patch**).

EBA. An Endemic Bird Area is defined as a specific area in which two or more restricted-range species occur together. BirdLife International has identified more than 200 such Endemic Bird Areas throughout the world.

eclipse plumage. A drab plumage (similar to that of females) that is briefly assumed by some male ducks immediately after the breeding season (from late summer to autumn).

El Niño. A climatic pattern affecting the tropical Pacific that occurs at intervals of about three to seven years. One result of this pattern is the failure of cold-water upwelling on the coast of South America, which greatly decreases food availability for many seabirds. During El Niño years, many seabirds from that region may wander north into Panama's waters in search of food.

endemic. Describes a species whose distribution is limited to a particular region. In this book, we recognize restricted-range species (defined by BirdLife International as those species with a total world range of less than 19,300 sq mi (50,000 km^2) as **regional endemics**. Most such species have ranges limited to Panama and the adjacent countries of Colombia and/or Costa Rica (a few have ranges that extend as far as Honduras). **National endemics** are those species whose distribution is limited to Panama alone.

epiphyte. A plant that grows on another plant without taking sustenance from it. In tropical forests, many trees are festooned with gardens of epiphytes (including ferns, bromeliads, and orchids), which are a favored foraging area for some species of woodcreepers, ovenbirds, and others.

eye-line. When the lore and the postocular stripe are of the same color and set off from the surrounding feathers, they form an eye-line (also called an **eye-stripe**).

eye-ring. When the very short feathers that form a narrow ring around the eye are of a different color than the surrounding ones, they are called an eye-ring.

fairly common. Abundance category that describes a species recorded on about half of all days in the field.

flanks. The sides of a bird's body toward the rear and below the wings.

flight feathers. The elongated feathers of the wing, including the primaries, secondaries, and tertials.

foothills. Areas from 2,000 to 4,000 ft (600 to 1,200 m).

forecrown (or **forehead**). The front part of the crown above the base of the upper mandible, particularly if distinctly colored.

forest. In habitat descriptions, indicates a wooded area with a closed canopy (the crowns of the trees are close enough to virtually touch).

forest edge. The boundary between forest and adjacent open areas, frequently characterized by thick tangles of shrubs, lianas, and vines.

form. A term used in this book to refer to a group of two or more subspecies that share similar plumage characters. For example, the "Mangrove" form of Yellow Warbler includes several subspecies which all have extensive chestnut on the head. Also used to refer to particular hybrid types, such as "Brewster's" and "Lawrence's" Warblers, names for distinctive hybrids between Blue-winged and Golden-winged Warblers.

frugivorous. Describes birds that feed on fruit.

gallery forest. A strip of forest found along water courses in otherwise mostly treeless terrain. In Panama gallery forests are especially common on the western Pacific slope.

graduated tail. A tail in which the central tail feathers are the longest, and in which the other feathers become progressively shorter towards the sides.

gorget. A patch of iridescent, brightly colored feathers found on the throat of some hummingbirds.

granivorous. Describes birds that eat seeds.

grassland. An area where grasses are the dominant vegetation and that mostly lacks woody vegetation; includes pasture as well as natural grassy areas.

Heliconia. A group of large, banana-like herbaceous plants with showy flower clusters (often red or yellow) that are often favored by hummingbirds.

highlands. Areas above 4,000 ft (1,200 m).

hood. The term hood has variable usage, but generally indicates that the crown and nape (and often also the cheeks and lower throat) are of a single color, and distinct from the color of the forehead, eye area, and chin.

insectivorous. Describes birds that feed on insects and other small invertebrates.

lateral throat stripe. A line that runs between the malar and the throat (also called a **submalar stripe**).

leaf litter. A layer of dead leaves covering the forest floor; a favored foraging area for many species of birds.

lek. An area where males assemble to display to females and court them. Some male hummingbirds, manakins, and flycatchers spend much of their time calling and displaying at such leks.

local. Abundance category that describes a species that appears to be absent from much of its potential range, not being found in habitat which otherwise seems suitable for it. This term is sometimes used in conjunction with other abundance categories, for example, "locally common."

loral. Referring to the lore.

lore. The area between the eye and the upper mandible.

lower levels. In descriptions of foraging height, refers to a range from ground level to about 10 feet above the ground.

lowlands. Areas from sea level to 2,000 ft (600 m).

malar. The area that extends from the base of the lower mandible through the area between the cheek and throat. When it has a distinct color, it is called a **malar stripe**.

mandible. One of the two segments that make up the bill, referred to respectively as the the upper and lower mandible.

mangrove. A forest type found between the low- and high-tide lines in coastal areas; the trees that grow there have special adaptations that permit them to thrive in salt water.

marsh. An area that has standing water most of the year and that lacks trees; dominated by grasses, large herbs, and other nonwoody vegetation. Also see **swamp**.

mask. A patch of darker color (usually black or blackish) around the eye, often extending to the area around the base of the bill and/or the ear coverts.

middle elevations. A general term that encompasses foothills and lower highlands.

middle levels. In descriptions of foraging height, refers to a range from about 10 to 30 feet above the ground.

migrant. A species that moves seasonally between its breeding areas and areas where it spends the nonbreeding season. Migrants can be either **transients** or **winter residents**. For migrant species with no clear pattern of seasonal abundance, the general term "migrant" is used without categorizing them as either transients or winter residents.

moist forest. Forest that receives moderate to large amounts of annual rainfall, and that has only a moderately long dry season. The majority of trees in such forests do not lose their leaves during the dry season. Also see **wet forest**.

montane forest. A forest type that occurs at higher elevations, usually above 4,000 ft (1,200 m).

morph. Within a species, a distinctive color variant that is not related to age or sex. Also known as a **phase**.

moustachial mark. A dark mark that extends below the eye and onto the malar area; found in some falcons.

moustachial stripe. A line of differently colored feathers just below the ear coverts and above the malar.

nape. An area on the back of the neck, between the crown and the back.

national endemic. See **endemic**.

neotropics. A biogeographical region that includes the southern parts of Mexico, Central America, and South America.

nonbreeding plumage. The plumage assumed by some species during the nonbreeding season; usually duller and less distinctive than breeding plumage.

nonbreeding resident. A species that does not breed in Panama, but that remains in the country for a significant part of the year.

nuchal collar. A distinctly colored area across the nape.

omnivorous. Describes birds that feed on both plants and animals.

open areas. A general term for areas without extensive woody vegetation (but which may include scattered trees), including grasslands, agricultural fields, golf courses, airstrips, parks, and gardens.

orbital ring. A ring of bare skin around the eye, often brightly colored.

orbital skin. A patch of bare skin around the eye area, often brightly colored.

pelagic. Describes birds that occur mainly on the open sea, away from coastal areas.

phase. See **morph**.

polyandrous. Describes species in which females pair with multiple males. Jacanas are a notable polyandrous species.

postocular spot. A distinctly colored spot behind the eye.

postocular stripe. A distinctly colored line of feathers that extends behind the eye.

primaries. On the outer part of the wing, the elongated feathers that extend from the bend of the wing outward.

primary projection. The distance that the tip of the outermost primary (on the folded wing) extends beyond the longest secondaries and tertials; a trait used in the identification of some flycatchers and other species.

quarter. With regard to flight behavior, refers to searching an area by crisscrossing it in various directions.

race. As used in this book, synonymous with **subspecies**.

raptor. A bird of prey. Includes vultures, hawks, kites, eagles, falcons, caracaras, and owls.

rare. Abundance category that describes a species recorded on fewer than 10% of all days in the field.

regional endemic. See **endemic**.

restricted-range species. As defined by BirdLife International, a species with a total world range of less than 19,300 sq mi (50,000 km²). Such species are referred to as **regional endemics** in this book.

rump. The part of a bird's body that lies between the back and the base of the tail.

scapulars. The feathers covering the juncture of the wing and body; corresponds to the shoulder of a mammal.

scrub. A habitat type with woody vegetation that is reduced to a short height due to such factors as burning or poor soil; found mainly on Panama's Pacific coast, often in drier or coastal areas.

second growth. As used in this book, refers only to very young woody vegetation, usually under five years old and less than 10 feet in height.

secondaries. On the inner part of the wing, the elongated feathers that extend from the bend of the wing inward.

shrubby areas. Areas composed mainly of shrubs, with few or no trees.

sides. That part of a bird's body that lies between the base of the wing and the breast.

spatulate. Refers to a bill that is spoon-shaped (wider at the tip).

speculum. A glossy patch on the upper secondaries of some ducks.

streaked. Marked with lines of color that run parallel to the long axis of a bird's body.

striped. Marked with sharply contrasting lines of color that run parallel to the long axis of a bird's body; the term describes lines that are more crisply delineated than in **streaked** birds.

submalar stripe. A line between the malar and the throat (also called a **lateral throat stripe**).

subspecies. A localized population of a species that differs from other such populations in details of plumage or in size. As used in this book, synonymous with **race**.

subterminal band. A distinctly colored band above the tip of the tail.

superciliary. The line of feathers extending from the base of the bill to above and behind the eye (includes the supraloral feathers).

supraloral. The area above the lore.

swamp. A wooded area in which standing water covers the soil for most of the year. Also see **marsh**.

tail corners. The tips of the outer tail feathers.

tertials. The three innermost elongated wing feathers.

throat. On the underside of a bird's head, the area extending from the base of the lower mandible to the top of the breast.

timberline. The altitude on a mountain above which trees do not grow. Vegetation near timberline usually consists of twisted, stunted trees and shrubs.

transient. Refers to those migrants that pass through Panama, during relatively brief periods, en route between their breeding and nonbreeding areas; unlike nonbreeding residents, transients do not remain in the country throughout their nonbreeding periods.

uncommon. Abundance category that describes a species recorded on substantially fewer than half of all days in the field, but that is more common than a rare species.

understory. The lower level of vegetation within a forest, consisting of smaller trees and shrubs growing beneath the forest canopy.

undertail coverts. The feathers that cover the base of the underside of the tail.

underwing coverts. The feathers that cover the underside of the fleshy part of the wing and the bases of the flight feathers.

upper levels. With reference to foraging height, everything above 30 feet, including the canopy.

uppertail coverts. The feathers that cover the base of the upper side of the tail.

vagrant. A nonbreeding species that has been recorded only a very few times in Panama, and that is not expected to occur with any regularity.

vent. The part of a bird's body between the belly and the undertail coverts.

vermiculated. Marked with a pattern of small wavy lines.

very common. Abundance category that describes a species that is recorded almost every day in the field, but usually not in such large numbers as an abundant species.

very rare. Abundance category that describes a species with few records in Panama; experienced observers may not encounter the species in years of field work, even though it may breed in the country or occur regularly as a migrant.

wet forest. Forest that receives abundant rain throughout the year, and that experiences only a mild dry season or none at all. Also see **moist forest**.

wet season. The part of the year with relatively greater rainfall; in most of Panama this occurs from mid-April to mid-December.

wing-bar. A bar across the upper part of the folded wing that is formed by the distinctly colored tips of the wing coverts.

wing coverts. The several rows of feathers that cover the base of the flight feathers.

wing edging. A lighter color on the edge of each flight feather (and often also on the wing coverts) that imparts a striped look to the wing.

wing-lining. The underwing coverts, which cover the fleshy part of the wing and the bases of the flight feathers.

winter resident. Refers to those migrants that remain in Panama throughout the northern winter (and usually during parts of fall and spring).

woodland. A wooded area in which trees are spaced so widely that their canopies do not touch; in woodlands, trees are usually shorter than in forest.

woodland edge. The boundary between woodland and adjacent open areas, frequently characterized by thick tangles of shrubs, lianas, and vines.

WS. Abbreviation for wingspan, the measurement from wing tip to wing tip of a bird in flight.

Checklist of the Birds of Panama

The order of this list conforms strictly to that of AOU.

Main List

Tinamous (4)	Tinamidae	location & date
Highland Tinamou	*Nothocercus bonapartei*	
Great Tinamou	*Tinamus major*	
Little Tinamou	*Crypturellus soui*	
Choco Tinamou	*Crypturellus kerriae*	

Ducks (16)	Anatidae	
White-faced Whistling-Duck	*Dendrocygna viduata*	
Black-bellied Whistling-Duck	*Dendrocygna autumnalis*	
Fulvous Whistling-Duck	*Dendrocygna bicolor*	
Comb Duck	*Sarkidiornis melanotos*	
Muscovy Duck	*Cairina moschata*	
American Wigeon	*Anas americana*	
Mallard	*Anas platyrhynchos*	
Blue-winged Teal	*Anas discors*	
Cinnamon Teal	*Anas cyanoptera*	
Northern Shoveler	*Anas clypeata*	
White-cheeked Pintail	*Anas bahamensis*	
Northern Pintail	*Anas acuta*	
Green-winged Teal	*Anas crecca*	
Ring-necked Duck	*Aythya collaris*	
Lesser Scaup	*Aythya affinis*	
Masked Duck	*Nomonyx dominicus*	

Curassows, Chachalacas & Guans (4)	Cracidae	
Gray-headed Chachalaca	*Ortalis cinereiceps*	
Crested Guan	*Penelope purpurascens*	
Black Guan	*Chamaepetes unicolor*	
Great Curassow	*Crax rubra*	

Quails (7)	Odontophoridae	
Crested Bobwhite	*Colinus cristatus*	
Marbled Wood-Quail	*Odontophorus gujanensis*	
Black-eared Wood-Quail	*Odontophorus melanotis*	
Tacarcuna Wood-Quail	*Odontophorus dialeucos*	
Black-breasted Wood-Quail	*Odontophorus leucolaemus*	

Spotted Wood-Quail	*Odontophorus guttatus*	
Tawny-faced Quail	*Rhynchortyx cinctus*	

Grebes (2)	**Podicipedidae**	
Least Grebe	*Tachybaptus dominicus*	
Pied-billed Grebe	*Podilymbus podiceps*	

Albatrosses (3)	**Diomedeidae**	
Gray-headed Albatross	*Thalassarche chrysostoma*	
Wandering Albatross	*Diomedea exulans*	
Waved Albatross	*Phoebastria irrorata*	

Shearwaters & Petrels (10)	**Procellariidae**	
Galapagos Petrel	*Pterodroma phaeopygia*	
Parkinson's Petrel	*Procellaria parkinsoni*	
Cory's Shearwater	*Calonectris diomedea*	
Wedge-tailed Shearwater	*Puffinus pacificus*	
Sooty Shearwater	*Puffinus griseus*	
Christmas Shearwater	*Puffinus nativitatis*	
Manx Shearwater	*Puffinus puffinus*	
Townsend's Shearwater	*Puffinus auricularis*	
Audubon's Shearwater	*Puffinus lherminieri*	
Galapagos Shearwater	*Puffinus subalaris*	

Storm-Petrels (6)	**Hydrobatidae**	
Wilson's Storm-Petrel	*Oceanites oceanicus*	
White-vented Storm-Petrel	*Oceanites gracilis*	
Wedge-rumped Storm-Petrel	*Oceanodroma tethys*	
Black Storm-Petrel	*Oceanodroma melania*	
Markham's Storm-Petrel	*Oceanodroma markhami*	
Least Storm-Petrel	*Oceanodroma microsoma*	

Penguins (1)	**Spheniscidae**	
Galapagos Penguin	*Spheniscus mendiculus*	

Tropicbirds (2)	**Phaethontidae**	
White-tailed Tropicbird	*Phaethon lepturus*	
Red-billed Tropicbird	*Phaethon aethereus*	

Boobies & Gannets (6)	**Sulidae**	
Masked Booby	*Sula dactylatra*	
Nazca Booby	*Sula granti*	
Blue-footed Booby	*Sula nebouxii*	
Peruvian Booby	*Sula variegata*	

| Brown Booby | *Sula leucogaster* | |
| Red-footed Booby | *Sula sula* | |

Pelicans (2)	**Pelecanidae**	
American White Pelican	*Pelecanus erythrorhynchos*	
Brown Pelican	*Pelecanus occidentalis*	

Cormorants (2)	**Phalocrocoracidae**	
Neotropic Cormorant	*Phalacrocorax brasilianus*	
Guanay Cormorant	*Phalacrocorax bougainvillii*	

Darters (1)	**Anhingidae**	
Anhinga	*Anhinga anhinga*	

Frigatebirds (2)	**Fregatidae**	
Magnificent Frigatebird	*Fregata magnificens*	
Great Frigatebird	*Fregata minor*	

Herons & Egrets (20)	**Ardeidae**	
American Bittern	*Botaurus lentiginosus*	
Least Bittern	*Ixobrychus exilis*	
Rufescent Tiger-Heron	*Tigrisoma lineatum*	
Fasciated Tiger-Heron	*Tigrisoma fasciatum*	
Bare-throated Tiger-Heron	*Tigrisoma mexicanum*	
Great Blue Heron	*Ardea herodias*	
Cocoi Heron	*Ardea cocoi*	
Great Egret	*Ardea alba*	
Snowy Egret	*Egretta thula*	
Little Blue Heron	*Egretta caerulea*	
Tricolored Heron	*Egretta tricolor*	
Reddish Egret	*Egretta rufescens*	
Cattle Egret	*Bubulcus ibis*	
Green Heron	*Butorides virescens*	
Striated Heron	*Butorides striata*	
Agami Heron	*Agamia agami*	
Capped Heron	*Pilherodius pileatus*	
Black-crowned Night-Heron	*Nycticorax nycticorax*	
Yellow-crowned Night-Heron	*Nyctanassa violacea*	
Boat-billed Heron	*Cochlearius cochlearius*	

Ibises & Spoonbills (6)	**Threskiornithidae**	
White Ibis	*Eudocimus albus*	
Scarlet Ibis	*Eudocimus ruber*	

Glossy Ibis	*Plegadis falcinellus*	
Green Ibis	*Mesembrinibis cayennensis*	
Buff-necked Ibis	*Theristicus caudatus*	
Roseate Spoonbill	*Platalea ajaja*	

Storks (2)	**Ciconiidae**	
Jabiru	*Jabiru mycteria*	
Wood Stork	*Mycteria americana*	

New World Vultures (4)	**Cathartidae**	
Black Vulture	*Coragyps atratus*	
Turkey Vulture	*Cathartes aura*	
Lesser Yellow-headed Vulture	*Cathartes burrovianus*	
King Vulture	*Sarcoramphus papa*	

Hawks, Eagles & Kites (41)	**Accipitridae**	
Osprey	*Pandion haliaetus*	
Gray-headed Kite	*Leptodon cayanensis*	
Hook-billed Kite	*Chondrohierax uncinatus*	
Swallow-tailed Kite	*Elanoides forficatus*	
Pearl Kite	*Gampsonyx swainsonii*	
White-tailed Kite	*Elanus leucurus*	
Snail Kite	*Rostrhamus sociabilis*	
Slender-billed Kite	*Helicolestes hamatus*	
Double-toothed Kite	*Harpagus bidentatus*	
Mississippi Kite	*Ictinia mississippiensis*	
Plumbeous Kite	*Ictinia plumbea*	
Black-collared Hawk	*Busarellus nigricollis*	
Northern Harrier	*Circus cyaneus*	
Long-winged Harrier	*Circus buffoni*	
Tiny Hawk	*Accipiter superciliosus*	
Sharp-shinned Hawk	*Accipiter striatus*	
Cooper's Hawk	*Accipiter cooperii*	
Bicolored Hawk	*Accipiter bicolor*	
Crane Hawk	*Geranospiza caerulescens*	
Plumbeous Hawk	*Leucopternis plumbeus*	
Barred Hawk	*Leucopternis princeps*	
Semiplumbeous Hawk	*Leucopternis semiplumbeus*	
White Hawk	*Leucopternis albicollis*	
Common Black-Hawk	*Buteogallus anthracinus*	
Great Black-Hawk	*Buteogallus urubitinga*	

Savanna Hawk	*Buteogallus meridionalis*	
Harris's Hawk	*Parabuteo unicinctus*	
Solitary Eagle	*Harpyhaliaetus solitarius*	
Roadside Hawk	*Buteo magnirostris*	
Broad-winged Hawk	*Buteo platypterus*	
Gray Hawk	*Buteo nitidus*	
Short-tailed Hawk	*Buteo brachyurus*	
Swainson's Hawk	*Buteo swainsoni*	
White-tailed Hawk	*Buteo albicaudatus*	
Zone-tailed Hawk	*Buteo albonotatus*	
Red-tailed Hawk	*Buteo jamaicensis*	
Crested Eagle	*Morphnus guianensis*	
Harpy Eagle	*Harpia harpyja*	
Black Hawk-Eagle	*Spizaetus tyrannus*	
Ornate Hawk-Eagle	*Spizaetus ornatus*	
Black-and-white Hawk-Eagle	*Spizaetus melanoleucus*	

Falcons & Caracaras (13)	**Falconidae**	
Barred Forest-Falcon	*Micrastur ruficollis*	
Slaty-backed Forest-Falcon	*Micrastur mirandollei*	
Collared Forest-Falcon	*Micrastur semitorquatus*	
Red-throated Caracara	*Ibycter americanus*	
Crested Caracara	*Caracara cheriway*	
Yellow-headed Caracara	*Milvago chimachima*	
Laughing Falcon	*Herpetotheres cachinnans*	
American Kestrel	*Falco sparverius*	
Merlin	*Falco columbarius*	
Aplomado Falcon	*Falco femoralis*	
Bat Falcon	*Falco rufigularis*	
Orange-breasted Falcon	*Falco deiroleucus*	
Peregrine Falcon	*Falco peregrinus*	

Rails, Gallinules & Coots (16)	**Rallidae**	
Ruddy Crake	*Laterallus ruber*	
White-throated Crake	*Laterallus albigularis*	
Gray-breasted Crake	*Laterallus exilis*	
Black Rail	*Laterallus jamaicensis*	
Clapper Rail	*Rallus longirostris*	
Rufous-necked Wood-Rail	*Aramides axillaris*	
Gray-necked Wood-Rail	*Aramides cajanea*	
Uniform Crake	*Amaurolimnas concolor*	

Sora	*Porzana carolina*	
Yellow-breasted Crake	*Porzana flaviventer*	
Colombian Crake	*Neocrex colombiana*	
Paint-billed Crake	*Neocrex erythrops*	
Spotted Rail	*Pardirallus maculatus*	
Purple Gallinule	*Porphyrio martinica*	
Common Moorhen	*Gallinula chloropus*	
American Coot	*Fulica americana*	

Finfoots (1)	**Heliornithidae**	
Sungrebe	*Heliornis fulica*	

Sunbittern (1)	**Eurypygidae**	
Sunbittern	*Eurypyga helias*	

Limpkin (1)	**Aramidae**	
Limpkin	*Aramus guarauna*	

Plovers & Lapwings (8)	**Charadriidae**	
Southern Lapwing	*Vanellus chilensis*	
Black-bellied Plover	*Pluvialis squatarola*	
American Golden-Plover	*Pluvialis dominica*	
Collared Plover	*Charadrius collaris*	
Snowy Plover	*Charadrius alexandrinus*	
Wilson's Plover	*Charadrius wilsonia*	
Semipalmated Plover	*Charadrius semipalmatus*	
Killdeer	*Charadrius vociferus*	

Oystercatchers (1)	**Haematopodidae**	
American Oystercatcher	*Haematopus palliatus*	

Stilts & Avocets (2)	**Recurvirostridae**	
Black-necked Stilt	*Himantopus mexicanus*	
American Avocet	*Recurvirostra americana*	

Jacanas (2)	**Jacanidae**	
Northern Jacana	*Jacana spinosa*	
Wattled Jacana	*Jacana jacana*	

Sandpipers & Allies (31)	**Scolopacidae**	
Spotted Sandpiper	*Actitis macularius*	
Solitary Sandpiper	*Tringa solitaria*	
Wandering Tattler	*Tringa incana*	
Greater Yellowlegs	*Tringa melanoleuca*	

Willet	*Tringa semipalmata*	
Lesser Yellowlegs	*Tringa flavipes*	
Upland Sandpiper	*Bartramia longicauda*	
Whimbrel	*Numenius phaeopus*	
Long-billed Curlew	*Numenius americanus*	
Hudsonian Godwit	*Limosa haemastica*	
Marbled Godwit	*Limosa fedoa*	
Ruddy Turnstone	*Arenaria interpres*	
Surfbird	*Aphriza virgata*	
Red Knot	*Calidris canutus*	
Sanderling	*Calidris alba*	
Semipalmated Sandpiper	*Calidris pusilla*	
Western Sandpiper	*Calidris mauri*	
Least Sandpiper	*Calidris minutilla*	
White-rumped Sandpiper	*Calidris fuscicollis*	
Baird's Sandpiper	*Calidris bairdii*	
Pectoral Sandpiper	*Calidris melanotos*	
Dunlin	*Calidris alpina*	
Curlew Sandpiper	*Calidris ferruginea*	
Stilt Sandpiper	*Calidris himantopus*	
Buff-breasted Sandpiper	*Tryngites subruficollis*	
Ruff	*Philomachus pugnax*	
Short-billed Dowitcher	*Limnodromus griseus*	
Long-billed Dowitcher	*Limnodromus scolopaceus*	
Wilson's Snipe	*Gallinago delicata*	
Wilson's Phalarope	*Phalaropus tricolor*	
Red-necked Phalarope	*Phalaropus lobatus*	

Gulls, Terns & Skimmers (32) **Laridae**

Swallow-tailed Gull	*Creagrus furcatus*	
Black-legged Kittiwake	*Rissa tridactyla*	
Sabine's Gull	*Xema sabini*	
Bonaparte's Gull	*Chroicocephalus philadelphia*	
Gray-hooded Gull	*Chroicocephalus cirrocephalus*	
Gray Gull	*Leucophaeus modestus*	
Laughing Gull	*Leucophaeus atricilla*	
Franklin's Gull	*Leucophaeus pipixcan*	
Belcher's Gull	*Larus belcheri*	
Ring-billed Gull	*Larus delawarensis*	
Herring Gull	*Larus argentatus*	

Lesser Black-backed Gull	*Larus fuscus*	
Kelp Gull	*Larus dominicanus*	
Brown Noddy	*Anous stolidus*	
Black Noddy	*Anous minutus*	
White Tern	*Gygis alba*	
Sooty Tern	*Onychoprion fuscatus*	
Bridled Tern	*Onychoprion anaethetus*	
Least Tern	*Sternula antillarum*	
Yellow-billed Tern	*Sternula superciliaris*	
Large-billed Tern	*Phaetusa simplex*	
Gull-billed Tern	*Gelochelidon nilotica*	
Caspian Tern	*Hydroprogne caspia*	
Inca Tern	*Larosterna inca*	
Black Tern	*Chlidonias niger*	
Common Tern	*Sterna hirundo*	
Arctic Tern	*Sterna paradisaea*	
Forster's Tern	*Sterna forsteri*	
Royal Tern	*Thalasseus maximus*	
Sandwich Tern	*Thalasseus sandvicensis*	
Elegant Tern	*Thalasseus elegans*	
Black Skimmer	*Rynchops niger*	

Skuas & Jaegers (4)	**Stercorariidae**	
South Polar Skua	*Stercorarius maccormicki*	
Pomarine Jaeger	*Stercorarius pomarinus*	
Parasitic Jaeger	*Stercorarius parasiticus*	
Long-tailed Jaeger	*Stercorarius longicaudus*	

Pigeons & Doves (28)	**Columbidae**	
Rock Pigeon	*Columba livia*	
Pale-vented Pigeon	*Patagioenas cayennensis*	
Scaled Pigeon	*Patagioenas speciosa*	
White-crowned Pigeon	*Patagioenas leucocephala*	
Band-tailed Pigeon	*Patagioenas fasciata*	
Plumbeous Pigeon	*Patagioenas plumbea*	
Ruddy Pigeon	*Patagioenas subvinacea*	
Short-billed Pigeon	*Patagioenas nigrirostris*	
Dusky Pigeon	*Patagioenas goodsoni*	
White-winged Dove	*Zenaida asiatica*	
Eared Dove	*Zenaida auriculata*	

Mourning Dove	*Zenaida macroura*	
Common Ground-Dove	*Columbina passerina*	
Plain-breasted Ground-Dove	*Columbina minuta*	
Ruddy Ground-Dove	*Columbina talpacoti*	
Blue Ground-Dove	*Claravis pretiosa*	
Maroon-chested Ground-Dove	*Claravis mondetoura*	
White-tipped Dove	*Leptotila verreauxi*	
Gray-headed Dove	*Leptotila plumbeiceps*	
Brown-backed Dove	*Leptotila battyi*	
Gray-chested Dove	*Leptotila cassini*	
Olive-backed Quail-Dove	*Geotrygon veraguensis*	
Chiriqui Quail-Dove	*Geotrygon chiriquensis*	
Purplish-backed Quail-Dove	*Geotrygon lawrencii*	
Buff-fronted Quail-Dove	*Geotrygon costaricensis*	
Russet-crowned Quail-Dove	*Geotrygon goldmani*	
Violaceous Quail-Dove	*Geotrygon violacea*	
Ruddy Quail-Dove	*Geotrygon montana*	

Parrots (22)	**Psittacidae**	
Azuero Parakeet	*Pyrrhura eisenmanni*	
Sulphur-winged Parakeet	*Pyrrhura hoffmanni*	
Crimson-fronted Parakeet	*Aratinga finschi*	
Olive-throated Parakeet	*Aratinga nana*	
Brown-throated Parakeet	*Aratinga pertinax*	
Chestnut-fronted Macaw	*Ara severus*	
Great Green Macaw	*Ara ambiguus*	
Red-and-green Macaw	*Ara chloropterus*	
Scarlet Macaw	*Ara macao*	
Blue-and-yellow Macaw	*Ara ararauna*	
Barred Parakeet	*Bolborhynchus lineola*	
Spectacled Parrotlet	*Forpus conspicillatus*	
Orange-chinned Parakeet	*Brotogeris jugularis*	
Red-fronted Parrotlet	*Touit costaricensis*	
Blue-fronted Parrotlet	*Touit dilectissimus*	
Brown-hooded Parrot	*Pyrilia haematotis*	
Saffron-headed Parrot	*Pyrilia pyrilia*	
Blue-headed Parrot	*Pionus menstruus*	
White-crowned Parrot	*Pionus senilis*	
Red-lored Parrot	*Amazona autumnalis*	

Mealy Parrot	*Amazona farinosa*	
Yellow-crowned Parrot	*Amazona ochrocephala*	

Cuckoos (14)	**Cuculidae**	
Little Cuckoo	*Coccycua minuta*	
Dwarf Cuckoo	*Coccycua pumila*	
Squirrel Cuckoo	*Piaya cayana*	
Dark-billed Cuckoo	*Coccyzus melacoryphus*	
Yellow-billed Cuckoo	*Coccyzus americanus*	
Mangrove Cuckoo	*Coccyzus minor*	
Black-billed Cuckoo	*Coccyzus erythropthalmus*	
Gray-capped Cuckoo	*Coccyzus lansbergi*	
Striped Cuckoo	*Tapera naevia*	
Pheasant Cuckoo	*Dromococcyx phasianellus*	
Rufous-vented Ground-Cuckoo	*Neomorphus geoffroyi*	
Greater Ani	*Crotophaga major*	
Smooth-billed Ani	*Crotophaga ani*	
Groove-billed Ani	*Crotophaga sulcirostris*	

Barn Owls (1)	**Tytonidae**	
Barn Owl	*Tyto alba*	

Typical Owls (14)	**Strigidae**	
Tropical Screech-Owl	*Megascops choliba*	
Vermiculated Screech-Owl	*Megascops guatemalae*	
Bare-shanked Screech-Owl	*Megascops clarkii*	
Crested Owl	*Lophostrix cristata*	
Spectacled Owl	*Pulsatrix perspicillata*	
Great Horned Owl	*Bubo virginianus*	
Costa Rican Pygmy-Owl	*Glaucidium costaricanum*	
Central American Pygmy-Owl	*Glaucidium griseiceps*	
Ferruginous Pygmy-Owl	*Glaucidium brasilianum*	
Burrowing Owl	*Athene cunicularia*	
Mottled Owl	*Ciccaba virgata*	
Black-and-white Owl	*Ciccaba nigrolineata*	
Striped Owl	*Pseudoscops clamator*	
Unspotted Saw-whet Owl	*Aegolius ridgwayi*	

Nightjars (10)	**Caprimulgidae**	
Short-tailed Nighthawk	*Lurocalis semitorquatus*	
Lesser Nighthawk	*Chordeiles acutipennis*	

Common Nighthawk	*Chordeiles minor*	
Common Pauraque	*Nyctidromus albicollis*	
Ocellated Poorwill	*Nyctiphrynus ocellatus*	
Chuck-will's-widow	*Caprimulgus carolinensis*	
Rufous Nightjar	*Caprimulgus rufus*	
Whip-poor-will	*Caprimulgus vociferus*	
Dusky Nightjar	*Caprimulgus saturatus*	
White-tailed Nightjar	*Caprimulgus cayennensis*	

Potoos (2) — **Nyctibiidae**

Great Potoo	*Nyctibius grandis*	
Common Potoo	*Nyctibius griseus*	

Oilbird (1) — **Steatornithidae**

Oilbird	*Steatornis caripensis*	

Swifts (13) — **Apodidae**

Black Swift	*Cypseloides niger*	
White-chinned Swift	*Cypseloides cryptus*	
Chestnut-collared Swift	*Streptoprocne rutila*	
White-collared Swift	*Streptoprocne zonaris*	
Chimney Swift	*Chaetura pelagica*	
Vaux's Swift	*Chaetura vauxi*	
Chapman's Swift	*Chaetura chapmani*	
Short-tailed Swift	*Chaetura brachyura*	
Ashy-tailed Swift	*Chaetura andrei*	
Band-rumped Swift	*Chaetura spinicaudis*	
Costa Rican Swift	*Chaetura fumosa*	
Gray-rumped Swift	*Chaetura cinereiventris*	
Lesser Swallow-tailed Swift	*Panyptila cayennensis*	

Hummingbirds (59) — **Trochilidae**

Bronzy Hermit	*Glaucis aeneus*	
Rufous-breasted Hermit	*Glaucis hirsutus*	
Band-tailed Barbthroat	*Threnetes ruckeri*	
Green Hermit	*Phaethornis guy*	
Long-billed Hermit	*Phaethornis longirostris*	
White-whiskered Hermit	*Phaethornis yaruqui*	
Pale-bellied Hermit	*Phaethornis anthophilus*	
Stripe-throated Hermit	*Phaethornis striigularis*	
White-tipped Sicklebill	*Eutoxeres aquila*	

Tooth-billed Hummingbird	*Androdon aequatorialis*	
Green-fronted Lancebill	*Doryfera ludovicae*	
Scaly-breasted Hummingbird	*Phaeochroa cuvierii*	
Violet Sabrewing	*Campylopterus hemileucurus*	
White-necked Jacobin	*Florisuga mellivora*	
Brown Violetear	*Colibri delphinae*	
Green Violetear	*Colibri thalassinus*	
Green-breasted Mango	*Anthracothorax prevostii*	
Black-throated Mango	*Anthracothorax nigricollis*	
Veraguan Mango	*Anthracothorax veraguensis*	
Ruby-topaz Hummingbird	*Chrysolampis mosquitus*	
Violet-headed Hummingbird	*Klais guimeti*	
Rufous-crested Coquette	*Lophornis delattrei*	
White-crested Coquette	*Lophornis adorabilis*	
Green Thorntail	*Discosura conversii*	
Garden Emerald	*Chlorostilbon assimilis*	
Violet-crowned Woodnymph	*Thalurania colombica*	
Green-crowned Woodnymph	*Thalurania fannyi*	
Fiery-throated Hummingbird	*Panterpe insignis*	
Violet-bellied Hummingbird	*Damophila julie*	
Sapphire-throated Hummingbird	*Lepidopyga coeruleogularis*	
Humboldt's Sapphire	*Hylocharis humboldtii*	
Blue-throated Goldentail	*Hylocharis eliciae*	
Violet-capped Hummingbird	*Goldmania violiceps*	
Pirre Hummingbird	*Goethalsia bella*	
Blue-chested Hummingbird	*Amazilia amabilis*	
Charming Hummingbird	*Amazilia decora*	
Snowy-bellied Hummingbird	*Amazilia edward*	
Rufous-tailed Hummingbird	*Amazilia tzacatl*	
Escudo Hummingbird	*Amazilia handleyi*	
Stripe-tailed Hummingbird	*Eupherusa eximia*	
Black-bellied Hummingbird	*Eupherusa nigriventris*	
White-tailed Emerald	*Elvira chionura*	
Snowcap	*Microchera albocoronata*	
White-vented Plumeleteer	*Chalybura buffonii*	
Bronze-tailed Plumeleteer	*Chalybura urochrysia*	
White-bellied Mountain-gem	*Lampornis hemileucus*	
Purple-throated Mountain-gem	*Lampornis calolaemus*	
White-throated Mountain-gem	*Lampornis castaneoventris*	

Green-crowned Brilliant	*Heliodoxa jacula*	
Magnificent Hummingbird	*Eugenes fulgens*	
Greenish Puffleg	*Haplophaedia aureliae*	
Purple-crowned Fairy	*Heliothryx barroti*	
Long-billed Starthroat	*Heliomaster longirostris*	
Magenta-throated Woodstar	*Calliphlox bryantae*	
Purple-throated Woodstar	*Calliphlox mitchellii*	
Ruby-throated Hummingbird	*Archilochus colubris*	
Volcano Hummingbird	*Selasphorus flammula*	
Glow-throated Hummingbird	*Selasphorus ardens*	
Scintillant Hummingbird	*Selasphorus scintilla*	

Trogons (11)	**Trogonidae**	
Lattice-tailed Trogon	*Trogon clathratus*	
Slaty-tailed Trogon	*Trogon massena*	
Black-tailed Trogon	*Trogon melanurus*	
White-tailed Trogon	*Trogon viridis*	
Baird's Trogon	*Trogon bairdii*	
Violaceous Trogon	*Trogon violaceus*	
Black-throated Trogon	*Trogon rufus*	
Collared Trogon	*Trogon collaris*	
Orange-bellied Trogon	*Trogon aurantiiventris*	
Golden-headed Quetzal	*Pharomachrus auriceps*	
Resplendent Quetzal	*Pharomachrus mocinno*	

Motmots (4)	**Momotidae**	
Tody Motmot	*Hylomanes momotula*	
Blue-crowned Motmot	*Momotus momota*	
Rufous Motmot	*Baryphthengus martii*	
Broad-billed Motmot	*Electron platyrhynchum*	

Kingfishers (6)	**Alcedinidae**	
Ringed Kingfisher	*Megaceryle torquata*	
Belted Kingfisher	*Megaceryle alcyon*	
Amazon Kingfisher	*Chloroceryle amazona*	
Green Kingfisher	*Chloroceryle americana*	
Green-and-rufous Kingfisher	*Chloroceryle inda*	
American Pygmy Kingfisher	*Chloroceryle aenea*	

Puffbirds (8)	**Bucconidae**	
Barred Puffbird	*Nystalus radiatus*	
White-necked Puffbird	*Notharchus hyperrhynchus*	

Black-breasted Puffbird	*Notharchus pectoralis*	
Pied Puffbird	*Notharchus tectus*	
White-whiskered Puffbird	*Malacoptila panamensis*	
Lanceolated Monklet	*Micromonacha lanceolata*	
Gray-cheeked Nunlet	*Nonnula frontalis*	
White-fronted Nunbird	*Monasa morphoeus*	

Jacamars (3)	**Galbulidae**	
Dusky-backed Jacamar	*Brachygalba salmoni*	
Rufous-tailed Jacamar	*Galbula ruficauda*	
Great Jacamar	*Jacamerops aureus*	

Barbets & Toucans (10)	**Ramphastidae**	
Spot-crowned Barbet	*Capito maculicoronatus*	
Red-headed Barbet	*Eubucco bourcierii*	
Prong-billed Barbet	*Semnornis frantzii*	
Blue-throated Toucanet	*Aulacorhynchus caeruleogularis*	
Collared Aracari	*Pteroglossus torquatus*	
Fiery-billed Aracari	*Pteroglossus frantzii*	
Yellow-eared Toucanet	*Selenidera spectabilis*	
Keel-billed Toucan	*Ramphastos sulfuratus*	
Chestnut-mandibled Toucan	*Ramphastos swainsonii*	
Choco Toucan	*Ramphastos brevis*	

Woodpeckers (20)	**Picidae**	
Olivaceous Piculet	*Picumnus olivaceus*	
Acorn Woodpecker	*Melanerpes formicivorus*	
Golden-naped Woodpecker	*Melanerpes chrysauchen*	
Black-cheeked Woodpecker	*Melanerpes pucherani*	
Red-crowned Woodpecker	*Melanerpes rubricapillus*	
Yellow-bellied Sapsucker	*Sphyrapicus varius*	
Hairy Woodpecker	*Picoides villosus*	
Smoky-brown Woodpecker	*Veniliornis fumigatus*	
Red-rumped Woodpecker	*Veniliornis kirkii*	
Rufous-winged Woodpecker	*Piculus simplex*	
Stripe-cheeked Woodpecker	*Piculus callopterus*	
Golden-green Woodpecker	*Piculus chrysochloros*	
Golden-olive Woodpecker	*Colaptes rubiginosus*	
Spot-breasted Woodpecker	*Colaptes punctigula*	
Cinnamon Woodpecker	*Celeus loricatus*	
Chestnut-colored Woodpecker	*Celeus castaneus*	

Lineated Woodpecker	*Dryocopus lineatus*	
Crimson-bellied Woodpecker	*Campephilus haematogaster*	
Crimson-crested Woodpecker	*Campephilus melanoleucos*	
Pale-billed Woodpecker	*Campephilus guatemalensis*	

Broadbills (1)   **Eurylaimidae**

| Sapayoa | *Sapayoa aenigma* | |

Ovenbirds & Woodcreepers (40)   **Furnariidae**

Tawny-throated Leaftosser	*Sclerurus mexicanus*	
Gray-throated Leaftosser	*Sclerurus albigularis*	
Scaly-throated Leaftosser	*Sclerurus guatemalensis*	
Pale-breasted Spinetail	*Synallaxis albescens*	
Slaty Spinetail	*Synallaxis brachyura*	
Red-faced Spinetail	*Cranioleuca erythrops*	
Coiba Spinetail	*Cranioleuca dissita*	
Double-banded Graytail	*Xenerpestes minlosi*	
Spotted Barbtail	*Premnoplex brunnescens*	
Beautiful Treerunner	*Margarornis bellulus*	
Ruddy Treerunner	*Margarornis rubiginosus*	
Buffy Tuftedcheek	*Pseudocolaptes lawrencii*	
Striped Woodhaunter	*Hyloctistes subulatus*	
Lineated Foliage-gleaner	*Syndactyla subalaris*	
Scaly-throated Foliage-gleaner	*Anabacerthia variegaticeps*	
Slaty-winged Foliage-gleaner	*Philydor fuscipenne*	
Buff-fronted Foliage-gleaner	*Philydor rufum*	
Buff-throated Foliage-gleaner	*Automolus ochrolaemus*	
Ruddy Foliage-gleaner	*Automolus rubiginosus*	
Streak-breasted Treehunter	*Thripadectes rufobrunneus*	
Plain Xenops	*Xenops minutus*	
Streaked Xenops	*Xenops rutilans*	
Sharp-tailed Streamcreeper	*Lochmias nematura*	
Plain-brown Woodcreeper	*Dendrocincla fuliginosa*	
Tawny-winged Woodcreeper	*Dendrocincla anabatina*	
Ruddy Woodcreeper	*Dendrocincla homochroa*	
Olivaceous Woodcreeper	*Sittasomus griseicapillus*	
Long-tailed Woodcreeper	*Deconychura longicauda*	
Wedge-billed Woodcreeper	*Glyphorynchus spirurus*	
Strong-billed Woodcreeper	*Xiphocolaptes promeropirhynchus*	
Northern Barred-Woodcreeper	*Dendrocolaptes sanctithomae*	

Black-banded Woodcreeper	*Dendrocolaptes picumnus*	
Straight-billed Woodcreeper	*Xiphorhynchus picus*	
Cocoa Woodcreeper	*Xiphorhynchus susurrans*	
Black-striped Woodcreeper	*Xiphorhynchus lachrymosus*	
Spotted Woodcreeper	*Xiphorhynchus erythropygius*	
Streak-headed Woodcreeper	*Lepidocolaptes souleyetii*	
Spot-crowned Woodcreeper	*Lepidocolaptes affinis*	
Red-billed Scythebill	*Campylorhamphus trochilirostris*	
Brown-billed Scythebill	*Campylorhamphus pusillus*	

Typical Antbirds (30)   **Thamnophilidae**

Fasciated Antshrike	*Cymbilaimus lineatus*	
Great Antshrike	*Taraba major*	
Barred Antshrike	*Thamnophilus doliatus*	
Black Antshrike	*Thamnophilus nigriceps*	
Black-hooded Antshrike	*Thamnophilus bridgesi*	
Western Slaty-Antshrike	*Thamnophilus atrinucha*	
Speckled Antshrike	*Xenornis setifrons*	
Russet Antshrike	*Thamnistes anabatinus*	
Plain Antvireo	*Dysithamnus mentalis*	
Spot-crowned Antvireo	*Dysithamnus puncticeps*	
Moustached Antwren	*Myrmotherula ignota*	
Pacific Antwren	*Myrmotherula pacifica*	
White-flanked Antwren	*Myrmotherula axillaris*	
Slaty Antwren	*Myrmotherula schisticolor*	
Checker-throated Antwren	*Epinecrophylla fulviventris*	
Rufous-winged Antwren	*Herpsilochmus rufimarginatus*	
Dot-winged Antwren	*Microrhopias quixensis*	
White-fringed Antwren	*Formicivora grisea*	
Rufous-rumped Antwren	*Terenura callinota*	
Dusky Antbird	*Cercomacra tyrannina*	
Jet Antbird	*Cercomacra nigricans*	
Bare-crowned Antbird	*Gymnocichla nudiceps*	
White-bellied Antbird	*Myrmeciza longipes*	
Chestnut-backed Antbird	*Myrmeciza exsul*	
Dull-mantled Antbird	*Myrmeciza laemosticta*	
Immaculate Antbird	*Myrmeciza immaculata*	
Spotted Antbird	*Hylophylax naevioides*	
Wing-banded Antbird	*Myrmornis torquata*	

| Bicolored Antbird | *Gymnopithys leucaspis* | |
| Ocellated Antbird | *Phaenostictus mcleannani* | |

Antthrushes (3)	**Formicariidae**	
Black-faced Antthrush	*Formicarius analis*	
Black-headed Antthrush	*Formicarius nigricapillus*	
Rufous-breasted Antthrush	*Formicarius rufipectus*	

| **Gnateaters (1)** | **Conopophagidae** | |
| Black-crowned Antpitta | *Pittasoma michleri* | |

Antpittas (4)	**Grallariidae**	
Scaled Antpitta	*Grallaria guatimalensis*	
Streak-chested Antpitta	*Hylopezus perspicillatus*	
Thicket Antpitta	*Hylopezus dives*	
Ochre-breasted Antpitta	*Grallaricula flavirostris*	

Tapaculos (3)	**Rhinocryptidae**	
Tacarcuna Tapaculo	*Scytalopus panamensis*	
Choco Tapaculo	*Scytalopus chocoensis*	
Silvery-fronted Tapaculo	*Scytalopus argentifrons*	

Tyrant Flycatchers (94)	**Tyrannidae**	
Yellow-bellied Tyrannulet	*Ornithion semiflavum*	
Brown-capped Tyrannulet	*Ornithion brunneicapillus*	
Southern Beardless-Tyrannulet	*Camptostoma obsoletum*	
Mouse-colored Tyrannulet	*Phaeomyias murina*	
Yellow Tyrannulet	*Capsiempis flaveola*	
Yellow-crowned Tyrannulet	*Tyrannulus elatus*	
Forest Elaenia	*Myiopagis gaimardii*	
Gray Elaenia	*Myiopagis caniceps*	
Greenish Elaenia	*Myiopagis viridicata*	
Yellow-bellied Elaenia	*Elaenia flavogaster*	
Lesser Elaenia	*Elaenia chiriquensis*	
Mountain Elaenia	*Elaenia frantzii*	
Torrent Tyrannulet	*Serpophaga cinerea*	
Olive-striped Flycatcher	*Mionectes olivaceus*	
Ochre-bellied Flycatcher	*Mionectes oleagineus*	
Sepia-capped Flycatcher	*Leptopogon amaurocephalus*	
Slaty-capped Flycatcher	*Leptopogon superciliaris*	
Yellow-green Tyrannulet	*Phylloscartes flavovirens*	

Rufous-browed Tyrannulet	*Phylloscartes superciliaris*	
Rough-legged Tyrannulet	*Phyllomyias burmeisteri*	
Sooty-headed Tyrannulet	*Phyllomyias griseiceps*	
Paltry Tyrannulet	*Zimmerius vilissimus*	
Northern Scrub-Flycatcher	*Sublegatus arenarum*	
Bronze-olive Pygmy-Tyrant	*Pseudotriccus pelzelni*	
Black-capped Pygmy-Tyrant	*Myiornis atricapillus*	
Scale-crested Pygmy-Tyrant	*Lophotriccus pileatus*	
Pale-eyed Pygmy-Tyrant	*Lophotriccus pilaris*	
Northern Bentbill	*Oncostoma cinereigulare*	
Southern Bentbill	*Oncostoma olivaceum*	
Slate-headed Tody-Flycatcher	*Poecilotriccus sylvia*	
Common Tody-Flycatcher	*Todirostrum cinereum*	
Black-headed Tody-Flycatcher	*Todirostrum nigriceps*	
Brownish Twistwing	*Cnipodectes subbrunneus*	
Eye-ringed Flatbill	*Rhynchocyclus brevirostris*	
Olivaceous Flatbill	*Rhynchocyclus olivaceus*	
Yellow-olive Flycatcher	*Tolmomyias sulphurescens*	
Yellow-margined Flycatcher	*Tolmomyias assimilis*	
Yellow-breasted Flycatcher	*Tolmomyias flaviventris*	
Stub-tailed Spadebill	*Platyrinchus cancrominus*	
White-throated Spadebill	*Platyrinchus mystaceus*	
Golden-crowned Spadebill	*Platyrinchus coronatus*	
Royal Flycatcher	*Onychorhynchus coronatus*	
Ruddy-tailed Flycatcher	*Terenotriccus erythrurus*	
Tawny-breasted Flycatcher	*Myiobius villosus*	
Sulphur-rumped Flycatcher	*Myiobius sulphureipygius*	
Black-tailed Flycatcher	*Myiobius atricaudus*	
Bran-colored Flycatcher	*Myiophobus fasciatus*	
Black-billed Flycatcher	*Aphanotriccus audax*	
Tufted Flycatcher	*Mitrephanes phaeocercus*	
Olive-sided Flycatcher	*Contopus cooperi*	
Dark Pewee	*Contopus lugubris*	
Ochraceous Pewee	*Contopus ochraceus*	
Western Wood-Pewee	*Contopus sordidulus*	
Eastern Wood-Pewee	*Contopus virens*	
Tropical Pewee	*Contopus cinereus*	
Yellow-bellied Flycatcher	*Empidonax flaviventris*	

Acadian Flycatcher	*Empidonax virescens*	
Alder Flycatcher	*Empidonax alnorum*	
Willow Flycatcher	*Empidonax traillii*	
White-throated Flycatcher	*Empidonax albigularis*	
Least Flycatcher	*Empidonax minimus*	
Hammond's Flycatcher	*Empidonax hammondii*	
Yellowish Flycatcher	*Empidonax flavescens*	
Black-capped Flycatcher	*Empidonax atriceps*	
Black Phoebe	*Sayornis nigricans*	
Vermilion Flycatcher	*Pyrocephalus rubinus*	
Pied Water-Tyrant	*Fluvicola pica*	
Long-tailed Tyrant	*Colonia colonus*	
Cattle Tyrant	*Machetornis rixosa*	
Bright-rumped Attila	*Attila spadiceus*	
Sirystes	*Sirystes sibilator*	
Rufous Mourner	*Rhytipterna holerythra*	
Dusky-capped Flycatcher	*Myiarchus tuberculifer*	
Panama Flycatcher	*Myiarchus panamensis*	
Great Crested Flycatcher	*Myiarchus crinitus*	
Lesser Kiskadee	*Pitangus lictor*	
Great Kiskadee	*Pitangus sulphuratus*	
Boat-billed Flycatcher	*Megarynchus pitangua*	
Rusty-margined Flycatcher	*Myiozetetes cayanensis*	
Social Flycatcher	*Myiozetetes similis*	
Gray-capped Flycatcher	*Myiozetetes granadensis*	
White-ringed Flycatcher	*Conopias albovittatus*	
Golden-bellied Flycatcher	*Myiodynastes hemichrysus*	
Golden-crowned Flycatcher	*Myiodynastes chrysocephalus*	
Streaked Flycatcher	*Myiodynastes maculatus*	
Sulphur-bellied Flycatcher	*Myiodynastes luteiventris*	
Piratic Flycatcher	*Legatus leucophaius*	
Crowned Slaty-Flycatcher	*Empidonomus aurantioatrocristatus*	
Tropical Kingbird	*Tyrannus melancholicus*	
Western Kingbird	*Tyrannus verticalis*	
Eastern Kingbird	*Tyrannus tyrannus*	
Gray Kingbird	*Tyrannus dominicensis*	
Scissor-tailed Flycatcher	*Tyrannus forficatus*	
Fork-tailed Flycatcher	*Tyrannus savana*	

Becard, Tityras & Others (13) — *Incertae sedis*

Thrush-like Schiffornis	*Schiffornis turdina*	
Gray-headed Piprites	*Piprites griseiceps*	
Rufous Piha	*Lipaugus unirufus*	
Speckled Mourner	*Laniocera rufescens*	
Barred Becard	*Pachyramphus versicolor*	
Cinereous Becard	*Pachyramphus rufus*	
Cinnamon Becard	*Pachyramphus cinnamomeus*	
White-winged Becard	*Pachyramphus polychopterus*	
Black-and-white Becard	*Pachyramphus albogriseus*	
Rose-throated Becard	*Pachyramphus aglaiae*	
One-colored Becard	*Pachyramphus homochrous*	
Masked Tityra	*Tityra semifasciata*	
Black-crowned Tityra	*Tityra inquisitor*	

Cotingas (9) — Cotingidae

Lovely Cotinga	*Cotinga amabilis*	
Turquoise Cotinga	*Cotinga ridgwayi*	
Blue Cotinga	*Cotinga nattererii*	
Black-tipped Cotinga	*Carpodectes hopkei*	
Yellow-billed Cotinga	*Carpodectes antoniae*	
Snowy Cotinga	*Carpodectes nitidus*	
Purple-throated Fruitcrow	*Querula purpurata*	
Bare-necked Umbrellabird	*Cephalopterus glabricollis*	
Three-wattled Bellbird	*Procnias tricarunculatus*	

Manakins (10) — Pipridae

Green Manakin	*Chloropipo holochlora*	
White-collared Manakin	*Manacus candei*	
Orange-collared Manakin	*Manacus aurantiacus*	
Golden-collared Manakin	*Manacus vitellinus*	
White-ruffed Manakin	*Corapipo altera*	
Lance-tailed Manakin	*Chiroxiphia lanceolata*	
White-crowned Manakin	*Pipra pipra*	
Blue-crowned Manakin	*Pipra coronata*	
Golden-headed Manakin	*Pipra erythrocephala*	
Red-capped Manakin	*Pipra mentalis*	

Sharpbill (1) — Oxyruncidae

Sharpbill	*Oxyruncus cristatus*	

Vireos (17)   Vireonidae

White-eyed Vireo	*Vireo griseus*	
Yellow-throated Vireo	*Vireo flavifrons*	
Blue-headed Vireo	*Vireo solitarius*	
Yellow-winged Vireo	*Vireo carmioli*	
Warbling Vireo	*Vireo gilvus*	
Brown-capped Vireo	*Vireo leucophrys*	
Philadelphia Vireo	*Vireo philadelphicus*	
Red-eyed Vireo	*Vireo olivaceus*	
Yellow-green Vireo	*Vireo flavoviridis*	
Black-whiskered Vireo	*Vireo altiloquus*	
Scrub Greenlet	*Hylophilus flavipes*	
Tawny-crowned Greenlet	*Hylophilus ochraceiceps*	
Golden-fronted Greenlet	*Hylophilus aurantiifrons*	
Lesser Greenlet	*Hylophilus decurtatus*	
Green Shrike-Vireo	*Vireolanius pulchellus*	
Yellow-browed Shrike-Vireo	*Vireolanius eximius*	
Rufous-browed Peppershrike	*Cyclarhis gujanensis*	

Crows & Jays (4)   Corvidae

Black-chested Jay	*Cyanocorax affinis*	
Brown Jay	*Cyanocorax morio*	
Azure-hooded Jay	*Cyanolyca cucullata*	
Silvery-throated Jay	*Cyanolyca argentigula*	

Swallows (16)   Hirundinidae

Purple Martin	*Progne subis*	
Gray-breasted Martin	*Progne chalybea*	
Southern Martin	*Progne elegans*	
Brown-chested Martin	*Progne tapera*	
Tree Swallow	*Tachycineta bicolor*	
Mangrove Swallow	*Tachycineta albilinea*	
White-winged Swallow	*Tachycineta albiventer*	
Violet-green Swallow	*Tachycineta thalassina*	
Blue-and-white Swallow	*Pygochelidon cyanoleuca*	
White-thighed Swallow	*Neochelidon tibialis*	
Northern Rough-winged Swallow	*Stelgidopteryx serripennis*	
Southern Rough-winged Swallow	*Stelgidopteryx ruficollis*	
Bank Swallow	*Riparia riparia*	
Cliff Swallow	*Petrochelidon pyrrhonota*	

| Cave Swallow | *Petrochelidon fulva* | |
| Barn Swallow | *Hirundo rustica* | |

Donacobius (1) — *Incertae sedis*

| Black-capped Donacobius | *Donacobius atricapilla* | |

Wrens (22) — Troglodytidae

White-headed Wren	*Campylorhynchus albobrunneus*	
Band-backed Wren	*Campylorhynchus zonatus*	
Sooty-headed Wren	*Thryothorus spadix*	
Black-throated Wren	*Thryothorus atrogularis*	
Black-bellied Wren	*Thryothorus fasciatoventris*	
Bay Wren	*Thryothorus nigricapillus*	
Riverside Wren	*Thryothorus semibadius*	
Stripe-throated Wren	*Thryothorus leucopogon*	
Stripe-breasted Wren	*Thryothorus thoracicus*	
Rufous-breasted Wren	*Thryothorus rutilus*	
Rufous-and-white Wren	*Thryothorus rufalbus*	
Buff-breasted Wren	*Thryothorus leucotis*	
Plain Wren	*Thryothorus modestus*	
Canebrake Wren	*Thryothorus zeledoni*	
House Wren	*Troglodytes aedon*	
Ochraceous Wren	*Troglodytes ochraceus*	
Sedge Wren	*Cistothorus platensis*	
Timberline Wren	*Thryorchilus browni*	
White-breasted Wood-Wren	*Henicorhina leucosticta*	
Gray-breasted Wood-Wren	*Henicorhina leucophrys*	
Southern Nightingale-Wren	*Microcerculus marginatus*	
Song Wren	*Cyphorhinus phaeocephalus*	

Dippers (1) — Cinclidae

| American Dipper | *Cinclus mexicanus* | |

Gnatwrens & Gnatcatchers (4) — Sylviidae

Tawny-faced Gnatwren	*Microbates cinereiventris*	
Long-billed Gnatwren	*Ramphocaenus melanurus*	
Tropical Gnatcatcher	*Polioptila plumbea*	
Slate-throated Gnatcatcher	*Polioptila schistaceigula*	

Thrushes (17) — Turdidae

| Northern Wheatear | *Oenanthe oenanthe* | |
| Black-faced Solitaire | *Myadestes melanops* | |

Varied Solitaire	*Myadestes coloratus*
Black-billed Nightingale-Thrush	*Catharus gracilirostris*
Orange-billed Nightingale-Thrush	*Catharus aurantiirostris*
Slaty-backed Nightingale-Thrush	*Catharus fuscater*
Ruddy-capped Nightingale-Thrush	*Catharus frantzii*
Black-headed Nightingale-Thrush	*Catharus mexicanus*
Veery	*Catharus fuscescens*
Gray-cheeked Thrush	*Catharus minimus*
Swainson's Thrush	*Catharus ustulatus*
Wood Thrush	*Hylocichla mustelina*
Sooty Thrush	*Turdus nigrescens*
Mountain Thrush	*Turdus plebejus*
Pale-vented Thrush	*Turdus obsoletus*
Clay-colored Thrush	*Turdus grayi*
White-throated Thrush	*Turdus assimilis*

Mockingbirds & Allies (2)	**Mimidae**
Gray Catbird	*Dumetella carolinensis*
Tropical Mockingbird	*Mimus gilvus*

Pipits & Wagtails (1)	**Motacillidae**
Yellowish Pipit	*Anthus lutescens*

Waxwings (1)	**Bombycillidae**
Cedar Waxwing	*Bombycilla cedrorum*

Silky-flycatchers (2)	**Ptilogonatidae**
Black-and-yellow Silky-flycatcher	*Phainoptila melanoxantha*
Long-tailed Silky-flycatcher	*Ptilogonys caudatus*

Wood-Warblers (54)	**Parulidae**
Blue-winged Warbler	*Vermivora pinus*
Golden-winged Warbler	*Vermivora chrysoptera*
Tennessee Warbler	*Vermivora peregrina*
Nashville Warbler	*Vermivora ruficapilla*
Virginia's Warbler	*Vermivora virginiae*
Flame-throated Warbler	*Parula gutturalis*
Northern Parula	*Parula americana*
Tropical Parula	*Parula pitiayumi*
Yellow Warbler	*Dendroica petechia*
Chestnut-sided Warbler	*Dendroica pensylvanica*

Magnolia Warbler	*Dendroica magnolia*	
Cape May Warbler	*Dendroica tigrina*	
Black-throated Blue Warbler	*Dendroica caerulescens*	
Yellow-rumped Warbler	*Dendroica coronata*	
Golden-cheeked Warbler	*Dendroica chrysoparia*	
Black-throated Green Warbler	*Dendroica virens*	
Townsend's Warbler	*Dendroica townsendi*	
Hermit Warbler	*Dendroica occidentalis*	
Blackburnian Warbler	*Dendroica fusca*	
Yellow-throated Warbler	*Dendroica dominica*	
Prairie Warbler	*Dendroica discolor*	
Palm Warbler	*Dendroica palmarum*	
Bay-breasted Warbler	*Dendroica castanea*	
Blackpoll Warbler	*Dendroica striata*	
Cerulean Warbler	*Dendroica cerulea*	
Black-and-white Warbler	*Mniotilta varia*	
American Redstart	*Setophaga ruticilla*	
Prothonotary Warbler	*Protonotaria citrea*	
Worm-eating Warbler	*Helmitheros vermivorum*	
Swainson's Warbler	*Limnothlypis swainsonii*	
Ovenbird	*Seiurus aurocapilla*	
Northern Waterthrush	*Seiurus noveboracensis*	
Louisiana Waterthrush	*Seiurus motacilla*	
Kentucky Warbler	*Oporornis formosus*	
Connecticut Warbler	*Oporornis agilis*	
Mourning Warbler	*Oporornis philadelphia*	
MacGillivray's Warbler	*Oporornis tolmiei*	
Common Yellowthroat	*Geothlypis trichas*	
Olive-crowned Yellowthroat	*Geothlypis semiflava*	
Masked Yellowthroat	*Geothlypis aequinoctialis*	
Gray-crowned Yellowthroat	*Geothlypis poliocephala*	
Hooded Warbler	*Wilsonia citrina*	
Wilson's Warbler	*Wilsonia pusilla*	
Canada Warbler	*Wilsonia canadensis*	
Slate-throated Redstart	*Myioborus miniatus*	
Collared Redstart	*Myioborus torquatus*	
Golden-crowned Warbler	*Basileuterus culicivorus*	
Rufous-capped Warbler	*Basileuterus rufifrons*	
Black-cheeked Warbler	*Basileuterus melanogenys*	

Pirre Warbler	*Basileuterus ignotus*	
Three-striped Warbler	*Basileuterus tristriatus*	
Buff-rumped Warbler	*Phaeothlypis fulvicauda*	
Wrenthrush	*Zeledonia coronata*	
Yellow-breasted Chat	*Icteria virens*	

Bananaquit (1)	**Incertae sedis**	
Bananaquit	*Coereba flaveola*	

Tanagers (44)	**Thraupidae**	
White-eared Conebill	*Conirostrum leucogenys*	
Common Bush-Tanager	*Chlorospingus ophthalmicus*	
Tacarcuna Bush-Tanager	*Chlorospingus tacarcunae*	
Pirre Bush-Tanager	*Chlorospingus inornatus*	
Sooty-capped Bush-Tanager	*Chlorospingus pileatus*	
Yellow-throated Bush-Tanager	*Chlorospingus flavigularis*	
Ashy-throated Bush-Tanager	*Chlorospingus canigularis*	
Yellow-backed Tanager	*Hemithraupis flavicollis*	
Black-and-yellow Tanager	*Chrysothlypis chrysomelas*	
Rosy Thrush-Tanager	*Rhodinocichla rosea*	
Dusky-faced Tanager	*Mitrospingus cassinii*	
Gray-headed Tanager	*Eucometis penicillata*	
White-throated Shrike-Tanager	*Lanio leucothorax*	
Sulphur-rumped Tanager	*Heterospingus rubrifrons*	
Scarlet-browed Tanager	*Heterospingus xanthopygius*	
White-shouldered Tanager	*Tachyphonus luctuosus*	
Tawny-crested Tanager	*Tachyphonus delatrii*	
White-lined Tanager	*Tachyphonus rufus*	
Crimson-collared Tanager	*Ramphocelus sanguinolentus*	
Crimson-backed Tanager	*Ramphocelus dimidiatus*	
Passerini's Tanager	*Ramphocelus passerinii*	
Cherrie's Tanager	*Ramphocelus costaricensis*	
Flame-rumped Tanager	*Ramphocelus flammigerus*	
Blue-gray Tanager	*Thraupis episcopus*	
Palm Tanager	*Thraupis palmarum*	
Blue-and-gold Tanager	*Bangsia arcaei*	
Gray-and-gold Tanager	*Tangara palmeri*	
Golden-hooded Tanager	*Tangara larvata*	
Speckled Tanager	*Tangara guttata*	
Green-naped Tanager	*Tangara fucosa*	

Spangle-cheeked Tanager	*Tangara dowii*	
Plain-colored Tanager	*Tangara inornata*	
Rufous-winged Tanager	*Tangara lavinia*	
Bay-headed Tanager	*Tangara gyrola*	
Emerald Tanager	*Tangara florida*	
Silver-throated Tanager	*Tangara icterocephala*	
Scarlet-thighed Dacnis	*Dacnis venusta*	
Blue Dacnis	*Dacnis cayana*	
Viridian Dacnis	*Dacnis viguieri*	
Green Honeycreeper	*Chlorophanes spiza*	
Shining Honeycreeper	*Cyanerpes lucidus*	
Purple Honeycreeper	*Cyanerpes caeruleus*	
Red-legged Honeycreeper	*Cyanerpes cyaneus*	
Swallow Tanager	*Tersina viridis*	

Saltators (5) | ***Incertae sedis*** |

Streaked Saltator	*Saltator striatipectus*	
Grayish Saltator	*Saltator coerulescens*	
Buff-throated Saltator	*Saltator maximus*	
Black-headed Saltator	*Saltator atriceps*	
Slate-colored Grosbeak	*Saltator grossus*	

**Seedeaters, Finches &
Sparrows (32)** | **Emberizidae** |

Blue-black Grassquit	*Volatinia jacarina*	
Slate-colored Seedeater	*Sporophila schistacea*	
Variable Seedeater	*Sporophila americana*	
White-collared Seedeater	*Sporophila torqueola*	
Lesson's Seedeater	*Sporophila bouvronides*	
Lined Seedeater	*Sporophila lineola*	
Yellow-bellied Seedeater	*Sporophila nigricollis*	
Ruddy-breasted Seedeater	*Sporophila minuta*	
Nicaraguan Seed-Finch	*Oryzoborus nuttingi*	
Large-billed Seed-Finch	*Oryzoborus crassirostris*	
Thick-billed Seed-Finch	*Oryzoborus funereus*	
Yellow-faced Grassquit	*Tiaris olivaceus*	
Slaty Finch	*Haplospiza rustica*	
Peg-billed Finch	*Acanthidops bairdii*	
Slaty Flowerpiercer	*Diglossa plumbea*	
Saffron Finch	*Sicalis flaveola*	

Grassland Yellow-Finch	*Sicalis luteola*	
Wedge-tailed Grass-Finch	*Emberizoides herbicola*	
Yellow-thighed Finch	*Pselliophorus tibialis*	
Yellow-green Finch	*Pselliophorus luteoviridis*	
Large-footed Finch	*Pezopetes capitalis*	
White-naped Brush-Finch	*Atlapetes albinucha*	
Orange-billed Sparrow	*Arremon aurantiirostris*	
Sooty-faced Finch	*Arremon crassirostris*	
Chestnut-capped Brush-Finch	*Arremon brunneinucha*	
Stripe-headed Brush-Finch	*Arremon torquatus*	
Black-striped Sparrow	*Arremonops conirostris*	
Lark Sparrow	*Chondestes grammacus*	
Grasshopper Sparrow	*Ammodramus savannarum*	
Lincoln's Sparrow	*Melospiza lincolnii*	
Rufous-collared Sparrow	*Zonotrichia capensis*	
Volcano Junco	*Junco vulcani*	

Grosbeaks, Buntings & Allies (20)

Cardinalidae		
Hepatic Tanager	*Piranga flava*	
Summer Tanager	*Piranga rubra*	
Scarlet Tanager	*Piranga olivacea*	
Western Tanager	*Piranga ludoviciana*	
Flame-colored Tanager	*Piranga bidentata*	
White-winged Tanager	*Piranga leucoptera*	
Red-crowned Ant-Tanager	*Habia rubica*	
Red-throated Ant-Tanager	*Habia fuscicauda*	
Carmiol's Tanager	*Chlorothraupis carmioli*	
Lemon-spectacled Tanager	*Chlorothraupis olivacea*	
Black-faced Grosbeak	*Caryothraustes poliogaster*	
Yellow-green Grosbeak	*Caryothraustes canadensis*	
Black-thighed Grosbeak	*Pheucticus tibialis*	
Rose-breasted Grosbeak	*Pheucticus ludovicianus*	
Blue Seedeater	*Amaurospiza concolor*	
Blue-black Grosbeak	*Cyanocompsa cyanoides*	
Blue Grosbeak	*Passerina caerulea*	
Indigo Bunting	*Passerina cyanea*	
Painted Bunting	*Passerina ciris*	
Dickcissel	*Spiza americana*	

New World Orioles & Blackbirds (22)	Icteridae	
Bobolink	*Dolichonyx oryzivorus*	
Red-breasted Blackbird	*Sturnella militaris*	
Eastern Meadowlark	*Sturnella magna*	
Yellow-headed Blackbird	*Xanthocephalus xanthocephalus*	
Great-tailed Grackle	*Quiscalus mexicanus*	
Shiny Cowbird	*Molothrus bonariensis*	
Bronzed Cowbird	*Molothrus aeneus*	
Giant Cowbird	*Molothrus oryzivorus*	
Yellow-hooded Blackbird	*Chrysomus icterocephalus*	
Black-cowled Oriole	*Icterus prosthemelas*	
Orchard Oriole	*Icterus spurius*	
Yellow-backed Oriole	*Icterus chrysater*	
Orange-crowned Oriole	*Icterus auricapillus*	
Yellow-tailed Oriole	*Icterus mesomelas*	
Baltimore Oriole	*Icterus galbula*	
Yellow-billed Cacique	*Amblycercus holosericeus*	
Scarlet-rumped Cacique	*Cacicus uropygialis*	
Yellow-rumped Cacique	*Cacicus cela*	
Crested Oropendola	*Psarocolius decumanus*	
Chestnut-headed Oropendola	*Psarocolius wagleri*	
Montezuma Oropendola	*Psarocolius montezuma*	
Black Oropendola	*Psarocolius guatimozinus*	

Goldfinches & Euphonias (14)	Fringillidae	
Yellow-crowned Euphonia	*Euphonia luteicapilla*	
Thick-billed Euphonia	*Euphonia laniirostris*	
Yellow-throated Euphonia	*Euphonia hirundinacea*	
Elegant Euphonia	*Euphonia elegantissima*	
Fulvous-vented Euphonia	*Euphonia fulvicrissa*	
Spot-crowned Euphonia	*Euphonia imitans*	
Olive-backed Euphonia	*Euphonia gouldi*	
White-vented Euphonia	*Euphonia minuta*	
Tawny-capped Euphonia	*Euphonia anneae*	
Orange-bellied Euphonia	*Euphonia xanthogaster*	
Yellow-collared Chlorophonia	*Chlorophonia flavirostris*	
Golden-browed Chlorophonia	*Chlorophonia callophrys*	
Yellow-bellied Siskin	*Spinus xanthogastrus*	
Lesser Goldfinch	*Spinus psaltria*	

Old World Sparrows (1)	Passeridae	
House Sparrow	*Passer domesticus*	

Ship-assisted Vagrants and Escaped Cage Birds

Crows & Jays (1)	Corvidae	
Common Raven	*Corvus corax*	

Chickadees & Titmice (1)	Paridae	
Great Tit	*Parus major*	

Starlings (1)	Sturnidae	
European Starling	*Sturnus vulgaris*	

Seedeaters, Finches & Sparrows (3)	Emberizidae	
Savannah Sparrow	*Passerculus sandwichensis*	
White-crowned Sparrow	*Zonotrichia leucophrys*	
Dark-eyed Junco	*Junco hyemalis*	

Goldfinches & Euphonias (1)	Fringillidae	
American Goldfinch	*Spinus tristis*	

Waxbills & Allies (2)	Estrildidae	
Nutmeg Munia	*Lonchura punctulata*	
Tricolored Munia	*Lonchura malacca*	

Index of Common and Scientific Names

About the Author

George Angehr grew up in the Bronx in New York City, where he began watching birds at the age of twelve in his backyard and neighborhood parks. He has worked on birds in Panama since 1977 and has lived there full-time since 1992. His publications include the *Annotated Checklist of the Birds of Panama* (Panama Audubon Society, 2006), and (with Dodge and Lorna Engleman) *A Bird-Finding Guide to Panama* (Cornell University Press, 2008). A Research Associate at the Smithsonian Tropical Research Institute, he is currently Curator of Exhibitions for the BioMuseo, Panama's new museum of biodiversity, now under construction in Panama City, and is also Director for Science for the Panama Audubon Society. In addition to birds of Panama, he has worked on birds in the United States, New Zealand, Peru, and Gabon.

About the Illustrator

Robert Dean has been studying and illustrating birds for more than twelve years, during which time he has gone on birding trips—both as guide and participant—throughout the Americas. Born and raised in London, England, he was a successful professional musician and recording artist for eighteen years, living for extended periods in the United States and Australia before finally settling in Costa Rica in the early 1990s, where he re-discovered his childhood passions for art and wildlife. He has executed art commissions for the Costa Rican National Parks, produced artwork for Rainforest Publications on the avifauna of Costa Rica, Panama, Peru, Belize, Guatemala, Mexico, and the United States. Dean illustrated *The Birds of Costa Rica: A Field Guide* (Cornell University Press, 2007) and was contributing artist to *The Wildlife of Costa Rica: A Field Guide* (Cornell University Press, 2010). He is currently working on a field guide to the birds of northern Central America.